THE CHINESE LOOKING GLASS

THE
CHINESE
LOOKING
GLASS

Dennis Bloodworth

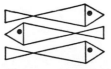

FARRAR, STRAUS AND GIROUX
New York

To my mother

Mea Culpa

This is not a book for the "China expert," real or imaginary, for he will find nothing in it that he does not already know or reject. It is for the ordinary reader who may never have been east of Suez, who has never argued with Chinese except over a restaurant bill, and who knows even less about them than I do.

Nor is this one of those travel manuals, dear to tourists, that will tell you everything about the Chinese from A to Zen. For it has a purpose, and the purpose is to try to explain what makes the Chinese tick, to trace across more than three thousand years of history, philosophy, literature, and day-to-day living those often invisible puppet strings of atavistic instinct and prejudice that may influence today the words and actions of one quarter of the people in this world—and their leaders. The choice of material, however frivolous at times, is therefore directed toward this end.

I do not apologize for the frivolities. I am not a Sinologue, but a journalist with a Chinese wife and three Chinese children who has lived in the Far East for twelve years, and who would like to see a broader, if necessarily shallower, understanding between the millions of East and West than works with a deeper but narrower appeal can foster.

The Chinese Looking Glass, then, is by way of being an *amuse-gueule,* an appetizer to tempt the more serious reader to tuck in to the solid fare listed in the bibliography at the back. There are no footnotes, or acknowledgments or attributions in the text, and I have often translated freely, contracting or paraphrasing quotations to bring out the essential pith and to avoid as many trailing sets of dots as possible, for this is a book designed for reading, not for study.

It presents, in any case, only one man's view, and must inevitably invite contradiction. How many Englishmen would turn furiously to the attack if a Chinese described them in terms of the adjectives which are so often applied to his own people: "insular," "cold," "arrogant," "hypocritical," "cautious," "cunning," "pragmatic"? Yet it is in terms of just these adjectives, in fact, that other people often do think of the English. My task has been to explain these characteristics and to counterbalance them with others, rather than to deny them.

The European or American reader, shocked by reports of rigid regimentation in Communist China and of the excesses of the Red Guards in 1966, may shake his head with disbelief when told that the Chinese are instinctively drawn to counsels of moderation and the Golden Mean, and repelled by "isms" and extremes. But all, I hope, will become clear as the scroll unwinds. Many Westernized Chinese may also feel that I have painted a picture of their people that is quite unrecognizable. But then I have not really been writing about them. There is no point in explaining Westernized Chinese to the West: someone should write a book that explains them, rather, to the Chinese.

I am not a research scholar and I dispose of no original sources or materials that go back more than thirty-five years. I am, therefore, immensely indebted to the writers and translators of the works upon which I have drawn so heavily to present my portrait of the Chinese—most notably, Mr. Maurice Collis, Professor H. G. Creel, Professor C. P. Fitzgerald, the late Professor Herbert A. Giles, the late Professor James Legge, Professor Joseph Needham, and the late Mr. Arthur Waley, together with all others whose relevant works are listed in the bibliography. If I myself am only the interpreter, I am at least in most illustrious company, for Confucius himself said: "I transmit, but I do not originate."

An impertinence? David Astor, the editor of *The Observer,* suggested the book and generously allowed me time in which to produce it. Frederic Warburg agreed to publish it. Only the unstinted help of my wife, Ching Ping (Apprehensive Ice, alias Chu Ti or Judy), made it possible for me to write it at all. But, in the last analysis, I must take the blame.

Singapore
September 1966

Acknowledgments

I would like to acknowledge my debt to the writers and translators of works from which I have quoted or taken extracts. (A full bibliography appears on page 423.) Arthur Waley's *170 Chinese Poems*, from which I have taken lines from the following poems: "The Rejected Wife" (p. 75), "Li Fu-jen" (p. 87), "Woman" (p. 71), "On the Birth of His Son" (p. 252), "A Protest in the Sixth Year of Ch'ien Fu" (p. 308); his study *Yuan Mei* (pp. 273, 276–277), and *Monkey* (p. 168); the translations of *The Chinese Classics* by James Legge (pp. 23, 85, 110, 213, 219); *A History of Chinese Literature* by Herbert A. Giles (pp. 213, 311–312, 379); the *Records of the Grand Historian of China*, translated by Burton Watson (p. 62); *Lord Macartney's Embassy to Peking in 1793* by J. L. Cranmer-Byng (condensed extract on p. 355); *The Romance of the Three Kingdoms*, translated by C. H. Brewitt-Taylor (pp. 230–231, 314); *Science and Civilisation in China* by Joseph Needham (p. 242, and much other material on Chinese science); *The Travels of Marco Polo*, translated by Ronald Latham (pp. 127, 175); *Europe and China* by G. F. Hudson (p. 265); *The Story of Chinese Philosophy* by Ch'u Chai and Winberg Chai (p. 380); the books of Morris Collis, including *The Great Within* (pp. 273, 297, 315, 346, 356) and *The First Holy One* (p. 63); *On a Chinese Screen* by W. Somerset Maugham (pp. 119, 382); *The Strange Case of Magistrate Pao* by Leon Comber (p. 115);

The Art of War, translated by Samuel B. Griffith (pp. 316, 318, 321, 322); *The Singapore Story* by Kenneth Attiwill (p. 326); *A Military History of Modern China* by F. F. Liu (p. 325); *Scratches on the Mind* by Harold R. Isaacs (p. 328, quoting from *The New Breed* by Andrew Geer, the historian of the U. S. Marines); *The Chinese Unicorn*, collected by Thomas L. Rowe (pp. 209 et. seq.); *Poems from China*, translated by Wong Man (p. 311). I should also like to acknowledge my debt to Yang Hsien-yi and Gladys Lang, to Rewi Alley, to J. H. Jackson and other translators of Chinese works published by the Foreign Languages Press and New World Press in Peking.

Above all, I must thank the editors of *The Observer* of London and The Observer Foreign News Service (OFNS) for allowing me to use in this book numerous extracts from articles I have written for them as a Far East staff correspondent over the past twelve years, and on which they hold copyright. Finally, I am most grateful to Hugh Howse, head of the Southeast Asia Office of the British Broadcasting Corporation, for reading the manuscript and making many valuable suggestions, and also to Edward de Souza, my assistant in Singapore, who typed, checked, and retyped the manuscript with such care and efficiency.

Contents

FROM THE INSIDE, LOOKING OUT

"I always thought they were fabulous monsters!" said the Unicorn. "Is it alive?" . . . Alice could not help her lips curling up in a smile as she began: "Do you know, I always thought Unicorns were fabulous monsters, too! I never saw one alive before!"

"Well, now that we *have* seen each other," said the Unicorn, "if you'll believe in me, I'll believe in you. Is that a bargain?"

—Lewis Carroll, *Through the Looking Glass*

From the Outside, Looking In

1

Dragons Nine

Ping has her own library of Chinese books in our Singapore bungalow, and casting around for some telling quote with which to open this chapter, I pulled out a volume entitled *The Merchant of Wei-Ni-Sz* by William Sha-Shih-Pi-Ya, and found what I needed. For, while intent upon his pound of flesh, the villain Sha-Lo-K'o asks a series of rhetorical questions that might be roughly translated like this:

> "If you prick us, do we not bleed? If you tickle us,
> do we not laugh? If you poison us, do we not die?
> And if you wrong us, shall we not revenge?"

The protest that Jews are also men—and the stern warning that they may therefore behave like human beings if provoked—seemed to apply admirably to the canny, pragmatic, hard-working, yet sensitive, often excitable, and sometimes deplorably stupid people who have in the past been dismissed humiliatingly in the West as the "Heathen Chinese with the Inscrutable Face."

And the Chinese share with us more than bleeding and laughing, death and revenge. There is the magical moment when a demure pigtailed little miss of six with eyes like chocolate almonds tells you a seemingly breathtaking story about how this maiden dressed in rags and plagued with two ugly stepsisters caught a magic fish whose bones would grant any wish, so she was able to go to this marvelous festival, but then her slipper fell off . . . and you realize you are hearing a version of Cinderella half a millennium older than the one you were read as a child.

The odd little similarities between China and the West accumulate, haphazardly. The Chinese have their own Noah in the legendary Sago-king Yü, who saved the country from great floods in about 2000 B.C. They have more than one version of the Judgment of Solomon, and can match *Pilgrim's Progress* with *Journey to the West*, the most hilarious piece of pious allegory that could ever have been based on a holy (and historically substantiated) expedition. Their thousand-page-long *Men of the Marshes* is *Robin Hood* in a Chinese mirror, and the delight of boyhood from Peking to Formosa.

It is curious to read that a thousand years ago the women of Hangchow buttoned on the left, and their men on the right; that the gentlemen of that time threw dice to decide who would pay for the next round of drinks. The Chinese Boxers (the "Society of Harmonious Fists") who stormed the foreign legations in Peking in 1900 grew whiskers for virility, but the corner-pub tradition of aggressive sozzling as a proof of masculinity is much older, and Lin Yutang has even dug up a story—*It's wonderful to be drunk*—about a wine so strong that it knocked you out for three months if you smelled it on someone else's breath.

This selection of mental bric-a-brac has not been assembled entirely at random, for it seems necessary even in the second half of the twentieth century to remind the West that any vision of China and the Chinese should include children entranced by Cinderella, and boys lying in the shade on a sunny afternoon daydreaming of adventure, and would-be poets, roaring drunk, rolling down the street in the night watches, bawling out their second-rate verse.

For the Western conception of the Chinese seems to be like a disastrous and dog-eared poker hand of unrelated cards, most of them left over from the last century.

There is the gorgeously clad and imperturbable mandarin of

suspiciously prosperous but benevolent mien, seated against a willow-pattern background of humped-back bridges and gracefully drooping bamboo. There are improbable mountains cut in half by thin skeins of cloud, a pagoda with upturned eaves, and you seem to hear the sweet tinkle of wind-bells, the sound of a gong. This, the most flattering of all the misconceptions, dates back to the eighteenth century. It is Dresden china, and it resembles the real thing just about as much as a Dresden shepherdess looks like a real shepherdess.

Then there is the eternal image of Dr. Fu Manchu and his friends, of the cultivated, callous, opium-smoking criminal, all long knives and little-finger nails enclosed in gaudily bejeweled sheaths; there are the petty crooks and dope peddlers with forty-two protuberant teeth, the comic laundrymen and the ship's cooks, the fat, greasy restaurateurs, and, most inscrutable of all, the potato-faced Mao Tse-tung with his boiler suit and his curious but well-known lifelong ambition to enslave his countrymen, make them all wish they were dead, and then grant a fair percentage of them their wish.

Cowards and cold-blooded torturers, the Chinese are positively known in Poughkeepsie and East Liverpool to eat unborn mice, monkey's brains hot from the hacked-off head, hundred-year-old eggs, and snakes cooked alive in boiling rice. You cannot expect an honest answer from people who invented the ivory backscratcher. You cannot expect them to know left from right when they cannot distinguish between "L" and "R." They laugh when they are sad, and cry when they are happy, and of course, as is widely known, their women are cut on the cross, so you never know where you are with them.

If they cannot talk the dog-American of Charlie Chan, they talk that murderous mixture of English, Portuguese, and bastard Cantonese strung together with Chinese idiom known as "pidgin," and it is assumed by many that this dead language is still the medium of Chinese who have any contact with civilization.

At a distinguished public dinner in London, the story goes

(in its most modern version), an elderly clubman was disconcerted to find himself seated next to a silent Chinese. Wanting to be courteous, however, he leaned toward him and asked, tentatively, "Likee soupee?" The Chinese looked at him briefly, nodded, but said nothing, and conversation lapsed. However, it appeared that the Chinese was a foreign guest of some note, for as coffee was served he was called upon to say a few words. He rose, bowed, and made a fifteen-minute speech in impeccable English about the sociological significance of the European Common Market. Amid polite applause he then sat down, turned to his abashed English neighbor, and, after the briefest of pauses, asked softly: "Likee speechee?"

The roles could certainly be reversed, however, for the Chinese conception of the Western "red-haired devil" is only too frequently something to frighten impressionable children with at night. "No good will come of allowing his sort in the house," our amah whispers urgently to Ping when a Roman Catholic priest calls. "Don't you know they don't believe in God?" But a more refined and authentic exercise in masochism is to ignore the grosser superstitions in which the ignorant envelop their image of the "barbarian," and simply look at a white man through narrowed eyes.

The barbarian then appears, on the whole, as a lamentable creature. Seemingly devoid of any philosophy that might enable him to live in harmony with the world as it is, he is at best a clever monkey, burning himself out in a feverish struggle to change everything all the time. The culture of the men who laughed at the bound "lily feet" of the ladies of Imperial China has produced a series of ludicrously unnatural and unhealthy distortions of the human frame and its packaging, from the Victorian wasp waist to the stiletto heel. And many of their habits hardly bear mentioning in mixed company. They kiss in public, pass you things *with one hand only* (extremely impolite among Chinese, who always use two), open presents you give them *in front of you*, and rudely say "thank you" all the time, in order—

quite obviously—to shrug off their obligations. They eat, as a viceroy of Canton remarked more than a hundred years ago, with kitchen implements. They take tea with milk and sugar and consume not only raw beef and rotten pheasant but also truly nauseating foods like cow's-milk cheese and kippers. The Chinese eat dog? But, surely, the French eat far more horse?

The newly arrived European can perhaps be forgiven for holding his conveniently long nose when he walks through a Hong Kong fishmarket, or past the stinking drains and trash heaps of Singapore's Chinatown. But the seasoned traveler in the East is used to this. What *he* often forgets, however, is just how highly seasoned he is. All that steak, Scotch, and after-shave lotion must make a difference, for it is well known that on Chinese territory the dog and the water buffalo—that docile friend of the unwashed farming family will react to the proximity of an odoriferous pale skin with dangerous violence. There is nothing odd about this, the Chinese say. A teetotaler from Peking who is almost as sparing with water as he is with wine once assured me that the Americans bathe so often only because, of course, they smell so much. On the principle that there are some things that a man's best friends must be bullied into admitting, I asked Ping what I smelled like to her. She thought about this for history's longest split second and then said with a nod of decision: "You smell like Banner." I sighed with relief, but, of course, she is prejudiced in my favor. Banner of Grandeur is our long-haired Alsatian dog.

The Westerner may nevertheless visit a modern Chinese home and ask, with a justifiable frown of happy disdain, what has happened to the exquisite taste of the Confucian mandarin with his scrolls, and his jade, and his artificially landscaped garden of rocks and pools and stunted trees. For here the ashtrays are by Cinzano and Guinness, the chairs are covered in red simulated leather, the tables with Formica, and there is a giant chromium-plated combination radio, record player, and TV set—all teeth and two-tone—surmounted by a mirror in the plastic grip of a garland of gardenias.

This, admittedly, is Honky-Tonk Han, the taste of the rice-patch-to-riches Overseas Chinese in Southeast Asia whose counterparts were turned out by the dozen after the industrial revolution in the English Midlands, cast in solid brass.

But there are other things to offend: pink flouncy dresses against taut yellow skin; velveteen cushions, embroidered with tiger heads, in the rear window of the passing Rolls-Royce; gold crucifixes on charm bracelets. Even a classic Chinese reception room, with its stiff rows of heavily carved blackwood chairs, its hanging scroll of graceful Chinese characters, its huge solitary Ming vase, and its painted silken lantern, is suddenly made or marred by a chamber-pot spittoon enlivened with the artist's impression of the Coronation of Queen Elizabeth II.

After this, the Caucasoid gazes with pride at his fashionably furnished "Chinese" lounge with its splendid twin paintings of a seated mandarin and his spouse, the elegant terra-cotta horse on the escritoire, the solid teak coffee table with the upcurled ends, the tall, pale green vase with its spray of dendrobium, and all the other appurtenances of Occidental gracious living in the Orient.

He is not, however, privy to the thoughts of his Chinese guest. This room is really terrible. The scrolls of the mandarin and his wife are ancestor pictures—but they are obviously not the ancestors of these people. What would my host say if I hung up a picture of *his* grandmother and grandfather in *my* house, I wonder? The T'ang horse is an obvious fake, of course. He doesn't seem to realize that the thing he's stuck the orchids in is not a vase but a cheap cylinder for holding rolled-up scrolls, and the coffee table is a copy of the kind Chinese butchers use for killing pigs on. As for those stools with the "long life" character carved into the seats in black and gold, they can only have come from an undertaker's. Why doesn't he bring a coffin into the room, and have done?

The best illustration of the dangers of cultural poaching was provided by an English girl whom we saw on the Star Ferry in

Hong Kong ten years ago, wearing a smart little cotton frock, the material plain except for the same string of Chinese characters repeated at intervals. Ping looked sad, and I asked her what was so funny. The stuff had evidently been hanging in a shop window, she said. I objected that there was nothing very odd about that. No, she said, except you see the characters say: "Good stuff inside: price cheap."

It may be argued that while there is a case for trying to tell the West something about the Chinese, it is at the same time an absurd proposition that can only lead to meaningless generalization, since one of the most bewildering things about them seems to be their infinite variety. No one can possibly include in one composite portrait the traits of the half-starved, steel-hardened Communist cadre who fought a bitter guerrilla war against overwhelming odds for twelve years in the implacable jungles of Malaya; the jovial overblown Hong Kong merchant, heavy with corruption and the importunities of his seven wives; the Cambridge-trained lawyer practicing putts in his downtown office; and the illiterate amah who thinks there's a rabbit in the moon. Moreover, would it not be true to say that there can hardly be a greater difference between two human beings than there is— in some families—between a Singapore Chinese mother and her Chinese daughter today?

Mother begins the day with a stentorian throat-clearing operation, a rubdown with a minute damp towel, and a breakfast of rice gruel. Her head is filled with gold teeth and much superstitious nonsense, but she has her favorites in heaven as on earth, and so she lights a joss stick before her little image of Kuan Yin, the Chinese Goddess of Mercy. (She will be horrified if you tell her that Kuan Yin was originally an Indian Bodhisattva called Avalokiteshvara, and that this is one of the earliest known cases of hagiological sex change: she thinks most Indians are really rather black.)

She reads with difficulty, but she will consult this year's astrological almanac to see if this is a good day for washing her hair.

She may switch on the radio, but quickly switch it off again—she finds all Western music utterly excruciating and cannot differentiate between Bach and the Beatles. But she loves Chinese opera with its shrieking female impersonators and earsplitting tambours, and she knows all the plots by heart. She is meticulously clean about her clothes, but incurious about the minatory smell of sour drains in her own kitchen—not that she is indifferent to scents, for she loves to sniff babies for the perfume of their flesh.

She is deferential to her husband—as long as he stays out of her household affairs—and respectful toward his old parents. She is rather frightened and mystified by big white foreigners—they seem to be a lot of money-wasting, ill-tempered lunatics—and if she is sick, she goes rather to a Chinese doctor and buys Chinese herbal medicines. Her main concessions to Western science are to use a sewing machine, travel by bus, and drink stout when she has her period.

Her great loyalty is her family, her greatest joy to have them all around her at Chinese New Year. She tends the tomb of her parents at the Ch'ing Ming festival, but she and her husband are not among those who practice this foreign heresy of putting flowers on their graves. She feels they should be trying to find a husband for her daughter. But then daughters nowadays . . .

The daughter is not one of those English-educated Beatle-screamers, but she is also not her mama. She is Chinese-educated but she speaks a clipped jerky English, heavily shaken by ugly, cockneyesque glottal stops. She dresses Western, can moan to the best tapes, likes dancing, James Bond movies, permanent waves, and ballet. She uses cosmetics, deodorants and peppermint-flavored toothpaste, and she thinks it might be smart to become a Christian, or at least call herself Mary instead of Mei Li. Sometimes she even dreams that she might actually marry a European. Anyway, West is best, and East is least, and Chinatown is dirty, smelly, uncomfortable, and overcrowded.

She went through a stage in which she wanted to join the

Communists, to be banished to Red China, jeering and shaking her fist as the Special Branch men put her on the boat, and then to become a dedicated doctor, or anyway a nurse in the service of Mao's 700 million head of population. She was disgusted with the fat cushions of a mercantile society, of forebears who never thought of anything but marriage and moneygrubbing, the contemptible role of the comprador in a colonial system upon which her parents set such store. And now her mother does not know which of her phases has in fact proved the more worrying.

People object that there is no such country as China and no such people as the Chinese, and point out that there are tall, slit-eyed, beaky-nosed northerners from Shantung who are slower, slovenlier, more stolidly courageous than the smaller, snub-nosed, bean-eyed, quick-witted and more fastidious Cantonese; that while the north eats noodles and sweeps the snow from the roof in winter, the south eats rice and sweats in clammy subtropical heat. But while Ping, with a northern face and southern eyes, has been mistaken for a Eurasian, a Portuguese, a Japanese, a Filipino, and a Mexican by her own people, any European or American can see with half an eye that she is Chinese. They never make a mistake.

The Chinese say the dragons had nine sons, each with its own distinctive character. The first is the dragon of burden, and is used as a base for monuments. The second is the dragon of fantasy and always stands on the roof, his head turned upward toward the sky. The third is a small loudmouth of a dragon and is frequently found on bells. The fourth is the strongest of all, has the face of a tiger, and guards the entrances of jails. The fifth loves his food and can be seen on many rice bowls. The sixth is a river dragon and adorns the parapets of bridges. The seventh is a great fighter and is carved on the hilts of swords. The eighth loves smoke and decorates incense burners. And the ninth is a recluse who appears on closed doors. All are different, but all are dragons.

To protest that there is no such thing as a Chinese is like saying that there is no such thing as a European, because a swarthy, garlic-chewing Calabrian seems to have little in common with a freckled Caledonian tackling his haggis. But from where an educated Chinese stands, they are both very much the heirs of a single recognizable culture—white men who in most cases may not even know the extent to which the hemlock of Socrates and the cross of Christ have given them a common heritage, full of strange habits and bizarre concepts that range from baking bread to chopping logic, and from churning butter to a sense of sin.

China, too, is a continent, and the Greco-Christian culture of Europe is balanced by the shared inheritance of disparate peoples in Eastern Asia who did not say they were Chinese but called themselves "the Hsia," much as the disunited city-states of Plato's day spoke of "Hellas." The story of China first emerges from the realm of sheer fable with the creation of the Hsia dynasty nearly three thousand years before Christ at a deep bend of the Yellow River in the modern province of Shansi. This was followed by the Shang dynasty, whose founder, according to traditional dates, overthrew the last Hsia tyrant in 1557 B.C. In 1050 B.C., Chou ousted Shang, and from the ninth century B.C. onward, Chinese history is accurately dated. Any examination of the source and course of a great river will tell the analyst what kind of sludge he is going to find at the estuary, and the universal characteristics, the beliefs, the prejudices, and the sometimes baffling reflexes of the Chinese can only be interpreted in the light of their long past.

If the contrary behavior of the Communists sometimes seems to show up this sketch of the Chinese as a poor likeness, it is precisely because Chinese Communism is a protest against that past. To have known the face is nevertheless to understand the face-lift. An ancient Chinese world of greed, cruelty, treachery, and gross excesses inspired prim Confucianism, with its ideals of moderation and men of propriety. In turn, the peculiar weaknesses of a corrupt Confucian China have determined the peculiar shape of Communist revolution. The Communists fight against some of the distinctive failings of their forefathers for the same reason that they succumb to others: they inherit them themselves. Like the noodle-eating northerner who is a "foreigner" to the rice-eating Cantonese, therefore, "un-Chinese" Communism remains stubbornly Chinese.

On the other hand, the more a Chinese is Westernized and detribalized, the less the findings of this book will apply. In principle, the Catholic, squash-playing Oxford undergraduate named Wong who speaks no Chinese at all is to be counted out as a true mutant. But, without plunging into arguments about blood and environment, even this supposition must be treated with a little caution. My Chinese friend Paul Strauss, aged five, was adopted when three months old by a Eurasian of Dutch and Ceylonese origin and his English wife, and he goes to a little kindergarten run in English on modern educational lines. When his mother tells him she will have no time to read him a bedtime story today because she must go out at six, his reaction is not to burst into tears but to wait until she has left the room, climb up on a chair, and put the clock back two hours. Warned not to cross the boundary line when taken to watch a cricket match, he does not wait until his mother's back is turned and then sneak over it. Instead, he walks up to the boundary and coolly opens up a yard-wide gap in it by rubbing out the chalk line with his feet. He reminds me irresistibly of Ping when I first told her about being placed below the salt. "I'd take my own," she flashed back at once. The influences in his life are overwhelmingly Western. But he is still a Chinese.

2

The Three Thousand Formative Years

In the past the European's choice of his own personal misconception of China and the Chinese seems to have depended on how devout a Christian he was and when he was born. To the agnostic of the eighteenth century we owe the golden legend of the great Confucian state moving majestically down the centuries, changeless, peaceful, inert, and practically embalmed beneath the rule of its godlike emperors and the government of its wisest scholars. To the Victorian churchgoer, on the other hand, China was the nightmare of the Protestant missionary, a godless kingdom of sinful rogues and heathens, for it was pious horror at the behavior of the benighted that first gave us the image of Dr. Fu Manchu.

The Chinese story is in fact an account of alternating periods of bloodthirsty upheaval and civilized splendor, and although this is not a history of China, it might be as well to give a synopsis of the plot at this point, with some emphasis on the sheer richness of a culture whose heirs may otherwise seem unaccountably pleased with themselves at times today.

One thousand years before the birth of Alexander the Great, the Chinese were carving jade and weaving silk, casting fine bronze and producing other alloys; they were growing wheat, millet, and rice, throwing and painting sophisticated pottery, fighting with war chariots, and recording past and prophecy in a written language of more than two thousand characters. In the first millennium before Christ, they were making fine armor and using the crossbow that Europe was only to discover in the Middle Ages; their astronomers noted the passage of Halley's Comet in 240 B.C.—it was observed with some justifiable misgiving in England in A.D. 1066—and they were already working with a calendar of 365½ days to the year.

The birth of Confucius in 550 B.C. heralded a golden era in philosophy, a sunburst of original thinkers whose wisdom was to illumine the land until today. But meanwhile the feudal Chinese kingdom ruled by the Chou dynasty was breaking up into petty states, with the seven biggest among them intriguing and fighting incessantly for supremacy across China's ravaged body. It was not for the last time that this was going to happen.

"Empires wax and wane," opens the *Romance of the Three Kingdoms* with the aphoristic pomp of a Shakespearean chorus. "States cleave asunder and coalesce." Forged into a single empire in the third century B.C., China split again four hundred years later into three states whose vicious struggle for mastery inspired this wonderfully inaccurate account of stratagem and swordsmanship under the banners of Wei, Wu, and Shu.

United at the end of the sixth century A.D., China began to splinter again in the eighth, after a rebellion that has provided one of the most terrible tallies of death and destruction in world history. Some two hundred years later a new dynasty arose but lost the northern half of the country to the barbarian Kins at the beginning of the thirteenth century and the whole of China to the Mongols of Kublai Khan before the end of it. It took these terrible Tatars more than half a century to overrun China, however, and just 106 years after they had made Peking their capital, they were thrown out again anyway.

Three hundred years of Chinese dynastic rule followed, but in 1644 the Manchus from across the northern border marched in and seized the throne. These usurpers were only evicted from power in 1912 in a Chinese revolution that laid the country open in turn to the pernicious warlords of the twenties, the three-cornered struggle between Chiang Kai-shek's Nationalists, Mao Tse-tung's Communists, and the Japanese in the thirties and forties, and the division of China into Communist Mainland and Nationalist Formosa in the fifties and sixties. It seems fair to say that this woeful tale hardly squares with the popular picture of China as an eternal Land of Smiles. But between catastrophies, the names and glories of great Chinese dynasties—Han, T'ang, Sung, Ming—ring down the centuries like great bronze bells.

First mention, however, must go to the short-lived dynasty of Ch'in, whose "First Emperor" welded the feudal states of China into an empire in 221 B.C. and constructed the Great Wall. Things are apt to be on a large scale in this country, and the wall is about 1,600 miles long as the crow flies. Twenty-four feet high, punctuated frequently by forty-foot towers, and wide enough for eight men to walk abreast on the top, it slides across the valleys and misty 5,000-foot hills of northern and western China like a colossal gray guardian serpent, belly to earth. The First Emperor's complex of palaces at the capital included 270 residences that extended over a distance of some seventy miles and were connected by covered corridors, for the emperor wanted his movements to be secret. Among these pavilions were precise replicas of the royal palaces of each of the states he had conquered, and in these he housed the harems and all the other treasure of their former kings. His main audience hall measured 500 by 100 paces and could hold ten thousand men.

At this time China was selling not only silk but fine-cast iron to an admiring and acquisitive Rome, and the Han dynasty, whose span includes Christ's lifetime, saw the invention of paper and the early beginnings of Chinese painting. Lacquerware and beautifully worked jewelry were to be found even in the farthest outposts of the expanding empire, and the troops were paid in bales of silk, which they used for barter trade with the nomadic Huns across the frontier.

In the fifth century, Hsieh Ho laid down the six rules of paint-

ing—rhythmic vitality, anatomical structure, conformity with nature, harmonious coloring, composition, and finish. In the seventh
century began the tremendous project of building a Grand Canal
connecting the Yellow River to the Yangtze and capable of taking
500-ton lighters. There is a detailed description of the Sui emper-
or's first progress along this waterway in a magnificent Imperial
barge 230 feet in length, built like a palace on four decks, with
a throne room and 120 cabins decorated with gold and jade. Nine
more barges of almost equal splendor carried the rest of the
court. When on land, this tyrant sometimes traveled with a palatial prefab which measured more than two miles around when
assembled, and once terrified the unsuspecting enemy during his
campaign against Korea by having it erected overnight on an
otherwise bare plain, it is said. And then came the great era of
the T'ang dynasty.

In a divided, primitive, and frightened England, men were
facing the first harassing raids of the Viking longships. Meanwhile, the T'ang empire extended from Vietnam to Mongolia,
from the shores of the Pacific Ocean to the fastnesses of Tibet.
The capital at Ch'ang An was nearly as big as modern Paris, and
the government under the emperor was divided into six boards
or ministries: Administration, Finance, Rites, Defense, Punishment, and Works. A census held in A.D. 754 records a taxpaying
population of nearly 53 million people, living in 321 prefectures.
China was not ruled by nobles and hereditary gentry but by a
professional civil service selected by an established examination
system which the British, well ahead of the rest of the field,
were finally to adopt and adapt some twelve hundred years later
when Queen Victoria was already middle-aged.

The arts flourished as never before, and the dynasty is famous
for its great poets, its early painting and hard-paste porcelain,
its music, and its drama school. Printing had been invented, and
before the dynasty fell, thousands of copies of the Confucian
classics were being published and sold cheaply to eager students
for whom education meant the civil-service ladder. The Chinese

were using whale or seal oil to make raincoats, stone lanterns, and waterproof covering on ships and carriages. They had discovered the principle of fingerprinting and the possibilities of the Lippizaner: "The Emperor ordered a hundred gentle horses to be brought to the gymnasium, and when the royal band struck up, all the horses followed the rhythm in unison, moving their heads, shaking their tails, curvetting and dancing."

Sung followed T'ang, and in A.D. 1005—a decade before Canute became king of England—a thousand-volume encyclopedia was published under the patronage of the Chinese emperor. "Quinsai is the greatest city that may be found in the world," wrote Marco Polo of Hangchow, the temporary capital of the Southern Sung emperors before the Great Khan came and conquered. There were 117 bridges within the walls of this fabulous Chinese Venice, which had a population of one million, according to the regular census, at a time when few European capitals held more than a hundred thousand people. Its streets were well paved with brick and stone, the main Imperial thoroughfare being three miles long and nearly two hundred feet wide, and fresh water for the inhabitants was channeled along terra-cotta conduits from six main reservoirs.

Throw together any twelve isolated facts about the Southern Sung, and a pattern of sophisticated luxury must emerge. This was an age of dalliance rather than dangerous living, and Hangchow was a city of pleasure gardens and pagodas, of leisurely excursions in painted lake barges, of taverns in which rice wine was served in silver cups and restaurants that specialized in this or that delicacy, including the ices that Marco Polo later introduced in Italy.

You could buy delicate silks, and brocades, and porcelain that was being shipped as far away as Zanzibar, gold and silver ornaments, or gems and pearls—and pay with treasury notes. There was a brisk business in antiques for wealthy connoisseurs, and dozens of shops sold merchandise unheard of in the West—ingenious toys, printed books, painted fans, anti-mosquito powder, toilet paper, drugs out of the capacious Chinese pharmacopoeia. A free dispensary, financed by the state, supplied medicines to the poor.

The striking statistics continue down the centuries: by 1762 there are 200 million Chinese (the population of the United Kingdom is well under seven million in that year). The enlarged Summer Palace of the emperor outside Peking consists of sixty thousand acres of cunningly contrived landscape whose architects built whole artificial hills in order to create an impression of dramatic scenery, turning the great depressions from which the earth and rocks had been removed into ornamental lakes. There are some two hundred pavilions and other buildings in this park, grouped into thirty different residential villages for the emperor (but all will be burned to the ground on the orders of Lord Elgin in 1860). And in case this tally should appear vulgar to the less materialistic, let it end with the stupendous work commanded by the Ch'ien Lung emperor in the eighteenth century —the compilation of an encyclopedia of literature containing the text of every book ever written in China, whether or not it had been printed before.

For more than a hundred and fifty years the West tended to be distrustful and contemptuous of the decadent and crumbling Manchu empire and the chaos that followed its downfall, so that Imperial China's impact on an open-mouthed eighteenth-century Europe has often been forgotten. At that time her painted silks and porcelains, her lacquers and landscapes were enthusiastically welcomed by a weary Continent bored with pompous baroque and ready for rococo. Watteau and John Cozens painted "Chinese," Chippendale made furniture in "Chinese taste," and as the pavilions and pagodas went up all over Europe, the vogue for *chinoiserie* extended from "Chinese-English" gardens to "Chinese" wallpapers, from goldfish, parasols, and tea to lacquered cabinets and sedan chairs, finally producing in "Chinese-Gothic" an architectural term whose powerful intimation of horror still makes the blood run cold.

Revolutionary thinkers of the day were profoundly influenced by the sometimes idealized accounts of China brought back by Jesuit missionaries. Leibniz urged that Chinese missionaries should be sent to Europe instead to teach natural theology. Voltaire declared, "The organization of the Chinese Empire is the best the world has ever seen," and cited the excellence of its secular government in his attacks against the Roman Catholic Church (which at that time owned one-fifth of France). Oppressive rule by nobles and clergy in Europe was cruelly compared with equitable administration by scholar-magistrates in China. Adolf Reichwein called Confucius the "Patron Saint of the Enlightenment."

What did he mean? The gaudy catalogue of China's disasters and dynastic glories, whose monumental scale has given the Chinese much of their character and should have earned them more of our respect, brings us to our true beginning. Confucius said: "When I have presented one corner of a subject to anyone, and he cannot learn the other three from it, I do not repeat my lesson." With all the humility of a philatelist separating a Blue Mauritius from its unlikely envelope, let us lift the first corner of the subject.

3

The First Gentleman

Today, at a distance of nearly twenty-five hundred years, Confucius might quickly be dismissed as a square: "When the Ruler was present, his manner showed respectful uneasiness. When he was passing the empty seat of the prince, his countenance appeared to change, and his legs to bend under him, and his words came as if he hardly had breath to utter them. He ascended the reception hall, holding his breath as if he dared not breathe. When he was carrying the scepter of his prince, he seemed to bend his body as if he were not able to bear its weight. His countenance seemed to change, and he looked apprehensive, and he dragged his feet along as if they were held by something to the ground." Confucius did not wear purple or puce or red, even in his undress, and he required his bed gown to be half as long again as his body. When eating, he did not converse. When in bed, he did not speak. When he was in his carriage, he did not turn his head quite around, and he did not talk hastily or point with his hands.

Evidently a model driver, certainly a stickler for etiquette and a careful respecter of persons, the Master drew upon himself the derision of his detractors, who laughed at his high, forked headdress, his wide cloak and broad belt of hide, his long sleeves thrown out like bird's wings, his bowing and scraping and sucking-in of breath, the court capers that included always mounting the royal dais with the same foot first but withdrawing from it with the other. For Confucius achieved the distinction of observing courtesies and fashions that were Old World and going out even in 500 B.C. It is recorded not only that the Master would not sit on his mat if it were not symmetrically arranged but even that he would not eat meat unless it were cut into precise squares.

But behind his old-maidish fussiness over the detail of daily ceremony lay the sound proposition that clothes and custom mold the mind. It is well known that prewar Englishmen who insisted on putting on a dinner jacket in the evening in fetid outposts of empire resisted the duskier temptations of dark continents rather better than those who ended up in rope-soled sandals and a sarong. For dinner jackets meant disciplined gentlemen. Outward form, contended Confucius, would lead to inward grace. When Ping was at school in China about twenty-four hundred years after Confucius died, the whole class began every week by bowing three times to a photograph of Sun Yat-sen, founder of the Chinese Republic, repeating the principles he had embodied in his will, observing three minutes' silence, and then singing the Nationalist Party song. And a dozen other ways were found of obliging students to show outward respect for the young state in order to make the new nationalism a subconscious habit. "It trained you to be loyal," Ping once said, and added, not too convincingly: "Like playing *God save the Queen* in theaters."

But the Sage preached that correct ritual was without merit unless it was heartfelt: "For mourning there should be deep sorrow rather than minute attention to detail . . . ceremonies conducted without reverence, mourning conducted without grief —how can I contemplate such ways?" "Even a bird pines for its dead," one of his successors pointed out. Confucius then asked men to extend their reverence for ritual to their daily acts and their relations with others until these also become sacred rites, to be practiced with a meticulous respect for moral and social obligations.

The virtually untranslatable word for this principle is "li."

What was "not li" was simply "not done," and its basis was the code of Chinese chivalry for the nobility, whose rigid rules could effectively replace law in a small, exclusive society. Suicide, not punishment, logically followed the disgraceful act once it was discovered, for its perpetrator would find it a far greater ordeal to try to go on living among his outraged fellows than to die. To the West, nothing seems so white and Christian, perhaps, as the medieval concept of chivalry, nor so far removed from the Chinese happy family of cherrystones: Mandarin, Gangster, Laundryman, Cook. But nothing could outdo the elaborate code of honor of the ancient Chinese, who believed that to take unfair advantage of the enemy or to treat a beaten foe harshly was to violate the laws of heaven itself, and to call down the celestial wrath.

"I am not the Lord of Sung," Mao Tse-tung has said more than once, and it is well to remember this. In 650 B.C. the retainers of the Duke of Sung faced a powerful invading enemy army over a river. The duke's aides urged him to attack at once and catch this force as it waded through the water, but the duke peremptorily replied: "You cannot." They then begged him to order the charge before the enemy could assemble on the hither bank. But again he tersely declined. Only when his adversary's forces were fully ready for the fray did the duke order the attack. He was wounded in the thigh, and his army disastrously defeated, but when his entourage upbraided him for his foolishness, the duke coolly replied: "The sage does not crush the weak, or assault the enemy until he is formed up."

This cautionary tale of folly and misplaced integrity is greeted with shining eyes by Chinese, who have a keen-edged sense of the heroic. But the Lord of Sung was not exceptional. We are told that when armies came face to face, opposing princes would exchange high-sounding greetings from their chariots, even drink a toast before the first blow was struck. A famous bas-relief records an incident in which a powerful charioteer protected his wounded lord in battle by breaking off the canopy of his chariot and holding it over him as a shield. Most significant in the group

are three figures approaching the scene, for these are the enemy
prince and his aides, who, in the middle of the fight, have come
to congratulate the charioteer on his loyalty and his feat of
strength.

Ping's favorite character is the temporarily dispossessed Duke
of Tsin, who, having received many kindnesses at the hand of
the future king of Ch'u before that monarch acceded to his title,
swore that if he ever found himself at war with Ch'u after he
came into his lands, he would retire thirty miles before turning
to fight. Some years afterward Tsin and Ch'u indeed went to
war. The duke kept his word, retreating for three days before he
turned about to give the army of Ch'u battle—and a sound thrash-
ing.

The tradition by no means died as the centuries crowded in.
In 1842 a furious Chinese general rejected as utterly despicable
a proposal to entice foragers from the British invading force at
Ningpo into capturing deliberately infected cattle (more than
seventy years before the first use of mustard gas). During the
Boxer Rebellion in 1900, when the foreign legations in Peking
were under siege and defended only by a handful of men, the
Chinese commander-in-chief consistently avoided providing the
investing force with the artillery that would have given it victory
and led to the massacre of men, women, and children from eleven
foreign states. In a telegram to the viceroys of South China, he
wrote: "When two countries are at war, it has been customary
from antiquity not to injure the envoys . . . I have argued with all
my strength [against such a course] and submitted seven me-
morials to the Throne . . . Death I do not mind, but the guilt I
would bear forever."

Confucius, however, lived at a time of treachery and disloyalty,
with the Chou dynasty monarch no more than an impotent chessboard king in a small, personal domain surrounded by the great
fiefs of ambitious lords who fought over China with increasing
ruthlessness, while they in turn were betrayed by their own ministers or underlings. But the Chinese have throughout history

seen the universe as a delicately balanced, infinitely complicated mechanism with whose motion man must also conform. China's own five sacred mountains might hold the world in place like so many eight-inch bolts, but any unharmonious action could still bring moving parts into collision and create chaos out of the cosmic order for which the Chinese have always had such a reverential regard. One event entails another, and even natural calamities may be the direct consequence of bad government. So Confucius preached that the times were troubled because men had lapsed from grace since the lost age of virtue when ancient sage-kings had ruled benevolently in accordance with "li"—the "li" that regulated not only the conduct between sovereign and subject, and father and son, but also the sacrifices which in turn ensured that rivers flowed within their banks, the rain fell opportunely, and the heavens wheeled. Salvation, therefore, lay in turning back to the past. Like all Chinese, Confucius believed in the power of precept. If a ruler would only follow the example set by the gentle kings of yore, all others would follow the example set by the ruler. There would be concord throughout the land, and the neighbors would be friendly.

The Sage was no egalitarian, however. He believed in a stratified society, in a harmonious pattern based on social differences. Loyalty should automatically be given to the concepts of brother, father, teacher, and prince, and therefore to the individual that happened at the time to personify these concepts, rather as a soldier observes discipline by impersonally saluting an officer's rank and not the hero or the son-of-a-bitch behind the stars or bars. All men should be classified, and their classification would fix their duties, their position, and their responsibilities toward one another. "Let prince be prince, minister minister, father father, son son," he said. Each must act as "li" dictates. This grid system would then reduce to orderly squares the social map of human anarchy over which Confucius laid it. The Master did not invent this quasi-military set of relationships. However, he injected into it not only the ideal of sincerity but also a sense of common humanity and consideration for others: "Deal with people as if you were assisting at a great sacrifice, and do not do to others what you would not wish to be done to yourself." And from those premises Confucius evolved the greatest of his ideas: the gentleman who is not a gentleman simply because he is the heir of a noble but because he has studied and emulated the wisdom and goodness of the ancients.

A Chinese gentleman lives in harmony with the universe and with his fellow men. He is generous of heart and is lenient toward the shortcomings of others. "Fine words and an insinuating appearance seldom associate with true virtue," notes Confucius, and his model man is essentially sparing of words, simple, and self-critical. He never loses his temper or shows an angry face in public. Above all, he is a man of "li." The Master said: "Respectfulness, without the rules of propriety, becomes laborious bustle; carefulness becomes timidity; boldness becomes insubordination; straightforwardness becomes rudeness." On the other hand, if the superior man is respectful to others and mindful of propriety, "all within the four seas will be his brothers." There emerges the picture of a poised, affable, somewhat reserved, if anything cautious man of integrity. He might or might not be born good, but since our betters and mentors lived in the golden age of the sage-kings, he could acquire goodness by studying the records of their times. Confucius wrote nothing original, but he compiled and edited five books that, to his mind, perpetuated the wisdom, the morality, and the "li" of the "good old days." And he founded the first private school for gentlemen, teaching any dedicated pupil that came to him, even if he arrived in a cheap, torn gown and paid for his tuition with a "bundle of meat."

His subjects? A knowledge of Rites, he said, regulated and disciplined the mind, and History taught the instructive events of the past. Poetry engendered ethical and improving thoughts, and Music a harmony of ideas. The Book of Changes (of which more later) revealed the dual forces of the Cosmos. Archery contests taught "li"—manners, restraint, the conduct of a gentleman—for the most formidable weapon of the day was not to be used for base ends. Confucius placed emphasis on moral and ethical instruction in order to fit young men for government, and any Englishman raised in the thirties must be irresistibly reminded of the hot summer form-rooms in which he took Latin as a mental discipline, the rainy and windy days on which his sports master patiently taught him the improving and intricate ritual, the inflexible etiquette of gentlemanly cricket. History, Rites (Christian), Poetry, and, alas, Music (singing)—he studied them all, while his doubtful parents were assured that the stress was not on book learning but "forming character," "improving the mind," "fostering *esprit de corps.*" Boys were to acquire decency rather than diplomas, and Confucius would have approved.

The Sage, who was not concerned with futile speculation about heaven but only to see an ethical social system reestablished on earth, cast the seed from which was to spring the thick and stubborn, if twisted trunk of a tremendous civilization—but he died a somewhat pathetic old man who felt he had thrown it away on stony ground. For about ten years he wandered among the rival states of feudal China, looking for a prince who would appoint him minister and listen to his words. But he had scant success. One can see those beefy blockheads, eager to learn from this peripatetic wise man with the overelaborate manners just how to encompass the downfall of their equally vile neighbors, only to listen with growing impatience to his tiresome message of a harmonious society and his platitudinous exhortations to conquer through kindness.

Two hundred years later, his great, if slightly flashy follower Mencius (Meng Tzu), living in the cutthroat era known in Chinese history as the "Warring States," was almost worse off. It is not difficult to imagine the reaction of the greedy feudal oaf whom Mencius told that even with his small state he could gain the control of all China, but went on to add: "For if you will but give the people benevolent government, reducing punishments and taxes . . . they will at your command fight with wooden sticks against strong mail and sharp weapons."

It is nevertheless said that Mencius was responsible for the first distortion of the Confucian precepts when in one sentence he destroyed the principle of the sanctity of kings and at the same time established the principle of popular revolt. Confucius, to whom the hierarchy was sacred, would describe even the just killing of a tyrant as "the assassination of the ruler," but when Mencius was questioned on the murder of the last king of the Shang dynasty, he remarked: "I have heard that a fellow called Jou was put to death, but not that a sovereign was killed." From this grew the legend of the "Mandate of Heaven": the ruler holds a celestial license as long as he rules well, but if he does ill, and another overthrows him and takes his place, it is because a frowning heaven has withdrawn its mandate and conferred it on the newcomer, who is, *ipso facto,* the better man. So all *successful* rebellions are automatically justified—nor is Mao Tse-tung, the present holder of the mandate, likely to disagree with this ancient tenet of Chinese faith in the context of modern Communist revolution and "just wars of liberation." (There is, moreover, strong evidence to suggest that the last Shang king was a reasonably well-loved ruler, whose name was successfully blackened by later propagandists to excuse his liquidation.) Mencius emerges, in fact, as the champion of the "people." "There is only one way to hold power and that is to hold the people," he said. "There is only one way to hold the people's hearts and that is to provide them with what they like, and to refrain from imposing upon them what they loathe."

Mencius contends that man is born good: "If men suddenly see a child about to fall into a well, they will without exception feel alarm and distress." But the misery and deceptions of daily life in times of misrule drive him to delinquency, and he can only regain his natural goodness through moral education. Mencius declared, therefore, that the learned man a king employed as his counselor was more important than the monarch himself. A ruler

who sought the services of a sage should hasten in all humility
to pay him a visit, and not wait until the wise man presented
himself at court. Mencius himself became involved in a ridiculous game of one-upmanship with the king of the Chinese state
of Ch'i, in which each swore he had a cold in order to oblige the
other to call on him first. For a king to interfere in government by
scholars, he said, was as absurd as if he tried to tell a skilled jade
carver how to carve jade.

A pattern now begins to emerge: people are born equal, but
their moral integrity depends upon their education in the uplift-
ing Confucian classics. It follows that the most learned is more
competent than the most royal, that scholars should be ministers
of government, and that kings should defer to their judgment.
As these principles are evolved, the wolfish wars between the
seven principal contenders for China's carcass are throwing on to
the remaining royal markets the dispossessed blood and brains of
smaller states that have already been swallowed up in the scramble. Many rulers are happy to employ able and disinterested men
from countries liquidated in the elimination rounds, instead of the
families of their own hereditary retainers, who are ever ready to
usurp power. They become the first "functionaries," the precur-
sors of the scholar-mandarins of Imperial China, who are as yet
only a gleam in the eye of Mencius, and so of the Communist-
indoctrinated cadres who are the obvious heirs, in turn, of the
scholar-mandarins.

On the principle that charity begins at home, Confucius believed that a disciplined filial son and loyal brother could be expected to behave with honesty and propriety in all his dealings
with men and monarchs. He has, therefore, been accused not only
of fossilizing Chinese society, of turning it into a stone image forever looking backward toward a Golden Age that probably never
existed, but also of perpetuating a traditional system of family
and clan loyalties under which a Chinese cheerfully cheats the
state in order to pocket five dollars for his third cousin twice removed. But criticism of Confucianism is more often than not a

measure of the extent to which the teachings of Confucius himself have been twisted: only fourteen centuries separated Geth-
semane and the Grand Inquisition, and Confucianism was no
more fortunate than Christianity. After his death, little was to be
heard of the old fellow who started it all in his inconveniently
self-questioning mood, in which he urged men to think for themselves. "If a man keeps cherishing his old knowledge in order
continually to be acquiring *new*, he may be a teacher," he said.
"Learning without thought is vain, thought without learning is
dangerous . . . If a man does not constantly ask himself what is
the right thing to do, I do not know what will become of him."
The Master confessed that he did not know the whole truth, but
only how to look for it. To his common humanity, his benevolence, and his moral rectitude must now be added his open mind,
his neglected spirit of free inquiry. His teachings were indeed to
help a tortured China to find peace and unity—but under the
most ruthless system of tyranny the world has ever seen.

For history is by no means skidproof.

4

Stick and Carrot

Mencius believed that men were born good, and the West conferred upon him the doubtful honor of a Latin name. But it was a man called Hsün Tzu who gave the Master's philosophy the sudden early wrench that was to send it down the centuries with a pronounced limp. For Hsün Tzu believed that all men were born crooks.

"The nature of man is evil," his most renowned chapter begins. "Man is born with a love of gain. If he indulges this love, he will be quarrelsome and greedy, shedding all sense of courtesy or humility. He is born with feelings of envy and hatred, and if he indulges these, they will lead him into violence and villainy, and all sense of loyalty and good faith will disappear. Man is born with desires of the senses, and if he indulges these, he will be licentious and wanton and will observe neither propriety nor principles." Continuing in this wounding vein, Hsün Tzu goes on to say that without guidance man will always take the wrong path: "If he is clever, he will surely be a robber; if he is brave, he will be a bandit; if he is able, he will cause trouble; if he is a debater, his arguments will make nonsense."

At first it seems that he is merely pointing once more to the key role to be played in civilization by good teachers and ancient example. But he carried matters further. Men were like warped wood that must be steamed and forced into the straight, he af-

33

firmed. They must not only be instructed through precepts but restrained by laws and disciplined by punishments. An authoritarian living in the turbulent third century before Christ, Hsün Tzu was nevertheless a brilliant Confucian, and for him moral education still remained the best depilatory for man's hairy heel. Hsün Tzu meant well, even if man meant evil. But history had to reckon with his two outstanding pupils.

Of these Han Fei had the most to say, and Han Fei makes lively reading. He contended that it was as absurd to model society on the anachronistic teachings of ancient sages as it would be to continue to live in trees or light fires by rubbing sticks together. For a man to believe that what had worked in the past would work now made him think of the farmer who once saw a rabbit charge into a tree and stun itself, and then neglected his harvest in order to spend his days futilely waiting beside the tree for other rabbits to do the same thing. Confucians who thought a state could be run on the simple principles of pious softies who had lived a thousand years before seemed to ignore the fact that where one man had owned and cultivated a given piece of land two generations ago, there were now twenty-five grandsons inevitably squabbling over their meager patrimony. A wise man studied his own age, and this ulcerous age required two things: one sovereign and one law. The law should be lengthy and infinitely detailed, and cover every possible contingency, so that none could twist its meaning. The king should be generous and prompt with his rewards but merciless and unrelenting with his punishments.

These virtuous reflections are very typical of the "Legalist" school of philosophy to which Han Fei belonged. He goes on to say: "In the state of the intelligent ruler there are no books, or precepts of past kings, but the laws serve as education, and the officials as the teachers." The people must not think, but simply obey, for they are incapable of governing themselves. The most perilous course a ruler can follow is to give the masses what they want. Nor is there any point in seeking honest or loyal officials, for not enough will be found, and sovereigns should not have confidence in their ministers anyway. A servant of the state does not work because he is faithful but because he is paid, and the king treats him well not because he loves him but because he needs him. It must be understood that subordinates will always murder their superiors and then supplant them, if they can get away with it. The more able a minister, the more likely he is to dispatch his sovereign with efficiency; the wiser he is, the more adroitly will he cheat him. Officials are mere maintenance men. Fallible humanity must be controlled by the infallible machine whose operator is the ruler and whose scientific principle is an iron law of wages for virtue or vice, paid on the nail in cash or castration.

When the ambitious king of the state of Ch'in heard of Han Fei's inspiring teachings, he at once exclaimed that he would love to win the services of such a man. He already employed Li Ssu, Hsün Tzu's other star pupil. But this was no coincidence, for Ch'in had been toying with Legalism for a century. If there is no coincidence in this story, however, there is nonetheless one of the most extraordinary parallels in the history of the world:

In 350 B.C., Macedonia, far away to the west, was a fringe country which separated the true Greek city-states from the barbarians farther north. Rapidly drawing away from its own lamentably wild origins, it was nevertheless a twilight civilization, still regarded in Athens and Sparta with some disdain. Macedonia, in fact, was hardly "Hellas." But change was in the air, for King Philip of Macedon had a son named Alexander, who was to be the pupil of Aristotle, the master of Logic, and to discipline and unite the Greek states before moving on to win history's briefest empire.

Now Ch'in: In 350 B.C., Ch'in was a fringe country, separating the six true states into which China was divided, from the barbarians to the west. Rapidly drawing away from its own suspiciously nomadic origins, it was still regarded by the others as scarcely civilized. It was, in fact, not quite "Hsia." But it was coming closer to the comity of kingdoms that represented "All under Heaven," and the day was near when the fastidious would cease to complain about its primitive music. "Beating on earthen pots, banging jars, and crying 'Wu, Wu' . . . has come to an end," a memorial notes of Ch'in with approval, its author happily ignorant of what is to come out of the barbaric West in future centuries.

But two years before Philip of Macedon succeeded to his throne there arrived in Ch'in from the state of Wei a brilliant exponent of early Legalism called Shan Yang, who quickly ingratiated himself with the ruling duke and persuaded him to give him office. This achieved, Shan Yang had a thirty-foot pole erected outside the South Gate of the Ch'in palace, and then told the assembled crowd that he would give ten measures of gold to any man who would move it to the North Gate for him. The people were skeptical and none stepped forward. Shan Yang then offered fifty measures of gold. At this, one husky fellow came out and carried the caber to the North Gate. Shan Yang, in the best traditions of Legalist thought, immediately gave the man his gold. And having shown that he was a man who would keep his promises promptly, he proceeded to promulgate an interesting decree, which he had already persuaded the duke to have drawn up, and which embodied some notable reforms.

The people of Ch'in were to be organized into groups of families which would be mutually responsible for each other's good behavior and would be punished collectively for any misdemeanor. Anyone who failed to denounce an offender would be cut in two at the waist; if he gave a miscreant away, on the other hand, he would be rewarded like a soldier on a per capita basis, so to speak. (Soldiers were paid per enemy head severed and duly submitted to authority.) Strong families were to be broken up by a clause which stipulated that a household with two grown men in it would have to be split, or pay double taxation. Titles would be awarded for military valor only. All must work at the two essential occupations of farming and weaving, and those who produced large quantities of grain or silk would be exempt from forced labor, while mere tradesmen and other idlers would become slaves.

The new laws were scarcely popular, and having made his own opportunity to show himself quick with the golden carrot, Shan Yang was soon given occasion to be equally swift with the stick. The king's son broke one of the new regulations, and Shan Yang had his tutors harshly punished. When timorous sycophants then hastily praised his rather distressing innovations, he remarked: "Men who have the impertinence to approve are no better than the disobedient who oppose," and banished them all to the inhospitable frontiers. Tyranny has never been so absolute since. Not even Stalin, on his bad days, actually sent his own supporters to the salt mines for daring to comment favorably on his administration.

Shan Yang pulled Ch'in together into a tight-knit state under a highly centralized government, a state in which the duke's idea of right was the definition of "right," and his idea of wrong was the definition of "wrong." The whole duty of men was to obey his laws; their education, to learn them. Subjects of Ch'in were not allowed to leave the state, were regimented for forced labor, terrorized by secret police. Mention of culture made Shan Yang reach for his sword, and he specifically condemned music, poetry, history, and all morality as being among the most corrupting of influences. He looked on love as the archenemy, and it is recorded that when the loyal people of Ch'in mistakenly sacrificed an ox in the hope that they could thus cure their sick duke, the sick duke punished them severely, for good government must not be endangered by any affection between subject and ruler. Officials who promised much but did little were penalized, and so were those who promised little but did much, for words must precisely suit actions. There was no favoritism, and no exception to the unbending mathematical law.

Nor did the ambitious duke or his coldly calculating counselor forget the end in view, the subjugation of the other warring states and Ch'in dominion over all "Hsia." Shan Yang taught total war. The entire people must be mobilized for conquest—men, women, and children. Since men did not want to go abroad and fight, life must be made so bitter for them at home that they would welcome the change. (This excellent tradition has been well upheld, for when I joined the army in 1939 and first heard of the disciplined horrors of home-based soldiering in England, a corporal explained kindly: "It's all deliberate, see? They make it like a proper bloody prison here, so's when your mob's posted five mucking thahsand miles away to Walla Walla, you're only too mucking glad to mucking go.")

Ch'in would win, Shan Yang said, by doing what the enemy would be ashamed to do, and in 341 B.C. gave an illustration of what he meant, by inviting the King of Wei to come and settle a dispute over frontiers amicably, as old friends should—then ambushing him, annihilating his army, and annexing the territory in question. The King of Wei must have bitten his lip when he remembered how, several years before, his dying chief minister had said of an assistant then in his employ: "You should either make that man my successor or kill him—above all, do not let him join the ruler of another state and plot against you." The man was Shan Yang. Nothing could have better justified the dictum of Mencius that kings should listen to their ministers.

Hated by the people, beloved by his duke, Shan Yang was made the Lord of Shang, but closely guarded.

And then the duke died.

The Lord of Shang knew what to expect, for the disobedient young man whose teachers he had branded was now the ruler, and a Confucian gentleman had already called on Shan Yang when the old duke was fading, and had made matters very plain: "Why not resign while you still can?" he suggested, with venomous concern. "For if the duke should leave us, how would it be with you, my lord? I fear you would die in no more time than it takes to lift a foot."

Shan Yang escaped his own secret police when they were sent to seize him, and rode hell-for-leather for the frontier of Wei.

Night fell when he was up in the mountains, so he stopped at a
lonely inn and demanded a room. When the innkeeper asked him
to write down his name, the hunted man tried to bluster his way
out of it, but the innkeeper insisted—for Shan Yang had himself
laid down the police regulations for the control of movement
and had stipulated that travelers must register at hostelries. "I
never would have thought," he observed ruefully, "that one of
my laws would prove so ill-devised." He pushed on to Wei the
next day, but his trail was now hot. Wei, remembering his past
treachery, threw him back across the frontier. Desperate, he
evaded capture once more and raised a minor revolt against the
new Duke of Ch'in. But he was killed in battle, and his dead body
was then torn apart with chariots.

Rarely has a man been hoist by such a fusillade of his own
petards. But Shan Yang is not entirely without his fans, for in
1961 the Chinese Communists, while somewhat reserved about
Confucius, approvingly described Hsün Tzu as "an outstanding
materialist," and both Shan Yang and Han Fei as "products of the
leftist school." It is to be noted, however, that Mao Tse-tung allowed open and frank debate on the subject, whereas anyone
who had proposed such a thing to the Lord of Shang would presumably have been chopped in two at the waist forthwith. A net
advance could therefore be registered.

Shan Yang was dead, but, between his coming and his going,
Ch'in had been converted into a formidable military machine
which now attacked the other Chinese states with calculated
ferocity. The domain of the Chou dynasty king was overrun, and
by the time Li Ssu had become minister of Ch'in, the brilliant,
ruthless, and power-hungry ruler of the day was no longer the
duke but the King of Ch'in and the time had arrived for the *coup
de grâce*. Using a combination of black treachery, bribery, assassination, and unprecedented savagery, this King Cheng annihilated his enemies in the field and massacred those who surrendered to him—on one occasion he is said to have had a hundred
thousand prisoners decapitated. The consequences of this sound
and realistic policy are soon related. In 229 B.C. he conquered

Han, the first of the six Chinese feudal states to succumb; in 228 he took Chao, in 226 Yen, in 225 Wei, in 223 Ch'u, in 222 Ch'i, and in 221 he became the First Emperor of all China, having conquered the whole civilized world of the Hsia "as a silkworm devours a mulberry leaf."

This was the terrible genius who built the Great Wall and the fabulous complex of palaces at Hsien Yang, his capital. But he did far more than that. He abolished the feudal system and divided the country into districts administered by the Imperial officials of his centralized government. He standardized the laws, the customs, the written language, the weights and measures, the agricultural tools, and even the lengths of cart axles (so that the wheels would always fit the ruts) throughout the empire, and built great strategic highways 250 feet wide to link up the different parts of the country. He worked like a man obsessed, "examining 120 pounds-weight of reports a day." But, fearful of treachery and heresy, he moved 120,000 leading families of the states he had conquered to the capital, so that they could not plot in peace, and ruled that any man who quoted from the Confucian classics should be executed. Nor was this enough. Persuaded by the crafty and insinuating Li Ssu, he sanctioned the atrocious act that has won him the undying detestation of more than sixty generations of Chinese: the burning of the entire body of Chinese literature, with the exception of a few works on agriculture, medicine, and divination. The precious heritage of the golden age of Chinese philosophy, which had so strikingly coincided with that of Greece, went up in the flames.

The Chinese did not stand the Ch'in reign of terror for long. Rebels rose to rend its authority to shreds from one end of the empire to the other and to establish a new dynasty which was to rule it for more than four hundred years. Alexander's swift and ephemeral triumphs have left the world with two dozen towns named after him. Ch'in's swift and ephemeral triumphs left behind one vast country named after him: China.

5

The Mask of Confucius

The rebel leader who now made himself Emperor of China was
not a prince but a peasant—a wily, rough-tongued, self-made general with a twinkling eye for village vulgarity and a hatred of
frills. It is related how he once approached a group of pompous
intellectuals decked out in full scholar's fig, seized the high hat
of the nearest, and, without further ado, pissed into it.

But history had, in fact, made no mistake in its choice: this
emperor was worthy of his hire. Behind the burly sweating body
and the surly manners—themselves examples of good "man-of-
the-people" image-building—was an essentially moderate and as-
tute ignoramus who ruled his subjects with studied clemency and
generosity. He knew that the scholars were popular with the
people, for many of them had been the destitute, persecuted victims of the odious Ch'in dynasty. For Han Kao-tsu, what was
important about these men was not that they were lofty, but
that they were learned and he needed them. He appointed the
best of them ministers and confided the administration very
largely to their hands. No Imperial decree was legal until they
had endorsed it.

The groove was cut, and as emperor succeeded emperor, the
principle of government by scholars produced in time a vast Imperial bureaucracy of educated officials chosen by written examination who were divided into nine grades of seniority and

whom the outside world was to call Mandarins. In the feudal days of Charlemagne, more than eight thousand students of the Confucian classics were competing at the Imperial University in the Chinese capital to qualify for posts in the administration. Confucianism, it seemed, had won a resounding victory. The nature of things that resound, however, is that they are hollow.

Confucius had recommended government by benevolence and the personal good example of the ruler: Han Fei had recommended a strict legal code. Successive emperors of China soon learned which of these doctrines enabled them to hold their thrones in comfort and keep order effectively in an enormous empire. For the would-be despot there was only one snag; Confucianism, like Christianity, was respectable and widely venerated; on the other hand, Legalism, like Fascism, was now a dirty word. However, Western authoritarians have had little difficulty in adopting the Cross as their emblem and finding up-and-smite Christian motives for their most impious acts, and the Chinese emperors could also "mix coal and ice" without a qualm. Scholar-officials were educated in the Confucian classics, therefore, but called upon to administer harsh Legalist laws. The early emperors "kicked upstairs" the more widely known Confucians, but surrounded themselves with Legalist confidants. Oppressive decrees were drawn up in fine Confucian language, especially where some really dastardly imposition on the long-suffering public had to be clothed in virtuous double talk, so that the advertised aim of an edict designed to make penalties even more severe was to "decrease punishment" (by discouraging crime, of course).

The great Emperor Han Wu-ti, who reigned in the days of Marius, shocked Imperial examiners by coolly moving the test paper of one scholar from the bottom to the top of the pile because his thesis had been strictly Legalist. Another scholar, when personally examined by the emperor, accused him to his face of presiding over a tyrannical administration inspired by the Ch'in dynasty. The emperor, careful not to strike at an honest Confucian directly, sent him to the court of a ruthless vassal who had a reputation for chopping up didactic critics when he became bored with them. The Confucian façade was preserved, but any criticism of the emperor was heavily punished, and at one time men so feared to hold prominent office that a profitable formula was worked out whereby they could be sold their right to refuse the honor of an Imperial appointment.

Meanwhile, since Ch'in had burned all the books, it was up to the scholars of the Han dynasty to rewrite the classics, piecing together the texts that had been buried or hidden in the walls of houses. This produced not only a tremendous tradition of fine and meticulous scholarship among honest Chinese literati, but also much fine and meticulous philosophical faking. Passages and whole works suddenly appeared to harmonize with the pragmatic teachings of the Legalists, or with the most superstitious aberrations of the Taoists (of whom more later), to please this or that emperor. As time passed, Confucian teaching became increasingly entangled with magic, and one great "Classic" was a mine of information on what color to wear if you were born in Gemini, and at what season a ruler should inflict the death penalty if he wanted to avoid floods. The mixed marriage between the Master's doctrine and peasant belief was not in itself more harmful than the fumbling that confused Christ's agony with Easter eggs, perhaps. But strip off this plaster-saint and penny-medallion aspect of "popular" Confucianism, so that the gaudy raiment of simple faith falls away, and what is revealed is the naked body of the philosophy itself—and the real damage that time and the scholars have done to it.

The Confucian teaching that Utopia was something that lay in the past, not something to strive for in the future, fostered a hidebound conservatism among Chinese that paradoxically betrayed Confucius himself. Even the revolution against the Manchu dynasty in 1911 was inspired by a subconscious slogan that would have read: "Restore the Old," the satirical Lu Hsün tells us, and "revolutionaries" were disappointed and surprised that a movement which was really aimed at bringing back the China of pre-Manchu days should fail to bring prosperity along with it. The coin had been thrust into the magic slot of the past. Why no goodies? "We have lost our pigtails for nothing," men said. (The pigtail was imposed on the Chinese by the Manchus, but it also symbolized a comfortable abdication from responsibility.) Lu Hsün adds that there were cries of dismay among Shanghai shopkeepers when the innovators cautiously ruled that the Chinese Republic should switch from the old lunar year to the Gregorian calendar. No good could possibly come of such a break with tradition, they complained.

This instinct for looking back has produced an outstanding race of copyists, to a point where a Moslem tablet found in a Chinese Mosque a thousand years old turns out to be a forgery executed at least five hundred years later, inspired by a Nestorian Christian slab. Artists know they would please if they imitated ancient or at least established designs. Fifteenth-century Ming porcelain was still being made in the K'ang Hsi emperor's reign of the Manchu dynasty two hundred years later, and most so-called K'ang Hsi porcelain was produced in the last century, two hundred years after that. Then there was the fast rally with Europe, when the Dutch copied Chinese porcelain in Delft, and the Chinese copied the Chinese Delft and exported it back to Europe as European Chinese, in competition with the Dutch, and then . . . But this exciting game, which the Chinese played simultaneously with other European and also English potteries, ended apparently with neither side really knowing the score, for today the Chinese origin of many European designs is completely unrecognizable. The Chinese, then, are driven by their conservatism to take a pride in honest forgery, so that earlier in the century the Chinese railways even advertised: "Counterfeit coins accepted at market rate." They would have just as much value as the genuine article—their worth in weight of metal.

But nothing can be forged better than spurious memories of the Good Old Days. For these, the counterfeiting goes on effortlessly right inside a man's head. And Confucius had left history wide open, for he had cited as exemplars certain venerable rulers of the Golden Age who were of unexceptionable virtue but insufficient antiquity. "What he calls ancient," the great philosopher

Mo Tzu said of the Sage, "is not really ancient at all." And here was the rub, for Confucius himself did not trace good government back to the earliest possible paradise, so others were free to write of older and therefore even better precedents. The immutable law of this form of gamesmanship is that the later a philosopher appears on the scene, the further back he has to go for his quotes and paragons, the more he fabricates, and therefore the more dogmatic become his assertions. Mencius already insists that the legendary sage-kings and Shun, whom Confucius mentions relatively briefly, must be so precisely imitated that taxes should even be leveled in accordance with the antediluvian and quite imaginary scales they notionally approved. Meanwhile, Hsün Tzu ("The Nature of Man is Evil") demands absolute reverence for the ancient works and so outlaws all intelligent skepticism. Study, he says, should be severely limited to uncritical learning of the Classics.

Nothing could have better suited the paltrier scholars and the more arbitrary emperors that were to come. The Classics stressed that education must be the basis of good government, and had thus inspired the rise of the scholar-mandarin. By enshrining them as the only required reading, then, the mandarins were making their own bureaucratic hierarchy sacrosanct. Moreover, as conveniently authoritarian tags of Legalist flavor could now be found in these reedited works, emperors were happy to lend their weight to the conspiracy. And the advent of "neo-Confucianism" and the Chinese renaissance of classical learning some nine hundred years ago only served to strengthen this association, instead of weakening it.

In Europe, Thomas Aquinas was soon to produce his *Summa*, which would justify Christian dogma in a world increasingly receptive to revived philosophical learning. But in China the Confucians were facing the opposite task of making dry philosophy satisfying in a Chinese world increasingly receptive to an exotic alien religion: Buddhism.

Buddhism reached China in the first century A.D., and was the only foreign creed other than Marxism ever seriously to challenge native Confucian orthodoxy. In its more florid forms, Chinese Buddhism offered something less arid than the teaching of the early canon—the gentle Madonna-like image of the Goddess of Mercy, the Laughing Buddha who is yet to come and bring good times with him, and Amitabha, whose name it is only necessary to invoke once (some day) in order to make sure of a place in at least an intermediate paradise. Unprettified, however, Buddhism teaches that Man is chained to this world of illusion by his own desires and endures a long series of reincarnations whose nature is determined by his karma—the sum of his record to date, good and bad. His aim must be to shed all desire and achieve Nirvana —the state of eternal bliss in which his light is extinguished and he is not born again. It may sound somewhat negative, but more men have poured gasoline over themselves and then flicked on a cheap cigarette lighter in this belief than in any other.

Buddhist metaphysics made the sociological do's and dont's of Confucianism seem uninspiring, workaday stuff. So the scholars set out to produce their own elaborate explanation of the universe in Confucian language, and came up with a new "li"—an unchangeable blind law of the cosmos with which all must conform. Whatever the emperor did, he did in accordance with "li." None could appeal against "li" itself, any more than a man with a bump on his head could lodge a complaint against the law of gravity. Thus, neo-Confucianism gave to the ruler and his counselors the unanswerable excuse for all their actions, and by the eighteenth century a great Chinese thinker was writing: "Those who have the advantages of influence and power and glib tongues always have 'li' on their side, it seems. The superior commands the inferior in the name of 'li,' and even when he is wrong, he will insist he is right. But if the inferior tries to argue that 'li' is on his side, he is condemned for being insubordinate." "Li," therefore, is the emperor's two-headed coin: Confucianism's greatest gift to tyranny, and a device well designed to turn China into a land fit for Neros.

6

The Judas Tree

Confucius had been most grievously betrayed. Nevertheless, since the Master had felt that education in the precepts of a perfect past must be the basis for future societies, his heart might have warmed to the Imperial system of scholar-officials that began to take clear shape in the new golden age of the T'ang dynasty, twelve hundred years ago. Government service was open to any man. Young hopefuls, whether from rich and cultivated families or self-taught while tending a neighbor's buffalo, could study the Classics and sit for the official examinations. The literature of China is full of stories of impecunious men setting out along the path to glory through a series of tiny examination cells, with a little money, a long way to go, but Confucius in the cranium and the future in a writing brush.

The provincial examination was held every three years, and if the wonder boy from the village wrote an essay that pleased the examiners at this stage, he moved on to the prefectural tests and then to the Metropolitan examination in the capital itself. This hurdle over, the now very senior scholar (and he might be anything from twenty-five to sixty-five years old) entered for the Palace examination. Brilliant careers were assured for those who came out at the top of the lists, and all who passed could apply for posts, the lowest of which was a magisterial appointment in the provinces.

Most scholars were only concerned with pleasing their examiners and thereafter entered the powerful club of the mandarinate with every intention of preserving its privileges and exclusivity. And for this they were invincibly armed with the Chinese written language, which had diverged sharply from the spoken, and whose laconic style was quite incomprehensible to anyone who had not put in years of concentrated study on it. For the millions it was alien, indecipherable, dead as dog-Latin. Imagine that the fitness of candidates for the civil service in Britain and the United States is judged almost entirely on their knowledge of the Greek Bible, their ability to write essays and commentaries on its different Books and to learn by heart and recite mechanically important passages and telling catchphrases. The thunder of Christ's meaning need not be heard in the heart: what the future undersecretary or ambassador must be able to do is to deal in dry words, to hairsplit and niggle at disputed texts in the approved scholarly way, to trot out the tags and the lifeless patter, to learn the dogma but not the dialectics, the answers but not the arguments.

This is how the emperor and the mandarinate preserved the husks of Confucianism, and their own power. In the first century of the era, the first critic is already voicing his lonely cry in the autumn wilderness of sere, rustling words: learning must not be limited to swallowing the Classics whole, or to the complacent study of so-called history that is patently falsified, he urges. Students must think, and argue, and reject what teachers cannot prove—not just imitate their forebears parrot-fashion. None listened. The slim library of standard and approved works was only slowly expanded to include collections of edicts, official histories, handbooks on ceremony, and commentaries on the Confucian writings themselves. And sometimes a fashion would be introduced, perhaps by the emperor, and scholars would be encouraged to write rhyming couplets in traditional style. "How can poetry prepare the mind for an administrative post?" the great progressive Wang An-shih demanded sarcastically in William the

Conqueror's day. But he was only echoing vainly the man whose free spirit they had all forgotten: "If a person can recite the three hundred Odes, yet does not know how to act when given an official mission, what is the practical use of all that study?" Confucius had asked.

The scholar who entered for the civil-service examination had been solemnly advised, in all probability, to learn the Four Books of Confucian teachings by heart, for he would be asked to write an essay on some section of them. The form of these carefully balanced compositions was specifically laid down, including the number of words in each paragraph and their inflection, the number of paragraphs and their length in each case, the language to be used, and the stages of the argument to be developed. This was the "eight-legged" essay, and anyone who could write one in a graceful style and with a good enough fist to win a passing mark became, *ipso facto,* a scholar and a gentleman, however much of an ignoramus he really was. Parents may complain today of the examination hurdles that oblige their muling and puling ones to learn the names of Canadian cities or the dates of the Plantagenet kings, but at least they do not live in a society which would accuse a fifty-year-old scholar of being a frivolous deviationist because he actually studied the Classics with something broader in mind than the desire to write an examination essay. Nor is the Communist term "deviationist" inappropriate, for from where the emperor sat, devices like these essays stopped the human poultry from thinking too much, kept their heads down to the chalk line of orthodoxy and their mesmerized minds healthily empty of questions.

The Chinese scholar might study one ridiculously outmoded work of mathematics only and, in consonance with the best Legalist practice of the First Emperor, could only have access to other scientific books with Imperial permission (in case he used his knowledge against the Dragon Throne). In consequence, by the seventeenth century the astrologers of the Ming dynasty who were responsible for calculating the all-important lunar calendar no longer knew how to use the astronomical instruments in Nan-king that had been installed during the Mongol overlordship nearly three hundred years before. All their dates for the Imperial sacrifices that kept the cosmos on an even keel had been wrong for generations, for it had not occurred to anybody that moving their astrolabes and armillary spheres down to the Yang-tze River from North China had automatically invalidated their polar elevation. The first Jesuit priest to arrive in China at the end of the sixteenth century was astonished to find many of these excellent but time-encrusted instruments dreaming away the centuries undisturbed by the tiniest inquiring mind.

During the early years of the Norman conquest, China produced one of her greatest innovators in the none-too-well-scrubbed shape of a cantankerous scholar who has already been quoted: Wang An-shih. This unfortunate man (for he was well ahead of his times) introduced a system whereby provinces exchanged their surpluses instead of sending tribute to the capital, so that gluts and famines were avoided and prices stabilized. He founded the first state credit banks for farmers, loans being granted in the spring and reclaimed from the peasant after the harvest. He taxed men instead of conscripting them for forced labor, and then used the taxes to pay for the hire of regular workers on public projects. He limited profits, pegged prices, and established state pawnshops to force the usurious private pawnbroker to bring down his frightening interest rates. He reduced banditry by obliging every family of two male members or more to arm and train one man as a soldier and, in riding country, to keep and feed a cavalry remount supplied by the state. His imaginative reforms lasted, off and on, for rather more than twenty years, but they were finally thrown out by the conservative Confucian clique around the emperor because they were something worse than bad—they were blasphemous, unsanctified by any precedent in the golden past. The supply of horses to the army was neglected, and in consequence, perhaps, the Sung emperor lost his capital and half of his country to the Kin barbarians from the north.

Narrow dogma again conquered common sense when scholars urged the new emperor to embark upon a war of revenge against the Kin, because the Confucian exhortation to filial piety taught that a son must revenge the death of his father—and the Emperor Hui Tsung had died while a prisoner of the Kin after the capital fell. This so bedeviled relations with the Kin that when their ruler sought an alliance with the Sung dynasty against new enemies threatening him from the north, in the famous words: "We are to you as the lips are to the teeth: when the lips are gone, the teeth are cold," he met with a chilly rebuff. In consequence, the Kin were overrun, and so was the whole of Sung China. For the new enemies were the terrible Mongol hordes of the Great Khan. (Communist leaders in Peking often repeat the seven-hundred-year-old "lips and teeth" formula when talking of North Vietnam and China. It does not, as many imagine, express their fraternal love for Ho Chi Minh and Hanoi. It merely emphasizes the hard fact that North Vietnam is a buffer on whose resistance to the American onslaught may depend the safety of China herself.)

Time brought no change for the better. The usurping Manchus who seized control of China in 1644 numbered only a few million that could easily have been submerged in the teeming population of their new empire, but they were quick to realize that they could best master this sea of humanity if they rode its currents rather than struggled against them. The Manchu emperors, therefore, outshone the Chinese in their rigid respect for all the conventions of the Classic age, placating the mandarins, whose cooperation they so badly needed to administer the huge state, by virtually embalming the Confucian system.

"Learn to handle a writing brush, and you will never handle a begging bowl," the Chinese said, for the scholar was universally honored and the candidate who came first in the Imperial examinations was as great a national hero as any astronaut today. When a man passed his examinations and it was known he would become a mandarin, he would be showered with gifts by his fellow villagers, and samples of his handwriting would be treasured like autographs. He enjoyed the privileges of a diplomat in his own country, and often behaved like one in consequence. In *The Scholars*, the great satirical eighteenth-century novel of Wu Ching-tzu, a successful candidate is detained for misappropriating some money, although no proceedings can be taken against him until he is first deprived of his status and thus of his immunity. "How ridiculous!" his fellow literati exclaim. "A salaried licentiate is a scholar; all he has done is to use some money belonging to some salt merchant; yet they want to deprive him of his rank and penalize him. Did you ever hear of anything so unreasonable?" The licentiate has only "lost" about 700 ounces of the salt merchant's silver, but his friends have not miscalculated the position and power that a little learning has conferred upon them. When a young woman is accused of being a runaway concubine and duly arraigned before a magistrate, she wins her case by producing not evidence but an elegant, impromptu poem of eight lines, each of seven characters. She is literate and therefore no longer the same under the law.

In this world of genteel academic contest, does the best man win? "At the Anching examinations some of the candidates found substitutes, and some slipped essays to each other. They were up to every conceivable trick: passing notes, throwing bricks, winking and making signs. One candidate, on the pretext that he must go to the latrine, slipped over to the mud wall which surrounded the school, knocked a hole in it, and put his arm through to receive an essay from an accomplice." Cribbing and cheating, like poking the tongue into a hollow tooth, are all-conquering habits that straddle continents and time, it seems. Examiners were bribed, or persuaded to favor the protégés of their friends. Essays of certain candidates—identified despite the rule of anonymity—were put at the top of the list without even being read. Confucius himself might well have failed ignominiously to pass even his provincial examination in some reigns, and his essays would certainly have been thrown out in others.

If he had been successful so far, further hazards faced the candidate once he was accepted into the mandarinate: for his first post might well be decided by drawing lots. What was a good post worth to a none-too-scrupulous mandarin with a sharp eye for the best cuts? "Three years of government—100,000 taels of silver [nearly four tons]," a senior prefect tells us. Even street-hawkers among the thrifty Chinese of Singapore and Hong Kong pinch and scrape to send their sons to the best possible schools, and sometimes to universities abroad. In the West, perhaps only French students have the passion for learning and the near neurotic approach to the baccalaureate that afflicts the young Chinese facing his senior examinations, for the instinct is in the blood.

If he did not qualify for a brilliant official career, a scholar was anyway a gentleman. Wrapped in the sanctity of his learning, he could buttonhole officials whom the ordinary people could not reach, he could sell his influence, demand bribes for small services and commissions as a go-between, hang around the magistrature, cadge from his peers, bully and cheat the ignorant with impunity, or wheedle a rich merchant into letting him write a poem or two for a fat sum of cash. Mencius had written: "Gentlemen are there to rule the people, the people to feed the gentlemen"; and the sacred monkeys, the "failed B.A.'s" of all China, made sure that nobody was going to be allowed to forget those few ill-chosen words.

There was no equitable law, for scholar-officials were treated as a morally upright class by definition—and they could not normally be charged, detained, or punished. They would not even be dismissed from office for their sins if they were well-enough connected. Unfortunately, narrow study of the Classics too often produced a punctilious fellow who observed all the outward forms of gentility but had no sense of *sagesse oblige*. Moreover, even if there had been enough gentlemen to go around, it could still be objected that China was too big for government by goodness. As it was, tag-end Confucians would simply produce the classical quotation that suited their current action: "Too many cooks spoil the broth" on this occasion, so to speak, and "Many hands make light work" on that. High officials in the distant provinces quietly shelved Imperial orders that they did not like and executed those that suited them. Corrupt mandarins spent much of their time deceiving the emperor and his ministers with false reports, particularly to cover up any local disturbance and to give the impression that their provinces were orderly and peaceful. For news of disorders would focus attention on the area, lead to the dispatch of officials or even troops from the capital, and an investigation that might expose the gangrene beneath the clean, neatly bound bandages. In a word, the mandarinate was in one sense a vast conspiracy for keeping up appearances, under which China too often found itself deprived of both the self-examining spirit of Confucius and the impartial, if brutal justice advocated by the Legalists.

Officialdom became a closed society in which considerations of nepotism and patronage, favor and face dictated the intricate social relationships, and corruption meant cash. At one end of the great chain of palms were men like Ki Shen, Grand Secretary of the Court in 1840, who was kicked out of his job for unnecessarily provoking the bloody-minded British and was then found to have enriched himself through his high office to the tune of approximately half a ton of gold, £6,000,000 worth of silver, shares in ninety lucrative businesses, and property covering nearly half a million acres. At the other end were the humble runners for the local magistrate's court who demanded tips even from the prisoners they escorted to the jail.

Mandarins were strictly enjoined not to go into business, and merchants were despised by the scholar classes. But like proud white empire-builders seduced by black satin skins, they performed that elementary exercise in mental adjustment whereby a colonial officer could contrive to be both lofty and lusty—keeping haughty looks for their trading partners but eager hands for the profits. It is fairly said that Western traders evilly promoted the sale of opium to China, but the British found in the eighteen-thirties that the Viceroy of Canton, who had been specifically charged with the task of killing the traffic, was making a fortune in it himself, and sent out his own boats to collect his share of the black cargo carried by the European and American opium clippers. In a gracious snub of a letter to Lord Napier, he nevertheless had the marvelous effrontery to write: "The Celestial Empire appoints its civil officials to govern the people. The petty affairs of commerce are to be settled by the merchants themselves; officials have nothing to hear on the subject."

More pernicious still than the abuses of the mandarins in decadent times was the influence of the eunuchs. Too often a young emperor grew up in a vast, secluded palace, surrounded by women and deliberately isolated from his empire by *castrati* who kept him in ignorance of the Chinese world outside, and, in particular, of their own little ways with it. He was coaxed from his earliest years into trusting these flatterers, and once he was ready to put his seal on their decisions, there was no limit to the excesses of greed and cruelty which they would perpetrate in his name.

At such times eunuchs exacted exorbitant annual tribute from mandarins, who would be dismissed and replaced at once if they defaulted. High official posts were sold to the best bidder, and any man who murmured against the system might well be banished or executed and his property confiscated. One ninth-century chief eunuch amassed a fortune in gold, silver, and gems whose value exceeded the entire annual budget of the empire. Another wrecked his young sovereign by almost suffocating him in beautiful women, and thereafter signed all edicts jointly with his exhausted Imperial victim. Whenever the palace eunuchs squeezed the mandarinate, however, the provincial governors, the prefects, and the magistrates were in turn obliged to squeeze the population; the country was ruined, its defenses neglected, and its scholar-officials and people ripe for revolt. The downfall of the dynasty was imminent. The Mandate of Heaven was about to be withdrawn.

Outfacing all threats of change, the scholars nevertheless stone-walled their way through the centuries. The written language moved—when it moved at all—on bound feet. During the later dynasties, poetry was stuffed rigid with classical allusions and quotations from older verse, and new writing was crammed stiffly into earlier styles. Except for serious prose, only poetry was regarded as literature. The drama and the novel that had developed from the marketplace storyteller's art were hardly respectable and often anonymous. Usually written by scholars for pleasure, as an escape from the *rigor mortis* of orthodox study, they frequently attacked authority or the social system, the author cunningly placing the story in an earlier dynasty in order to escape punishment. They were read secretly, as were the notebooks of anti-Confucian philosophers. However, the more brazen-faced would not hide their bedside delinquencies but, having eagerly swallowed the latest satire, would loudly boast that they had performed this duty and were now in a far better position to denounce it than they had been before.

In 1965, Communist leaders in Peking spent much time sternly admonishing the masses that feudal and bourgeois books must be shunned, and the "poisoned weeds" of reactionary culture rooted out from among the "fragrant flowers" of improving Socialist literature. Ostensibly, the Chinese trembled and obeyed—in fact some, expressing the fear that they might make the common mistake of confusing flowers and weeds, immediately stopped reading books altogether. Indoctrination lost way, until exasperated Communist editors told their readers that the "positive and revolutionary" thing to do might, after all, be to read even the "poisoned weeds," since they would afterward be better equipped to recognize heresies and more effectively immunized against them.

There is no real coincidence here. Confucius had said: "The superior man is catholic and not partisan, the mean man is partisan and not catholic," but by the end of the Sung dynasty, Confucianism had become doctrine, and by the Ming dynasty it was dogma. The empire severely discouraged liberal thought and was ever watchful for any deviation from the orthodox line. Religion was tolerated, although Buddhists and Taoists were constantly supervised to prevent any dangerous subversion. But Confucianism was the fixed, official ideology of the empire, as propounded by its masters in Peking, and was to be accorded loyalty (or lip service) according to performance. Nothing would change unless Confucianism itself lost the Mandate of Heaven to another creed, which in turn would be accorded loyalty (or lip service) according to performance. This, of course, is what has happened.

7

Men of Distinction

For those who think that the case against the Chinese as a race of rapacious, conniving, double-crossing Asiatics has now been proved, it is as well to recall the appalling corruption in British politics in the eighteenth century, the ghastly conditions in English prisons, the indictments contained in the novels of Dickens and the drawings of Hogarth, the St. Bartholomew Massacre, the horrors of the American slave trade, and a few more of the rather more tangy aspects of Western social history to restore the perspective. It is perhaps not even necessary to call upon reserves like the more recent extermination of six million Jews, or the long agony of the crucifixion of Christ's gospel that followed the shorter agony of Christ.

Moreover, the early Confucian teachings survived all betrayal in the minds of many soldiers, scholars, officials, and even sometimes emperors who were worthy of the Sage's doctrine, so that their common humanity and moderation pervaded court and county yamen. Nothing brings out good better than evil, and the horrors of Chinese history have been well matched by the heroes who died defending or upholding Confucian ideals with the courage, the hard pride, and the loyalty of the Roman. The Chinese use a four-character phrase to describe the terrible act of the First Emperor in destroying all literature—"Burn book, bury scholar"—for many disobeyed his minatory edict that all who failed to surrender their copies of the Classics would be executed, and hid the compromising bamboo strips. And of these at least 460 are known to have been put to death and their corpses thrown into pits.

No body of distinguished men in history, probably, had a more dangerous task than the Imperial censors of China, part of whose moral duty it was to remonstrate with the emperor if he did wrong. Their ideal was Ch'ü Yüan, a famous Confucian states-man whose blunt criticisms of the ruling Duke of Ch'u earned him perpetual banishment in the year 195 B.C. While in exile, he wrote one of the most celebrated poems in the Chinese lan-guage: "Falling into Trouble." Urged on the banks of a swift-flowing river that he should abandon his principles if they only earned him disgrace, Ch'ü Yüan exclaimed: "I would rather the fish had me!" He had learned that thanks to the foolish policies urged upon his duke by treacherous rivals, Ch'u had fallen to its enemies, and he therefore threw himself into the water and was drowned. Legend adds that many boats at once converged on the spot to try to rescue Ch'ü Yüan and frighten off water serpents, and that people threw dumplings into the river to tempt away the fish, so that they would not attack his body. On the fifth day of the fifth lunar month, nearly twenty-three hundred years after Ch'ü Yüan's death, the narrow, gaudy, high-prowed dragon boats with their long lines of paddlers still race against one another, to commemorate the integrity and poesy of this upright man, in Formosa, in Hong Kong, and even in North Borneo, where the Chinese community then settles down to steamed dumplings like those their ancestors had originally fed to the fishes.

Some two thousand years after Ch'ü Yüan, an equally blunt Imperial censor memorialized the Ming emperor who had al-lowed a vicious chief eunuch to usurp his power. Fearlessly setting down a long catalogue of evils committed in the emperor's name, he concluded: "Why do you nourish a tiger to work mis-chief at your very elbow?" For this indiscretion he was arrested and imprisoned, nails were driven into his ears, and then heavy sacks heaped upon him until he was squashed to death. Numerous censors stood up to implacable, all-powerful emperors and their favorites, with nothing between them and flogging, banishment, disgrace, and extinction but the forlorn hope of striking a spark of conscience in a mind that was perhaps already spongy with the wet rot of corrupting power. And many, having reproved the emperor, decorously committed suicide to add weight to their protests.

Nor was outspoken criticism of Imperial injustice or foolishness confined to the censors. It is possible that a man called Ssu-ma Ch'ien, of whom few west of Singapore have ever heard, has been the most influential, if not the greatest compiler of history the world has yet seen, for as Grand Historian to the Emperor Han Wu-ti a hundred years before Christ was born, he had access not only to the entire body of Chinese historical literature in existence but to all the official documents of the empire. After unremitting research over many years, he wrote his comprehensive, minutely authenticated, and above all unique *Historical Records*, upon which all future historians would rely. One can visualize this devout Confucian in his voluminous robe, the descendant of Ch'in military aristocracy, a distinguished traveler and respected high official engrossed upon a tremendous task which must bring him immortality. And then, like any other, came the year 99 B.C.

The emperor's favorite general was Li Kuang-li, a man who had already proved a mediocre tactician in the long-ranging, wearisome wars against the ever present Huns beyond the Great Wall. But, as plans were being laid for a new offensive, a distinguished young cavalry commander named Li Ling begged to be allowed to mount a flank attack on the enemy in support of Li Kuang-li, not with horsemen but with archers armed with the new deadly weapon that only the Chinese possessed, the trigger-operated crossbow. In his *Historical Records* Ssu-ma Ch'ien curtly tells what happened: "In the autumn of that year General Li

Kuang-li led an army of thirty thousand cavalry in an attack on the Huns at the Heavenly Mountains. He meanwhile ordered Li Ling to lead a force of five thousand infantry and archers northward, and to advance about a thousand li [330 miles] into enemy territory. In this way he hoped to split the Huns.

"Li Ling had already reached his objective and had begun to march back when the Hun leader surrounded him with eighty thousand men and began to attack. Li Ling and his army fought a running battle for eight days, retreating as they fought, until all their weapons and arrows were gone and half the men were killed. In the course of the fighting they killed or wounded ten thousand of the enemy.

"When they reached a place only a hundred li or so from their starting point, the Huns cornered them in a narrow valley and cut off their retreat. Li Ling's food supplies were exhausted and no relief was in sight. The enemy pressed their attack and called on Li Ling to give up. 'I could never face the emperor and report such a disaster,' Li Ling told his men, and so finally surrendered. Nearly all his soldiers had perished in the fight; only some four hundred managed to escape and straggle back to safety. The Hun king had already observed Li Ling's bravery in battle, and as a result treated him with honor. But when the emperor received news of all this, he executed Li Ling's mother and his wife and children. From this time on, the name of the Li family was disgraced." Ssu-ma Ch'ien said no more of this matter in the *Historical Records*, but he took action. While from the safety of the Chinese court sycophants at once vilified Li Ling, the Grand Historian sprang to his defense in an open and laudatory appeal to the emperor, which somewhat cuttingly concluded: "He did not die on the field, for he longed to wipe out his defeat and show his gratitude for his emperor's clemency, upon which he dared to count with a clear conscience." Emperor Han Wu-ti, furious, ordered that Ssu-ma Ch'ien be arraigned for "attempting to mislead the Ruler." He was tried, sentenced, and castrated.

In China, this dreadful punishment—which the more humanitarian emperors only ordered to be carried out symbolically—
ruined the man not only physically but socially. Ssu-ma Ch'ien the
Grandee was now a eunuch, a creature that even Confucius himself had viewed with disgust. "I have a body that is degraded,"
the historian wrote, "a presence that soils. I am cut off from
life, and in my loneliness am a broken man. Since my virility
has been taken from me, I can never be accepted as a man of
honor. To attempt to act like one would only expose me to more
ridicule." Why did he take such an awesome risk for Li Ling? "He
had admirable qualities," he explained. "He was not an intimate
friend of mine, for he was a soldier and I a civilian. But all I saw
of his character pleased me: he was honest in money matters, just
to his dependents, respectful to his superiors, devout at the Rites.
When I heard him belittled after his defeat, I could not keep
silent." Ssu-ma Ch'ien lived on stubbornly to finish the work that
alone was breathing life into him, then died.

Nearly one thousand years later the tradition was upheld by
the renowned Confucian Han Yü. Han Yü is famous above all
for his stinging memorial to an emperor who, having become
infatuated with Buddhism, planned to house for a few days in
his palace a holy relic of the Lord Buddha and to mark the occasion with solemn processions and public celebrations. The great
Confucian shared the irritation and distrust of many of his fellow
officials for the imported foreign mumbo jumbo that was catching on so outrageously in court and country, and showed it to
his Imperial master at the risk of his neck: "On Your Majesty's
accession it was hoped that Buddhism would be stamped out,
and no further tolerance extended to it," he wrote. "Alas, these
expectations were disappointed. For it seems that instead of sup-
pressing this religion, the Court is to patronize it. Yet Buddha
was only a barbarian from the West who could not speak Chinese and wore outlandish clothes, and who violated the loyalty
that the subject owes to his prince, and the son to his father
[for Buddha, heir to an Indian kingdom, had one day quietly

abandoned his father and his heritage]. Were he alive today, Your Majesty might accord him an audience and a banquet, instruct him to behave with propriety, and have him escorted to the frontiers after giving him something suitable to wear. How different from this correct procedure are Your Majesty's present proposals. This barbarian has been dead and decomposed for twelve hundred years, and now a dried and rotten bone, said to be his finger, is to be admitted to the precincts of the Palace, although, disgusting object that it is, it may well give off evil emanations. Your servant asks rather that this bone be given to the magistrates to be burned or ground down and cast into the river. And if Buddha has power over men's happiness and unhappiness, I am prepared that all the ills that may accrue from this act shall befall myself alone. Tremblingly submitted for the Benign Glance . . ."

The face of the emperor saddened when he saw this document, and so Han Yü was banished to Kwangtung Province, whose capital today is the great city of Canton, but which was then one of the farthest outposts of empire. However, less than twenty-five years later the next emperor—during one of the rare spasms of religious intolerance that shook China—relentlessly cut the Buddhist church down to size, and more than a quarter of a million nuns and monks were forced to return to secular life.

Confucian precept nevertheless lays down that although a minister should admonish an erring sovereign, he must still give him—by virtue of the title he holds—his unswerving loyalty. When in the seventeenth century the eunuchs betrayed their Ming ruler, and the Forbidden City in Peking fell to rebels, the emperor wrote a valedictory message on his yellow robe and strangled himself with his silken girdle. Loyalty, like disloyalty, obeys the falling-domino principle. The empress had already hanged herself; the emperor's one loyal eunuch now strangled himself in his master's presence, and when the news flashed through the palace, the president of the censors and at least six other senior ministers and officials committed ceremonious suicide (in some cases with their womenfolk) after changing into formal dress, for they were about to serve their emperor in another world. Meanwhile, no fewer than two hundred ladies of the court, following the example of one Imperial concubine, drowned themselves in the Royal Canal.

A true Confucian would not ask whether a Chinese emperor deserved such loyalty. A worthy whose father had been executed for defying the Imperial eunuchs in these catastrophic times nevertheless fought hard against the invading Manchus, despite his personal hatred for the Ming emperor he served. Afterward he refused, like so many other scholars, to take office under the barbarian usurpers once they had overrun China, and metaphorically slapped the face of the foreign Manchu ruler who now sat on the Dragon Throne with a suicidal essay in which he wrote: "The great scourge of the empire is its sovereign. How can one suppose that the monarchy was intended to produce the conditions we have today? In former times, the people loved and supported their ruler, looking upon him as the father that he was. Now the people hate their ruler, regarding him as a thief, and an enemy, without any right to demand their fidelity."

The Confucian died for his ideals, not for other men. When the Manchus had already taken Peking, but a Ming emperor still sat on a throne in Nanking to the south, the Manchu regent privately sent a grandiloquent, yet wily letter to General Shih K'o-fa, who commanded the Chinese armies now defending what was left of the empire. Couching this in impeccable Confucian phrases (for he was a very literate barbarian), the regent promised General Shih the highest possible rank and the greatest rewards if he would persuade his ruler to drop all further resistance to the invaders and if he would himself change sides. General Shih dispatched an elegant, gem-encrusted reply, whose burden was that he hesitated to send a definite answer because (as any Confucian should know) the Master had himself laid down in his *Spring and Autumn Annals* that an official of one state must not exchange private messages with an official of another. He went on to make a quite obviously unacceptable compromise proposal and ended by saying: "I treat with silent contempt your ignoble endeavor to lure me with promises of rewards and honors." He then informed the emperor and at the same time asked for arms and equipment so that he could build up his army during the winter and prepare to meet the full weight of the Manchus one hundred miles north of Nanking when they inevitably attacked in the spring.

At this moment the emperor, his head full of girls rather than the grim realities of Manchu acquisitiveness, assigned the business of organizing military supplies to a corrupt and jealous toady who sent nothing. The spring of 1645 came, and it was still another Confucian's turn to memorialize his spineless and irresponsible fop of a monarch. "While Your Majesty is banqueting on rare food and drinking wine from jade cups, the soldiers are starving. If you remain lolling in Nanking, favoring flatterers, forgetting your troops, and talking of secret state plans in a loud voice, and if you do not discriminate between loyalty and treachery, then destruction is inevitable." But General Shih was wasting his time. The Manchus attacked, and he was forced to fall back on Yangchow, a walled city of one million souls which stood like a keep forty miles north of the capital. He had forty thousand men, their morale and discipline still uncertain after their lean winter of discontent in the defense line. But when a Manchu herald appeared and suggested that he abandon the cause of his frivolous and ungrateful sovereign, Shih cursed him roundly from the city wall and aimed an arbalest at him.

The Manchus mounted an assault and after ten days broke through the wall. Shih ordered an officer to run him through and, when the trembling fellow missed, seized the sword and drove it into the bungler's neck. Others then stopped him before he killed himself, and he was taken before the young and chivalrous Manchu prince commanding the enemy forces. The prince offered him a high post—"Now that you have done all that duty could demand"—but Shih replied: "Do you expect me to play the

traitor? You can decapitate me, but you cannot subdue my will."
After three days of argument during which the general remained
adamant, loyal to those iron rules of conduct beside which the
disciplines of European chivalry seem merely attractive terms of
service, they chopped his head off.

Men were loyal not so much to their prince as to the principle
of princedom. In 1841 the British first learned that the Chinese
were not all the poltroons they had thought, when the town of
T'ing Hai fiercely resisted their assault, matching an absurd collection of outdated weapons against modern arms, and was taken
only after the military commander had been mortally wounded
and the prefect and the chief of police had committed suicide.
After the Boxer Rebellion of 1900 the Manchu court sentenced
119 officials to death for their alleged responsibility in the affair.
These mandarins were serving in provincial towns throughout
the vast empire. Some of them were more than a thousand miles
from Peking and could easily have made a break for it. Not one
tried to escape, however. All patiently waited to meet their end.

The *trousseau* that opens the locks to the character of the Chinese also holds this key: that he is inspired by fine traditions of
loyalty but must first be quite sure of its object. Englishmen do
not make friends easily, nor Chinese give their allegiance with
a shrug. If this is a problem for men like Mao Tse-tung, it is a
thousand times greater problem for men like Lee Kuan Yew,
the prime minister of Singapore, whose predominantly Chinese
citizens are loyal enough—but to what? Some to China, more to
Chinese culture, some to newly acquired Western civilization,
some to Communism, a few to Chiang Kai-shek, but most of
them to their family and their clan, and probably not much else.
This explains the half-starved but defiant Chinese guerrilla in the
Malayan jungle at one end of the scale, and the wheezing, pig-
eyed pawnbroker gulping dumplings in Chinatown at the other.
But how long will it take before these disparate, stubborn, conservative, cautious, and suspicious people give their loyalty to
the little island state of Singapore, which has a largely immigrant

population of Indians, Malays, Eurasians, Pakistanis, as well as Chinese, and, embracing all cultures, has none of its own?

It will happen in time. During the reign of the Dowager-Empress in Peking at the turn of the century, many Chinese officials accepted, after two hundred and fifty years of foreign rule, that the Manchus had been granted the Mandate of Heaven and gave their loyalty to the ruling house; other Chinese were just as loyal to the lately arrived "foreign devils" whom they served in the Legation Quarter of Peking. There were courageous men who offered unasked to smuggle messages through the lines of the besieging Boxers on behalf of the besieged diplomats in the British legation, and were captured and cruelly killed. In 1958 I was in this same British legation in Peking when Mao ordered mass anti-British demonstrations because London had dispatched troops to Jordan. Once more the old compound with its twelve-foot walls and great red doors was under siege—this time from nearly two million highly disciplined, Communist-directed "spontaneous" demonstrators, who jam-packed the avenue outside day and night in shifts tens of thousands strong. The small British staff took it in turns, two by two, to stand at the open main entrance on a round-the-clock roster and face the roaring crowds, the blinding arc lights of the TV vans, the insulting slogans and the shaking fists, the torrent of mechanical Marxist abuse. But when the Chinese servants of the embassy were called upon by the Communist cadres to join in the general vilification of their foreign employers, they refused, and would only go out to join the mob after Duncan Wilson, the able British chargé d'affaires, had virtually ordered them to obey for their own sakes. No bunch of stage demonstrators in a fifth-rate school production in French could have looked more shamefaced and unconvincing.

Chinese may be good, bad, and stonily indifferent, but they are capable of stoical self-sacrifice for their beliefs and principles, which do not include such definitions as "beyond the call of duty," for either a thing is meet to be done or not. When the pitiful son of the Dowager-Empress died in dubious circumstances and none went to offer sacrifices at his grave, a former Chinese censor, horrified that there was no one to attend upon and defend the Imperial scion's spirit in the next world, killed himself near the sepulcher so that he could join him. In his customary farewell memorial he explained: "Fear is my private weakness; but Death is my public duty." This, unquestionably, was the equation of true integrity.

8

The Female of the Species

A plaintive, far-off voice whispers down seventeen centuries: "How sad it is to be a woman. Nothing on earth is held so cheap . . ." From time immemorial she rose earlier in the morning, and her toys were few and poor. When she was older she might learn to read the Classics, but she must be careful not to be clever. Boys were "like gods fallen out of heaven," but Confucius had long since put the girls—when they were not drowned at birth like unwanted kittens—where they belonged. "Only women and small men are hard to keep," he declared pontifically. "If you allow them close, they show no respect. If you keep them at a distance, they bear a grudge." Dogs, he almost implied, made easier pets. But he would not have added that pigs made more profitable ones. For a few head of the female of the species could always be reared to some purpose in a Chinese family. They could be placed as servants, as cooks, nurses, or companions in wealthy and important households, as musicians, and even as concubines that might, in powerful, if prying hands, win great advantage for all. They could become matchmakers, or midwives, or be sold for singsong girls, but best of all, of course, they could be married off blindly to the man of their father's heart, and so provide another link in the latticework of family relationships with which a Chinese screened himself from a hostile world.

Since no parents would sign a marriage contract for the supply of damaged goods, a girl had to be good, and this is still true today. Communism may, paradoxically, offer freedom of choice to lovelorn Chinese, and the jukebox set may walk around with the pill in their pants' pockets, but the ordinary Chinese girl, rich or poor, observes the decencies and indecencies of tradition.

When our personable young wash-amah, Ah Mui, got married, the betrothal was entirely arranged by a go-between who acted for both the bride's parents and the groom's. His first job was to check their horoscopes with a Taoist priest to make sure the match was suitable, and then to fix an auspicious day for the wedding. These essential preliminaries out of the way, the boy came to the bride's parents' house—a cement-floored wooden shanty with a corrugated-iron roof—and formally asked for Ah Mui's slightly reddened hand. A business discussion followed, with some fairly hard haggling, at the end of which the parties had settled precisely how much was to be paid for the girl ($28 to $35 would have been a reasonable guess) and just how many fittings and fixtures in the way of furniture, clothes, and trinkets went with her. A contract was signed, and the groom's parents supplied innumerable small cakes, which the bride's parents sent out, as an earnest of the coming nuptials, to their families and friends.

The wedding feast was thrown in a good restaurant and was attended by more than one hundred guests, and as they all got down to an eight-course dinner, as the brandy began to circulate and the crimped metal bottle tops started to spring off the orange-pop bottles on all sides, a stranger might have wondered how in the world these modest chicken-farming peasants were going to pay for all this. The answer is simple. When Chinese get married, friends do not usually give bedside alarm clocks or fireside rugs or picnic baskets to the couple, but a present of money, and most of this money is then spent on a banquet for the givers. (As the employer of the bride, by traditional responsibility was to provide all the brandy.) The lucky pair have a marriage feast for nothing, the donors are paid back with a dinner, and all are content.

It only remained for the young couple to link arms and toast each other. Next morning the groom and his bride knelt before the boy's parents and presented them with a ceremonial cup of tea: "For one cup of tea, I have given away my son," is often the first ominous ranging shot that opens life's battle between mother-in-law and daughter-in-law. Three days later the parents of the groom, duly apprised of his findings at the moment of truth, presented to the bride's family a number of edible young porkers to signify that she had in fact been a virgin. Not to have done so would have been a deadly insult.

Throughout the centuries, Chinese women played the complaisant domestic to three generations of males—their fathers, their husbands, and then their sons—often living a housebound life in the women's quarters, peeping at visitors from behind a screen. For a woman to have ideas of her own or to voice an independent point of view was regarded as a minor catastrophe, for Confucius had declared, in his usual misogynic fashion: "The woman with no talents is the one who has merit." In the Sage's state of Lu, men and women walked on opposite sides of the street, it is said, and in Imperial China strict propriety dictated that when they appeared in public, women must avert the gaze, be cool, withdrawn, grave, their beauty "like winter plum blossom in the snow," not some great saucy-eyed sunflower. Have they changed? Walking through the streets of Singapore in 1965, a colleague fresh from Europe makes his first comment on the East: "These girls never look at you, and they never smile."

A T'ang dynasty manual on the training of females lays down: "A chaste woman must not go out often, but must be ready to obey commands. If asked to come, she must come at once; if asked to go, she must go quickly. If she fails to submit to any order, reproach her and beat her. She should be instructed twice daily, morning and evening. She must work very hard, her duties including sweeping, looking after the cooking, sewing, burning incense, and weaving cloth. When others are present, she must preserve a modest demeanor and, after bringing them tea or soup, walk slowly backward and retire to her own room. When she is distressed, she must not weep or scream, for this brings ill-fortune to the family; and when she is happy she may not sing, for this encourages lewdness." And a thousand years thereafter this was still her lot.

In a man's civilization, feminine chastity became something of an obsession. The first virtue of a woman was goodness, morals were strict, and the lady who lapsed would be thrown straight out on to the street. During the Ming dynasty, chaste widowhood was part of the dogma, and for a woman to remarry after her first husband's death was a punishable crime. In all periods, widows who killed themselves became national heroes, and ceremonial arches were raised to those who lived out the rest of their lives in solitude.

The modern Chinese girl looks back on this bleak stretch of her cultural inheritance with forgivable horror, but she is still far more hesitant than her white or black sister to indulge in the joys of premarital sex. She may choose her own fiancé and go out courting with him, but she does not make jokes about marriage. She will still look askance at public necking, kissing, moist eyes and loose-lipped speech, well-it-seems-there-was-this-commercial-traveler, and titillating movies. Tradition dies slowly, sometimes agonizingly. On some days the streets of Singapore are suddenly full of cars decked in pink ribbon, each containing a Chinese bride in a white European wedding dress, and they can later be observed clustering around church doors, or lining up in an orderly fashion at the back of the aisle, waiting with their grooms for their turn at the altar. They are all being married according to Christian rites. But they are all being married on the same day because the Chinese almanac says this is a good day for marrying. And the Chinese almanac is based on a pagan work of divination that was old when Confucius (who thoroughly approved of it) was born.

Marriage was no real lottery for the Chinese girl, or even at worst a gold-brick sale, for no deception was involved. She knew exactly what to expect: a thoroughly one-sided deal, of which she would get the dirty end. Most Chinese men, completely spoiled by their mothers from childhood, expected to be waited on hand and foot and to be paid in sons annually. It was entirely accepted that the man would play around with courtesans or "flower girls," that he would spend nights out with his rowdy friends and leave his wife at home, as he still does today. Yet among the reasons for which a man could obtain a summary divorce, or in some eras simply send his wife back to her parents' home or into a nunnery as a reject, was ordinary jealousy. She could also be dismissed for being too talkative, for being chronically sick, for neglecting her father-in-law, or for being barren, as well as for stealing, or adultery. Although in modern Hong Kong most Chinese respect the English divorce laws where their first wives are concerned, there are still many who will arbitrarily shed the rest of the harem in accordance with an unceremonious old custom.

However, rigid discipline does not exclude emotional loyalty, nor contractual mating, love; and the cruel Chinese marital system broke hearts over more than just the loss of a roof and a bowl of rice:

> Entering the Hall, she meets the new wife;
> Leaving the Gate, she runs into her former husband.
> Words stick: she does not manage to say anything:
> She presses her hands together and hesitates.
> Agitates moon-like fan—sheds pearl-like tears—
> Realizes she loves him just as much as ever;
> That her present pain will never come to an end.

These lines read like the directions in a film script; they seem poignantly familiar and alive even today, yet they were written 1,400 years ago. But this type of sentimental poetry is regarded with contempt by the Chinese, who for the most part had stopped writing love poems about women some four hundred years before that. Critics are also quick to point out that this tender little verse was composed by the Emperor Yuan Ti, a monster who only won the throne after murdering his own brother.

The inequalities of a Chinese marriage were not enough: Chinese wives also had to accept a design for living that included polygamy and concubinage—and still have to in many cases. The concubine has influenced the course of Chinese history almost as much as has Confucius, some contend—usually disastrously, occasionally for the good. The number of Imperial concubines ran into hundreds, sometimes thousands, so that many lived out their lives as reservists who never saw the emperor at all, let alone any action. But they represented another exercise in what might misleadingly be called "Chinese democracy," for just as any village lad could in theory rise to become prime minister if he studied and passed the Imperial examinations, so any lass could rise to become empress in the same way, although the nature of the examinations might be a little different. Precious Pearl, strong-willed consort of the last Ming emperor, was in fact a foundling.

All girls between thirteen and sixteen were eligible for this early form of beauty contest. In an account of a selection made in the seventeenth century, we read that eunuchs were responsible for weeding out the non-starters, until only four thousand girls were still in the running. Vital statistics and voice tests cut this number down to about two thousand candidates, who were then examined on their deportment, and the successful among them stripped naked, pinched, prodded, carefully scrutinized, and their points noted. The three hundred who survived this ordeal were all retained in the Imperial palace as ladies-in-waiting for a month, during which their characters were studied. At the end of this period, 250 were rejected, and the fifty winners all became Imperial concubines.

If the scholar system, at its best, kept the government and

people in contact, the Imperial concubines injected a fine flow of vulgarity into the veins of the Imperial family, and introduced something of the spirit of the millions outside into the sheltered precincts of the palace. But otherwise their rivalries, their ambitions, their extravagances, and their whims played the devil with empire and more than once brought China to the brink of ruin. Chinese women are capable of a tigerish jealousy rarely seen in the West, and at court observed exacting standards in revenge set by such exemplars as the Imperial princess who cut off the nose, ears, and breasts of her husband's mistress, and then threw them at him.

More dangerous were capricious darlings like the lady whose favorite occupation was tearing up vast quantities of silk, and whose failure to smile proved a national catastrophe. Determined to wring a laugh from this gloomy beauty, the infatuated emperor ordered hilltop beacons to be lit in the recognized alarm signal that the Huns had invaded. All over the country, men dropped their plows, seized their swords, and followed their feudal lords in forced marches to defend the frontier and the capital. When the joke was sprung and the tired, mud-stained feudatories learned they had been the victims of a harmless little hoax, the concubine's merriment knew no bounds. But sheepish though they may have appeared, they would not respond twice to the same cry of "Wolf," and when the beacons had to be fired in earnest shortly afterward, the lords and their armies stayed at home and let the Huns light the biggest beacon of all by burning down the capital.

Time and time again an imperial favorite started a vicious struggle for supremacy by persuading the emperor to give the most important posts in the land to members of her family, hoping that when he died they might seize power before the rival faction—probably the mother of the heir-apparent and *her* family —had them all exterminated. Yang Kuei-fei, fattest and most famous of all Imperial concubines, combined most of their characteristics. For this statuesque but grasping and imperious bitch, relays of horsemen fetched litchis from nearly one thousand miles away in the far south of the empire, so that she could indulge her taste for these fruit at the daily breakfast table. Doted on by a sexagenarian emperor who had enjoyed a brilliant reign up to the moment when he ill-advisedly filched her from one of his princes, Mistress Yang brought hundreds of her clansmen under the shade of the Imperial favor, and had her brutal and stupid brother made prime minister. Ruinously extravagant—a new summer palace with sixteen marble bathing pools had to be built to please her—she was also unfaithful to the Emperor Ming Huang, favoring a gross Tatar general, who, having insinuated himself into a key Chinese command in consequence, mounted a military insurrection and forced the court to flee the capital. By the time the retreating Imperial cortege reached the bleak uplands of western Shensi, its demoralized armed escort had had enough. At Ma Wei Slope the soldiers mutinied, murdered Yang Kuei-fei's sister, fed her brother's head to the birds, and demanded the life of the woman who had broken the empire with her extravagances and her treacherous infidelities. The besotted emperor at first begged for her life but finally sanctioned her execution. She was then strangled with a silk cord, in accordance with established practice.

These are the bare facts, but this was the golden age of the great T'ang dynasty poets; the story of Ming Huang and his plump minx was converted into lyrical legend and celebrated in a famous romantic narrative poem that ends:

> Heaven and Earth, long-lasting as they are,
> will some day pass away,
> But this great wrong shall stretch out to eternity . . .

Statistics, though dull, restore a sense of balance. The emperor was seventy-two when his favorite died: the war lasted ten years and, according to admittedly rather improbable official estimates, cost thirty million lives.

It has been argued that in less exalted circles concubinage reduces the divorce rate, for the dissatisfied husband is not compelled to make a choice between his outworn love and his latest passion. He can keep his wife and "keep" his mistress and still be the soul of propriety. It was customary for a barren wife to give her formal consent before her husband brought a concubine under the roof (so that he could have children), and if she was smart, she would pick the girl herself. As first wife, she remained the mistress of the household, and against horrendous tales of savage jealousies can be set the many authenticated examples of an affectionate relationship between a man's two or more womenfolk.

In some ways the practice of polygamy has become even more elaborate than before, "so that," as one indignant champion of women's rights complained a few years ago in Singapore, "Chinese men are now degenerating into doing such unheard-of things as taking two wives at a single wedding ceremony." It is less common for the women to be shuffled around under one roof, however. The modern polygamist sets up his ladies in separate establishments, and in consequence wears himself out keeping to a tight schedule that enables him to spend enough time with each to avert tears, accusations, and endless nagging. Moreover, tricky situations arise when, for example, a first wife encourages her husband to take a third wife in order to counterbalance the rising influence of the hated second wife (who was of course chosen by his mother).

But sometimes all works out smoothly. I once asked a young Chinese friend why his father kept five wives (and twenty-one children) in five different establishments in five different cities. "He had to travel constantly on business, you see," he answered, and then added confidingly: "And he hated staying in hotels." To those accustomed to the rationing systems of the West, it sometimes comes as a shock to realize that Chinese friends who may be scrabble addicts and wizards with the number 3 iron hold exotic views on marriage that have little in common with practices widely acclaimed in Arkansas and Yorkshire. And sometimes it is the Chinese who is shocked, for having settled comfortably in England or the United States with one wife, he is astonished to find himself regarded with sorrow by authority when he tries to bring a second wife with six children from Singapore to join him. Nor are all these wives necessarily a burden. Arriving at Kai Tak Airport in Hong Kong, Ping and I were once given a lift into town by a smart but sad-faced Chinese waiting to meet a passenger from Saigon who was not, as it turned out, on the plane. "Of course he is not happy," Ping told me after he had dropped us and driven off. "He's stuck in Hong Kong with no money and three wives."

"Who was he coming out to meet, then?"

"His number-four wife. She is famous singer and working in Saigon. She makes all the money for family."

Under customary Chinese law, only the first wife is entitled to inherit. The feckless little nightclub hostess, whose marriage ceremony probably consisted only of a hilarious wedding party at which her lover publicly took her as his wife but signed no contract, finds when he dies that she and her children get nothing (although in Singapore the number-three widow of a murdered biscuit manufacturer set a new precedent when she won a claim on his estate in 1965). Modern law is catching up with polygamy in deference to twentieth-century prejudices about the equality of the sexes, but the old Chinese custom will be with us for a generation yet.

In the prudish West, a mistress may have importance; in the profligate East, where girls have been bought and sold since the beginning of recorded history, a stricter morality supervenes: wives have status, but concubines cut no ice. "I have never heard such nonsense," an old Chinese lady said to me scornfully at the height of the scandal that linked the name of Christine Keeler not only with a British cabinet member but with a Russian attaché. "If a government minister takes a fancy to some chit of a girl with undesirable outside associations, he must shut her up in a house with trustworthy servants who see that she receives nobody but him. Expense? Well, I have never been to England, but surely the Conservative Party would have been happy to pay?" (The moral aspect of the matter was, of course, dismissed as so much irritating Western hypocrisy).

The courtesan was perhaps the only truly free woman in China. Witty, talented, and beautiful, she was at her best a mistress of elegant repartee, versed in all the niceties: chess, eroticism, versifying, the Classics, contraception, and music—in fact, at some periods of history the development of Chinese music lay entirely in her practiced little hands. In Yuan dynasty China, she was "attired with great magnificence," says Marco Polo, "heavily perfumed, attended by many handmaids, and lodged in richly ornamented apartments." But this particular hell has many mansions. After the luxurious courtesan came the "singsong" girls, adept at filling the wine cups, playing childish games with drunken carousers, singing and strumming in the private rooms of taverns and teahouses; the "flower girls" in the ornate lantern-lit boats on the West Lake; their sisters in the brothels, each advertised by a bamboo shade over the light at the entrance.

A man's wives might be dutiful and dull, but out in the city among Marco Polo's "multitude of sinful women," he and his male friends could find entertainment, excitement, smart conversation, and studied caresses. He was free as the air, for he suffered from no sense of solecism or sin, and if in a more rustic setting plainer fare was to hand, he enjoyed this too without a qualm of conscience: "He had hired two big-footed countrywomen and was carrying on with both of them," we read in an eighteenth-century novel. "All the men are accustomed to sleeping with these big-footed maids. Even in respectable families, people laugh at this custom until their eyes are slits, thinking it great sport and nothing in the least to be ashamed of. But the two maids in Ling's house had grown jealous, and after smashing all the bowls, plates, and dishes in the kitchen, they kicked over all the tubs with their big feet."

Chinese love of "lily feet," the tiny, steep-instepped hocks which give a sensuous undulating motion to a woman's walk and are formed by binding the toes under the sole from childhood, is more than a thousand years old. It was inspired by a delicate little Imperial dancer who gyrated seductively on her points upon a golden lotus six feet high, after stringing her feet with a twist of silk so that they resembled curved longbows. The fashion for plump women with soft, fat feet gave way to a taste for slim, willowy girls in loose gowns, their sleeves far longer than their arms, and their chests tightly bound to restrain the natural exuberance of the feminine flesh. But the Chinese would protest that these abuses of the natural form were no more extraordinary than the invention of the hourglass figure in the West.

Since the pre-Christian era, Chinese women have been plucking and penciling their eyebrows and painting their nails, as well as putting powder and rouge on their cheeks, and they have developed their own distinctive tricks, like hiding little hot-water bags in their muffs in winter, and holding them surreptitiously to their faces from time to time to bring roses to their cheeks. Modern medicine has now persuaded the Chinese to break out in breasts, and Manchu influence has left them the tight-fitting *cheong sam* with its high collar and slit skirts, but both they and their clothes retain their tremendous traditional asset: durability. The foreigner is repeatedly astonished to meet fragile little creatures with girlish figures who turn out to be the mothers of five, six, or even eight children. Their clothes—the unchanging *cheong sam* and the pajamalike *sam foo*—can also be worn year after year. In North China it was common for poor women to pledge their winter dresses regularly every spring and to redeem them in the autumn, while in well-to-do houses clothes were kept in four trunks respectively decorated with the characters for the four seasons.

If a sense of beauty is governed by anything, it seems to be perversity. Western women spend much time sweating uncomfortably in the sun in order to bake themselves brown, and making up their eyes to give them a mysterious Oriental slant. On the other hand, the Chinese regard the girls of Soochow as the most beautiful in the land largely because their complexions are pale as alabaster, and minor quacks and beauticians coin small fortunes by nicking the lids of Asian girls to make their eyes round like a European's, and dyeing their hair red or blond. We end up with two freaks: a wide-eyed, flaxen-haired, apparently Nordic girl who in fact first saw the light of day in Hong Kong, and a sultry, slit-eyed seductress who positively oozes subtropical glamour, but was in reality born in Sheffield to Mr. and Mrs. Smith. The first seems to be two sizes too small for her cotton frock, and the second looks curiously cylindrical in her silk *cheong sam*. The basic Chinese build is flatter than the European, so that a Chinese girl may often appear broad from the front, yet astonishingly slim from the side.

The move from chest-binding to the fleshly assertion of the *cheong sam* was a bold one, for the female nude had hardly figured in China's painting and sculpture throughout her long history, the women had always been up to their necks in flowing drapes, and there is no such art form as Chinese cheesecake. But the Chinese girl who will happily sit down and let her slit skirt fall open to the garter belt still clings to her high Prussian collar, for she would—in many cases—rather show a bare thigh than a bare throat.

However, concealment is of course a gimmick to entice, and a Chinese woman's modesty in public should not be mistaken for sexual shyness. It is the Chinese men who tend to suffer from a possessive prudery of their own, and while the wife may coolly ask a male doctor to fit her for a contraceptive, the husband will blush with fury when he finds out. He likes to be thought a devil of a fellow among the taxi-girls, but at home he will not discuss sex, and in the marriage bed he is sometimes more notable for his retiring nature than for his outstanding qualities as a lover. His wife, on the other hand, is in her element. "When is she mistress of the situation if not that moment?" as Ping asks logically.

In Chinese society, sex was an essential but readily procurable commodity, like salt or detergents, and not some gift-wrapped bauble to swoon over. Chinese women looked upon love-making as an obvious, unmysterious, sometimes delightful activity, but only important for its occasional, equalling results. It is true that pairs caught in adultery were sometimes strangled under the law, but this severe punishment was designed to protect the family. For sex was part of the system: it had nothing to do with sin. The Taoist temples themselves served as retreats for superfluous girls, and nunneries became brothels in China as unself-consciously as monasteries became distilleries in France. Not that the Chinese were indiscreet. Chu Hsi, the famous neo-Confucian scholar who lived some eight hundred years ago gave this sly little piece of advice to young folk: "When going upstairs, utter a loud 'Ahem.' If you see two pairs of shoes outside the door and hear voices within, you may enter; but if you hear nothing, remain without."

The shyness that sometimes afflicts Chinese men in feminine matters does not spring from any lack of sexuality, but from a certain unsureness. They are frequently obsessed by a fear of impotence, or a desire for more swaggering virility. They provide a ready market for fortifying Korean ginseng, and also for powdered rhinoceros horn, the stand-by of Asian aphrodisiacs. Some are touched by tantric Buddhist beliefs that to hold back in the sexual act is to preserve one's precious potency, and there are even those who have a morbid terror of finding (or not finding, so to speak) that they have a regressive penis that disappears back into the body. But these are all signs of preoccupation, not disinterest, and many are enviously fascinated by the account of the paramour of the First Emperor's mother who could fit a cartwheel over his organ and then spin it rapidly without noticeable loss of poise (he was a present from an indulgent husband).

Chastity counted for nothing in the days of Confucius, and incest was common. In earlier centuries, peasants mated freely at festival time and only set up house together if the girl became pregnant. There is a description of orgiastic goings-on under the last king of the Shang dynasty at which men and women pursued each other stark naked around a pool of wine and among trees hung with meats. There was much free intermingling, and guests were often courteously invited into the harem of their host. From the Classical Book of Odes comes the sweet song of a wanton perhaps three thousand years dead:

> On the moor is the creeping grass,
> And how heavily is it loaded with dew.
> There was a beautiful man,
> Lovely, with clear eyes and fine forehead.
> We met together accidentally,
> And so my desire is satisfied.

In later times, many hypocritical, moralizing scholars were renowned for their lubricity, and some of the Sung women of Hangchow were so ardent that their overworked husbands allowed them "complementary spouses" to help gratify their gluttony. There is a tale that during the reign of one elderly emperor most of the imperial concubines fell sick, and no one could cure them until a brilliant doctor produced his own special prescription: a quantity of lusty young fellows, to be taken daily as directed. The emperor reluctantly agreed to the treatment, and a few days later he went into the women's quarters to see what had happened. He found all his concubines in glowing health, in sharp contrast to a number of haggard and emaciated men who now kowtowed shakily before him. "Who are these?" the startled emperor asked, to be met with a giggle and the coy answer from the ladies: "Sire, these are the dregs of the medicine."

Nevertheless, despite tales of delicious excesses, the Chinese approach to sex is balanced and matter-of-fact. The lengthy and amusing Chinese novel *Chin P'ing Mei* (variously translated as *Golden Vase Plum* and *Golden Lotus* and even *Chin P'ing Mei*) is considered so pornographic that whole pages of the first unabridged English version had to be rendered in Latin. But the Chinese author was not trying to be dirty: he was simply describing the salacious antics of his hero in the same detail that he devoted to all his other activities. Why not? Sensual ecstasy is all part of a day's pleasure. It may even be all in a day's work. Asked about his morals, Eliza Doolittle's father replies stoutly: "Can't afford 'em, Guv'nor," and this often expresses the Chinese attitude. In *The Scholars*, the reader is introduced to a new character in this undramatic fashion: "Her father-in-law, who had played women's parts in a theatrical company, had been extremely popular with men in his time, but after his beard grew he had to give up that sort of thing. So he married a wife, hoping that she might take over his clients, but she was so fat and swarthy that not a ghost came through the door. At last there was nothing for it but to adopt a son and find a child bride for him. By the time she was sixteen, this girl had grown into a beauty, and customers crowded the place."

Young actors were frequently catamites, and some of the leisured class bisexual, but during the Sung dynasty homosexuality could be punished with one hundred strokes of the rod, and there was always the usual prejudice against queers. Infuriated by some careless act of his hip-wiggling neighbor, a red-faced surgeon in *The Scholars* shouts contemptuously: "Your place is a house of amphibians. Are you all ass and no eyes?"

9

More Gentle Sex

"Be moderate in all seven passions," a disciple of Confucius urged upon the Chinese, for he knew he was dealing with a people capable of violent and romantic obsessions. The Emperor Han Wu-ti, whose conquests and achievements and puerile search for immortality are all part of the same monumental tapestry worked by a ruler of unbridled ambition, pined inconsolably like a lovelorn boy for years after the death of his favorite concubine, of whom he wrote:

> The sound of her silk skirt has stopped,
> On the marble pavement dust grows.
> Her empty room is cold and still,
> Fallen leaves are piled against the doors.
> Longing for that lovely lady,
> How can I bring my aching heart to rest?

He employed necromancers from all over the empire to try to summon her spirit, until one alchemist produced a shadowy apparition whose movement toward the concealed emperor was accompanied by the familiar swish of a skirt before it vanished. Weeping with emotion, Han Wu-ti conferred high honors on this ingenious charlatan, who had seemingly brought back the beloved dead for one brief instant.

Blind love, defeating all honor, rang the knell for the great

Ming dynasty and opened the frontiers of China to nearly three hundred years of foreign domination. When the last ruling Ming emperor took his life and the rebel leader Li Tzu-cheng seized the Dragon Throne in Peking, an Imperial army some two hundred thousand strong was still stationed on the frontier at the coastal end of the Great Wall to prevent the Manchus to the north from invading the country.

The commanding general was a man called Wu San-kuei who was naturally expected at this point to march on Peking, throw out the rebel leader, put the Ming heir apparent on the throne, and return to the frontier to stop the Manchus from trying to take advantage of the situation. But Wu San-kuei was deeply infatuated with a round-faced singsong girl whom he had made his concubine, and this Lady Ch'en—the "Full Moon Beauty"—had now fallen into rebel hands. So Wu stayed put on the border, arguing that if he made no move the rebels would look after her carefully as a hostage for his good conduct, but if he once marched on the capital, they would murder her.

He next sent word through his father, who was also in Peking, that he would swear allegiance to the rebels if they first gave up to him the Ming heir and the Lady Ch'en. The contemptuous rebel reply was first to offer Wu San-kuei a bribe and then to demand that he surrender in any case ("Otherwise, we will defeat you in the morning and decapitate your father the same afternoon") and finally to inform him that the Lady Ch'en had been handed over to the captive Ming heir.

The distracted Wu San-kuei now invited the Manchus to join him in annihilating the rebels, and those grasping barbarians, their covetous eyes on the whole Chinese empire, eagerly crossed the frontier and helped him inflict an initial defeat on his tormentors, who promptly sent him the heir apparent and the Lady Ch'en as he had asked. With the girl back in his hands, Wu San-kuei turned his coat again and secretly entered into an agreement with the rebels to expel the Manchus and then share the empire. The rebels became suspicious, however, and—so outraged Confucian historians hint—played another trump by threatening to hack off Wu San-kuei's father's head unless he handed back the Lady Ch'en at least temporarily as a token of his good faith. The old man himself then wrote, begging his son to remember his duty to his father, but with the Lady Ch'en safely in his camp, the general was taking no more chances. And when the rebels realized that she was not going to be sacrificed as a pawn in the game, they killed Wu's father and all his family. Infuriated, Wu again switched back to an alliance with the Manchus, who seized Peking and established their dynasty on the throne of China, leaving their dishonorable Chinese confederate to pursue and exterminate the fleeing rebels.

This disagreeable tale of passion and treachery has a curious sequel which would have given Shakespeare—dead only a few years before—his last act. Wu San-kuei, treated as a viceroy by the Manchus, set himself up in kingly style in a great palace in southwest China and offered the Lady Ch'en the title of queen. But his mistress, bitterly disappointed that he made no attempt to fling the foreigners out, rejected the rank and entered a monastery. We have a picture of this weak, yet able man, his bones growing old, visiting his shaven-headed beauty in her cell from time to time to discuss some problem of state, until finally he decides to attack the Manchus after all. She warns him it is too late, that they are now too strong, but in vain. The aging general dies during the long campaign that follows, and on hearing the news, the Lady Ch'en throws herself into a lotus pond. The Manchus, from now on victorious, then butcher the entire Wu clan.

Chinese festivals faithfully reflect the sentimental and romantic side of Chinese womanhood. Women's clubs throughout Malaya and Singapore celebrate the Feast of the Seventh Evening, on the seventh day of the seventh month, at which time their members pray for the happiness of all lovers, and also for fine weather so that the River of the Milky Way will not become dangerously swollen with rain. For legend has it that the angry father of the

Weaving Maid (Vega) has sternly ruled that she may only join her lover the Cowherd (Aquila) across the Milky Way on this one evening of the year. The origin of the Feast of Hungry Ghosts, the All Souls' night of China, when all uncared-for spirits of the dead rise out of the earth in search of food, is said to lie in the sad little tale of two disconsolate lovers who, separated by their disapproving parents, flung themselves into a river and drowned. The Chinese have their own tradition of sighs and secret signals, of perilous assignations and wild elopements and love-will-find-a-way. Theirs is the sentimental symbol of the never separated mandarin lover-ducks, matching the turtledove metaphors of the West, and the most charming of all romantic concepts—the two one-winged birds that can only fly if they are joined together. But it is a common mistake to look with slight contempt upon poor, downtrodden Chinese woman, for there is more to her than sentimentality and submission. Take, for example, the case of the Empress Wu.

In the days of the Venerable Bede, this demure lady first appears as a marginal note on the page of history when she enters the Imperial palace of the great T'ang dynasty Emperor T'ai Tsung as one of his uncounted concubines, aged twelve. Although not entirely neglected by the reigning monarch, she is of a speculative cast of mind and therefore buys forward by sleeping with the heir apparent also. When the emperor dies, she piously enters a nunnery, but her high infidelity now pays off, and his young successor, madly in love with her, takes her out of the cloisters and back into the concubinate again. In 655, this weakling divorces his first wife, installs his *beguin* in her place, and lets her assume full powers as his consort. It is now a bad time to be a crown prince. No fewer than three are eliminated in succession in various ingenious ways, so that when the emperor also expires in his turn, Wu the regent becomes Wu the ruling empress.

Wu Chao was not only beautiful but talented and thorough. She had supplanted her rival, the original consort of her Im-

perial husband, by framing her as the instigator of a plot to
poison him with the help of another palace beauty. Once these
two ladies had fallen from favor, Wu showed her genius for con-
clusive action by first having them beaten until they were half
dead. Next, their hands and feet were lopped off, and their pollarded bodies tossed into a brewing vat, where they were left
to die. Their corpses were then hacked to pieces and their heads
were cut off, after which Wu Chao appears to have been satisfied
for the moment.

She is further credited with the poisoning of one of her sons,
and she certainly murdered her niece. Two of her brothers also
died in suspicious circumstances after making slighting remarks
about her interference in the running of the government while
the emperor still lived. Once he was dead, she executed or exiled
almost his entire family because they challenged her right to
rule, and to be on the safe side, she wiped out twelve collateral
branches also, after an unsuccessful revolt. She was responsible
for the violent killing of a fantastically long list of princes (but
was compassionate enough to allow the husband of her favorite
daughter to starve to death). Living in terror of her secret police,
men who held positions of any importance thought themselves
lucky if they were only exiled to the farthest frontiers for life.

At sixty, this energetic usurper fell for a lusty, big-limbed lout
of a peddler and so indulged the strapping fellow that he became
aggressive and arrogant, beating an Imperial censor who objected to his behavior almost to death without being punished
for it. In her seventies, she was showering extraordinary favors
on two fattish brothers of delicate gait whose precise relationship
with their Imperial mistress no one has ever quite worked out.

The queasy Caucasian is perhaps horrified by such manners,
but the Chinese measure of good rule is the public good done for
the greatest number. To them, the sometimes displeasing quirks
and fancies of this greedy and merciless woman are of little account. And they are not without arguments. While the emperor
still lived, Wu Chao won his approval for a series of edicts

whereby the army was reduced and a policy of peace pursued, taxes were axed, salaries of officials were raised, low-grade civil servants were promoted on merit, retired mandarins were assured of a secure living. Agriculture and the silk industry were given a new impetus, and royal lands near the palace were turned over to husbandry.

Once she became supreme empress, Wu ordered a bronze suggestion urn to be set up in public, into whose four slots any citizen might slip a petition, or a letter of criticism of the administration, or a demand for redress, or a private prophecy. If she knew her critics to be able men who had something to give to the country, she frequently pardoned them, and in later years she disbanded her odious secret police. She was ruthless in weeding out inefficient time-servers and crooked climbers in government service, but she promoted to high office many humble men whose brains belied their barnyard origins, and in consequence hers was a long, peaceful, and equitable reign. At seventy-six, we find her weeping bitterly at the death of a great and honest minister whom history knows as Ti Jen-chieh and lovers of detective fiction as "Judge Dee." She died at eighty-one, having usurped the Imperial authority for more than half a century and done the empire a power of good.

Nearly twelve hundred years later, China was dominated by another small woman of iron, Tzu Hsi, "The Last Empress"—an amusing, quick-witted, extravagant, and stony-hearted assassin with an equally good eye for a fine piece of embroidery or a rival to be chopped down. Beginning public life as a third-grade concubine, the captain's daughter (for that is what she was) gave birth to the heir apparent and so became regent when her Imperial husband died in 1861. She then perpetuated her power by allowing eunuchs to pander to the crown prince's profligacy to a point where he expired, seemingly exhausted, and contriving an obscure death for his dangerously pregnant widow. Tzu Hsi next put her nephew on the throne illegally, but virtually imprisoned him when he showed a disconcerting zeal for reform and West-

ernization, and made her outraged conservatism further felt by
having fifty-three of his servants executed. This poor, faltering
fellow was to stand by in 1901 while his unforgiving aunt ordered
two eunuchs to wrap his favorite concubine in a carpet and
throw her down a palace well. Tzu Hsi's gentle sister also died
after eating certain pastries, having foolishly revealed that she
held a compromising letter which might strip the Dowager-
Empress of her power if published.

Tzu Hsi was a woman of admirable poise and decision. When
two rebellious princes accompanied by a group of sixty armed
Boxers pushed their way into the palace, out for blood, and
bawling for the young emperor himself, Tzu Hsi met them with
nothing but a small, frightened entourage of eunuchs, and her
Imperial fury. "Only I have power to make or break a sovereign,"
she told them bluntly. She then commanded the immediate de-
capitation of all the Boxer leaders present, instructed the princes
they were docked one year's allowances for their effrontery, and
told them to get out forthwith and to return in future only when
summoned. In a few minutes, nothing remained of this dramatic
scene but the blood and the silence. Tzu Hsi had gone back to
finish her early morning tea (it was about 6:30 a.m.).

If this indomitable little Victorian figurine clad in her stiff
brocade and her despotic power seems as strange, if not as remote a symbol of womanhood as the Empress Wu, Yü Hsüan-chi
can be seen a thousand years after her time in a hundred London
or New York bars, head bowed, hair curtaining another one for
the road.

With an itch to be free and a grimace for the straight and narrow path along which her wellborn sisters tottered on their tor-
mented toe knuckles, Mistress Yü was a pensive, studious, wonderfully talented young wanton who knew her Classics like a
scholar, played the Chinese lute like an angel, was a graceful
calligrapher and a poetess of mark. Her early life at the T'ang
capital consisted largely of study and seduction in the amusing
and invigorating company of Imperial candidates, many of whom

were as much concerned with making the most of the gay, un-
inhibited city of courtesans and taverns as with entering the mandarinate. But she made the mistake of becoming the concubine
of one of these lady-killers, who took her out of the city and back
not only to his conventional home in the country but to his
shrew of a first wife. Unable to stand soulless domestic drudgery
under this virago, she went to live and write her poems in a lonely
hut in the mountains, and when her lover neglected her there,
withdrew, seemingly heartbroken, to a nunnery in the capital.

Here chastity was commended but not imposed, and the disillusioned young woman, who had meanwhile learned to drink
like a man, was not seeking anyone's commendation. Young men
came to wine and versify and copulate with this somber but
eager partner, until she teamed up with an ugly devil of a poet,
a great drinker and brawler and kicker of convention who led
her an exciting dance around the country, hailed by topers and
vagabonds and pursued by gypped landlords. Back once more
in the capital after this extended jag, she set herself up as an
artistic and enchantingly sophisticated courtesan, but she was
ever generous to her wine-bibbing old loves, so that fornicators
of sobriety and discretion began to desert her, and as the years
skimmed off the yeast, and dissipation the distinction, she sank
into the sediment of rascals and whores and tippling, unwashed
failures of the city. Pulling herself together, Mistress Yü returned to her nunnery, to write a sorry but immortal poem about
herself called "Selling wilted peonies." Now on the books of the
police, she was accused of the murder of a personal maid who
had stolen her latest and last amour, confessed under torture,
and was executed. She had been ready to toss the lees out in
any case. She was not yet thirty.

There have been other great poetesses in China, great women
painters, and renowned women musicians. There was also General Mu Lan, who was offered the hand of the emperor's daughter as a reward for twelve years of outstanding military service,
an honor which finally obliged this exceptional officer to confess

that he was really a certain Miss Hua. In modern times no woman in the West, with the possible exception of Evita Perón, has asserted her influence and wielded so much power in public affairs—thanks to a taut, tigresslike quality compounded of will and courage, wiry energy and implacable ambition—as lissome Asian ladies like Madame Chiang Kai-shek or (to take an example from a mandarin family in the best Chinese tradition) Madame Ngo Dinh Nhu of South Vietnam.

There were matriarchal communities in early China, and every open lorry that bounces down a Singapore road crammed with leather-faced females in faded blue denims and stiff red head-dresses proves that the tradition is not dead. For these Sam Sui women from South China, with their horny hands and even hornier feet, glimpsed padding swiftly up a steep ladder with a heavy load of bricks or balanced high on some flimsy bamboo scaffolding, take on the toughest construction work in the community for less than a dollar a day, while daddy minds baby at home. Nor is the matriarch absent from man-dominated Chinese society, and no figure of fiction is truer to life as it was lived until very recently than the splendid old autocrat of a grandmother in *The Dream of the Red Chamber*, probably China's finest novel of the eighteenth century, who rules the affairs of the magnificent, collapsing house of China from the privacy of her apartments.

"Look at their faces," a Singapore politician once murmured to me while we were watching a pro-Communist youth meeting, and I obediently glanced down the rows of earnest, bespectacled Chinese youths. "No, not those. Over there." I turned to the other side of the central gangway, and there sat the contingents from the Chinese girls' schools—lines of intent, immobile, snub-nosed faces under black fringes cut so severely that they looked as if they ought to bleed, their unsmiling expressions as stiff as their starched white blouses and skirts. "Yes," said the politician. "They're the ones I'm really afraid of." And I knew just what he meant.

Fired in the terrible crucible of Chinese social custom, the

Chinese woman has in the past either crumbled into submission or, more often, melted without but hardened within. Docile, demure, modestly silent, and deferential as a guest accompanying her husband to the houses of others, she knew how to use every weapon she could lay hands on in order to remain mistress in her own home. If her husband was infatuated with her, she might sell her favors dearly for greater powers. If he was a fool, she would start keeping his accounts, then advise, then manage him. The best marriages are still run on the principle that the home of a Chinese is not his castle but his wife's fortress. "She may act like a slave," a Chinese said to me calmly once, as his wife declined to sit at table with us but stood to serve us with food. "But she is the real Minister of the Interior here." I glanced at this elderly mother of eleven as she bent to ladle me out some duck's-foot soup, and caught something in the warm opacity of her onyx-black eyes that seemed to be a marvelous mingling of love, derision, and hard, hard confirmation of this admission. Many Chinese are comically frightened of their tough, jealous wives. The Americans invented the gold digger and the English the henpecked husband, but the Chinese made their own graphic contribution to the terminology of the sex war with the "teapot"— the nagging wife with one hand on her hip, in the time-honored gesture of righteous indignation, the other stabbing an accusatory forefinger at the defendant. One arm is the handle, of course; the other, the spout.

The woman's almost aggressive insistence on her rights in the household frequently engenders harmony, however, for it makes for a well-defined division of labor which Chinese men today are learning to appreciate. "Keep out of kitchen," Ping shouted the first time that, in the foolish way of the Western washer-upper, I wandered in with a dirty glass or something. "You are not *allowed.*" And there was a note almost of distress as well as urgency and indignation in her voice. "Go to sit down and rest. You work too hard." Life could hardly have held a more delicious moment for an expatriate from the sinks and stews of

Europe. For the first time, in a rice-eating household, I had achieved the dignity due to the breadwinner.

The Chinese woman will stifle her feelings and present a placid countenance until, like some inverted *bombe Alaska,* she is in fact red-hot with resentment within, if icy without. She will then explode into sudden hysterical fury that few of her Western sisters could hope to match. She is hard-working, her delicate structure often a soft sleeve for the steel beneath. Nothing is more absurd than to see six feet of trained British or American soldier offering to help ninety pounds of poor little refugee from Communism who is trotting indefatigably down the quay in Hong Kong or Saigon with two heavy-laden baskets slung on to her bamboo carrying-pole. Ten to one, he will barely be able to lift the load, however important it is to win the hearts and minds of the people, let alone run with it.

The Chinese woman is abstemious, clean-living, mean with money, full of a peasant, sock-under-mattress urge for security; in business she is flinty, as a shopkeeper, positively metallic, but she can weep to read in *The Red Chamber* how heartbroken Black Jade dies on Pao Yü's wedding day, and she will indulgently let the children squander money on firecrackers at New Year, to the fury of the non-Chinese. Today, in the newfound freedom of a new era, she is often almost intoxicated by her own liberty. She has learned by bitter experience to conquer servitude, and she may easily have in her vitals, therefore, the gritty little irritant that starts the itch for power.

Ah Fu, dragon of our kitchen in her gleaming white jacket and black cotton trousers, her hair up in a neat bun and her pendulous lobes pierced for the absurd coquetry of two tiny gold earrings, personifies the early emancipation of Chinese womanhood. For an amah's dress is not so much the uniform of a servant as the habit of a proud sisterhood founded on the principle that husbands are hell. It seems that in the second half of the last century certain countrywomen decided that they were crazy to allow themselves to be bound over to one man, to be obliged to clean, cook, and clear up after him and bear him a seemingly ever rolling stream of infants, to put up with his egoisms and his tantrums and his sickening importunities in the thankless name of "wife," and to be repaid solely with the objurgations and insults of some Tartar of a mother-in-law. These perceptive ladies therefore formed their own lodge and thereafter arranged to go out and cook and clean and clear up for complete strangers, who did not saddle them with babies or mothers-in-law but, instead, actually paid them for their services in good silver.

This refreshing arrangement, infinitely more advantageous and tasteful than the old, primitive institution of marriage, attracted a considerable following, and the Hong Kong or Singapore amah of today is the devout spiritual descendant of its first pioneers. Ah Fu observed the custom of "putting up her hair" at a ceremonial party when she first became an amah, to signify that she would never marry. Others only marry so that they will have a family name—relatives in heaven to go to when they die, relatives on earth who will pray for their wandering souls in front of their ancestral tablets. They usually leave their husbands shortly afterward, compensating them for any inconvenience in cash. And that is that.

Ah Fu and her colleagues are touchy about their sorority and relentless in their ostracism of any jumped-up kitchen greenhand who assumes their uniform without due justification. Younger amahs are usually inducted because they belong to the families of older ones, who then teach them all their tricks, from exacting the just and fair amount of squeeze from the mistress's marketing money to making the horripilant dish that may be a European master's favorite. Often these "aunties" adopt their "nieces," and leave all their hoarded piles of crumpled dollar notes to them when they die. (When Ping finally persuaded Ah Fu to open a bank account in Singapore, she made an initial deposit worth over seven hundred dollars.) Lesbianism is neither ruled out nor rampant.

For the equivalent of US $11 a week and her food, Ah Fu rises at 6:30 and finishes work when dinner has been cleared away in the evening. She is goodhearted, cantankerous, penny-counting, yet full of little presents for us when feast days come around. She has a fast Cantonese tongue for anyone who invades her kingdom, but from her smooth, round, middle-aged face also emerge carefully garnered gems of English of which she is inordinately proud, like her resigned "All ri' "—the response to any request—and the brighter "Flend come," which means unexpected and inconvenient callers. She cooks good plain European food by the numbers (she would never dream of tasting the stuff), and succulent Chinese dishes for all the family, including three boys, three dogs, and two cats. She asserts herself by being excessively obstinate, so that it is almost impossible to stop her from putting the dog biscuits in with the home remedies, keeping the marmalade in the deep freeze, and cleaning the milk shaker with the latest detergent.

In a Chinese household she would be treated almost as one of the family, and in ours she enjoys such prerogatives as loudly interrupting any conversation between ourselves and our guests in midsentence, and driving us out on to the terrace by monopolizing the TV in the lounge to watch some excruciating Chinese soap opera. She likes animals, tolerates men and Europeans, but her bright, acquisitive eyes really gleam when she looks at the wives who come to the house. She is illiterate, but she envies none of them. To show who is boss, she treats the wash-amah to some particularly earthy specimens of Cantonese vituperation for not ironing her dishcloths. "Now then," says Ping, "we all know you're the queen, so why not talk like one." Ah Fu is entirely happy. For in her bare little amah's quarter with its shower and lavatory, its wooden bed with a rush mat for a mattress, its one creaking wicker chair, its monstrosity of a clothes cupboard, and its toy transistor radio, she is above them all. For she is an independent woman.

Empress Wu and Amah Fu, what do they share? They share the watchful, murderous patience, the pliant exterior, and the razor-sharp, if retractable, talons of a feline that has been at bay for three thousand years. There are perhaps 350 million of these for Mao Tse-tung to mold. And much though he may have given them, they are likely in the long run to provide Marxism-Leninism in China with its most exhausting operation in mental surgery.

10

The Tribal Custom

Every month Ah Fu sends about a quarter of her salary to relatives in Communist China whom she has not seen for at least ten years, and one day she will doubtless retire among the strangers who are her innumerable nieces and nephews in the village of her ancestors, taking her enviable bank balance with her. She has escaped the servitude of family life as a young bride: but, Communism permitting, she will return to its compensations with the power and position of a wealthy grand-aunt. She has no other vision of happiness.

It is customary in the West to say that the Chinese have a "strong sense of family," that relatives "stick together," but these watery expressions are so diluted that they betray rather than suggest the spirit of the truth. Traditionally, the Chinese family was not simply a cozy collection of jolly, warmhearted relations, of fathers and mothers, and sons and daughters, aunts and uncles, and nephews and nieces and cousins all kissing and fussing and gossiping and backbiting in affectionate good humor until someone mentioned money. Nor was it even the aristocratic Christmas tree of the Western nobility, whose ornaments best upheld the family honor by doing their duty to their country. The Chinese family was itself the state, a state with its own stiff hierarchy, its procedures, its laws and its obligations, its religion and its church, its customs and its economy. The family came first, the individual second, much as among the best of the West the nation comes first and the individual second. As for the country, that ran a bad third with the Chinese, just as the remoter interests of a United Europe or Pan-American cooperation still run a bad third in any race for our loyalty. And the bigger and more powerful the Chinese family, the more its individual member was its well-beloved prisoner.

To Ping, "the house where I grew up as a young girl" was neither a country cottage nor a Georgian mansion with a well-tended herbaceous border and a monkey-puzzle tree, but a vast walled enclosure within which more than one hundred houses and pavilions of stone and sun-dried brick and upcurling tiled roofs were connected by a maze of courtyards and round moon-gates. Behind the guard whose lookout was located above the red double doors of the great main entrance lived, ate, and slept four generations of the Liang family, with their wives, their con-cubines, their children, and their numerous servants—about eight hundred souls in all.

Beyond a huge courtyard, in which opera companies performed on festival days, stood the first hall, where the sedan chairs were housed and the children played if it rained; after that came a second hall, very formal with its long center table and rows of curved chairs against the walls; and then a third. This was the Ancestral Hall. Red and gold wooden tablets commemorating Liangs dead and gone covered the wall at one end above a dais and an altar on which stood incense burners and vases of flowers. A special committee within the family was responsible for acting pastor and verger to this sanctum, keeping it in order and organ-izing prayers, drawing upon an allocation of the common budget for any necessary expenses. Outside the curved wall of the Liang household, whose bowstring was a river over which a bridge led to the village, lay an ancestral temple and a vast family burial ground (an entire hill being reserved solely for Ping's father), tended by the older servants. And then came the extensive rice

fields—for this family had its wealth in land and not money—
each with its solidly built granary.

The houses and pavilions, painted and whitewashed, were
usually one-storied, with a built-on eyrie for the daughters' bedroom. Young girls slept on wooden boards fitted across iron beds,
their mattress an old eiderdown. But married couples enjoyed
the ornate Chinese red-and-gold four-poster that is almost a room
in itself. In the dining-room area of each house, the table was
round and flanked by a long, high Chinese sideboard on which
stood the silver jug that a bride always brought to the house
when she married. The house would also have a sitting room,
and a small courtyard of flagstones with flower beds, a caldron
of goldfish, and jars of jasmine, chrysanthemum, and lotus which
were taken indoors when they flowered.

To serve the hundred-odd kitchens of this family home, an
endless stream of small girls brought charcoal from storage or
brushwood and rice straw from the nearby fields and hills. Huge
pans of water were kept boiling night and day on stoves whose
precise position and angle had been fixed by a geomancer, for
above each one hung a plaque inscribed *Lord of the Stove*,
representing the Kitchen God of the Chinese household, who
reports to heaven on the conduct of the family every New Year's
Eve.

Clothes were washed in the river by the servants of each individual house, and peddlers, allowed through the gate by the
guard, would set up shop in the Second Hall and announce their
presence with a rattle, so that maids could be sent to buy British
soap, or American toothpaste, toothbrushes, towels, and all the
other Kleenex-age commodities that Western intrusion had
brought to China.

There was nevertheless much that it had not yet brought.
Carriers transported the water for the bathrooms in large jars
from the wells and the river. Some would bathe in these small,
stone-floored chambers, scooping the water over themselves from
a big basin and drying with the usual minute Chinese towel. But

many had a round wooden tub brought to the bedroom and filled with hot and cold water from buckets carried in by the servants. The older folk always used a commode in the bedroom also, instead of the nearby non-flush, porcelain lavatory down which water had anyway to be poured. The servants, four or five to a room, shared a sanitary bucket. But within the walls were two large ponds or small lakes, and over the middle of one of these had been built an elegant little enclosed platform with a cut-out seat, standing high above the water and connected to the bank by a gaily painted bridge. And here, if nature called, Ping liked best to go in the evening, accompanied by a maid who would wait on shore with a lantern, while her mistress surveyed the moonlit scene from her trap-door throne, caressed most intimately by the soft, cool breezes of summer.

This pond was noted not only for its fat carp, but also for its suicides, for pregnant young servant girls who had been forbidden by the household elders to marry, and maids who would rather die than become the meanest concubine in the jealous harem of some lubricious Liang, would end their sorrows by throwing themselves into the water. The household proliferated young servants who were little more than female slaves, and every new bride that married into the family brought six or eight more of these little things with her, along with the great procession of goods and chattels that included her future marriage bed. Anywhere from seven to seventeen years old, they were frequently given away or exchanged as presents, or married off under arrangements made by the family, or sold as concubines, or simply taken to bed. They followed their mistresses everywhere with fans, were to be tripped over at every corner as they ran messages to and from this or that Liang, and generally ensured that no one enjoyed any privacy at all. Ping's father shocked his relatives by treating these chits for the first time as if they were fully qualified human beings. The leading Republican rebel in his own district and an associate of Dr. Sun Yat-sen, he believed that revolution must begin at home.

The patriarch of the family was Ping's grandfather, and because his youngest concubine was still alive, the women of this rigorously disciplined family, whatever their seniority as first wives, were obliged to kowtow to the girl. Position in the hierarchy was the subject of precise mathematical calculation, so that Ping was known as "Number seventeen's eighth young mistress"— eighth child of the seventeenth son of the patriarch, but born of his first wife and not of a concubine. Today in exile she is still "Eighth aunt."

Within this communal society that numbered more than three hundred vociferous Liang children, and included further cohorts of domestics who lived in special quarters nearby, the Brueghel effect was offset by cold ritual. If one unit of the family wished to visit another, a servant would first be sent with a small gift of cakes or candy. There was no casual dropping in, even within the same walls. Class distinctions were rigidly respected, so that the wife of one branch would not greet the concubine of another. Strict order of precedence prescribed that unmarried members of the clan, however aged, should still be treated as children, and old and raddled spinsters could be seen wearing the costume of a bride on feast days, for they had never passed beyond that rank. "We were one hundred years behind the times," Ping said.

Poor peasants did not, of course, live together in great blocks of blood relations. Fathers were often virtual serfs, brothers might be sold, kinship and contact sadly lost. But most hovels would nevertheless be shared contentedly by three generations, the respected grandparents doting on a platoon of their descendants, the son's sense of obligation to the father as strong there as among the educated and the wealthy.

In August 1961, four students of Dublin University stepped out of a car at the gate of their home in North Malaya and humbly covered the twenty- yard distance to the front door on their knees. They were the two sons and two daughters of a Chinese millionaire tin miner, and they were observing a Chinese custom which decrees that if a parent dies while they are absent, children must approach the body on their knees from the entrance of the home in order to pay homage. For at the core of the sacrosanct family system is the duty of filial piety, eloquently symbolized by a large, gaudily painted piece of cement statuary in Singapore's Tiger Balm Gardens which shows a young woman suckling her own father. One of the best-known improving works in any Chinese library is a book which contains twenty-four tales of outstanding filial piety, about which the Chinese were above all sensitive and punctilious, sometimes to a point of absurdity. Confucius had insisted that when a man's father died, he should retire from office and go into mourning for three years, wearing sackcloth, eating gruel, seeing nobody, and never going far from the grave. A timely sabbatical in middle-age in its modified form, this severe obligation could wreck a man's life if meticulously fulfilled.

For a child to testify against a parent was a criminal offense in Confucian China. A Chinese should not even pain his parents with unpalatable truths, and on our own lacquered settee in Singapore there is a painting illustrating the ridiculous moral story of a dutiful sixty-year-old son who romped around the floor pretending he was only three in order to conceal from his parents that they were getting very old and therefore near death. In Singapore I have seen Ah Fu nod with sorrowful understanding as the modern Chinese TV heroine sells herself to the villain to pay for her mother's funeral. Not only virgins, however, but whole families have frequently been ruined in the past by the cost of sending the revered forebear to his last rest in fitting style.

Filial piety was simply the first rung on the ladder of ancestor worship. Every family treasured the sacred tablets on which were inscribed the names of its antecedents, and in Singapore or Hong Kong many Chinese still have an altar in the house, or at least papers inscribed with the names of their forebears on the walls. If they live in rented rooms, they may set up the ancestral tablets in a nearby temple. At the festival of Ch'ing Ming, which usually falls in April, Chinese may be seen driving out to the big sprawling cemeteries which are always part of their environment, to tend the graves of their parents and grandparents. Afterward a small flag is often raised over the graves to show that the living have done their duty to the dead, for filial piety is primarily a matter of respect and is not necessarily inspired by love.

The family dictated marriages, for these were strictly contracted and mutually advantageous alliances between households. When a young bride entered the home of her husband, she became part of a closed world and rarely saw her own parents again. She was not regarded as a new wife so much as a new daughter-in-law, and when she gave birth to the babies that would win her the honored rank of "mother," they would in fact be regarded not as children but as grandchildren. If she could not have any, she must allow her husband a concubine, for had not Mencius said: "The most unfilial act of all is to have no offspring"? There must always be children, and more children, to extend the power of the family and to tend the ancestral graves. The wife should not love her husband too much, therefore, nor he her, for nothing must transcend the loyalty that they owed to the group.

Only recently have these attitudes started to change, so that while the rich may still indulge their instinct and produce enormous clusters of diminutive progeny, the middle-class Chinese in Southeast Asia are beginning to balance joy in the child against sorrow in the checkbook, to take at least a hit-and-miss interest in the Pill. But the poor, opposing superstitious prejudice to the mechanics of family planning, are still with us in ever increasing numbers.

Within the family system, the duty of the individual to the collective, of the ant to the hill, has inhibited the Chinese throughout his history, so that any show of selfish initiative has demanded far more strength of character, conviction, and determination than a European would have required in the same circumstances: China has had her Romeos and Juliets, but young people who fall violently in love have had to be very sure that indeed they were a perfect match, and cool reflection has often led to second thoughts. For to marry against the wishes of the parents may still mean, even today, not only that the couple will be cast off and disinherited but that they will be socially ostracized and thrown out of their jobs by disgusted employers. A brilliant scholar but a bad son commanded no respect in Imperial China and could hope for little advancement. Confucian moral law was founded on conscience, and across the Chinese conscience was written one word: *Chia*—family. A man could be a Scott, a Lawrence, a Gauguin, a Schweitzer—but only if he left his family secure and his activities brought upon them honor, not destitution and disgrace.

A Chinese may have a taste for adventure, a dewy-eyed admiration for the brave and the chivalrous and the public-spirited. But before he starts righting wrongs, plunging into fights, rescuing drowning dogs, or denouncing the abuses of authority, he must remember that if in consequence he ends up in the hospital, the grave, jail, or simply a ridiculous and humiliating situation, he will be betraying his family and his ancestors, and his good deed will earn him the well-deserved disapproval of all decent-minded people.

The prudent paterfamilias looks after his own business so that his kinsfolk may prosper. He leaves trouble to those whose trade it is and who support their families out of it—the soldier, the policeman, the militant revolutionary, the secret society "tiger general." They sell courage, as a whore sells her body, but he sells broiler chickens, or Shanghai furniture, or Japanese tape recorders. To each his last. It is not easy to recruit a family-minded Chinese into the ranks of the army or the police, not because he lacks courage but because from a family point of view such activities are both dangerous and unprofitable. But once he feels that the fame or advantage that will accrue to his folk may outweigh the hardship or the risk in an enterprise, he will not hesitate to act. In Imperial times, thousands entered for the official examinations so that, as mandarins, they might bring greater glory and influence to their families, and many made great personal sacrifices for the sake of the honor of their house. All wanted their particular family to be looked up to "as a crane among chickens."

Conversely, a Chinese does not seek comfort at the expense of his own. The elderly Americans who totter from one air-conditioned hotel lobby to the next in the course of some luxury tour of Asia that is costing them a small fortune are often regarded in Eastern waters as egotistical renegades. A rich Chinese never goes on a cruise, or takes any kind of expensive holiday, and he rarely throws away money on any type of perishable goods, with the two exceptions of food and firecrackers, for he would otherwise simply be squandering the patrimony of his progeny. The Chinese look askance at the selfish monster of a European who appears to think that his responsibilities end with his two parents, his wife, and his few children.

The great extended Chinese family was a happy system for the venerated elders, it gave the fecund matrons positions of power, but it reserved for the young bride the hundred chores of the drudge and the ordeal of domination by mother-in-law. However, it was also a give-and-take commonwealth, in which the rich paid and the poor worked, so that a destitute relation could be sure of a bed and food and company and security (even if she performed the duties of a menial in exchange), and in which the well-behaved older children looked after the younger, and the younger respected the older. Everywhere in East Asia, solemn little nine-year-olds may be seen carefully carrying solemn little four-year-olds, tears are rare, bullying rarer. Children are brought up to be obedient, submissive, gentle, conventional, polite, and sometimes rather dull.

One thousand years ago the law provided that a son who lifted his hand against his father should be beheaded and that a younger brother who struck his elder brother should be condemned to two and a half years of forced labor. When a disciple asked Confucius what a son should do if his father were murdered, he replied: "He must sleep upon grass matting, with his shield for a pillow; he must refuse to take office; he must not live under the same sky as the killer. When he meets him in market or court, he must have his weapon ready to strike." Other relatives should "stand behind with weapons in hand" to support him when he exacts vengeance. It sounds like the Law of the Far West rather than the Wisdom of the Far East, and no Montague or Moses could have put it better.

Throughout most of recorded history, Chinese law has left prerogatives with the family, has condoned blood revenge, has allowed clan customs to overrule Imperial legislation. The family and the clan have therefore been the seedbeds of violence and rebellion. When one man wronged a rival, he had a horde of his kinsmen to fear, and if he were an emperor, he must savagely exterminate hundreds of his victim's clan in order to buy security from revolt. In this gentler nuclear age, vendettas are not usually carried to the knife except among criminals, but for his family a Chinese will place stupid cousins in sinecures and corrupt nephews in positions of trust, systematically rob the state to enrich his relatives, cover up his kinsmen's crimes, steal and lie and mislead authority. "Sweep the snow from your own door, but not the frost from the roof of your neighbor," goes the old Chinese adage. Traditionally, the Chinese family felt little obligation to the outsider, whatever his extremity.

Confucius is often blamed for the negative nature of his nearest approach to the Christian doctrine of universal love: "Do not do to others what you do not wish to be done to yourself." But the Classical Book of Odes, whose songs existed long before the Sage, had already laid great stress on family solidarity as the basis of society. Moreover, it can be argued that Confucius calculated that the family would be the pattern for the state, and from the good son would come the good citizen. "Those who love their parents dare not show hatred to others," he said.

If this is so, then the old man failed miserably. Next, the Legalists, with their materialistic principle of the supremacy of the state, broke up the big families, set son to spy on father, and again tried to compel the Chinese to extend his sense of duty and loyalty to cover the wider conception of the nation as just one big unhappy family. But their success was ephemeral, for the family proved too strong for them. Mao follows in these footsteps two thousand years later, at a time when rebellious, revolutionary youth is kicking over the traces of tradition, and in a world of changing values he may win where they lost. Except that perhaps no period of Chinese history up to the turn of this century better deserved to be described by that selfsame, creaking old cliché—a world of changing values—than the turbulent era of Ch'in.

11

The Chinese Antisociety

Asked whether you should return good for evil, Confucius, un-hampered by Christian qualms, replied forthrightly: "What then would you return for good? No: return good for good; for evil, justice." And in many respects the Imperial Chinese administration that his teachings inspired seemed so excellent that the stubborn persistence of the family as a fenced city armed against a threatening world appeared slightly absurd.

Beneath the ministries, the chancery, the censors, and the Imperial College at the capital, the country was divided into provinces, circuits, prefectures, subprefectures and counties, whose officers saw that justice was done in accordance with laws that revealed a sharp eye for loopholes. Portuguese prisoners of the Chinese reported nearly five hundred years ago that Chinese governors were chosen for their integrity and scholarship, and that sons only succeeded their fathers if they had the same qualities. To ensure impartiality, no man was sent to govern or judge in his home province, and all were paid enough to discourage the taking of bribes, which was in any event heavily punished. Magistrates were not allowed to drink before sessions, they were responsible for noting down all important evidence in their own hand, and their professional behavior was verified by commissioners who visited them on circuit every six months. All punishments had to conform with the fixed law. Moreover, judges were warned not to rely entirely on the testimony of witnesses but to make a careful investigation of each case, and this explains why the detective in earlier Chinese whodunits was always the local magistrate. One thousand years ago the corpse of the victim had to be produced before a murderer could be convicted, and death sentences had to be reviewed by the Imperial government before they were carried out.

But there were other, less edifying elements at work. The history of Chinese justice opens on a note of cold-blooded cruelty, for in the Warring States period a man could be convicted of any one of so many thousands of crimes that it hardly seemed possible for him to escape all the trip wires of the law—and the punishments were death, castration, to have both kneecaps and elbows broken, the nose severed, the feet and hands removed, or just the fingers and toes chopped off. During the T'ang era, flogging remained the lightest punishment (the culprit frequently died), and the only other sentences for crimes were banishment and execution.

The curious equity of the Legalists survived, so that an innocent person who was falsely denounced was still guilty of having disturbed the peace, and so was the victim of any public violence, as well as its instigator. Once a man was accused, he was thrown into jail, but his accuser was treated as a suspect also. If a suspect were not caught, his neighbors might be detained in his place. If the peace of the region was violated, the judges on the spot were taken to task, and they therefore turned harshly on everyone in sight connected with any breach. The ordinary people learned to fight shy of the law and the courts, and to settle their differences privately as ancient custom had dictated. The law was in any case expensive, for whatever the ruling about bribes, no man would get a fair hearing if he did not give to the judge the "presents" that courtesy demanded.

The accused, innocent or guilty, would spend long periods in foul prisons, fed by relatives who had to bribe the guards in order to get his rice to him. Since a confession had to be obtained before a man could be convicted, the prisoner would be flogged and tortured, beaten with bamboo rods, or locked into a cangue so sturdy that he could not get his hands to his mouth and had to be spoon-fed by friends if he were not simply to starve. The number of strokes of bamboo or whip was supposedly limited, but theory and practice sometimes diverged, so that the flesh of a man's face might be systematically beaten into pulp while fingers or ankles were squeezed between slowly compressed wooden blocks. Criminals were decapitated, or condemned to the excruciating "death of a thousand cuts." There are horrifying stories of men chopped through at the waist whose severed upper halves, duly labeled with their crimes, were then carried through the streets on a platform until—perhaps as many as twenty minutes later—they toppled over in death.

Just as ghastly were the illegal tortures, which included smoking the suspect's head in a cylinder, or burning the skin off his torso by winding a soft pewter pipe around it like some great serpentine musical instrument and then pouring boiling water through its convolutions. Most diabolical of all, perhaps, was the "iron shirt" described by Leon Comber: "This consisted of a garment made of very fine wire mesh with interstices rather like those of a fishing net. It was put on a prisoner and squeezed tight by pulling on a cord attached to it so that the skin would protrude through the mesh of the wire. A sharp instrument was then passed over the shirt which cut or scraped off the protruding flesh." The rack, the bastinado, and all the tortures of Torquemada, the iniquitous circumstances of the first electrocution in the United States, the legal system in early nineteenth-century England under which a man could be hanged for stealing goods to the value of five shillings and disemboweled for treason—all these seem hardly more inhuman than the horrors of earlier Chinese justice at its worst. In the city of Hangchow, which Marco Polo so admired, there was a curfew, and a list of the inmates had to be pinned up at the door of every house. The words "police state" did not exist, but the old Chinese saying

"Clear conscience never fears midnight knocking" reminds one chillingly of twentieth-century Europe.

The ordinary Chinese people have suffered for three thousand years from the brutality of warring soldiery, the rapacity of privileged officialdom, and the catastrophe that is a despot's whim. Eight hundred years after the First Emperor sacrificed the Chinese millions to the Moloch of the Great Wall, the Emperor Yang Ti had more than three million men and women press-ganged into working on his project for a Grand Canal joining the Yellow River and the Yangtze Kiang. For centuries, under the crippling tribute system, the people of the provinces had to supply immense quantities of silk and grain to the capital and pay the fantastic cost of their transportation. The farmers lived in penury, at sowing time the prey of greedy moneylenders and magnates who would foreclose mercilessly if they were not repaid with outrageous interest after the harvest. They were regularly conscripted for forced labor, and more than two hundred years after the Grand Canal was completed, another one million Chinese found themselves working on the drainage of the Huai River marshes under conditions of vile servitude.

One of the less happy examples of provincial government was provided by the compulsive butcher who seized control of the province of Szechuan in the sixteen-forties. This maniac is said to have raised a stone tablet in the city of Cheng Tu inscribed with the one word *kill*, and then to have acted on its instructions. He liquidated more than fifty percent of the population, it is estimated, and eighty years passed before the province recovered. Even today, most of its inhabitants are descendants from immigrants who came in from other provinces. Many of these were, in their turn, massacred by Manchu troops in Cheng Tu in 1911, when the people rose against the tyrannical administration of the local Chinese governor. With the advent of the Republic, little seemed to change. The bitter little proverb "Officials protect officials" still rang true, as warlords, soldiers, and bandits again became hard to tell apart, appalling corruption went unpunished, and tax monopolies were farmed out to imaginative Confucian literati who enriched themselves by slapping imposts on everything from pigs' troughs to coffins. The people were, as ever, pitifully grateful to any honest local administrator who took no bribes and only had "clean wind in his sleeves."

However, the instinct to close ranks with men of one's own blood who can be trusted has sprung not only from misgovernment but from the long toll of calamity and poverty and misery and uncertainty that have beset the Chinese throughout their history. High on the list of adversities, of course, must come man's own unremitting efforts to annihilate man. We read that when the first Han dynasty emperor mounted the throne after years of devastating civil war he could not find four horses of the same color in the entire Chinese empire to pull his chariot. There is a hardy myth that in the Good Old Days prices were excitingly low, but at that moment in history more than two thousand years ago a horse was worth 300 pounds of gold in the ravaged Middle Kingdom, and even a hundredweight of rice cost one pound of gold.

In the fourth century the Huns captured the Chinese capital, and of the populous life of that gorgeous city there afterward remained one hundred families, four carts, and a forest of weeds. In the eighth century the city was sacked again by the Tibetans, and during the single decade in which this happened the recorded population of all China dropped from 52 million to 16 million. In the tenth century the capital was once more completely wrecked and deserted. Under the Sung dynasty the population of China rose to 100 million taxpayers, but after the Mongol invasion in the thirteenth century—in which one million people were slaughtered in the taking of one city alone—it had dropped to 58 million again: the rest of the survivors were so poor that they no longer figured on the tax lists. Lengthy and destructive civil wars followed during the Ming dynasty, and in the Taiping rebellion against the Manchus in the nineteenth century all the central provinces of China were ruined in thirteen years of vicious fighting.

But that is not all. The monstrous waterways of China have flooded disastrously throughout the centuries, bringing catastrophe and famine on a scale unheard of elsewhere. The vast Yellow River—aptly nicknamed "China's Sorrow"—has achieved fantastic and violent changes of course that have left its old valleys dust bowls of drought and made its new bed the axis of a half-drowned community. As late as 1929, more than three million people died of starvation in a Chinese famine, for which there had been a hundred calamitous precedents, nor is the country safe from these terrible scourges today. No one knows how many died between 1959 and 1962. Chinese ways often seem too dark to the well-fed Westerner simply because he cannot see over his waistband to the millions of small men on the map of Chinese civilization who have, generation after generation, lived on the rim of the unlivable and whose inspiration has been the specter of starvation.

The Caucasian, well fed on an abundance of edibles, may take for granted his daily intake, but most Chinese simply cannot afford to. If he is thrown out of a job, a Chinese says his "rice bowl has been broken." When he worships his ancestors, his first thought is to take them food. If he envies the rich man, it is above all for his girth and the good things he can put on his table. In the course of his intimidating history he has evolved the greatest and most imaginative cuisine in the world—strictly from hunger. For he has learned to make the most of grasses and fungus, wild plants and insects. He has fed on snakes, and cats, and moles, on silkworm pupae, and rice-field grubs, on rats and cicadas, bamboo and seaweed. Famine has forced him into cannibalism in North China, and he has even developed a taste for his fellowmen on occasion, for during the Sung dynasty there were restaurants that served human flesh in Hangchow. In that great saga of bandit-heroes, *Men of the Marshes*, we meet the engaging couple running a tavern enticingly called "Three Cups and You Cannot Cross the Mountain," who serve not only a rice-based Mickey Finn to their victims, but bits of their last customer to their next. Ping's first reaction to the magnificence of Venice was: "How is it nobody eats all these fat pigeons?"

Peasants without a grain of rice left in the home sold their children into domestic service, concubinage, and slavery. More often, distracted Chinese simply killed off the latest baby in order to have one less mouth to feed, one less claim on the meager inheritance to be shared out among the next generation. Sometimes a bucket of water was kept ready beside the bed of childbirth so that the period from delivery to death by drowning need only be a matter of moments. Marco Polo describes how the Chinese "expose babies," and half a millennium later, Somerset Maugham tells us in *The Sights of the Town* how he came upon a little tower on a Chinese hillside with a single small hole in its wall, from which came a nauseating odor. This was a baby tower, and it covered a deep charnel pit into which parents threw their unwanted children through the aperture or, if they were more gentle, lowered them in a basket on a piece of stout string. As he stood there, "a lively little boy came up to me and made me understand that four babies had been brought to the tower that morning." The year was 1920. The League of Nations was meeting for the first time.

On the other hand, it is enormously difficult to persuade the self-conscious, dog-tired people of Singapore's Chinatown to go through the mechanics of birth control, for example, when they may live fourteen to a room, or similarly to influence refugees in Hong Kong, who are sometimes packed in three thousand to the acre. One Singapore maternity hospital alone handles about three thousand or more cases of furtive, botched abortions every year—performed despairingly by a people to whom procreation is theoretically sacred. Perhaps nothing measures the enormous abyss between Chinese living and Western understanding than a passage from a Chinese book of travel that was quoted to a skeptical emperor in the last century: "England is so short of inhabitants that the English rear every child that is born. Even prostitutes who bear children do not destroy them." But who could believe such stuff? Small wonder if in his poverty a Chinese inches his way to financial security with the single-minded dedication of a marooned man climbing a sheer cliff to safety, acutely alive to all the hazards that may dash him on to the rocks below.

Ah Fu cooks for seven humans and five animals in our household, all of whom eat at different times, although only the two cats are really fussy about their food. But she is very reluctant to teach the wash-amah a little simple cooking so that she can help out. For Ah Fu undoubtedly reasons that once the wash-amah can do her job, she herself may be looking for work. Ideally, she would like the household to be in a state of chaos the moment she steps out of the gate on her day off, and she will never take more than two days' holiday, for fear that we will find we can manage without her.

Then there are the perquisites. Every working Chinese is a born rag-and-bone merchant, and it was a sore trial to Ah Fu when I gave up smoking, for there is a brisk trade and money to be made in the round fifty-cigarette tins the British affect— the Chinese use them for everything from sending morning coffee to outside customers to selling tropical fish. But she does a regular business in my gratifying accumulation of newspapers every month, and in the excellent bottles with their patent removable tops with which distillers of Scotch beguile the public. Furthermore, there are bonuses like non-returnable kerosene cans, which, halved diagonally and fitted with handles, will make *two* excellent dustpans. There are medicine bottles and pickle jars and old shirts and empty insecticide bombs; in fact, all the trash of the wasteful white at one end, and a cent-snatching Chinese market at the other. And lucky Ah Fu is in the middle. Carl Crow remarks how in Shanghai in the thirties the newsboys would cut out the sample coupons in the daily papers, sell the mutilated copies for their normal price, and apply for the samples themselves. He describes courageous scavengers who collected brass shell-cases in barrows in the middle of battles, and the bumboatmen who kept the Whangpoo the cleanest river in the world. For poverty made the Shanghainese a veritable mackerel of a man.

However, the penurious Chinese has had to suffer not only from acts of God but from acts of government. The Taoist sage Lao Tzu said: "The ruler of a great kingdom administers it as you would cook a small fish: meddle too much with either, and it falls apart." From quite a different standpoint, Confucius encouraged the same masterly inactivity at the top by advocating a harmonious community founded upon orderly personal and class regulationships that would become instinctive. No system of rigid, all-embracing national laws would be necessary in an ideal society based on "li," he implied, and the Chinese, repelled by the early Procrustean experiments in Legalism, developed a healthy dislike of fixed codes and a possessive affection for the Confucian concept of justice administered with humanity. The old English Justice of the Peace who dismisses the case against the poacher because he knows his son died three weeks ago, after the medical expenses had taken his last penny, represents the Chinese idea of equity. Judges, the Chinese felt, should have a fatherly approach to misdemeanor. For them, "blind justice" would be a contradiction in terms, and their attitude toward a mechanical code was: "For each new law that is devised, a way of cheating it will also be found."

In good times, scholar-magistrates judged according to these humane principles. But the Chinese have not been molded by good times. If the prince set a good example, Confucius had said, his people would imitate him. It followed that when the emperor was bad, the poison of his rule coursed down the veins of the administration into the finest capillary, and little was heard of "reasonable" justice. The chronic degeneration that set in as each successive dynasty aged taught the Chinese that even when you had a good emperor all you could expect after him was a bad one. Moreover, since customary law prevailed in most matters, even in better times the government was known to the millions only as the agency that collected taxes, exacted tribute, imposed forced labor, and conscripted sons for soldiers. There was no redress to hand: "Heaven is high, the emperor is far," the people learned to echo—at the same time that they learned to distrust the whole concept of superior authority, with an implacable, enduring distrust. The Chinese ideogram for an official looks like

this: 官 and the Chinese said that, as you can see from the drawing, "an official talks with two mouths under the same roof." They did not ask for democracy. They only asked for a fairer contract—to receive a little more, to pay a little less. "Chinese always felt there was no good government," Ping once said, "and no government that would protect you."

There was an immediate and vehement protest in Singapore's Chinatown when the administration proposed to take over the highly organized monopoly of death which arranges that for a modest monthly payment a Chinese can assure himself of a sound coffin, a slap-up funeral, and enough prayers to get him to heaven when he dies. "Naturally people don't like it," a Chinese friend commented indignantly. "They know they can trust the private monopoly. But whoever heard of a government that kept its promises of paradise?" The government quickly dropped the idea. The Chinese has tended to regard the law as his enemy, as something not to be trusted but to be broken without compunction in self-defense. He vastly prefers TV films about joyous brigands and outlaws to detective dramas in which authority wins.

Where government does not interfere, a Chinese enjoys his true heritage of happy anarchy: his concept of a society kept in balance by mutual accommodation and compromise, by a smooth live-and-let-live-or-die relationship, whose wheels within wheels are oiled occasionally out of a drumful of dollars. One of the commonest sights in Singapore is a Chinese on a wobbling bicycle riding along the curb on the wrong side of the road and crossing an intersection on the red light because it saves him a detour. In London, Paris, or Chicago, the ulcerous air would be filled with cries, groans, insults, and shrill whistles, and the law would take its course. In Singapore, everyone swerves round the cyclist—the simplest solution for all parties—and no one would dream of bringing in the law "as a matter of principle," since any such principle would be considered utterly depraved. Men must help each other against bureaucracy, not help bureaucracy to divide and rule men.

In the old Roman camp of the Chinese defensive society, the innermost ring of earthworks was the family and the second was the clan. Now, the Chinese language has about 420 monosyllabic sounds in all (Ching, Chang, Fu, Wu, etc.), and only about a quarter of these are used as surnames. And of the "hundred names"—an expression that describes all the Chinese—only thirty are really common, and these are spread among several hundred million people. No Wong believes himself related to all the other Wongs in China, therefore. But the closer their ancestral homes, the greater the sense of clan between any two of them. In stricter families, people of the same name from the same commune or county will normally not marry one another, just as first cousins rarely marry in the West. If a Lee meets a complete stranger from the same province who is also a Lee, he will quote the polite formula: "Five hundred years ago we were of the same family," and at once the two men will be drawn together as kinsmen against any third character called Mao or Chiang. Any starving Teochew-speaking Lee in dire need in Singapore will get money, or food and comfort, from the offices of the Singapore Teochew Lee Clan Association, for rich members of the clan have financed this excellent institution for the specific purpose of looking after their own. The Malaysian peninsula is particularly peppered with these clan organizations, for the Chinese immigrants into the alien lands of Southeast Asia naturally banded together even more closely than did the Chinese in China. The colder it is, the more men huddle for warmth.

As ancestor worship made the Chinese family long in time, so the clan system made it wide in space. A clansman was very much "one of ours." If he committed an offense against an outsider, he must be forgiven and protected, and his fate was always inextricably entwined with that of his fellow clansmen. When a great man fell in Imperial China, his whole clan might be slaughtered, and all the kinsmen of any group of conspirators could expect extinction also. Condoning the wholesale revenge exacted by a Ming emperor against the kin of a rebel, a scholar explains: "The severest punishment meted out under Han dynasty law was to wipe out three clans: the father's, the mother's, the wife's. But the nine branches of the clan executed with Fang Hsiang-ju were the families of the great-great-grandfather, great-grandfather, grandfather, father, sons, grandsons, great-grandsons, and great-great-grandsons. They were all the father's clan. His mother's and wife's clans were not involved, much less his pupils." He did not say how few lost their lives in a massacre so tempered by Imperial clemency, however.

Village loyalty interlocked with ties of family and clan, for in a vast empire ruled according to Confucian precepts, nine out of ten problems in a village were settled by the elders themselves according to custom and usage and in a humane and flexible fashion. It was here, above all, that the Chinese governed themselves better than the Chinese government governed them. There was a venerable tradition of cooperation among villagers, and since the Chinese have always been close to the earth and so to those from the same land, village ties and communal feeling are strong. Among overseas Chinese, there are schools financed by the people and for the people from this or that village in China, clubs where they meet, and guilds for their protection. Like the man whose name is Lee, the boy from the same village is part of the inner, if not the innermost defenses against the world, and he will be accorded his due measure of favor. Moreover, the

man from the same county, the same district, the same province
is always to be befriended before the man from the next county
or district or province, the fellow Chinese from the south before
the fellow Chinese from the north (or vice versa), and, finally,
any fellow Chinese before any outer barbarian.

When the Communists seized control of China from the Nationalists in 1949, two British consular officials in a major town
in the southwest were one day ordered to report at 7:30 in the
morning to a police station on the far side of the city from their
compound. Arriving early, they found the gate still locked and
had to wait while a crowd from this unfamiliar part of the town
gathered around them, staring at their bearded faces in astonishment.

"Who are these people?" they heard one of the mob ask
another.

The other hesitated and then replied: "I don't know. But they're
foreigners, all right. Maybe they come from the next province."

"There's more to it than that," objected another suspiciously.
"I don't believe they're foreigners from the next province. I don't
believe they're even foreigners from the north. I think they're
foreign foreigners, from right outside China."

"Could they be our glorious Russian comrades, then?"

"Russian comrades?" echoed the other, derisively. "When our
Russian comrades move about, they travel in big shiny cars with
uniformed drivers and all the curtains drawn. These fellows came
on foot, just like any coolie, and so it's my belief that they're
nothing but rotten Western imperialists and capitalist exploiters
of the proletariat." At this, things began to look ugly, but fortu-
nately the police opened the gates and the two footsore plutocrats
limped through them to safety.

12

The Outer Defenses

The fishnet of families and friends that is the very fabric of Chinese life is still finer than all this, however. Marco Polo says of Quinsai: "The city was organized in twelve main guilds, one for each craft, not to speak of the many lesser ones. Each of these twelve guilds had twelve hundred establishments, each employing at least ten men and some as many as forty . . ." In this city of Hangchow during the Sung dynasty, before the somewhat imaginative Marco Polo and the Mongols ever arrived, the immensely rich rice, silk, and bankers' guilds had houses like palaces, with shrines to their patron gods, and enormous cash reserves, from which they would dispense generously in times of famine. There were also impressive guild houses for antique dealers, for jewelers and gilders, cutlers and gluemakers, bootmakers, and "companions of the double thread," for dealers in ginger and honey and olives and crabs, even for scavengers, soothsayers, doctors, and similar rabble.

There were guilds for burglars and beggars which honorably fulfilled the roles of insurance companies. Shopkeepers paid protection money to the thieves' guild and were then guaranteed against robbery, since these contributions enabled the thieves to live without having to steal. The morality of this was unimportant: the live-and-let-live principle was the thing. If any thief broke these contracts, his guild would deal with him, and heaven help him. The deity of this guild was the God of War (who in Chinese doublethink is actually the God for the Prevention of War, and thus the God of Peace), and the thieves magnanimously shared him with the police services. The insurance activities of the thieves' guilds have only tapered off noticeably since World War II in Singapore, and it is still possible to approach a King of Thieves in Hong Kong, to explain that a certain diamond brooch, stolen in a dark alley at 10:30 p.m. on the first of June, is of particular sentimental value and please can I have it back— and to have it returned punctiliously on payment of a nominal fee. In 1966 it was discovered that pickpockets had their own insurance companies which would bail them out and provide them with competent legal counsel if they were caught, for a premium of twenty dollars a day. (The Hong Kong dollar is worth about eighteen American cents.)

The beggars' guilds, run by a King of the Beggars, were administered along similar lines. The king made his rounds every week, collecting contributions and dividing the take among his followers. Subscribing shopkeepers and householders were then immune from the importunities of beggars until the next collection day. In March 1966, a somewhat lordly young man showed that time had not spoiled this market, when he walked into a Hong Kong restaurant and reserved a whole floor for a banquet to be thrown in honor of the King of the Beggars' birthday, paying half of the estimated bill in advance. The beggars turned up promptly on the evening, waded through an eight-course dinner that cost about a hundred Hong Kong dollars a table (without wines), and drank enough whisky and brandy to double the original bill.

The state dealt directly with the masters of the mercantile guilds on all matters affecting their product or their personnel, and where the customary right of a guild and the law of the land were in conflict, it was common for judges to give a verdict in favor of the guild. There were few lawsuits, as the guilds normally arranged settlements between disputing parties out of court. But if local officials were stupid enough to quarrel with them, they would find a "trade stoppage"—otherwise a strike—on their hands, even during the Sung dynasty. The very first contribution to the finances of the revolution that overthrew the Manchu dynasty in 1912 came from the merchant guilds of Wuhan, whose leadership had been in the same families for centuries and whose accumulated wealth ran into millions.

Nothing has happened in this compassionate century of national health services and social-security cards to curtail these brotherhoods. On the contrary, the defense system has been immeasurably complicated and fortified among overseas Chinese. In addition to the guilds, we have the clan organizations, the chambers of commerce, the Old Boys' associations of Chinese schools, and the provincial patriotisms that sometimes make it almost impossible for a Cantonese steersman to be employed on a Hokkien fishing boat, or for a Hakka to buy a shop in a Singapore side street monopolized by Teochew landlords.

That very British system of interstices, the Old Boy net, has been drawn to a fine, muslin gauge. Any bona fide Chinese businessman who is suddenly short of hard cash to buy a shipment of goods can appeal for an immediate loan to a mercantile "Hui" —a chamber of commerce group that meets every month to help the lame dog in the pack over the stile and so keep the team intact. In the same way, when the impecunious want to marry, there is always a friendly group ready to lay out the necessary money against repayment in the future. Chinese society is so highly organized for the struggle against Chinese society that by the time you are Mr. Wong from Tai Po village in Kwangtung Province, a paid-up member of the frog merchants' guild, and a registered Old Boy of the Chung Shan High School Association with a sister married into the Lim family, you are so sewn up with householder's comprehensive loyalties that you begin to believe you are more powerful than the commissioner of police. And you are probably right.

On her day off, Ah Fu sets out for the headquarters of her

own little *kongsi,* a modest room in Chinatown permanently rented by sixteen Cantonese amahs who are their own mutual-aid club. Many of them keep their real valuables there, for the place is looked after by a trusted superannuated "auntie," one of the group who is too old for outside work and is therefore pensioned off with the job of taking care of the room and retailing all the latest Chinatown gossip. The sixteen amahs fill the kitty with enough money every month to pay the rent and the "auntie," and if one of them loses her job, she can live and eat there until she finds another. The others will support her without question.

"Auntie" and "uncle," "nephew" and "niece" are magical terms in the nomenclature of the Chinese net, passwords and counter-signs that gain admittance to this vast, yet invisible trelliswork of trust. Down a side street in Cholon, Saigon's predominantly Chinese twin-city, we pay off the cab, climb a steep, rickety staircase to enter a barely furnished, whitewashed room with a small balcony occupied by a green multitude of potted ferns and one bowed old gentleman in a watered-silk coatee. Greetings and then introductions follow. The old man fingers his few thin strands of graying beard and smiles at me through small, pink, drop-curtain eyelids. "Her father and I"—he laughs throatily, nodding at Ping —"were in jail together in this very city. Dangerous revolutionaries, the French said. And they were right. Her father was a brother to me. And so now, it seems, I have a new nephew in you." "Yes, Uncle," I say, feeling slightly foolish. But I only know later how foolish I am to feel foolish, for this is open sesame. A whole skein of new connections across Asia is unraveled for me— as a nephew and not as a journalist. There is the political widow in Hong Kong ("Call me Auntie"), the general in Bangkok, the business tycoon in Java. And from the first row of avuncular relationships extend further rows, knitted up to it by introductions: "You have a letter for me from my old friend Chang? Aah . . ." No further questions are asked. This complete stranger will entertain me with embarrassing generosity and give me whatever help he can.

Nor are the Chinese exclusively a race of shallow, conspiratorial, one-good-turn-deserves-another acquaintances, for few peoples have such a keen sense of the value and rarity of true friendship. "Yellow gold is plentiful compared to white-haired friends," the proverb runs, and a Chinese believes himself a lucky man if he has one friend worthy of the name. He asks for no further props: "With true friends, even water is sweet enough." There are more Chinese poems about parted friends than there are moon-June verses and laments of sundered lovers. A favorite illustration of the unspoken sympathy which the Chinese value above all is the anecdote about the man who never failed to grasp at once what mood or image his friend was expressing when he improvised on the lute. One day, however, he died, and the musician at once seized his instrument and smashed it, for: "Since there is no longer anyone to understand, why play?"

However, in everyday life there seems much to admire in the complex nervous system of relationships and obligations that runs and branches and proliferates just beneath the skin of organized society. The activating principle of this system is that the have's acknowledge a moral debt to the have-not's on the same net, a debt to be paid promptly in hard coin in time of need, for there is nothing that stings a Chinese quite so subtly as a useless promise. When the Prince of Wei tells the starving Taoist sage Chuang Tzu that he cannot give him a bowl of millet now but will lend him three hundred pieces of silver after he has collected his dues from his vassals, Chuang Tzu indignantly compares him to a man who sees a fish gasping for water on dry land and comforts it by promising to dam a river later in the year, so that it will in due course flow down the cart track on which it is lying.

The needy do not ask for pity: they have a right to take. But it is incumbent upon them not to take more than they need, for otherwise they become mere beggars. Big gifts are corrupting and put the recipient under an obligation, and Chinese sometimes win an unfair reputation for meanness among Westerners when they carefully scale down their presents so that they neither burden their beneficiaries with a sense of debt nor incur suspicion of bribery.

The former Chinese Nationalist soldier, now a refugee in Hong Kong, hops along the narrow, stinking, muddy little lanes of a hillside shantytown above the harbor, knocks on the door of a shack improvised out of beer crates and flattened-out kerosene tins, and greets the hungry stick of a man inside who was once his captain. It is the time of the Moon Festival, and the soldier needs a little money. His wife is sick. The captain reluctantly fishes a few dog-eared dollars out of his pocket and says he cannot spare more but will see what he can do. He goes in turn to the old colonel, who has a good job now selling entrance tickets at the Happy World Amusement Park and cannot slip off when he sees him coming, cap in hand. The general will help the lieutenant, the professor his former student, the ex-official his junior clerk even when they are all hard up in Hong Kong and Mao has been ruling China for nearly twenty years.

Old China hands will at once object in angry chorus that Chinese may be counted among the meanest, most ruthless exploiters of sweat labor in the world and that Chinese inhumanity to Chinese is a byword in all clubs east of Calcutta. But within his own social web the system of interlinked responsibilities exerts its moral pressure on even the avaricious Chinese, and he will give if only to save his face. Chinese millionaires found schools and hospitals to pay for their past exactions in the sacred name of business, to honor their parents, and to earn a good name for themselves and their families. There is no statistical breakdown available to show how many are genuinely philanthropic. Whatever their individual motives, the Chinese are obedient to the rules of a highly complex give-and-take system. They have an instinct for moderation and therefore for a leveling operation that demands that no man for whom you are responsible should be stamped into the ground. A good employer hesitates to dismiss anyone, for his family will suffer, and in particular he hesitates to dismiss a stupid employee who may be incapable of getting another job.

"Squeeze" and "tea money" are other great substitutes for democracy among the Chinese, and the cautionary tale of Wang Ch'ao-chün has for two thousand years served as a warning to those who try to flout these venerable institutions. During Julius Caesar's last years, China was ruled by an emperor who had no time to inspect his thousand-odd concubines personally and therefore employed a court painter to produce portraits of them, so that he could judge from afar which might be worthy of closer attention. Now, this scoundrel operated a system of squeeze widely practiced by artists in the West whereby he would paint the most flattering portraits of those who paid him the fattest fees. But the Lady Wang refused to tip him at all, and he therefore submitted to the emperor a picture of her whose ugliness was compounded by a purely imaginary mole under the right eye, for this was a sign of ill-omen.

In consequence, Lady Wang languished for seven long years while the emperor distracted himself with others, and when the king of the Huns came to him for a wife, he thumbed over his portraits and at once decided to give him this seemingly unattractive lady. It was only when the time came for him to bid her a ceremonial farewell that the overstaffed emperor first saw Wang Ch'ao-chün. He fell in love with her immediately and tried to ransom her from the Hun, but that rude barbarian's only response was to clutch his bargain closer to him and ride with it out into the steppes.

Squeeze means that wealth goes percolating down from pocket to pocket, through a series of increasingly fine strainers, so that the rich still retain the bulkier nuggets, but some of the thinnest dust nevertheless reaches even the abjectly poor. At the top end of this filtration system we find that at the turn of the century eunuchs were charging the Dowager-Empress twenty-four silver taels (about $8) for poached eggs in ordinary chicken broth— a favorite, almost daily dish of hers that was sold for a few copper coins in any Peking restaurant—and were submitting accounts for $700 a day for feeding her relatively small personal family. At the other end are the amahs of Singapore and Hong Kong who will exact fair squeeze from their white mistresses and still save them money. For if I go down to the market to buy a chicken it may cost me the equivalent of nine shillings. If Ping goes in a European dress, it will cost eight; in a *cheong sam,* seven and six; in Chinese pajamas, seven shillings; and if the amah goes down instead of either of us, it will cost only six shillings. If the amah then charges me six and ninepence, I am still in pocket. This is a ritualistic exercise in income-bracket adjustment, and is devoid of any malice, so that at New Year and on feast days, or when any younger member of the family is going away, the amah is the first to give her small presents.

Outside the system it is very cold indeed, however. The Chinese—especially the Chinese poor—will help neighbors who are in dire need or distress, and they will take them food or medicine, or club together to buy a coffin for their deceased parent, or do anything else that does not involve any great expense or risk. But they have no tradition of charity toward a stranger, whose approaches they will instinctively treat with suspicion until he has proved himself innocent. There are Good Samaritans in Chinese legend, but as a family man the Good Samaritan is suspect: how much might he have endangered himself and his kin by irresponsibly helping an unknown man who had been mixed up with brutal thieves? The Chinese, therefore, has no civic sense. His conscience may urge him to call a doctor or telephone for a fire engine if he sees a fire, but he has no real conception of the public weal. If he knocks someone down with his car and is sure he has either badly injured him or killed him, he will usually keep going. He cannot do more for the victim than the bystanders can, but if he stopped and were identified, his whole family would indirectly suffer.

In China he did not feel that the law protected him, and he therefore shrank from committing himself to an act that might make him enemies. There were wrongs he could never right, and he remembered the Taoist story of the praying mantis "that lay in a rut and tried to stop a chariot by waving its forearms, for it did not realize that although they had always been most useful, this was a task beyond them." There is no greater folly than to try to change what you cannot, the Chinese say. In Singapore a crowd of some fifty people stood by while secret-society thugs stabbed a hawker to death. None ran for help, none tried to save the victim, and none supplied the police with any information that would help identify the killers afterward.

A Chinese shuns contact with authority, never wishes to report anybody, for fear of blame or reprisals. For blame is an arrow of erratic flight in the eyes of a people in whose history one chief minister has been denounced for getting himself murdered and another for not doing so. As for reprisals, the wary Chinese, for millennia deprived of equality before the law, warn their children: "Before you beat the dog, be sure to learn the master's name."

In her wooden-soled shoes, Ah Fu clops her way down the narrow Chinatown street beneath the multicolored washing of a hundred families that flaps from bamboo poles thrust out of the windows on either side overhead, like a wedding arch of signal flags. As she turns into the narrow doorway of her *kongsi*, shopping basket in hand, she brushes past a stocky, pock-marked fellow in singlet, cotton trousers, and sandals, with a gold ring on his finger, a jagged scar down one cheek, and a switchblade in his pocket. He is a secret-society "fighter," and he is on his way to his club too. Both have their cells within the great Chinese antisociety, but while the amah's is negative and defensive, the gangster's is by tradition positive and aggressive. The early Chinese Republicans claimed that they managed to break through the fine mesh of linked but limited Chinese loyalties, yet they did not succeed in weaving a strong fabric of national feeling in its place. And Mao still faces this problem in a Communist China in which former classmates of the thirties, senior administrators, and academic leaders spread throughout the country will even now form funeral committees, mutual-assistance groups to insure that each old friend has a fitting burial when he dies.

But this is not the whole tale of Chinese society, as volumes of examples would attest—from the outstanding heroism of a Chinese boy who wins a national life-saving medal in Malaysia to the whole fighting history of the Chinese Communist revolution. Not every man is a Gulliver staked out and tied down by a thousand cutting bonds of family responsibility, or an armchair adventurer ready to leave action to others. There have been impatient men whose very refusal to mind their own business or to neglect public duty or ignore public wrong has restored honor, wealth, and security to their families. There have been men who had nothing more to lose, or who burned with indignation, or who yearned for revenge or adventure, or for that mystique which the Chinese are ever ready to accord to the hero and the champion of the downtrodden. And throughout the long history of his country the lean and hungry Chinese has indeed proved that such men are dangerous. For every dynasty has fallen when he has played the catalyst, converting the inert mass compounded of the Chinese millions and their misery into a violent and unstable explosive of appalling destructiveness.

13

The Unheroes

The man with the scar and the shiv in his pocket pushes past Ah Fu and makes for another doorway along the street, to be stopped by a lounger leaning casually against the lintel, and the odd question: "How many meals have you had?" Pockmark's answer is even odder: "Three and a half." But it pleases the stranger, who waves him inside, for that "half" is a coded reference to the bizarre initiation ceremony at which he drank from an unappetizing brew that included some of his own blood. It proves he is a secret-society member.

The secret society absorbs young and active men, for it is essentially an energetic organization of multifarious interests, and it operates in a highly competitive field. In 1966, for example, the Singapore police had on their books six major groups of secret societies, whose eight hundred branches directed about nine thousand loyal followers in a community of less than two million people. And these figures are in no way exceptional, for in the earlier postwar years the Hong Kong police were principally devoting their energies to preventing the secret societies in the crown colony from linking up into one iniquitous cartel of crime that would have enjoyed a following of about three hundred thousand Chinese. The notorious 14-Karat Society alone at one time had nearly eighty thousand men and women on its registers.

The myriad tentacles of these Triads (as they were loosely called after the parent body from which they claim descent) spread through Chinese society with a cold, all-embracing touch that in communities like Hong Kong is felt by one man in every three. They employ a horde of "snakes"—amahs, shop assistants, keycutters, gas and electricity inspectors—who will tip them off to an easy burglary and supply them with floor plans of wealthy houses. They arrange for girls to entice rich men into marriages so that the bride can let them in to rob the happy home on the first suitable night. Sometimes the Triad gangsters enforce their taxation with a certain humor, occupying all the chairs indefinitely in a dance hall whose owner has refused to make a "voluntary contribution," or staging violent and embarrassing scenes about shoddy goods in smart downtown shops whose proprietors refuse to pay protection money.

But for the most part they prey savagely upon the flocks of poor who have no means of defending themselves, demanding money week after week from respectable little dance hostesses and prostitutes, from shoeshine boys, hawkers, harbor boatmen, and drivers of pirate taxis who are themselves outside the law, from small shopkeepers and café owners, stevedores and waiters, and from the mild old menaces who run opium dens. And when these fail to pay up, the bullyboys set upon them and the terrified herd swiftly shies off, leaving the isolated victim alone to take his slashing or smashing. In addition to taxation, there is commerce. Secret societies are involved in every form of smuggling, in piracy on the high seas, dope peddling, white-slave traffic, stealing and selling children, and the kidnapping of millionaires for ransom—an occupation that became so common in Singapore in 1961 that the rich were obliged to hire permanent bodyguards from the police, and hardly dared move between their offices and their nearest palatial villas.

The system seeped into the schools, until no father could be sure that his son was not submitting to threats and paying regular dues out of his lunch money to some juvenile thug. In 1959 a fourteen-year-old urchin was found to be the leader of an adult Triad mob in Singapore, where one half-demented woman admitted that she chained her ten-year-old grandson to his bed every night for fear that he would be corrupted or kidnapped by secret-society adolescents. In Hong Kong the Triads were meanwhile exploiting children by terrorizing them into peddling their blood to clinics, and taking a percentage of the established fee (US $21 for 500 c.c.).

At one end of their tariff of abuses are the great gambling enterprises run by Singapore's rival "24" and "108" gangs, the betting farms and illegal lotteries. At the other end is the killing for cash down. Secret societies will take on any task of violence and intimidation if the price is right. A Singapore secret society of women called The Red Butterflies specialized a few years ago in wreaking bloody vengeance on husbands who cheated or ill-treated their wives (the paying clients), while better-known bandits worked secretly for vengeful dignitaries, some of them honored in their time by the queen. Triads also sold their expert services to rival political parties at election time, wrecking meetings, buying and selling blocks of votes, and leaving canvassers for dead in a drain. And when they are not fighting anyone else, they are fighting the police and each other.

A group suddenly turns into the big, open-sided Singapore café on the corner, and the tables empty quickly, for some of the men are carrying bicycle pumps and others electric lightbulbs, and this means trouble. The secret-society gangster uses a switch-blade, sometimes a pistol, and quite often a parang or Malay machete, but he reinforces his armory with more exotic weapons. He will fight with motorcycle chains trimmed with razor blades, linked steel rods, stilettos in bicycle pumps, ball-bearing guns contrived out of gas piping, and he industriously hones down steel bars to make heavy spears and swords. Everyone flees as two shrieking Chinese youths stagger blindly out into the road while a distracted mother shouts: "Can you see? Can you see?" For there are also the acid bombs. These require no complicated apparatus. Simply puncture the base of an electric lightbulb while it is submerged in hydrochloric acid; the acid is sucked into the bulb, and the hole is then sealed. For maximum effect, shake well before use.

The secret society has its special "killer section" under the control of a military-affairs officer with a title curiously reminiscent of more gracious gatherings in royal surroundings: Red Rod. Beneath him are five Tiger Generals, each in charge of a squad which is licensed to kill. Involved in a vicious struggle against this formidable hydra-headed enemy, the law has taken off the gloves and donned knuckle-dusters. A special ordinance promulgated in Singapore in 1954 provided that a suspect could be arrested on the basis of a simple certificate from a police officer stating that "to the best of his knowledge" the man was a Triad member, since none dared come forward to identify these human scorpions. In Malaysia, special Black Cross identity cards have been issued to secret-society toughs, who may be summarily arrested and jailed for loitering, for sitting in a café in the company of a man who has a knife, even for being in a place of public entertainment with insufficient excuse. They can be restricted to their towns, or even to their homes, and subjected to dusk-to-dawn curfews. There are fifty-seven offenses for which they may be given double the maximum sentence the law normally allows, including possession of a "corrosive substance" or a knife with a blade more than two and a half inches long.

These are no ordinary racketeers. Overseas lodges of the Triads have been set up during the past century in Hawaii and San Francisco, in Chicago, in London and Liverpool, Australia and India, Indonesia, Thailand, and the Indochina states. Up to 1870, the British administered the entire Chinese community in the Straits Settlements through "kapitans," who were in fact secret-society headmen. In 1867, thirty thousand Chinese became directly or indirectly involved in a battle in Penang in which rival secret-society factions fought it out for ten days with everything from clubs to cannon while the colonial government looked on helplessly. Five years later, the "Larut Wars" broke out, with Triad gangs taking sides in a dispute over the succession to the sultanate of Perak in North Malaya. These ended only after the British had been called in to restore order—the event which first extended British suzerainty to the Malay States.

After the Chinese revolution in 1911 and the subsequent overthrow of the Manchu dynasty, the secret societies were quick to give allegiance to left or right wing among the new republican movements. Dr. Sun Yat-sen, later the first president of China, manipulated the Triads throughout Southeast Asia, operating from a headquarters in Singapore and traveling about disguised as an itinerant fortuneteller. The Marxists were not too squeamish to fish in the same murky waters either, so that by the end of World War II the Chinese Nationalists were supported by two of the biggest Triad movements in Malaya and Singapore, and the Communists by the third. But when Mao became master in Peking, the Triads tended to veer further to the left. The subsequent pull-devil, pull-baker struggle for Triad support culminated in the wild "14-K" riots of 1956 in Hong Kong. The criminal secret societies provided the yeast for this upheaval by forcing Nationalist or Communist flags on to the Chinese community at exorbitant prices, savagely beating those who would not buy, and whipping mobs into a frenzy of furious and bloody rioting which effectively covered their own looting operations. Some five thousand were arrested, exasperated members of the public began at last to provide the police with a thin trickle of useful information about these scum, and for the first time the authorities were able to hit the Triads where it hurt—below the belt of harmless-seeming Chinese clan, village, and charitable associations which had hitherto acted as their cover.

That is not to say that in Singapore, Hong Kong, and all the other insanitary cities of the gorgeous East the secret society was then trodden into the sidewalk. Once the Communists were firmly established in power in China proper, the "pro-Nationalist" secret societies went into the refugee business, selling safe passage from

China to Macao and Hong Kong by underground routes, fixing the authorities (the Triads spend a considerable percentage of their income on bribing officialdom), "welcoming" the rich from Shanghai, and threatening those who would not cooperate with them with banishment back to the Communist mainland. Refugee money began to pour into such private enterprises as heroin production, the distribution of taxi-girls, and "accident insurance" for wealthy émigrés. And now the Triads also exploit the other refugees, the American and European tourists who are running in the opposite direction, for they have their sharp hooks into nearly every tout and dubious travel agent, every girlie bar and gin palace in Hong Kong whose object is to extract dollars painlessly from unwary visitors.

The police do not delude themselves into thinking that they can rip this evil out of Asia as simply as a shaman might exorcise a devil, all in one piece. Their more limited ambition is to achieve the moment when they have to face nothing more than a criminal enemy of the kind the Western countries make such a fuss about—gangs of teddy boys or train robbers, rats in the granary activated by nothing but their greed and against whom any man's finger may confidently point—instead of the huge, cancerous Triad organization with its blood oaths and braggadocio. Nor is this an idle dream, for the more the secret society has degenerated into a purely criminal organization, the more it has lost the sources of its past intimidating strength—its prestige, its mystique, and the unquestioning loyalty of its members.

A Triad, says the *Concise Oxford Dictionary*, is a group of three: in chemistry, an element with the combining power of three; in music, a chord of three notes. In the vocabulary of Chinese conspiracy it is a secret society whose symbol is a triangle representing the harmonious blending of Heaven, Earth, and Man. Each of these elements has its own secret cipher, which is always a multiple of three—36 for Heaven, 72 for Earth, 108 for Man—and these are respected within the Triad to a point where even the entrance fees paid by new members are $1.80,

$3.60, $7.20, or $10.80, according to the size of their wallets. Bastardized Taoist numerology further prescribes the ciphers for all ranks within a secret society, whose symbolism is a chop suey of religious, mystical, and moralistic leftovers. The names of the five principal ranks are taken from the five virtues enjoined by Confucius (among them, "li"), while the five Tiger Generals represent the five elements in ancient Chinese cosmology: Wood, Fire, Earth, Metal, and Water. The Triads, like the Freemasons, are organized into lodges, which for the purposes of initiation are arranged as walled "Cities of Willows."

The candidate for membership makes a symbolized journey through the city of his future lodge, answering questions with the correct password ("Where do you come from?" "The East"), and swearing an initial oath of fealty. He passes the "Mountain of Knives," the "Red Flower Pavilion," the "Circle of Heaven and Earth" (a bamboo hoop), the "Fiery Furnace" (burning joss paper), the "Stepping Stones," and the "Two-Planked Bridge," to arrive at the sacred altar bearing the memorial tablets of the Five Ancestors. At the altar the novice kneels while his finger is pricked and the blood mixed with that of a sacrificed cock in a bowl containing other, nameless ingredients. A machete is laid across the bowl, and a small cup which has been dipped into the soup is then balanced on its blade. With his hands now tied behind his back, the initiate bends forward and drinks from it. As a glowing joss stick is suddenly extinguished, he demands that his life may be snuffed out in like manner if he breaks his oath of secrecy.

The Triads have a complicated system of hieratical tattoo marks, and a multitude of slogans and test phrases, secret finger and hand signs, recondite ways of holding everyday objects like teacups and umbrellas and chopsticks, or arranging matches or cigarettes or saucers on a table to identify themselves in obedience to an established code. The trick is to use the right number of fingers at the right time when grasping an object, for the number may vary not only according to rank but according to whether it is before or after the twentieth of the month.

Within their lodges, secret-society office bearers don the elaborate paraphernalia laid down for their hierarchy, and a headman is a phantasmagoric figure solemnly clothed in what appears to be the ceremonial regalia of a slightly absent-minded high priest. He wears a red headband with five loops in it and a red robe inscribed with the mystic symbols of Chinese cosmology. His left fist is laid across his breast, the middle and little fingers extended in the secret sign that indicates his rank. But on his right foot he has a perfectly ordinary leather shoe, while on his left is a straw sandal, fastened with thongs over a parti-colored sock, and when he moves, it can be seen that his left trouser leg is also rolled up above his somewhat knobbly knee, but his right is not. The eccentricities of this attire have an impeccable history, however, for the single grass sandal—which is also to be found on the altar of the lodge, together with the rosary, the clappers, and the begging bowl of a monk—represents a relic of the great Zen Buddhist Master Bodhidharma, who first brought the faith to China in the sixth century. The trouser is rolled up so that the Triad official may kneel like a humble friar, his bare flesh touching the earth.

The impression that something has slipped askew, that reverence and racketeering seem to have become most oddly mingled, increases on further acquaintance with the Triads. The secret-society member swears thirty-six oaths of loyalty and fraternity toward all his brothers. He promises that he will always offer them hospitality and help whenever they need it, that he will respect their wives, that he will be honest, charitable, and steadfast in all his dealings with them and their families, that he will strictly observe the disciplines of the lodge. He will be guilty of no treachery, and if his brothers offend, he will not inform the government. He also swears to keep most strictly the secrets of his order, and prays that if he breaks these oaths he shall be annihilated by "five thunderbolts" or skewered by "ten thousand daggers" or "a myriad swords." Security is remarkably good, and even illegal lottery runners in Singapore cheerfully go to jail when caught, rather than reveal more than their names (rank and number are already secret, of course).

The curiously mathematical apparatus on the altar of the lodge discloses the true nature of the Triad, for in addition to the "magic mirror" that indicates the good and the bad, there are scales, a ruler, and an abacus. The scales are for weighing the virtues of the Chinese Ming dynasty against the iniquities of the foreign Manchu dynasty that usurped its power in 1644 and thereafter held the Dragon Throne until 1912. The ruler is for measuring the extent of the land to be wrested back from these Manchus, and the abacus is for totting up their debts and crimes. There is also a censer inscribed: *Overthrow the Ch'ing. Restore the Ming;* Ch'ing was the title of the Manchu dynasty. The original Triad was, in fact, a secret patriotic organization pledged to rid China of her barbarian conquerors. The forerunners of the cowardly thug who cut the throat of a mother of five in Singapore with her own kitchen cleaver were men like the headman of the Small Dagger Society. This worthy captured and held the great South China port of Amoy for three years in the middle of the last century and was subsequently tortured to death before he would give away the smallest secret of his fraternity.

The story of the Triad begins in a monastery, as do so many stories of violence in China, the traditional home of the fighting monks. The art of judo can be traced to these pious, yet pugnacious fellows, who traveled the bandit-infested roads without any weapons and therefore worked out their own system of unarmed combat. It is also said that the basic elements of "empty-handed" karate, including the spectacular trick of smashing a thick piece of timber with the edge of the palm, were evolved in the kitchens of Buddhist monasteries where the monks were forbidden by their faith to use a knife or ax, and therefore chopped up the wood for their stoves with their bare hands. "We may not have knives, so make every finger a dagger; without spears, every arm must be a spear, and every open hand a sword," the venerable brother who invented the art is recorded as saying.

Esoteric history that no one dared to put in writing at the time has it that the Triad was founded in the seventeenth century by an abbot of Shao Lin monastery who had raised an invincible company of 128 warrior-monks to quell a force of Tibetan "rebels." Jealous voices whispered that by their exploits the fighters of Shao Lin were really trying to inspire the Chinese to rise up against the Manchus, and the emperor therefore agreed that the monastery should be set on fire and blown up. This was achieved with the help of an unfrocked traitor who was number seven in the Shao Lin hierarchy, so that even today secret-society gangsters never use this number in their ritual. Eighteen heroes escaped the conflagration, but after many battles and privations, only five of these survived. These are the Five Ancestors to whom homage is paid in every Triad lodge, and their progress through fire and water is the journey symbolically imitated in the "City of Willows" by every secret-society novitiate. According to this quasi-Arthurian legend, the dispirited five, hotly pursued, were able to go on after a shining sword had sprung magically out of the earth before them, bearing the mystical inscription: *Overthrow the Ch'ing. Restore the Ming.* Thereafter, they raised the standard of the Ming claimant to the throne in a widespread revolt in South China but were defeated by the Manchus and forced to scatter. Biding their time, however, they formed the Triad of Hung League as a secret underground movement for the destruction of the usurpers.

Triad insurrections were not infrequent in the centuries that followed, and when the revolution against the Manchus broke out in 1911, some twenty thousand secret-society brothers fought in South China for Dr. Sun Yat-sen, who had earlier founded an "Association for Changing the Mandate." Once the Manchus were thrown out, Sun Yat-sen solemnly presented himself at the tombs of the Ming emperors outside Peking to inform the Imperial dead that the order to "Overthrow the Ch'ing" had been executed. But victory proved the ruin of the Triad. Enjoying heady powers as pressure groups in political affairs under the Republic, and tempted on to the mucky highways of grand-scale racketeering and vice, the lodges broke into warring factions and rival criminal empires. Today the secret marks are blacked out to baffle the police, the rituals are severely curtailed for fear of raids, the mumbo jumbo is minimized since it is too compromising, and the average secret-society gangster is an ignoramus who flunks his numerology and cannot get even his own call sign straight. The instrument of patriotism has indeed become the refuge of the scoundrel.

At least, that is the harsh Western reading of the case, but the Chinese refugee who believes in guilds before governments often sees things differently. The Triad looks after its own, he says, and if you pay your dues you get protection; but pay your dues to the government and you will get no protection from the Triads. For the man fleeing Communist China into Hong Kong in the nineteen-fifties, it seemed that whether you were under a Chinese or a British administration you could still starve in the street in the same way. But make contact with the more responsible Triad officials (and there were still such people) and you would be welcomed, you would lose your sense of loneliness in a strange land, and in your destitute and desperate condition you would get rice and a roof of sorts against payment at some future date. With secret-society help, Ping organized some twenty penniless ex-officers and students into a lumberjack and wood-chopping group with its own saws and axes, able to scratch an honest living by selling its services in the New Territories of Hong Kong. "How?" echoes Ping. "Because they give us two hundred dollars. Who else give refugees two hundred dollars?" (Two hundred Hong Kong dollars are worth about US $36.)

If a secret-society gangster is good to his family, loyal to his clan, and leaves his neighbors alone, he is given credit where credit is due, for the fact that he shot a police detective dead in broad daylight on the other side of town a week ago has nothing to do with the Chinese uncitizen. It is an abstract sort of evil to be met only with an abstract reproach. There is nothing really curious in this. The West is bulging with people who unaffectedly enjoy the society of crooks, cheats, racketeers, and ruthless businessmen, cannon-fodder generals and bloody-minded gendarmes ("Well, he's always been so nice to me"). It is full of men who are not horrified by catastrophe, or who hear with complete indifference that three thousand people have been drowned in a flood in Pakistan, or Sudan, or Burma, or Laos, or anyway one of those places.

Moreover, the secret society, however vestigial and obscene a stump it may so often be today, is part of an ancient heritage that never fails to stir the Chinese and still casts its shadow over contemporary events: the hallowed tradition of bloody rebellion.

14

The Blessing of Bandits

"When the emperor errs, the peasant quakes," the Chinese say, for if he offends heaven, fire and flood and famine will ensue. The evil is compounded, so that if the emperor neglects the sacrifices at New Year and the solstices, and inflicts cruelty and hardship on the people, they may rather unfairly have to expect a follow-up of natural calamities from an angry deity. But the principle of the Mandate of Heaven provides that revolution is hallowed by its own success. There is, therefore, always recourse to revolt.

This is an exceptionally well-worn track, for all dynasties, it seems, pursue the same depressing clogs-to-clogs course. The first emperor of the new line, having overthrown his tyrannical predecessor, brings fresh blood and vigor to the throne at a time of general rejoicing and relief. As sovereign follows sovereign, however, the corruption of power and riches, the isolation of the monarch from reality within some monstrous high-walled palace, the greed and the cruelty of jealous eunuchs, and the rivalries of extravagant and ambitious concubines progressively produce a sort of vicious, imbecile degeneration at the center and administrative ataxy in the provinces. The Chinese millions observe this inevitable process with bland, closed faces and deceptive patience, but the time comes when the abuses and the distress have become insupportable, and the country, like the individual

Chinese, suddenly goes berserk. Bloody revolution follows, a new man receives heaven's mandate, a new dynasty starts down the peony path to perdition, and two or three centuries later it all happens again. Sometimes a period of anarchy and fragmentation intervenes, but this always provokes a new revolutionary impulse toward unification. At such times the agency that transforms the Chinese peasant into a partisan—and five Chinese out of six are still peasants today—may be one man, but may also be a mystical movement.

More than four hundred years before Christ was born, the great Chinese philosopher Mo Tzu preached a doctrine of universal love and at the same time founded an esoteric society of fighting freemasons. These two activities were not as contradictory as they might appear, for Mo Tzu believed that the truculent were to be deterred less by the moral reprimand of the turned cheek than by a perfect system of defense that would make any aggressor pay dear. When the powerful Duke of Ch'u was contemplating an attack against the capital of the smaller state of Sung, Mo Tzu went to dissuade him, but the loveless duke refused to cancel his program for the assault. Whereupon, "Mo Tzu took off his girdle and laid it down to represent a defended city, and seized a little stick as his weapon. He then successfully repulsed nine different attacks, and still had plans for defense in reserve when the others had exhausted their stratagems for taking the city." The duke gave up his project.

Mo Tzu's society was founded to champion the poor and defend the weak, and he frowned on chivalrous treatment of the enemy as a convention that simply handicapped the good and the honorable: in a "just war" it was righteous to be ruthless. His society enforced the strictest discipline on its members and demanded of them a spirit of unquestioning self-sacrifice, so that its Grand Master, the agent of the Will of Heaven, could "order the faithful to enter a fire or walk on sword blades."

The society faded away, but ever afterward their sprang up in times of misery a succession of movements whose revolutionary ideals were enfolded in a voluminous rainbow cloak of secret signs and oaths and mystical beliefs, blood brotherhood and magical immunity from blade or bullet, sacred numbers and Taoist portents, and all the gaudy ritual in which the Chinese instinctively enshrine their dedication and their loyalties. This is the Confucian principle at work again: the outward manifestation inspires the inward grace.

During Christ's lifetime, a usurper who had plunged the country into a lamentable state of disorder and economic distress provoked a great peasant uprising led by the secret society from which Triad officials today derive their red headbands. This was the Red Eyebrows, a farming freemasonry whose members painted their eyebrows red as a token of their eternal loyalty to the cause of rebellion. Hordes of impoverished and desperate Chinese closed in on the capital, plundering and massacring mandarins as they moved, and years of atrocious civil war followed, in which millions died. The upstart was finally beheaded, and the Han dynasty, whose throne he had seized, was restored —but it was typical of this historical formula that the new sovereign also had to fight the Red Eyebrows, for the milling peasantry had developed an insatiable appetite for loot. The Triad was not the first society to abandon patriotism for plunder.

Some hundred and sixty years afterward, the wheel of Chinese history turned full circle once more. Rascally eunuchs and their creatures had won control of the country and were exterminating scholars and pillaging the provinces in the name of a cloistered, impressionable young emperor who never saw the truth behind their fat friendly faces. However, in Central China a traveling magician had found a sure cure for a prevalent pestilence, which consisted of drinking ordinary water over which he had recited a secret incantation. He was quick to gain disciples and trusting adherents among downtrodden peasants only waiting for a savior, and rapidly built up a great, popular revolutionary movement. These Yellow Turbans were organized into rural communities whose members ate together, practiced public confession, and trained for war eighteen hundred years before Mao Tse-tung introduced his system of people's communes and made them the basis for a people's militia. Their leaders also promised an era of happiness in the future, which would justify the sacrifices and hardships of the moment, just as he has done. Fortified by a magic that was supposed to ward off death, the Yellow Turbans flung themselves into the insurrection, perishing to the number of half a million in one year alone. The revolt was crushed, but it brought down the dynasty with it.

The White Lotus society, whose origins remain part of its mystery, was a secret Buddhist organization that carried out clandestine weapon training during the Mongol overlordship of Kublai Khan more than a thousand years later and is said to have helped the founder of the Ming dynasty to rout these barbarians and establish a Chinese line on the Dragon Throne once more. True to form, the White Lotus mounted another bloody insurrection against the Ming dynasty when it went rotten on China nearly three hundred years afterward, and in the eighteenth century impartially launched a third against its Manchu successors. One hundred years ago, the Taiping rebellion— this time of quasi-Christian inspiration—swept through China, and finally the Society of Harmonious Fists rose at the turn of this century. These Boxers besieged the foreign legations in Peking and murdered more than two hundred white missionaries and sixteen thousand Chinese Christians ("second-class red-haired devils"), having been deflected by the Dowager-Empress from their original purpose of annihilating the Manchus to annihilating other barbarians.

This murderous rabble, a curious bedfellowship of xenophobia, patriotism, banditry, superstition, and sadism (some Boxers hacked their victims to pieces as human sacrifices in Buddhist temples) was a bastard creation that drew its members from several secret societies. Behind the Taiping rebellion was not only a distorted vision of Christianity but a Triad quarrel in which Hakkas were pitted against Cantonese. An alternative

account of the founding of the Triad itself ascribes its origins
to the White Lotus, and all these conspiracies claim descent from
the Yellow Turbans. The northern Tongs, some of which have
links with the southern Triads, will sometimes ingeniously trace
their lineage right back to Mo Tzu (who no doubt turns in his
grave). Across the pages of twenty-five hundred years of carefully edited popular history, the secret society is depicted as the
strong arm of the millions against the cruel excesses of government.

Sometimes, however, it was a single man who appeared as
the champion of justice and unity and led ragged armies to victory against Imperial tyranny. Han Kao-tsu was a common peasant, but his birth was said to have been accompanied by many
outstanding celestial portents, and when another rebel provided
the curtain raiser for his insurrection by shouting his defiance of
the Ch'in tyrant in 209 B.C., "the empire answered him like an
echo." A sixteen-year-old boy inspired the seven-year-long revolt
that ended the despotic Sui dynasty and reunited all China under
the great T'ang dynasty. And when the Chinese rose against the
Mongol Khans, one man led them and founded the glorious Ming
dynasty—a son of poor peasants, an ex-shepherd, Buddhist monk,
and beggar. For the Chinese, great leadership has nothing to do
with class. "Do not ask where the hero comes from," they say.
"The lotus rises from the mud, but does not smell of it." Nor has
heroism anything to do, of course, with "goodness" or "honesty"
as defined by a government whose Confucian moralizing may
simply be pap to disguise the poison of its abusive rule.

The knight-errant of China, extolled and beloved throughout
the centuries, is a swashbuckler and a bold assassin. Expert in
the eighteen methods of fighting, he pursues the vendettas of
the widows and orphans of murdered men, he takes from the
rich and gives to the poor, but he may be anything from a duke
to a dog butcher, and he is likely to get blind, swearing, stag-
gering drunk in the lowest company between his missions of
mercy. The "Hsieh" is a freelance, selling his sword to this and

that prince, and he is usually "errant" simply because there is a price on his head in the place he has just left. He by no means sublimates his sexual appetite by worshipping maidens in distress from afar, and, being Chinese, he actually *likes* dragons.

Furthermore, the Chinese hero is allowed his moments of mercilessness for it is a cutthroat world in which defeat may mean a swift death not only for the vanquished but for his entire clan. An ambitious warlord fights for power as he would fight for his very life, and once he holds that power, he must diligently chop off at the wrist every clutching hand that reaches for it. The pitiless General Ts'ao Ts'ao slaughters the entire family of his host, having quite wrongly imagined that they were conspiring against him, and then justifies his vile act by retorting: "I would rather betray the whole world than let the world betray me." The act fixes him as the villain of the piece, but his words—the most famous quotation in the *Romance of the Three Kingdoms*—establish him as a hero, a man who will succeed where nothing succeeds like success. When he leans forward and says flatteringly to Liu Pei: "You and I are the only heroes now," the Han pretender drops his chopsticks in fright, for he knows that what he has just heard is a declaration of war to the knife. On the other hand, Ts'ao Ts'ao the chivalrous commander is so struck with admiration by the gallant conduct of an opposing captain that he exclaims: "A very tiger of a leader! I must get him alive," and orders his bowmen in ambush not to shoot. The captain escapes—with the baby heir apparent under his breastplate. When he died in A.D. 210, a poet wrote an epitaph for Ts'ao Ts'ao that could be the definition of his species:

> The thoughts of heroes are not ours to judge
> Nor are there actions for our eyes to see.
> A man may stand the first in merit; then
> His crimes may brand him chief of criminals.
> And so his reputation's fair and foul.
> In all things great, his genius masters him.

It is often almost impossible to tell a hero from a brigand, since in the Chinese tradition of left-handed loyalties, the one so frequently begins or ends life as the other. The man who was to be the Emperor Han Kao-tsu started out as a farmer and a village headman, a vinous, womanizing, bonhomous individual who saw trouble ahead when half of the band of convicts he had been ordered to escort escaped. Under the Draconian laws of Ch'in, he could only expect slavery or death as the punishment for his negligence. He therefore unfettered the rest of the gang and urged them to escape too, saying he fully intended to take to the hills himself. Some ten of the prisoners joined him as outlaws. These were the first recruits of an army that was to free the empire and establish a dynasty that would last four hundred years.

Life in China was for millennia like a lethal board game in which a blind destiny threw the dice, and to land on the wrong square at the wrong moment could mean sudden ruin and repulsive death. The victims of greedy or malevolent oppression, of a debt forced upon them, of a change in favor at court—these were the men who turned outlaw in the hospitably inhospitable mountains, where the born leader could await his moment in security. Every educated Chinese understands the principle of revolution, for the whole history of his race is perforated by a series of bloody insurrections that broke out when the masses, having "nothing to lose but their chains," fell upon their absurdly intemperate abusers.

The rich man was regarded with deep suspicion and the robber with sneaking sympathy, for there must be some excellent reason why he turned bandit which doubtless reflected not upon him but upon the fat and righteous. That is not to say that his depredations were appreciated, and the ordinary peasant, caught between soldiery and outlaws, was often reduced to rags himself and driven to become a bandit in turn. Then would come the final breakup of society that set moving an avalanche capable of burying dynasties in their own rubble. And it was at this point that the "family" man who instinctively recoiled from trouble made his crucial and revolutionary decision—that the interests of his family would be served best if he joined the ranks of the desperate. "Whenever the officials move against the bandits," says Yüan in *Men of the Marshes*, "the people at once suffer. As soon as they enter the village, they seize our pigs, sheep, chickens, and geese and eat them, and then demand money for their soldiers. But the soldiers are stupid, and although the bandits commit great outrages, they are not punished. It is we who become distressed and poor, and so, if only someone would help us, we would become bandits ourselves." (Which he duly does.)

A weariness of books from *Das Kapital* to *Mein Kampf* may be blamed for the bloodier chapters of modern history, but nothing ever printed perhaps has provided so tiny a spark capable of igniting an inflammable world as a few seemingly trite lines from this seventeenth-century Chinese novel, based on a record of Sung dynasty bandits. In Chapter 10 a competent and honest officer, framed and forced to flee by a corrupt minister whose adopted son covets his wife, is advised where he can find asylum by a well-wisher: "It is a village surrounded by a lake of reeds and called Liang Shan Po," his friend says softly. "It has a stronghold in the center, and a circumference of nearly three hundred miles of waterweed and rushes . . ." In the passages that follow, we are in a baffling marshland of hidden creeks and paths and secret waterways in which bewildered government troops with their armor and horses are disastrously ambushed by bandits who know every inch of these treacherous fens. Beyond is the natural inner fortress of the brigands, set above a forest of enormous trees and surrounded by an impregnable wall of indignant peaks, its twisting approaches protected by great traps of overhanging boulders and suspended avalanches of heavy logs.

This is the Sherwood of the Chinese Robin Hood, conceived on a grand scale and every bit as beloved and famous as its Western equivalent. In this warm, wet womb of a robber's lair, there assemble no fewer than 108 (the magical Triad number for Man) great heroes, all of whom have been the victims of their instinct to protect the weak, their own impulsive and often horrifying ferocity, and the injustices of officials. A band of able swordsmen and dead-eyed archers, accompanied by a wily schemer and a fat (if bellicose) Friar Tuck, the outlaws take us through a series of exciting, if sometimes distastefully gory adventures (for these are no Technicolor renegades in Lincoln green with a manicured and deodorized Maid Marian among them). And then comes the incontestable proof that crime pays, when all these excellent ruffians are vouchsafed celestial immortality and duly celebrate with one final, gigantic binge.

Among the many young men who have carried this tale in their knapsacks was at one time a somewhat rebellious, taciturn student called Mao Tse-tung, who had bitterly resented the authoritarian bullying of his father and who was imbued with a keen sense of injury. *Men of the Marshes* enveloped this resentment in a vision. It was a vision of modern man responding to a centuries-old call to revolt which taught that salvation came from poor, cotton-clad figures descending from the mountains in the driving rain, from men stigmatized as bandits who, by definition, represented invincible right against the might of Imperial injustice.

It is impossible to say to what extent history might have been different if Mao had not been fascinated by the Chinese tradition of the Liang Shan Po, the prototype of the "liberated area" and the "revolutionary base." In 1927 he retired with his few followers to the misty heights of Chingkangshan, a mountain stronghold on the crenelated frontier of two separately administered Nationalist provinces. From the region of Chingkangshan, and later from the caves of Yenan, Mao pitted the guerrilla heroes of his own twentieth-century Liang Shan Po against Chiang Kai-shek. And in the end he won. To him it is axiomatic that the Men of the Marshes, maneuvering in their familiar fens with the support of the local people, must always win by their ruses and ambuscades against blundering, conventional forces of officialdom ignorant of the treacherous terrain. Today those forces are equipped with napalm, jets, amphibious craft, and rocket-firing helicopters, and no Vietcong would deny that these later versions of the war stallion and the crossbow are also more formidable. But, just as the British have believed with absolute confidence that they will always win the last battle, so Mao and his hard-line supporters believe that guerrillas will always make idiots of their enemies—in Vietnam as in China. Moreover, it is inconceivable to Mao that a decadent imperialism should subdue the forces of rebellion once the Mandate of Heaven has so obviously been removed. It simply has never happened in all history.

This is the spirit that divides the world today. For while the Western half thinks in terms of cops and robbers, the Eastern half is conditioned to revere the holy mission of the outlaw. Nothing could better dovetail with the Communist convention that all non-Communist governments are evil, and therefore to be overthrown.

15

Heaven Does Not Speak

In despot or desperado, the educated Chinese conscience is a noble thing, for, unlike its Western counterpart, it is not swayed by fear of celestial balance sheets. It does not insult God by believing that He is a merciless Legalist, a stick-and-carrot deity who rules through a system of unimaginable rewards and awful punishments, and that therefore we must act piously in order to be recompensed on earth or in heaven. Destiny, said Confucius, distributes riches and long life irrespective of merit, or, as one of his early critics put it so trenchantly: "Man is like lice in the fold of a robe—Heaven no more hearkens to him than he himself would listen to an inquiring flea."

Chinese are of the earth, earthy. Their sages propounded practical rules for living in this world with a minimum of grief, but they promised no paradise and drew no maps of kingdoms above or below. For them there was a Will and so, of course, a Way, but no anthropomorphic benevolence with a long white beard. "Heaven does not speak," declared Mencius, and the words echo convincingly across the vast silence of the ages. Confucius, who declined to discuss "extraordinary phenomena, feats of strength, disorders, or spiritual beings," once tartly chided a disciple who had opened the forbidden subject of the metaphysical, by saying: "You do not understand life; how can you understand death?" Those among his Taoist rivals who believed in a universal blind force for once agreed with him. Like the vicar who refused to be reassured when told that a savage-looking dog never bit parsons, they objected: "I may know I have a soul, and you may know I have a soul, but does the dog know I have one?"

Since heaven was not a place you went to when you died but only a term for the rather forbidding moral mechanics of the universe, the sales talk of Taoist charlatans who claimed to hold the secrets of immortality on earth itself met with a ready response from the public. Fourteen centuries or more before their Western brethren went into the business, Chinese alchemists were producing formulas for the philosopher's stone that would transmute base metal into gold, and for the elixir that bestowed everlasting life.

The great Emperor Han Wu-ti, who made the mastery of his arms felt more than two thousand miles away across Central Asia, proved the biggest of royal fools at home when wheedling magicians came to whisper in his long ears. Although one old swindler who swore he held the key to immortality died right after, and the magical message on silk found in the stomach of a bull turned out to be in the calligraphy of another trickster who had predicted it would be there, the emperor never lost faith. To the end of his days, he listened eagerly to rogues who talked mysteriously of the Fortunate Isles off the coast of China where the Immortals lived, or who coyly admitted to 550 if pressed for their age.

The Western stranger, narrow-minded know-all that he so often is about the hereafter, tends to assume that if the Chinese do not believe in a heaven they do not believe in an afterlife. But to the Chinese, afterlife does not have to be lived in the intimidating palaces of omnipotent and omniscient deities, any more than life on earth is lived with popes and kings. The dead sink into the soil to find themselves in a world of their ancestors not unlike our own. In January 1963, a twenty-four-year-old Chinese girl and her twenty-eight-year-old groom were married in

a temple on Penang Island, off North Malaya, after all the for-
malities had been observed. A go-between had arranged the
alliance, gifts had been exchanged, the dowry agreed, and the
banns had been posted in advance. Once the bride and groom
were before the altar, the bride's mother took the lighted candles
that each held, tied them together with a red cord, and placed
them on a bowl of incense to symbolize the union. Man and wife,
the couple were conducted to a bridal chamber set up outside
the temple—and then set on fire, together with half a million
dollars in fake currency.

For this was a wedding of departed souls, of babies that had
died shortly after birth twenty-four and twenty-eight years before, respectively. They were represented at the ceremony by
effigies, their bridal chamber was made of paper, their money
probably stamped "Bank of Hell." Their wedding had been
arranged for the usual reason: their spirits had been possessing
their living younger sisters, confiding to them their love for each
other, and demanding their parents' consent to a marriage. A
medium confirmed their identities and thereafter acted as match-
maker. The parents raised no obstacles. It was quite natural for
an elder sister to want to marry first, dead or not. Such marriages
are not regarded as extraordinary, though more commonly the
dead groom is represented by a cock and the bride by a tablet
inscribed with her name. In March 1966, for example, a young
man in Formosa embraced a wooden board wrapped in a pink
wedding gown, at the end of an elaborate ceremony during which
he was married to a young girl who had fallen to her death from
a four-story building the week before.

Life below has its heartaches and hardships, and the helpless
shades must not be left solitary, or hungry, or poor and despised.
They must be able to pay their way and buy themselves out of
trouble if necessary. (For, like life on earth, it can be hell as
well as heaven.) When they come of age, dead babes should be
married off; and when the old die, they should be pushed out
into the next world with every advantage. Ah Fu pays three

dollars a month (about fifty cents) to a competent, trusted, and discreet old man who runs his customers into the ground on a sound, businesslike basis, and who is known as "Mosquito." If she is old and ill and cannot go back to China, he will house her in one of the upper rooms that overlook "Death Street" (Sago Lane in Singapore's Chinatown), or will pay her hospital bills. When she dies, he will move her down to street level, where most shops are of four kinds: coffin-makers, gaudy little Taoist and Buddhist chapels, open-fronted sidewalk cafés, and funeral chandlers or "paper shops" dealing in all appurtenances for obsequies from blue-ideogrammed mourning lanterns to paper servants, cars, and houses for the dead. Mosquito will see that in one of the cafés her family and friends are given a good funeral feast. He will see that she gets a stout coffin, that the necessary riches —if only on paper—are burned to accompany her into the next world, that enough prayers are said for her in the little chapels to ensure her happy entry into hell-and-heaven (monks and nuns chant for up to forty-nine days, according to the subscription the deceased client has paid), and he will give her an ear-splitting send-off with a hired band to a well-chosen burial plot.

When the feast of Ch'ing Ming comes around, the period of formal remembrance that follows the vernal equinox, families take food to the graves of the dead. Since they may draw on a special nest egg reserved for ancestral rites, they can buy suckling pig and poultry and rose-petal wine, humbly offer it all up to their forebears and then eat and drink it themselves with a concious pride in their own piety and damn the expense. It is not a gloomy occasion, but a picnic outing to be shared with the departed. For the Chinese, the dead are very near, and so is the whole realm of the supernatural.

The emperor communed with heaven, plowing a sacred furrow at the beginning of spring, observing the solemn rites of the seasons and solstices. But from time immemorial the people have had no truck with God, only with gods. And these gods have for the most part simply been the spirits of wood and spring and

hill and village, little local animistic deities that have sometimes
—but not always—achieved nationwide fame. Under the direction
of sorcerers, sturdy peasant folk in earlier times were known to
tie virgins to ornamental beds and push them out on to the
turbulent waters of the Yellow River as "brides" to placate
"China's Sorrow," but this practice has since ceased.

On the other hand, the inquiring mind is apt to be thrown
into almost epileptic contortions by any study of "popular" Chinese religion of later centuries, for it is the one stew in the world
that has everything in it, *including* the kitchen stove. A Chinese,
it seems, will worship Confucius, Buddha, the Goddess of Mercy,
the Kitchen God of the Stove, the Jade Emperor, the Mother of
the Western Heaven, the Queen of the Sea, his own grandfather,
the Eight Immortals, a piece of red paper inscribed with the
name of a man who once lent him twenty dollars at a difficult
moment, the Monkey God, the Big Dipper, and the man who
killed a tiger in the street of his home village and subsequently
emigrated to the United States, where he appears to be doing
very well. They say there is a rabbit pounding out the pill for
the Elixir of Life in the moon, together with the woman who
first filched it from her husband. This man was a general who
was given it as a reward for shooting down nine out of the ten
suns that once surrounded the earth, thus leaving only one. And
the first thing I knew of an eclipse in Singapore in 1960, was a
tremendous rattling and banging of gasoline cans set up by all
the people in a nearby Chinese kampong. They were shooing
off the Sky-dog to stop him eating the moon, which is, of course,
made of cake.

This list can be extended almost indefinitely. The Chinese will
pray to different myths for different things, and they have absolutely no sense of dogmatic exclusivity or of our own great and
gory traditions of religious bigotry in the West. There is always
room for an extra god, therefore, and the incense can be made
to go around. The Taoists have been largely responsible for
turning the Chinese cosmos into a celestial Disneyland that has

apparently been the scene of an appalling population explosion in distorted deities. But many of these are no more than a curious apotheosis of figures in parables and fables invented to make piety more comprehensible to the peasant. It is as if we suddenly filled our churches with garish plaster saints that included the Man Who Did Not Bury His Talent, the Prodigal Son, the One Lost Sheep, the Pillar of Salt, perhaps a somewhat confused Lazarus going through the Eye of the Needle, and possibly peripheral Christian characters of an improving nature like old Scrooge and Little Eric. Aesop and La Fontaine would supply the moralistic animal life, and we would be in no wise different from the Chinese, or any worse Christians than we already are.

The Chinese pantheon is further swollen, moreover, with patron deities like the sage who was famous for his siege ladders and his "wooden bird that flew for three days" and who is now enshrined by the corps of Chinese carpenters, the Immortal Swordsman beloved of barbers, and "Lee Iron-Crutch," the God of Beggars, and the purely fictitious heroine of Chin P'ing Mei who is now the Goddess of Brothels. The Chinese worship of men that once lived is only different from our calendar of saints in that canonization has been more haphazard. The Christian and the Moslem look upward to a God in heaven, for theologically they are monarchists. But a Chinese is a sort of metaphysical Marxist. His gaze is horizontal, not vertical, and is directed toward a mass organization of spirits, and animistic deities, and saints living or dead, and ghosts and goblins, dragons and unicorns. The hungry deceased are beneath the earth; devils fly at a height of only one hundred feet (it is said the great gates of Peking are just ninety-nine feet high). The partition between the living and the dead, the natural and the supernatural is as thin as the ash of incinerated counterfeit dollar notes, and the big curve in the Great Wall was caused, when it was being built, by a dragon that fell asleep against it, unnoticed during a workers' lunch break.

The ghosts of Chinese fiction hardly seem to belong on "the other side," for they are frequently robust creatures by Western standards, pretty girls (with a fox or two hidden among their ancestors) who marry, quarrel with their mothers-in-law, make their husbands rich, bear them bouncing boys (in one famous case, twins), before they finally fade out somewhat disconcertingly over a pile of rotten bones in some deserted ruin. Chinese ghosts have not only been laid, however, but bought and sold, cheated, bullied, and even killed. The Communists have published a slim anthology of traditional and modern tales called *Stories of Not Fearing Ghosts* which puts the spook into his miserable place. "Actually, we ghosts are afraid of men," one of them sighs, while another is scared silly by a scholar who somewhat unfairly haunts him back. "To stamp out the fear of ghosts," said a Communist Party newspaper in a review of this book, "is the serious fighting task of every revolutionary."

It is a peculiarity of Chinese literature that since ghosts, ogres, and marvels are all around us, even a straightforward, realistic novel may suddenly introduce a supernatural figure. The sociological *Dream of the Red Chamber* has its Taoist spirits; *The Scholars* has walking dead and a dreadful ghost bear on a lonely mountain path. In the *Romance of the Three Kingdoms*, armies are put to flight by phantom cavalry, and in great detective stories like those of the Magistrate Pao or Judge Dee the hero most unfairly solves a number of his cases by literally dreaming up the solution or learning it by ghostly means, and no disgusted Chinese reader accuses him of cheating.

The Communists urge the masses to treat such menaces as imperialism, revisionism, the Tito clique, and bourgeois and landlord elements at home as so many insubstantial ghosts that should be boldly outfaced. But they are on delicate ground here, because they may easily discredit the bogies they have themselves raised in order to persuade the millions to close ranks behind them: for the more discerning Chinese knows that believing is seeing, that it takes two to make an effective ghost—the ghost himself and his credulous viewer. A story that may be fifteen hundred years old makes this point neatly: One day a rat in the dress of a high official came out of the wall to tell the Prince of

Chungshan that he would die on a certain day. But the prince made no reply. Early on the day in question, the rat appeared again in formal costume and said quite distinctly: "You will die at noon." The prince again said nothing, and the rat went rather slowly back into its hole. In the next few hours he returned several times to repeat his warning, but the prince ignored him. Finally, at noon, the rat came out and shrieked: "If you will not respond, what can I say?"—and fell down dead. Its clothes vanished, and it turned out to be an ordinary rat, just like any other.

The Chinese have a bold, familiar way with their naturalistic gods, ghosts, and ancestors, treating them as beings full of human failings with whom it is always possible to arrange a little sharp business. Since the Kitchen God reports to heaven every New Year on the behavior of the family, the less scrupulous will at this time burn quantities of paper money to bribe him to speak fair of them to the Jade Emperor, and have even been known to fuddle him by rubbing opium, rice wine, or neat cognac on his lips. "Money can move even the gods," say the Chinese, who do not pray for salvation but for solid bank accounts or more children. The living will strike bargains with the dead, promising to sacrifice fat ducks to them if they vouchsafe a lucky number from the other world, and then shaking dice at the graveside to see what comes up. Only Buddhism in China promised any sort of eternal bliss, and this did not deflect the practical peasant from thinking in terms of cash down rather than credit in the hereafter. Christians who feel themselves comfortably aloof from all this Oriental haggling with heaven should nevertheless consider the canny fifth verse of the Second Paraphrase on Genesis, so dear to Scottish churchmen:

> Such blessings from Thy gracious Hand
> Our humble prayers implore.
> And Thou shalt be our chosen God
> and Portion evermore.

(And it is still a deal: the Scots remain Christian to this day.)

Chinese worldliness about the other world is well brought out in the sixteenth-century novel *Journey to the West*, translated by the late Arthur Waley as *Monkey*. This has fairly been called the Chinese *Pilgrim's Progress*, and is based upon the holy journey that the monk Hsüan Tsang made to India in the seventh century to bring the teachings of Buddha to China. But it is hardly one for the Victorian Sunday bookshelf. Monkey is a celestial rebel against meaningless rules and regulations, hypocrisy and pious humbug, who falls from grace after eating the Jade Emperor's Peaches of Immortality and drinking the Elixir of Life in an absurd bureaucratic heaven that simply mirrors misgovernment in this world. To work out his penance, he is confined to earth, where he accompanies the devout monk Tripitaka on his pilgrimage to the Holy Mountain of Buddha in India. He is joined in his role as escort and disciple by Pigsy, the former Marshal of Heaven, who has been changed into a pig after getting drunk and making hay with the Moon Goddess.

The party reaches its destination after a number of boisterous adventures that spare no blushes, but there is up to this point an unmistakable moral overtone in the devotion of Tripitaka, and also in Monkey's conscience—the steel band around his head that Tripitaka can tighten excruciatingly whenever the Simian "Sage equal to Heaven" starts to misbehave. We now climb the holy mountain and arrive at the sacred precinct, and in a reverential passage it is related how the Lord Buddha "opened the Mouth of Compassion and gave vent to the Mercy of his Heart." He then instructs his disciples to present the Chinese monk with scriptures from the Buddhist canon, so that they will be a boon forever in the benighted East. Once alone with the pilgrims in the treasury, however, Buddha's followers Ananda and Kasyapa unsuccessfully try to cadge a tip from the poor monk before handing over the texts, and after they have traveled some distance on their homeward journey, the hapless pilgrims discover that these pinchpenny disciples have taken their revenge by fobbing him off with rolls of blank paper.

They return to the sanctuary and complain, whereupon the Blessed One on his Lotus Throne retorts: "I quite expected those two would ask for their commission. As a matter of fact, scriptures should not be given on too easy terms or received gratis. On one occasion some of my monks went down the mountain with some scriptures and let Chao, the Man of Substance, read them aloud. The result was that all the live members of his household were protected from all calamity and the dead were saved from perdition. For this they only charged gold to the weight of three pecks, and three pints of rice. I told them they had sold far too cheap . . ." In the end, Tripitaka gets his 5,048 scrolls (although not before he has given up his begging bowl as a *douceur*). But it is hard to imagine an irreverently reverent Western work in which God Almighty reads Moses a lecture on the propriety of paying a fair commission before handing him the tablets inscribed with the Ten Commandments.

When Chinese pay lip service to a religion, it is often because they are afraid to err through omission. At New Year, Ah Fu and four other amahs hire a taxi first thing in the morning and then do a lightning tour of every temple in Singapore they can possibly visit before lunch, paying a few dollars for incense oil and praying for a moment or two while the cabby keeps his engine running. They are not to be caught out. It is considered perfectly legitimate for a Chinese, to make sure that he is not forgetting any deity, to pray to a piece of paper on which has been written: "All the Gods."

It is this admirable impartiality that produces the Chinese macedoine of faiths in which Confucius becomes a bodhisattva, and the Buddhists and Taoists borrow each others' saints, although they are rival confessions. The Chinese feel that in a balanced world no creed should have a monopoly, for what would happen if everyone were a good Buddhist, killed no life, ate no meat, and went into a monastery, they ask. And surely in terrible times the world needs all the schools of ethics and all the possible forms of heavenly intercession that it can summon?

Furthermore, it is inadvisable to be on the side of any particular set of angels if you end up by having to share the point of a moral needle with them. There were at least "three ways to one goal," the Chinese said: Confucianism, Taoism, Buddhism.

Religious persecution was nevertheless not unknown. The Confucian mandarins regarded Buddhism as heretical, for it advocated a celibacy that offended the principle of filial piety, and it denied a man's debts to his ancestors by preaching that his personal karms was the key to his destiny. In the ninth century, the emperor struck at all foreign faiths, and in 1511 an anti-heresy law was passed which permitted the repression of any non-Confucian movement but was specifically directed against the Buddhists. These were pulled threads, however, on a broad tapestry of tolerance. Scholars had to be Confucians, but they might dabble in anything they liked on the side, provided it had no political nuisance value. Emperors welcomed the champions of new creeds, sometimes pitting one against the other in philosophical argument to see which was the more convincing. In A.D. 635, while the Moslems were intent upon showing their piety by peremptorily putting those that ventured to disagree with them to the sword, the ruling T'ang emperor issued this decree:

"The Way has more than one name. There is more than one Sage. Doctrines vary in different lands, but their benefits reach all mankind. A man of great virtue has brought books and images from afar to present them in our capital. After examining his doctrines, we find them profound and pacific. This religion does good to all men. Let it be preached freely in the empire." It is believed that the "man of virtue" was named Reuben. The doctrine he brought for the first time to China was certainly Christianity.

Christian churches of the Nestorian sect were built in every prefecture, and meanwhile Jews, Moslem Arabs, Zoroastrian Persians, and Manichaeans from the Middle East were free to practice their religions. In China today there is still a strong minority of many million Moslems, and near Kaifeng on the Yellow River may be seen the ancient tablets of the last Jewish synagogue. Nestorianism died out, but from the sixteenth century onward Jesuits were welcomed in Peking. The last Ming empress, it is claimed, was converted to Christianity before she died, and her son was baptized Constantine. Although the Roman Catholics were full of righteous indignation about the fetters that continued to hamper free missionary work in the rest of China, they were on ridiculously weak ground. For this was the sorry period in which the Catholics were butchering the Protestants of the Netherlands, the Huguenots were being tortured by the thousands in France, and the Holy Office was busy burning heretics from Granada to Goa.

To the literate Chinese, gods were only for ignorant peasants. As a prominent neo-Confucian had laid down: "There is no man in the sky judging sin." Religion was the opiate of the "stupid people." For the rest, there was no personal salvation or, come to that, damnation. The scholar therefore appreciated only the ethics of Christianity and otherwise regarded the Jesuits as clever technicians. At the popular level, the Taoists were perfectly ready to take Christ to their capacious cosmological bosom—along with the Dragon King of the Sea and the Pole Star and other celestials. This no missionary could countenance, of course. For him China must be divided into Christians and heathens. But the difficulty was that the Chinese simply had no word for "heathen," for religions had rubbed along well enough together in the Middle Kingdom on the strict understanding that Confucianism was the only official creed. Nevertheless, it gradually became clear to the slightly astonished mandarins that these Christians were not prepared to be stitched into the patchwork quilt made up of the rest, but were challenging Confucian doctrine itself with a rival set of rules of their own.

This was heresy. A Chinese who became a Christian could no longer be regarded as Chinese. Missionary enterprise was hampered, then forbidden, then permitted again. The "Christian"

fanatics of the Taiping rebellion perilously compromised the
faith by smiting scholars in the name of Jesus, and when it was
the turn of the missionaries to be manhandled and murdered by
other Chinese mobs, the Church did not earn sympathy in Peking,
but even greater distrust, for it seemed that the Western powers
always made these excesses against their men of God the pretext
for seizing more concessions in China. The missionaries could
not win either way. After the revolution in 1911, Christianity
enjoyed a certain vogue, for it was confused in the muddled
minds of eager Chinese republicans with liberty and democracy.
But disillusion soon followed. The frightful toll of World War I
persuaded Oriental onlookers that a gentle cult productive of
so much mass murder held no salvation for them, and the atroc-
ities of World War II confirmed the initital impression. The
trouble with Christianity, it appeared, was the Christians. And
it was therefore struck off the list of official solutions.

Christianity had already, in fact, missed its one, bizarre chance
in China. In 1837 an unsuccessful Hakka scholar, who had a
chip on his shoulder about the way civil-service candidates from
North China were always given preference over those from the
south, began to see visions. He was inspired by Chinese translations of the Holy Gospel, prepared in his spare time by a contemporary Protestant priest of Prussian extraction whose main
occupation was acting as interpreter to a prestigious British
enterprise engaged in opium smuggling. Since these translations
were incomplete, the vision of Hung Hsiu-ch'üan was somewhat
distorted, but he founded a Society of Worshippers of God, based
on Christian stories, and when the Manchus tried to suppress his
movement he announced the accession of the Great Peaceful
Heavenly Dynasty in 1851, and proclaimed himself Heavenly
King. Mr. Hung—schoolmaster and witch doctor—then set out to
destroy the Manchu usurpers and within nine years controlled
half of China from his captured capital of Nanking, supported
by a disgraceful percentage of deserters among the Imperial

troops and by his own vast mass of followers, many of whose captains were admirable men and soldiers.

His revolt, although inspired by anti-Manchu sentiment, was above all a religious revival. The Taiping (Great Peace) movement distributed its bible free, believed in the one Christian deity, preached the Ten Commandments, and was faithful to the un-Chinese traditions of its Middle Eastern confession by being utterly intolerant of other beliefs. Its Heavenly Leader was an absolute monarch, an inspired prophet who arbitrated when orthodoxy was challenged and whose word was law. He called himself "Younger Brother of Jesus," and although his enemies made much of this seemingly blasphemous title, he did not mean it to signify more than fraternity in Christ. But to narrower Christians his unorthodox assertions that the Holy Ghost entered into his living followers and that the other members of the Trinity had wives were enough to condemn him. In particular, they were enough to discredit him with his Protestant co-religionist and very Christian contemporary, that eminent and devout Victorian, General Charles George Gordon.

Gordon was a man of a rectitude hardly imaginable outside the gray confines of the nineteenth century. Lent to the Manchu government by the British to help put down the dangerous conspiracy of men whose sin was, roughly speaking, that they believed in the same God as himself, he strode fearless and unarmed into battle as Commander of the Ever Victorious Army (and defender of the nonexistent Manchu faith). At first he refused any salary for his services, and later would accept only £1,200 a year. Stiff, single-minded, repelled by what he considered the blasphemous curlicues of Taiping Christianity, Gordon taught the Chinese that Western barbarians could be men of principle and honor, and proved of inestimable value to his heathen masters in the northern capital.

In the course of the great Taiping rebellion, which was only crushed in 1864, the exotic "Christians" routed the Manchu trash wherever they met it, took Nanking and all the cities along the

Yangtze River, and created panic in Peking. Burning Buddhist and Taoist temples, and substituting Christ for Confucius as they went along, they could almost certainly have overrun the whole country had they made up their minds to do so. Six hundred cities and towns were destroyed in the course of their crusade, and an empire that had a population of 400 million in 1850 was down to 267 million by 1862, it is said. A brilliant general, a simple, brave, blinkered sort of a Christian such as they bred in those days, Gordon finally crushed the remnants of the Taiping movement, presented himself at court in the full regalia of a top-flight mandarin, and then unobtrusively left China without enrichment. He had been greatly assisted by the French and the British, who had supported the Manchus against the Taiping uprising in the belief that Peking could in this way be persuaded to open up the country to the missionaries and the merchants of the West.

It is to be remarked that, as the Manchus were pagan and corrupt, the Taiping armies were, in their fashion, Christian and continent. They never pilfered or ravaged as they advanced, they abolished opium smoking and foot binding wherever they conquered, they put women and taxes on a more equal and fairer footing. But they were in turn crucified by the bigoted missionaries, by the heathen Manchus, and by the impeccable Charles George Gordon. For the West, this was the mercy killing of a horrifying mutant. For many Chinese, the perspective was different, however. The Western Christians had allied themselves with usurpers to crush the only movement that might have given China a new impetus toward both morality and modernization. The Chinese had taken Christianity and, in the best traditions of their ragbag religiosity, had transformed it into a faith peculiarly their own. But in the fog of complete incomprehension that lay between the dogma of the West and the harlotry of the East, barbarian backed barbarian, and so brother killed brother. Missionaries mumbled on in China for another century, but the great fight was all over, and no one to this day knows what Christ thought of it.

The Chinese dragon therefore continued to sleep, until awakened by the shaking of others. Today the Communists frown upon reasonless, animistic superstition, tolerate in the best traditions two to three million Catholics in China, who "lead a proper spiritual life" without the blessing of Rome, and patronize a much bigger Buddhist movement led by men who understand they must "first bear their socialist responsibilities and fulfill their patriotic obligations" before indulging in the luxury of religion. The foreign observer may sift seeds of counterrevolution here, but the Chinese remember that subsidiary religions were only tolerated in the past provided they did not represent some sort of ideological danger to the regime. They see no change when Mao castigates the Christians, but only when the harmless Kitchen God comes under fire—instead of over the stove, where he belongs.

16

The Business End

Expecting no rewards hereafter, the Chinese are intensely practical, and it is typical of them that whereas Jesus preached universal love as the manifestation of God, their own Mo Tzu prescribed it as a compulsory social exercise. Emotional love should be abolished, he implied, but it should be drummed into people that as a mental discipline love was beneficial, useful, and to their own advantage—like observing the highway code. Men should be made to love one another as a matter of sound policy, and coerced into doing so when necessary "with punishments and fines."

In a sense, the Chinese have responded to Mo Tzu's urgings, for they practice a deliberate, limited charity dictated by the enlightened self-interest that characterizes most of their actions, rather in the spirit in which state treats with state. The rich merchants of the Sung dynasty looked upon philanthropy as a form of moral taxation that would win them security from revolt, and Marco Polo records how they gave generously to the poor, the orphaned, and the aged, and in freezing weather would "go round from door to door to find out which families are worst off, take note of their distress, and, when night falls, push through the cracks in their doors some scrap of gold or silver, or else cash coins or notes. So that when the people open their doors in the morning, they find these presents which seem to them to have dropped from Heaven."

Buddhism taught that men gained merit hereafter if they performed good acts, but native Chinese philosophy is full of the dispassionate calculations of a people who do not fear damnation in hell so much as discord on earth, not the wages of sin but of solecism. Mencius admonished one king for thinking only of profit when he should have been practicing benevolence and righteousness—not, however, because these would win the approval of God, but because the profit motive led to such dangerous situations on earth. Confucius himself had exhorted his disciples to act correctly, for since only heaven bestowed long life and riches, their own greed would get them nowhere. And Hsün Tzu adds: "A man who pays undue attention to material things is always anxious in his heart, and when the heart is afraid, the mouth may be filled with delicious food but will not taste it, the body may be clad in warm garments and rest upon a fine mat but it will feel no comfort." A man of moral principles, on the other hand, will be content even if he has only simple rice, coarse clothing, and hemp sandals. It is practical to be proper, therefore, and the Chinese appreciate the story about the greedy monkey that could not get its closed fist out of the jar because it had grabbed too many nuts. During the great Cultural Revolution of 1966, the Communists declared that there was no such thing as a "good" bourgeois. If a mandarin treated the peasants kindly, he only did so to keep them quiet. Many Chinese would agree.

On the other side of this coin, however, lies the belief of most Chinese that the end justifies the means, and their keen sense of advantage sometimes produces effects that may seem bafflingly contradictory. The great strategist Wu Ch'i, born one hundred years before Alexander the Great, murdered his wife to prove to the Duke of Lu that he was not a security risk and could be safely appointed commander-in-chief of an army that was about to attack her native state. His outstanding military career began that day. On the other hand, he undoubtedly approved of the exceptional clemency that Chinese kings and commanders some-

times showed to the most able officers among their prisoners—
for these could then be suborned and used against future enemies.
He was not prompted by brutal instincts but by accurate calculations. In the *Romance of the Three Kingdoms,* the Han pretender
launches a vengeful campaign against the state of Wu, whose
ruler has killed his sworn brother-in-arms. He is defeated and
himself dies. Serves him right, say most Chinese. His ruthless
adviser Chu-ko Liang had told him he had no business to be
wasting his time fighting Wu when his plain interest lay in con-
centrating his forces against the usurper Ts'ao Ts'ao to wrest
from him the control of the empire. The dead prince's desire for
revenge is weighed against Chu-ko Liang's cold judgment and is
found to have been praiseworthy but sinfully counterproductive.

At the end of 1936, Chiang Kai-shek was planning still another
drive to exterminate Mao Tse-tung and his Communist forces,
then established in the fastnesses of Yenan in North China. But
while visiting the wavering Nationalist troops that were to be deployed against them, Chiang was made prisoner by mutineers
and soon found himself being given an ultimatum personally by
the Communist leader, Chou En-lai. The Communists offered to
recognize Chiang as head of state and as generalissimo of their
forces as well as his own, if he formed a united front with them
to fight against the Japanese. The alternative was death.

But the Communists had no desire whatever to kill this archenemy who had fallen into their clutches, although, nine years
before, he had ordered their slaughter in Shanghai, and Chou
En-lai had only just escaped with his life himself. So when he
agreed to their terms they immediately released him with full
honors. The civil war was over for the time being, and no Chu-ko
Liang could complain of fruitless fratricide while the Japanese
enemy stood at the gate. There was more to it than this, however.
For both sides were thinking many moves ahead. Chiang Kai-shek
felt that with the Communists "pacified" he could make a stand
against Tokyo that would rally to his rather discredited Kuomintang the full support of the anti-Communist Western democra-

cies, so that the Japanese would be overwhelmed and he could afterward cut the throats of the Communists at his leisure. Mao, on the other hand, foresaw that the Japanese would knock out the conventional forces of Chiang and that meanwhile he would strengthen his own hold over the vast Chinese countryside, which the enemy could not hope to occupy and control in the face of his small but expanding guerrilla armies.

The West was astounded when the Chinese Communists invaded India in 1962, apparently throwing away all their good will in Asia, and then withdrew. Only afterward did it dawn slowly on the world just what China had achieved with one swift stroke. She had discredited India as the rival, neutralist leader of Asia, for New Delhi had at once been compelled to call upon the Western powers for help. She had won the friendship of President Ayub Khan, and so twisted a chisel in the anti-Communist Southeast Asia Treaty Organization, to which Pakistan belonged. And she had taught a frightened continent not to backchat the Chinese behemoth.

For the average Chinese the conundrum that worries the delicate conscience of the Western democrat is no conundrum at all: which is more dangerous to democracy: to allow a Communist Party to operate, knowing it is dedicated to the overthrow of the democratic state once it achieves power or to betray democratic principle yourself by banning it? Ban it, or subvert it, or emasculate it by throwing all its ablest leaders into jail, say the Chinese Nationalists. The object of the game is not the game but checkmate.

Pragmatism colors most aspects of Chinese character, just as the same candle flame will be reflected in all facets of a diamond. The Japanese have almost as big a reputation for cruelty as have young children, yet during World War II they in turn employed Koreans (in whose sadistic ferocity, it seems, even greater confidence may be placed) for their more grotesque feats of torture. The Chinese also have an unenviable record of vile treatment meted out to Westerners during the past hundred years. Much has been made of the vandalism of Lord Elgin for burning down the Imperial Summer Palace outside Peking in 1860, but it is often forgotten that this was a reprisal for the unforgivable murder of envoys from his force who were first sent to the Chinese capital under a white flag. The envoys were bound with thin ropes that were wetted to make them tighten, and thrown down in an open courtyard. If they spoke or cried out in their torment, they were stamped on, and if they begged for food, their mouths were filled with ordure. The cords slowly cut into the flesh, as day followed ghastly day, until gangrene set in; and of the thirty-eight unfortunate men, more than half died and were left to rot among the living.

In 1900 the Boxers set houses on fire and forced their victims into the flames at bayonet point, and on occasion seized and bound young women, soaked them in petrol, and put a match to them. At Tientsin they cut the breasts off European wives and pushed them out on to the city wall, where they were left until they died. At Taiyuan an eyewitness later described how soldiers helped a Chinese executioner to hack off the heads of missionaries in front of their womenfolk and children, and then to decapitate the wives and children after them, forty-five dying in all. However, it should be noted that while the soldiers botched this terrible job through inexperience, the executioner killed each victim cleanly and mercifully, with one blow. Moreover, the soldiers had been called in to help only because the governor wanted the task done quickly. He was out to please his empress, not to gloat over foreigners, who in fact comported themselves with faultless courage.

For to the Chinese even *Schrecklichkeit* is often simply the solution on the slide rule. The Boxers were for the most part a bloodthirsty hooligan rabble, and man in the mob becomes a many-headed monster in any continent, but the individual Chinese is callous rather than cruel. When he sets out to hurt, he does so in order to achieve his object by the most efficient available means, but he takes no pleasure in it. The whole tradition of

Chinese torture has been largely inspired by a principle of criminal law that was originally conceived to be just: that a man should not be condemned until he had confessed.

Chinese thugs appear to show a certain cold-blooded genius for inflicting pain, and Lu Hsün in his essays quotes from a news item of the thirties describing this recipe for ransom, employed by bandits who had kidnapped a father and son: "Cloth strips, pasted over their backs, were painted with unboiled varnish. When this had dried a little, the cloth was pulled off, bringing the men's skin with it . . ." But bandits are, after all, bandits. It does no harm to remember that when a number of monks were caught stealing royal treasure worth £100,000 that was stored in Westminster Abbey in 1303, their secular accomplice was first hanged and then flayed, and his skin was subsequently nailed to its great doors. It is only some two hundred years, in fact, since the rusty nails were pulled out and the last loathsome vestiges of generations of smashed humanity, pinned to them for acts of sacrilege, disappeared from those blessed portals. The Chinese approach to torture is not eager but clinical as a rule. Set grim examples, the pundits advise: "Kill the chicken to show the monkey"; give the more intelligent a lesson that will teach them to conform, and so spare them punishment. The Chinese have little love for lost causes, and little sympathy for the fallen, and they are ready to be disagreeably tough in a tough world. But they are not fierce just for the fun of it.

Nor are the Chinese consciously cruel to animals, although they are often insensitive and ungentle and even jealous of them. Lu Hsün describes the usual black bear in a small traveling circus in China as "so starved and thin it barely has enough strength to move. Half dead and alive as it is, its nose has still to be pierced with an iron ring to which a rope is attached, and by this it is dragged along to do its tricks. While the bear is still alive and performing, we can see it is so shriveled that it no longer looks like a bear. Indeed, in some places it is called a 'dog-bear,' showing the utter *contempt* in which it is held."

At the other end of the spectrum are Ah Fu and Ah Keng, the wash-amah, who constantly assault the air with affectionate cries for our three dogs and two cats, fill them up with Cantonese food (they are far too fond of them to foist some European muck on to them), and tend them with admirable devotion when they are sick. Ah Fu has even taught Rusty (Lus-teee!) to eat vitamin pills off a saucer as if they were dog biscuits, and she is the only person alive who can hold a cat gently by its four feet and somehow pour medicine into its mouth from a teaspoon at the same time, singlehanded. The whole household of six Chinese bends upon me the same regard of unbearable reproach if I dare to give Banner a beating for siting his latrines badly. Ping has lovingly nursed back to woolly health a stinking, raw-skinned mongrel whose very presence I could hardly bear, and fed daily for a month a whining, thin-tempered dog in the deserted garden next door that an American subtenant had abandoned on departure.

Chinese, like Europeans, come callous and kind. But basically their approach to animals is far more matter-of-fact than ours. The miserably poor have not been able to allow themselves the luxury of showering expensive affection on animals, and their envy of the rich and privileged often extends to their well-covered, coiffed, and pomaded pets. A passage that creaks with class war in the Chinese socialist play *Sunrise* describes how a penniless bank clerk with a hungry family at home pleads vainly for his job and then kills his children and himself, while a Westernized fop complains bitterly that he cannot get anything fit for his American dog to eat now that he is back in Shanghai— and this is quite a problem, because it must have four pounds of meat a day. People whose ancestors have sometimes starved by the million, or eaten roots or grubs or each other, find themselves involved in an unequal struggle for existence in a world of fat dogs and sleek horses whose upkeep may cost enough money to feed several of their families. And they tend to resent it. Ideological passions may therefore be roused against the four-footed.

Many thousands of ragged Shanghai coolies, who vainly wished the white man would at least treat them like dogs, developed a deep sense of resentment toward his aristocratic fox terrier as well as himself when he refused to do so.

But not all dogs are aristocrats or foreigners. Like humans, the vast majority of those in China were poor, underfed, and Chinese. A Chinese has little sense of duty toward the man next door, and he has no feelings about the dog next door either. But his own watchdog—a good, trusted worker that earns his keep—he will treat with care and kindness, and rank him second only to his invaluable farmhand, the water buffalo. The Chinese tend to honor the animals by behaving toward them much as they behave toward humans, treating them as family or strangers, friends or parasites, workers or wasters. And just as Ah Fu, being our cook, wants me to be fat so that she will gain face, so she wants Polly ("Porreeee!") to be fat, too. There is always a purposefulness about the Chinese attitude toward anything, and they domesticated the pig before the dog, for of course no part of the pig goes to waste.

It is their practical instinct that persuades the Chinese to build their honeycombs of mutual aid against adversity, but it also dictates that these cell structures of family and clan and guild and group shall be a defense against disaster, not a form of social insurance that justifies loafing. The power of the club is the power of its most influential and ambitious member, and the Chinese therefore often emerge from their communal background as individualists of initiative, enterprise, and boundless energy. Outside their honeycombs they have little feeling for teamwork and will contend against each other within the same ministry or corporation almost as fiercely as army, navy, air force, and marine officers are said to fight each other within the Pentagon. They are not afraid of competition, and admire the tycoon who makes a fortune "out of his empty hand" as a real man. They have to be broken to the Western spirit of the pack (or flock) before they can take an interest in football, rugby, bridge, or passing an orange from chin to chin. They instinctively prefer badminton, boxing, mah-jongg, chess, and musical chairs. Exasperated that he could not get them to conform and cooperate within a new national society, Sun Yat-sen described his own people as "a heap of sand." He was dealing with the Jews of Asia, a race whose struggle for survival across the centuries had produced a prominent vein of compulsive commercialism.

However, the synagogue and not the pawnshop is the focal point of a Jewish community, and Chinese civilization was not built upon a chamber of commerce. Imperial society was divided into five classes—scholar, farmer, craftsman, merchant, soldier— in that order, and it is only in modern overseas communities that the merchant has achieved a better rating. His relationship to the scholar was forcefully described by the four-character phrase: "Fragrant book—stinking copper," and for a great beauty to marry a businessman was considered the very definition of a damned shame. Too often in history, nonetheless, the tael wags the dog, and there is even a legend that the father of the First Emperor himself made a fortune by "buying things up when they were cheap and selling them when they became dear," which means that Imperial China may have been founded by the son of a commercial speculator. Certainly from earliest times the Chinese have had a keen, sophisticated nose for finance and business, and an attitude toward riches as the source of fame and power expressed in the phrase: "With money, a dragon; without money, a worm."

Nearly two hundred years before Christ cast the money-changers out of the Temple, rich merchants in China were manipulating the rice market to such a disastrous degree that the emperor, believing they were taking advantage of a shortage of coin, authorized private mints. In almost no time at all, an aristocrat who found a copper mine on his land had made himself "richer than the emperor," and before the ruler had learned to show a little more healthy respect for the unscrupulous business acumen of his subjects, there was so much cash on the market that it was hardly worth anything. Forty years later, it was the powerful magnates who, having cornered the salt and iron industries, were to be described as "richer than princes," and meanwhile the continued counterfeiting of bathtub coinage on a grand scale after minting had been prohibited was still causing catastrophic fluctuations in prices. The Emperor Han Wu-ti tried to remedy the situation created by all this boodle-faking by inventing the first treasury notes, which were cut out of the skin of a rare white stag and theoretically could not be imitated. The pieces of skin were each sold for 400,000 copper cash, and in this way white-stag currency—a foot square, fringed, and stenciled—went into circulation backed by a treasury reserve. Han Wu-ti also introduced a new pewter coin, but this the counterfeiters copied as fast as they had forged the old copper ones, at the same time multiplying in number so rapidly themselves that coining soon became a major cottage industry.

The officials finally beat the forgers by introducing coins worth no more than the value of the metal, the salt and iron profiteers were curbed by the establishment of a government monopoly, and in 110 b.c. an outstanding if controversial economist stabilized prices by organizing a government department to stockpile when produce was abundant and to sell in times of shortage. By the time the Saxons were nailing the devaluated skins of flayed Vikings to the church doors of East Anglia, the Chinese were already beginning to use paper currency widely. The early notes were really private receipts for cash deposits and were known as "flying money," but by the thirteenth century, treasury notes printed with government serial numbers and backed by silver or gold were in free circulation.

It was in this period that the merchants began to put on airs, to ape the benevolent and ponderous mien of scholars, to dress sumptuously and behave with academic decorum. There was indeed a certain magnificence about Chinese foreign commerce, for from the pre-Christian era to the nineteenth century the Middle Kingdom sold unique and celebrated manufactures to the

outside world: iron tools to Rome, silk to Byzantium, porcelain to
an admiring Europe, and cotton of unrivaled quality to the in-
dustrialized modern West. In return, however, the Chinese only
deigned to buy from the barbarians luxuries and curiosities from
the inventories of Masefield—like apes and ivory, precious stones
and feathers (peacock).

The mandarins did not tolerate this self-promotion from the
commercial ranks. But while their scholars may have been disdainful of merchants, the Chinese have never been disdainful of
money, and in this they are closer to the Americans than to the
more elderly British, with their furtive wallet manners and their
finicky belief that cash is a dirty word. Nor do they imitate the
Western custom of giving useless objects to one another on prescribed occasions; they give naked dollars, concealed at best by
no more than the fig leaf of the "Hung pao," the red envelope for
good luck in which presents of money are normally offered.
Nothing was commoner in Imperial China than for people to
press upon one another a few ingots or broken pieces of silver,
whereas the European would send some unwanted knickknack
for the mantelpiece, or grapes, telegrams of good will, a bouquet
of roses, or a wreath of lilies. To the Christian, there is something
peculiarly odious about the sound of thirty pieces of silver, so
that after two thousand years the neat slither of debased nickel-
alloy coins of even size still affronts the ears when they are paid
out to others. But the Chinese are heirs to no such tradition.

Splendid bas-reliefs on tombs in North China, erected by devout sons for their fathers when Marcus Aurelius was in the
cradle, are decorated with archaeologically fascinating inscrip-
tions that seem to bring down to us the sweet breath of an age
of noble simplicity. But translated they may read: "Made by the
sculptor Li Ti-mao at the cost of 150,000 pieces of silver (Sun
Tung made the lions for 40,000 cash)." When in 1840 the commissioner of Canton commands that a corps of vigilantes be formed
to meet the menace of an approaching British fleet, he does not
prate of king and country but rouses his compatriots with a price

list: $20,000 for a "74" of the line captured (with $100 knocked off for every gun less), $5,000 for a naval commander taken alive (one-third of this sum if taken dead), $100 for white ratings, $20 for Asian ratings. As a further incentive, it is understood that the usual ten percent for the officials paying out the rewards would not be deducted. Recompense is, in fact, to be tax free. In 1860, similar prizes are offered for white and colored British troops, but by the Boxer rebellion of 1900, the market slumps to $50 for a white male, $40 for a white female, and $30 for a child (only heads need be produced in evidence). It is nevertheless reliably recorded that on one occasion no fewer than eleven Chinese were killed in a struggle for the possession of one Russian corpse.

Neither do the Chinese have our hypocritical approach to matters of usury, moneylending, and pawnbroking, for it is assumed that the client is smart enough to service his debt and still earn a well-cushioned profit. High rates of interest have always been the rule, and nearly one thousand years ago merchants at Zaitoun were paying up to half the value of their cargo in freight charges and duties, according to Marco Polo, but still made millions. The Chinese thought it perfectly normal to charge one percent a day on capital loaned, and rates of interest ranged from twenty percent to as much as fifty percent a month (where the collateral was the harvest). Even today, a man may pay between ten percent and eighteen percent a month to a reputable moneylender. And this is regarded as fair. For a Chinese appears to believe that money should breed about as fast as he does. Give him goods on three months' credit and he will immediately resell them on one month's credit, or even peddle them at a loss for hard cash, and so wind up with at least two clear months in which to play with your money—and if a man has $10,000 in hand like this and still he cannot make a quick million, he must be either a moron or a European. Naturally a creditor demands his percentage; he would be a fool if he did not. Even stars on the United States flag accumulate interest, if at a low rate.

Prices and discounts are never fixtures, but movables. In 1960,

I advertised an old car that Ping had been driving, and the first person who called was a Mr. Wang. "My name's Wang," he said sharply, and then added all in one breath "I-see-you-are-offering-a-Fiat-for-eight-hundred-dollars-how-much-do-you-want-for-it?" I thought this over carefully, did a little mental arithmetic, and finally replied: "Eight hundred dollars." "Eight hundred dollars?" he echoed incredulously. "What color is it?" "Green," I replied. "Oh, well," he commented sadly, and hung up.

How straight are the Chinese? "If you can't cheat, you're no merchant," says the fastidious scholar. But in the ninth century Arab traders to South China ports praised their scrupulous honesty, and a thousand years later skeptical Caucasians were grudgingly admitting: "A Chinaman's word is his bond." Until the fine, clean-living, upright Victorians introduced him to the thirty-five articles in small print that automatically presupposed that the party of the second part was a rascal and a swindler and a thief, the devious Shanghainese did not bother about written contracts but simply shook hands on a deal, and then kept it—why waste money on idle lawyers? In the old crafts, the merchants have always shown a dignified indifference to cheeseparing and cheating. A Chinese silk dealer will take a match and burn a sample to nothing to prove the quality of his goods, Carl Crow notes, and silversmiths will buy back even battered pieces at only a slightly reduced price, if they are stamped with their own chop. They are solicitous of the good will and repute of their trades.

Not all feel the same concern, however. In the Sung dynasty, soldiers and workers ordered to dig the mud out of silted-up canals made their mad money by demanding bribes from rich householders, and dumping the evil-smelling sediment around their houses if they refused to pay. It was perhaps this precedent that recently persuaded a Chinese landowner in Singapore to try to oust his tenants by churning their entire garden into a sea of mud with an excavator, and then running a bulldozer around their marooned house until they capitulated. (This piece of pragmatism cost him the equivalent of US $25,000 in compensation.) In the days of Confucius it was forbidden to water beasts before driving them to market, so that peasants would not cheat by making them heavier in this way before selling them. This was evidently a wise precaution, for in the less ordered days of 1962 a severe outbreak of typhoid that killed a number of people in Formosa was traced to watermelons into which peasants had pumped ditchwater to increase their weight.

Singapore food and drug inspectors—often far more finicky than their counterparts in the West—have proudly demonstrated to me the ingenuity of their race by opening up cans of coffee that were ninety-five percent ground maize, bags of grain that were mainly sand, cans of sardines that had been punctured, slimmed down from their nauseatingly potbellied condition, and neatly resealed once the gases of corruption had been let out. The British only drink Indian and Ceylonese tea today because the Chinese, who originally dominated the Western markets, threw away their advantage by juggling with the quality of their consignments. Chinese builders specialize in excellent plasterwork—for it can cover a multitude of sins far more effectively than any metaphorical whitewash—and the false weights of Chinese marketmen are a specialized study that requires much time and application.

The pattern is not unfamiliar: the men at the top in stable businesses with great traditions of probity know that their renown is worth more than freak profits, and so make a necessity out of virtue. But the men on the way up are fighting for financial fingerholds with a whole family roped in behind them. A great body of law bears witness to the esteem in which the West holds the old adage that a fool and his money are soon parted. The Chinese shopkeeper also respects this venerable principle, but further contends that the burden of proving that his victim is not a fool is up to the victim, not to himself. This means that for a European, shopping with an Oriental wife can be an excruciatingly slow and thirsty business, for even a gift horse must be looked carefully in the mouth. The biggest mistake I ever made was to take Ping to help me buy a set of Chinese chess, for there are thirty-two pieces to a set, plus the board and the box, and all had to be counted and checked for redundant, substituted, or missing men, and then minutely examined individually for flaws, cracks, discoloration, and other evidence of sharp practice. The shop assistant took pity on me and gave me a straw and a bottle of rather nasty orange crush, while I congratulated myself on not having started out with Ping to buy a bingo set. The morning wore on, and finally, after much haggling (Ping had found an ink stain on the box), a price was agreed. Ping then asked the assistant to gift wrap a cigarette lighter and a bottle of cologne we had bought next door and, this done, paid for the chess. The set cost five Hong Kong dollars, or about ninety cents. And I am bound to admit that there was in fact nothing wrong with it.

Chinese merchants will splash money on big dinner parties, they will buy jewelry for their concubines, houses for each of their sons, diamonds for their wives, and in these matters they will never be mean. For they are investments that bring returns, and it is known that dollars are like small fish in a fast-flowing river: difficult to catch and not to be thrown back except as bait for something bigger. In Imperial China, merchant apprentices were paid nothing and given no more than their bare keep. But their parents were perfectly content: they were spared the expense of feeding their son and he was meanwhile being taught a trade by a man who obviously knew the value of money. Chinese shopkeepers and restaurateurs are still loath today to pay out good profits on gimmicks and expensive decorations—unless, of course, they give the owner "face." For "face" is not just "image," but the collateral of the speculator, a source of credit and confidence, which in turn open up new vistas of high wire and trapeze for the giddy aerial antics that often constitute the Chinese way of business.

The overseas Chinese merchant is loyal first and foremost to his family and his finances, in the great tradition of the burghers of London and Amsterdam and Novgorod. He is the Chinese at his most pragmatic, but he is only one of the nine dragons. For his doctrine that to grasp is to gain, that power lies in possessing, is counterbalanced by a philosophy which lies deep in the Chinese spirit and which preaches that to grasp is to lose, that power lies in throwing all away.

17

The Unspeakable Way

According to one unconfirmed report, the fabulous Emperor Yao decided that, as he was imperfect himself, he would abdicate the throne and offer it personally to one of two Taoist hermits of exceptional virtue who, he had been told, lived on the same high mountain. Advised that both old gentlemen were fairly cross-grained but that the one who lived higher up the hill was the more amenable of the two, he rode up to the cloud-wrapped cottage of this sage and invited him to become emperor of China.

Without uttering a word, the disgusted recluse strode quickly to a nearby mountain stream and began washing out his ears vigorously. Much offended, Yao left at once and made his way to the simple dwelling of the second hermit, which lay a short distance down the slope, only to find him giving urgent orders to his one rustic servant. "Don't let the calves drink from the stream," he was shouting. "The water has been poisoned by Ch'ao Fu higher up the hill—he has been washing some filth he heard out of his ears." Shortly afterward, the affronted Yao was persuaded to return to his capital without repeating his obscene offer of the throne to any other anchorite.

In theory, every well-read Chinese is a potential schizoid, for the Chinese mind has been dominated by two powerful, contradictory philosophies for nearly twenty-five hundred years. In the West, only the devout Roman Catholic Communists of Italy, perhaps, feel the same tight squeeze on both temples. Confucianism was unashamedly square. It was the custom, in fact, for scholars to adopt a "square walk": a curious gait whereby men of distinction kept the two feet well apart, yet both pointing straight forward, swinging each leg wide in turn as if suffering from a particularly excruciating itch in the crotch. But where Confucianism was the religion of an ordered, carefully articulated society, Taoism was the advocate of anarchy, and if Confucianism produced the square, Taoism bore the beatnik.

It was foolish of the Emperor Yao to offer a post in a man-made administrative machine to a Taoist hermit, for he would be bound to feel that it sullied his ears on two counts. First, he would believe that all ambition, wealth, and worldly glory were contemptible and harmful; second, he would say that man must act entirely in harmony with nature and that all artificial organization, all government, all laws and moral codes were discordant and therefore dangerous. Confucian pratings about education in "goodness" and "duty" simply disturbed the natural course of men and things, the Taoists complained. Sages should shut up and leave well alone: "The swan does not need a daily washing to stay white; the crow does not need a daily inking to stay black." To try to change men's nature was like painting the crow white and the swan black.

Good intentions are a terrible hazard. It was the sages who taught bandits their jobs by forever expounding the cardinal virtues, a brigand explains in one Taoist passage. For a bandit chief must have Insight in order to guess where the valuables are kept in a house, he must have Courage in order to break in first, and a Sense of Duty to be the last of his band to leave. He must have Wisdom; otherwise, he will be rash and get caught. And he must have a Sense of Goodness to divide the loot fairly and so keep the loyalty of his gang. All these qualities he learned from the sages. Had there been no sages, there would have been no bandits. Meddlers are a menace, and so the only good government is one that does not govern: the ruler does nothing, the people are fed but otherwise left in their simple, natural state, without knowledge or ambition. For crooks are a product of social institutions. Civilization, therefore, is the path to perdition.

Everything—earth, heaven, the whole cosmos—must conform to Tao, and Tao is the Way of Nature, which alone obeys the basic principle of the universe. Can it be further defined? Lao Tzu, the semi-legendary founder of Taoism, says: "Tao is vague, impalpable—how vague! How impalpable! Yet within it there is Form. How vague! How impalpable! Yet within it there is Substance. How profound! How obscure! . . ."

This rapidly becomes somewhat trying to the eyes, but "vague," "impalpable," and "obscure" well describe both the origins of Taoism and the writings of its venerable sage. The story goes that Lao Tzu—the "Old Master"—lived at the same time as Confucius and was Keeper of Imperial Archives at the capital. He compiled a work of five thousand words the very title of which is untranslatable, and, this done, flew up into heaven without further preliminaries. But no one really knows who wrote this slim volume, or when, or whether it is genuine or a fake. Taoism emerges as still another gnarled and twisted growth from the original seed of inspiration, like Confucianism and Christianity, but its basis is still best expressed by its principal symbol:

The circle represents the **oneness of a cosmos that is always,** however, in a state of flux. The Taoists do not believe in a rigid universe bolted together by some supernatural mechanic; it grew without trying and without knowing how it grew, spontaneously but in obedience to a basic natural law, much as humans do. Nothing stands still or is fixed, and so there can be no static standards or conventions. Chinese philosophers use the character

"Tao"—a Way of Road along which you progress—to express what in Europe would be a system of immovable moral principles.

The unceasing change in the cosmos is due to the interaction of the two opposite forces, Yin and Yang. Yin is earth, feminine, negative, passive, dark, weak, even, moon. Yang is heaven, male, positive, active, light, strong, odd, sun. Yin contracts and Yang expands, and so the universe "breathes." Yin and Yang do not divide the world into warring forces, but unite it, just as in the Taoist symbol they do not conflict but intertwine, and there is a small spot of Yin in Yang's sector, and of Yang in Yin's. Yin and Yang mean completion in the sense that a coin must have two sides, there can be no good without bad, no left without right, and no heaven without earth.

Pekinologists have sometimes fallen into the trap of concluding that because Mao Tse-tung has come out with some new and horrifying example of Communist intransigence at one moment, and Chou En-lai has spoken soothing words on the same subject the next, there must be a division among Chinese leaders. But this does not necessarily follow at all. Each may well be acting in a complementary role to the other. The West is perfectly accustomed to the civilized principle of political interrogation whereby some harmless bully kicks his hapless prisoner around for an hour or two after midnight while he is standing in a four foot six high cubbyhole with arc lights directed upon him, but then the bully is suddenly replaced by a diabolically disarming character who is all soft speech and cigarettes, dim lights and do-sit-down. This, again, is so much Yin-and-Yang.

From the Great Void, then, comes the natural impulse of the universe, stimulating a flip-flop action between these two opposites, and all automatically move in harmony with the great, developing equation—except for synthetically civilized man. Naturally, the West would say, for thinking man, master of his own destiny, is the one item that is outside the computer. Unnaturally, says the Taoist, for he also is part of the eternal oneness and so one of its components.

Being one with the universe, "though you die, you are not lost," for you are still an indestructible part of the cosmos. Man simply moves on, possibly reappearing in his next existence as "a rat's liver or a beetle's claw," or some ingredient from *Macbeth*, Act Three, Scene One. But there must be no discourteous complaints. Metempsychosis, like marriage, is a lottery. The bronze in the crucible cannot leap up and protest that it does not want to be a plowshare but a sword. So man cannot be so injudicious as to try to insist that in his next role he must again be man. In the *Book of Chuang Tzu*, most stimulating and enchanting of a line of persuasive Taoist works of dubious authenticity, one character says: "If my buttocks were changed into wheels, and my spirit into a horse, well, I would drive. What other carriage would I want?" When his wife died, Chuang Tzu shocked his friends by singing and drumming on a water jar, for "death and life, end and start, are no more disconcerting than the passage of night and day."

Since man must not struggle against nature, the superior person eats when hungry, sleeps when tired, does what has to be done in his daily life, but otherwise simply allows himself to be swept along by the current of universal change. Magisterial in his inertia, he knows above all when not to act, and that to do more than the necessary minimum when he does act is just to create still more things to be done. Non-action, say the Taoists, is preferable to action. Nothing existed before something, and so something comes out of nothing, not the reverse. Emptiness is all. The one absolutely essential part of a cartwheel is the axle hole, and it is the hollow in the middle that is the all-important part of a beer bottle. Were it not for the spaces between, objects would have no shape and could not even be told apart.

Almost any Chinese landscape painting is a demonstration of the power of nothingness. At the top right-hand corner of the scroll there is one of those improbable Chinese mountains, all peaks and precipices, and at the bottom left-hand corner is a spit of land, a pavilion, perhaps a moored boat. In between there is morning mist on the lake which the sunlight from a clear sky is just beginning to penetrate. It is this that so successfully conveys the mood. But look again, and the lake, the mist, the sunlight, and everything else that occupies two-thirds of the entire picture are simply not there. The silk is blank. The artist has painted it by ignoring it. It follows that all striving is futile and even peril- ous, say the Taoists. Achieve contentment by not chasing after it. The eye perceives without effort—in fact, you have to shut it to stop it from doing so. The ear hears, the lungs breathe, the body grows, all without conscious intervention by the mind of man.

Nothing could be more horrifying to these gentlemen than the hellish vision of the scrambling West, an inferno of ticker tape and traffic jams, snatched self-service lunches, split-second one- upmanship, sales graphs and security ratings and competitive commercials, inhabited by a pitiful horde of lost souls all fighting for short cuts in space and time along the rat-racetrack. These are the damned, who have forgotten that only God can make an instant instant. Ill-treated slave to worldly possessions, worked to the bone in the higher interests of the split-level apartment and the two-tone Cadillac, the American is a phenomenon whose acrobatics in pursuit of his death wish are too exhausting even to watch. "He who stands on tiptoe does not stand on firm ground," the Taoists warn in their complacent fashion. "If you do not want to spill the wine, do not fill the glass to the brim." They agree with Confucians in advocating moderation in all things, the philosophy of the golden mean, satisfaction with what comes, and let others pay supertax.

This sense of moral vertigo may seem strangely absent from the make-up of the friendly and familiar figures of relentless, coldly ambitious Chinese who have fought tooth and nailsheath for control of an empire or a corner pitch in Chinatown, but in fact Taoist renunciation of rank and riches has been a common event in Chinese history. Once he had been solemnly installed as a provincial governor, one of China's greatest poets immediately played the ceremony backward by stripping off his newly ac-

quired insignia of office in front of the startled assembly of dignitaries, bowing, and backing out. He then wandered idly through
the countryside, making doubly sure that he had no visible means
of support by concealing his fame under a false name. In the
same reign, a noted author who had taken Imperial office also
forsook his emperor to become a recluse, and showed his contempt for greed and achievement by spending much of his contemplative life angling without bait, for although he loved fishing,
he had shed all desire to catch fish by artificial means.

Since there must be no conscious striving, all action must be
spontaneous, for to be spontaneous is to be natural. Take the case
of drunks. "If a drunken man falls out of a carriage," Chuang Tzu
remarks encouragingly, "he may be shaken up, but he will not
be killed. His bones are the same as any other man's, but he is
not hurt because his spirit is calm. He does not know he is riding
in a carriage, nor does he know anything about it when he is
thrown out. He feels nothing of life, death, bewilderment, or
terror, and so he does not suffer when he hits something. If this
integrity can come from wine, how much more is it to be gained
from being natural?" All that is done well, say the Taoists, is
done instinctively, without thought. Get an archer to compete
with others when the prize is a common piece of pottery, and his
shooting will be excellent. But offer him a brass knuckle, and you
will see him aim carefully, concentrate upon his target—and miss.

Here again Taoist philosophy strongly influences art, for the
Chinese usually paint with watercolors on paper or silk, and
these are sometimes so absorbent that the paint must be laid on
with swift, spontaneous strokes of the brush that cannot be corrected later. Natural rhythm is the pulse of the universe, and
man can only be with it if he stops trying to live by numbers,
and lets himself go—relaxed, unresistant, flexible, yielding, intuitively responding to the beat in all things:

> The centipede was happy, quite,
> Until a toad in fun

Said, "Pray, which leg goes after which?"
This worked his mind to such a pitch,
He lay distracted in a ditch,
Considering how to run.

The King of Wei's royal carver was so deft and swift when cutting up a bull that he seemed to dance through the work, but as he explained to his admiring monarch: "When I first began to carve, I looked at the bull as a whole animal. Three years later I still looked at the bull, but as if it had already been cut up. Now I no longer see it with my eye at all, I only feel it with my mind. I cut instinctively along the natural divisions, and since my action is in harmony with the build of the beast, I never find myself forcing my way through tendon or muscle . . ." This little surgical homily is one of many Taoist fables that make a virtue out of taking the line of least resistance, the principle that Taoism has contributed to the art of judo and other forms of fighting in which the small man does not try to stand up to his charging opponent like some squared-off Regency pugilist but gives way as he comes and brings him down heavily with the force of his own momentum. Soft beats hard, the tongue outlasts the teeth, and to Taoists water is the ideal substance: it does not batter itself against stone, but percolates through the cracks, and the more you try to clutch it, the more it evades you. A Taoist believes that man should not beat a path from birth to death, but trickle to his end after seventy-odd years of gentle osmosis.

Anyway, why struggle, when life itself may be an illusion? "Chuang Tzu once dreamed he was a butterfly that fluttered about happily, quite unaware that it was Chuang Tzu. But then he woke up, and after that he never knew whether he was Chuang Tzu who once dreamed he was a butterfly, or a butterfly now dreaming it was Chuang Tzu." Imaginative, romantic, or just bone-idle, Chinese frequently prefer to retire into an ivory tower of their own and invent a dream world of success rather than fight for it on earth, and most Chinese scholars would rather commune with the great minds in their books than with the tiny little ones they meet out of them. "Only fools know they are awake and just what they are," says the *Book of Lieh Tzu* (who almost certainly never existed himself anyway).

In a cosmos that may itself be purely imaginary, no absolute truth can be known, for everything depends upon the point of view. The whole world is a speck in the universe, yet the tip of a hair is not insignificant, says the *Book of Chuang Tzu*. It is useless to explain the grandeur of the ocean to a frog whose world is a well, or to try to convince the skeptical wren that the roc can fly hundreds of miles, for they are like men who believe that the only truth is the evidence of their own senses. Since infinity and eternity are endless, the largest thing must be contained in something larger, and the smallest thing is always divisible into two smaller things. What is "big" to one must always be "little" to another, and vice versa.

"Suppose," says Chuang Tzu, "that we argue. If you win, does that mean you are right and I am wrong? Or if I win, am I really right and you wrong? Is one of us necessarily right and the other wrong, in fact? Or might not both of us be right, or both wrong? Whom shall I ask to arbitrate, since we cannot agree? If I ask someone and he agrees with you—or agrees with me—how can he make an objective decision? Or if he differs from both of us or agrees with both of us, how can he decide? So to whom can we go for a decision?" Do not seek one, say the Taoists. Man made his big mistake when he invented right and wrong, "is" and "is not." For all is one, and "when there is life, there is death, and when there is possibility, there is impossibility."

It follows that logic, deduction, and all the other activities of the mental sorting office are absurd and misleading. Man must only feel things intuitively, not try to break them down into the wretched rubble of language. He must apprehend instinctively, through contemplation, not analyze everything out of existence through intellection. He talks far too much anyway. "The four seasons observe clear laws, but do not discuss them," says the Taoist. "Those who talk do not know, and those who know do not talk—a man should know without knowing how he knows," and so: "The Tao that can be spoken is not the eternal Tao." Banish wisdom, discard knowledge, there is no truth to be explained in words. To register things in the mind is dangerous. When we are conscious of our shoes, they are not fitting properly, and when we are conscious of our trousers, they are too tight. You are only a man when you stop thinking about it.

"The fish trap exists only because of the fish," concluded Chuang Tzu. "Once you have caught the fish, you can forget the trap. Words exist only because of meaning. Once you have caught the meaning, you can forget the words. Now where can I find a man who has forgotten words so that I can talk to him?" Dreadful damage was done when men split the unity of the universe by inventing ten thousand separate names for everything, for this mental scratching in the dust for what should be apprehended automatically as a whole gets in the way of understanding. "The five colors will blind a man's sight," it is said. Propositions should accord with the universal law, not logic; with nature, not nomenclatures.

Millions of modern Chinese would agree. The profound influence of Taoist teaching is to be seen in more than painting and judo. It is to be discerned in the principles of flexibility in Chinese guerrilla warfare; it accounts for Chinese readiness to make a pious *potage* of the major Asian religions, for while one may be right, the other is not necessarily wrong; it is to be found in Chinese reverence for knack rather than know-how, for poetic justice rather than law, and in a calm acceptance of the ups and downs of life. But it has achieved more than that. Confucianism maimed the spirit of progress by teaching the Chinese that only what was ancient was good; Taoism then smilingly lured them away from the solid path of scientific method and left them a mighty heritage of mumbo jumbo, an aversion for the rational and contempt for Q.E.D., a distrust of dogma and deep-frozen truths, and a marvelous talent for spurious argument. In a word, this side of the coin is essentially Yin-equals-female.

18

The Triumph of Unreason

"That won't last two minutes," remarked Ah Fu, happily exon-erating herself from a future breakage when I bought an imi-tation cut-glass salad bowl made of plastic. "It will go in no time. It's not like glass. Glass has juice in it, and that holds it together. That's why it's heavy, you see. But this is dry and brittle." We saw only too quickly. It may be argued that Ah Fu is not an educated woman, but "juice in the glass" is no more striking a piece of nonsense than "wind in the bone," which is a Chinese doctor's explanation of rheumatism. Favoring instinct rather than scientific tests, the Chinese for long believed that the heart (possibly confused with the liver) was on the right side of the body, and when they read in a Jesuit work of anatomy that it was on the left, they not only assumed that Europeans were constructed differently but argued that this meant that Chinese could never be Christians. For centuries the Chinese also hugged to themselves the agreeable delusion that a hectic sex life was good for old age.

It was evidently dangerous to be a doctor in old China, for when one famous physician told Ts'ao Ts'ao that he could cure his splitting headaches by neurosurgery while he was anesthe-tized with hashish (this in the third century A.D.), the suspicious general had him tortured for plotting his murder. The doctor left his precious black bag of prescriptions to his kindly jailer before he died, but this man's wife burned it by mistake. Furiously upbraided by her husband, she retorted: "If you also became learned like the doctor, you would end up in prison, too. What good did all that knowledge do him?" The husband on reflection agreed, and many Chinese today would say her argument was unanswerable.

During the Sung dynasty, it is recorded, men would take drugs, swallow charms, get themselves cauterized, and pray in three different denominations of temple, all on the same day for the same bellyache. Which of these multifarious activities cured it? The patient could take his pick, and this became his personal contribution to medical truth. It was also common for writers in Imperial China to fill "notebooks" with childish assertions which they made no attempt to prove, for hunches were better than higher mathematics, and reasonableness more important than reasoning. And this tradition stubbornly persisted. Many twentieth-century Chinese revolutionaries were convinced that if they simply introduced a system of general elections and parliamentary rule into China, this arbitrary imposition of Western democracy would naturally give their country all the advantages of a Western democracy. It would somehow put an end to foreign concessions, give China back her lost territories, and turn her into a formidable military power and a rich, modern industrial state. In these calculations, the problem of know-how came nowhere. Not surprisingly, Western democracy, inexpertly grafted on to the tortured old trunk of the Imperial system, failed miserably to produce these strange blossoms. Which is one of a hundred reasons why Mao Tse-tung is where he is today.

Repeated conflicts of mind between the West and China on questions of law have resembled a series of nonsensical bouts of blindfold boxing between two deaf-mutes. In 1921 a special commission of inquiry, formed to study Chinese objections to the establishment of foreign concessions in Shanghai, solemnly ruled that China had no legal claim whatever, since these little exercises in daylight robbery had been fully provided for in properly ratified treaties. The Old China Hands were shocked and bewildered when the Chinese showed that they did not give a fig for the legalities: they were only concerned with the simple fact that someone else had stolen their property, and they were going to get it back. A treaty that sanctioned theft made no more sense to them than would a housebreaking permit issued to a cat burglar.

Law, to the Chinese, consists mainly of a series of mean catches designed to deprive the individual of his rights. The intricate shape of these rights should be recognized intuitively, and should not be distorted into oversimplified geometrical patterns of "wrong" and "right." When in 1965, therefore, the Singapore government simultaneously hanged eighteen thugs convicted of the brutal murder of a detention-island superintendent and two of his guards, the Westernized Chinese nodded approval, while the "Chinese" Chinese shook their heads and muttered those stony imprecations against authority that have been worn smooth by centuries of scandals. Who cared what the law provided? The prisoners must have been unbearably exasperated; otherwise, they would not have rebelled. It was a crime to string up so many luckless rapscallions on the same morning, more than two years after their lapse. There ought to be a law about laws.

British Hong Kong dangles freakishly from the great underbelly of Communist China like some small but surprising anatomical monstrosity, and many are astonished that its almost entirely Chinese population should so passively accept British rule most of the time. There are, in fact, many reasons for this, but one underlying explanation is that the Chinese and the British inhabit two quite different Hong Kongs. To Mr. White, Hong Kong is a crown colony ceded in perpetuity by Peking (only the additional New Territories are on lease) under a legal treaty signed in 1842, and so inalienably British forever. To Mr. Wong, the treaty is irrelevant. His Hong Kong is a piece of China. It is under reasonably competent foreign jurisdiction (just as a city in Gaullist

France might have a Communist mayor), with which he has little direct contact. Otherwise, it is inalienably Chinese.

The Taoist may be master of the specious argument, but his greatest contribution to Chinese unthink has been negative. By sanctifying intuition and scorning reason, Taoism has encouraged an addiction among Chinese to a more comprehensive irrationality that is no longer always loyal to the Tao, and sometimes even turns against it. As a philosophy, in fact, Taoism has proved to be something of a second Frankenstein, and has in its turn muffed its monster. The laborious ritual of grinding a stick of Chinese ink on a stone block, and mixing it with water to a consistency suitable for the writing brush, is a time waster in a telecommunicative world, and has long been recognized as such. "Man does not grind ink, but ink grinds men," the Chinese have said. Yet in a burst of anti-foreign foolishness in the thirties, the more militant Chinese Chinese threw away their Western fountain pens and reverted to the brush—which at once cut their efficiency as militant Chinese Chinese by one-third.

Examples of this sort of nationalistic nonsense can, of course, be found elsewhere, even among those Britons who boycotted Beethoven during World War II for being a Hun, if a harmonious one. But the affair of the swords has, by contrast, the distinctive flavor of Chinese folly. During the Sino-Japanese war, pitifully underarmed Chinese troops in one part of the country were reduced to fighting the well-equipped "Dwarfs from the East" with old-fashioned broadswords, and acquitted themselves with such courage that the story was widely published in the press, and many a tear of pride shed. Patriotic organizations were then inspired to do something about this situation, and to do it energetically and quickly. Funds were rapidly raised, and it looked as if some lucky foreign firm was about to receive a big order for modern rifles. But no. The money was spent on forging more broadswords to give to more hapless Chinese soldiers fighting against the well-equipped "Dwarfs from the East." A hundred homilies of the Confucian sages of the Good Old Days persuasion could certainly be quoted to prove that brushes and broadswords are better than pens and pistols. But that would only compound the lunacy.

Taught that all is relative and each case must be judged in a common-sense way on its own merits, the Chinese nevertheless are adept at basing sweeping judgments on the flimsy evidence of feminine intuition, and of arguing from the particular to the general. "I can recognize the Irish anywhere," a Chinese woman once told me confidently in Hong Kong. "They're all red-haired and blind drunk." Very frequently a newcomer will not be judged by what he does, or even what he says, but by the shape of his face, the cut of his calligraphy, the way he walks (square or otherwise), and even what he eats (modest heroes are particularly fond of fresh-boiled dog). It is related that a famous enchantress of ancient days (claimed by the Vietnamese as well as the Chinese) was frowning and beating her breast when she happened to be observed by an ugly woman who wanted to steal the secret of her beauty. "Aha," said this creature. "Now I have it," and thereupon went about frowning and beating her breast, frightening everyone around her so much that the rich hastily bolted their doors, and the poor—having no bolts—fled into the surrounding countryside.

The besetting Chinese sin of overconfidence conspires with this fatal illusion that one man's meat is also sauce for the gander. In the nineteen-twenties a succession of Chinese Communist leaders kowtowed to Marxist doctrine, imported in whole cloth from the Soviet Union, which laid down that the industrial proletariat must lead the revolution and that the cities must be seized first. They were well aware that underdeveloped China could hardly be said to have anything so sophisticated as an industrial proletariat of any consequence, and that for more than two thousand years successful insurrections had depended upon the desperate and bloody resolution of her normally docile peasants. But the revolution had been led by the workers in Russia, and so it must be in China. In consequence, the Chinese Communists suffered a series of absurd setbacks until Mao cut through this magic ring of moronity and—to the fury of the orthodox— rallied the peasants to him in the wilds of Kiangsi, instead of attacking the towns.

In 1927 Chiang Kai-shek suddenly broke his uneasy alliance with the Communists, turning upon them without warning and crushing their movement in Shanghai. In perpetual memory of that day of refined treachery, Mao has harbored a deep distrust of all nationalist movements, and although he has sometimes found it expedient to tolerate non-Communist leaders in the emerging African and Asian continents, he sees them only as rotten rungs on the ladder to revolution, to be left behind as quickly as possible. China has therefore tried to maintain a pleas- ing, if protocolar relationship with the woollier geopolitical won- ders of Afro-Asia while fomenting revolt within them at the same time, simultaneously feeding flattery to their prime ministers and firepower to their rebels. But in the apparent belief that all Men of the Marshes are by definition ideological heroes, Mao has sometimes armed and trained drunken and discredited tribesmen from the dimmer provinces of young, struggling African states, mistaking a bunch of common cutthroats for an organization of respectable revolutionaries. The result has been a humiliating failure for Chinese policy in Africa. For while leaders in Peking may have seen themselves as arbiters of national revolution above any moral law, the Africans do not, as it happens, regard China as the umpire upon whom sin never sits.

In 1956, North Vietnamese Communist leaders directed a Peking-inspired purge of landlords similar to those that had so drastically reduced the rural population of China. However, a shamefaced Hanoi government was later obliged to admit that well over ten thousand innocent men had been quite unneces- sarily murdered. For, intent upon their ideological vermifuge, Chinese-trained dogmatists had once more generalized from the particular and had ignored the fact that the North Vietnamese pattern of property and tenure was not the same as the Chinese, that land was more evenly distributed, and that few of the small-holders who had been so savagely parted from their socage could be classed as feudal exploiters at all.

In 1958, Communist leaders in Peking gave the signal for a Great Leap Forward that would convert China almost overnight from a poor backward country into a rich, modern industrial state—only to see her fall flat on her face. Muddle, dislocation, bottlenecks, and deviationist weather all helped to bring the country to the very brink of ruin in the years that followed, but one of the fundamental reasons for the spectacular failure of this great plan lay in the Chinese tendency to mistake one swallow for a summer.

At the beginning of the Great Leap, I talked with cadres on cooperative farms in North and West China who assured me that thanks to "socialist methods," which included deeper plowing, more fertilization, closer sowing, and other agricultural abuses, rice output on their land would be doubled that year, quadrupled the next, and thereafter, who knew? Anything was possible. A little earnest inquiry revealed, however, that this pipe-dream arithmetic had been inspired by increases of production already achieved by experts on small, special experimental plots of land elsewhere whose conditions could not possibly apply to the whole country. It was nevertheless assumed that what could be done in Iowa could be done in Nevada, and moreover that if 400 tons of natural fertilizer had been available to produce exceptional results on one acre in Shantung, 400 million tons would be available, for example, for one million acres in Szechuan. Gravely following the printed instructions, and without thought for the local environment, some cadres, inspired by reports of land reclamation in swamp areas elsewhere, drained off the water tables of rich, well-irrigated paddyfields that had produced two crops of rice a year, leaving them looking like the grittier sections of the Gobi Desert, and just about as productive.

When Mao Tse-tung describes the Americans as arch-enemies

of Communist China who would add her yellow stars to Old Glory if given half a chance, most mainland Chinese probably feel instinctively that this is correct. They do not examine all the facts or attempt to analyze the situation. There are anyway too many facts, all moving and changing faster than you can arrange them, some would say. But this does not make the individual Chinese into a sheep. If he is outwardly conformist, it may often be because skin and safety depend on it, but it may also be that on a given issue his truth harmonizes with Mao's. For he still believes that each man must make his own truth in a world in which there is no standard model of the article, and this do-it-yourself doctrine gives him a stubbornly independent private outlook which his readiness to agree when he agrees should not obscure.

In an evolving universe, then, objective truth is as hard to come by as a Tyrannosaurus Rex, and usually just about as ugly a customer. And where a Chinese truth is concerned, there is the added hazard of the Chinese language. *How vague! How impalpable!*

19

Shrink-Think

Turn the pages of the smallest Chinese-English vocabulary I know, and you will find useful, everyday words and phrases like these:

Hoo. To find bail for the lighter offenses of females.
Ch'he. Devoid of intelligence, deficiency of wit, silly, idiotic. Also used for borrowing and returning books.
Maou Tsaou. A scholar not succeeding and giving himself over to liquor.

This is all doubtless very illuminating, for the experts (who, as usual, are too busy quarreling to note that their very differences condemn them as inexpert) assure us either that man makes his language or that the language makes the man. These extracts from *The Chinese Unicorn,* which is based on a mid-nineteenth-century Chinese-English dictionary, therefore open a fanlight on to Chinese society through which we can glimpse its curiosities if we are like *pa* ("a short man standing as high as he can").

On closer examination, however, we find more puzzling entries in the *Unicorn.* For example:

Wan. A small mouth. Some day a large mouth.
Chen. To stand still. To gallop at full speed.

Pee. A dog under the table.
A dog with short legs.
A short-headed dog.

You dismiss these contradictions as the bet hedging of an English missionary working on a little-known tongue more than a century before Suzie Wong, and consult a modern Chinese-English dictionary for the correct meanings—only to find something like this:

E (in the *Unicorn*): Pig, some say a fox.
(in the modern dictionary): Emulate, strive after.

At this point, even *heaou* ("a well-informed female mind") feels as if her brain has gone a bit *sih* ("water dried up so as to make it difficult to sail a boat"), and pitches the *Unicorn* into the trash can. She may then with some sense of relief look up a very simple or common Chinese character in the modern dictionary, with this result:

Nai. Then, now, so, also, and, but, if, i.e., namely, accordingly, to be, your, theirs, his, her, its, that, those.
or *Tui.* Push, extend, refuse, shirk, hand over to, trace, investigate, infer, promote, elect, praise.

By now it will be realized that the Chinese written language may sometimes be a little imprecise.

The ancestor of the modern Chinese character was the straightforward pre-Christian pictogram, like this one:

$$\text{𠨞} = Nu. \text{ A woman}$$

The arm and leg positions, in particular, were supposed to indicate that this was a female. Man was (and is):

人 (or 亻)

But as writing became gracefully stylized, woman came to be written:

Pictograms were then combined with others to express more sophisticated, if sometimes debatable ideas like:

安　(A woman under a roof) = Peace

好　(Female with male child) = Good

and 姦　(Three Females) = Adultery, fornication, debauch, ravish. (Some say a four-letter word.)

The pictogram of a woman is one of 214 "radicals," at least one of which will form part of any Chinese character. The radicals are supposed to give some indication of the meaning of the character, much as *phil* at the beginning of a romance word in English tells us that it is about love—but no more. A stranger to the word *philately* may guess wildly at erotic connotations and be faintly astonished to find it means stamp collecting after all. In Chinese, the pits are dug even deeper. A character may have five component parts, including two or three possible radicals, its meaning may have nothing to do with the radical nor its sound with its phonetic element. Or it may be highly allusive:

如　Woman + mouth

originally meant "follow" (a woman obeys orders from the mouth). From "follow" it came to mean "like" (to follow, to be like), and from "like" it came to mean "if" (like supposing).

The basic character:

 (*piao*)

means "to display." Put the "man" radical on its left:

(*piao*)

and it means "to distribute." Put the "woman" radical there:

(*piao*)

and it means "prostitute." But in the old days radicals were not attached to all characters as they are now to make these fine shades of meaning obvious. Sad errors could therefore creep in. And did.

Ideograms are in turn combined into pairs or groups to express more complicated meanings or phrases, and this system of word building may on occasion produce interesting results when a Chinese is struggling with English. ("And now," says Ping happily at the London Zoo. "Now we go to see the—the—the pocket mouse." "The *what?*" "The *pocket* mouse. *You* know. Put-in-the-pocket, *that* kind mouse!" And she traces the two characters for "pocket" and "mouse" on her palm. I am still in the dark, until she adds: "That bigger-than-you jumping-around boxing mouse. In *Ao-ta-li-ya.*" Light dawns, and we set off for the kangaroos.)

But literary Chinese has been essentially a laconic affair, with one character sometimes standing for a spoken word of three syllables which could only be fully expressed by three characters. It is just as if we wrote *autocracy* as "auto" and left the reader to work out that we did not mean "automobile." It can well be imagined that this terse style in the hands of sub-editors produces a form of cypher language that is a study in itself.

Seizing the first Chinese newspaper to hand and glancing at the headline, I find: *Eminent Outside Like Country Protect Like Yesterday Fly Beautiful Commerce Far East Protect Necessary.* Decode and you get: "British foreign and defense ministers yesterday flew to the United States for discussions on Far East defense matters."

No one would in fact misunderstand this, given the narrow context of our daily disasters, for combinations of characters are as readily comprehensible to the educated Chinese themselves as is the word "porcelain" to a European who is fully aware that it has lost its original connection with pigs. But take these two translations of a slightly offensive passage in the Classical Book of Odes:

> "Those from whom come no lessons, no instruction
>   are women and eunuchs."—Legge

> "Among those who cannot be trained or taught
>   are women and eunuchs."—Giles

Not only do two eminent Sinologues flatly contradict each other, but some Chinese say they are both wrong: there is no mention of eunuchs anyway. The character for "eunuch" should be interpreted in its broader meaning of "serve," and the sense is that a ruler is not taught evil but learns it from listening to the women who serve him. Who is right?

A university student must be familiar with some six thousand Chinese characters and their complex system of association with one another, and he has no alphabet to guide him through a dictionary. An ordinary Chinese typewriter looks more like a printer's type-setting machine. It has 2,590 "keys," and blank settings into which slugs of the rarer characters, taken from a reserve of an additional 3,432, can be fitted as they are needed. A telegram in Chinese characters must be enciphered into a number code, the numbers transmitted in Morse, and then the groups translated back into characters by the recipient. Through-

out history, the Chinese written language has been difficult to learn, and it was estimated even in the nineteen-
thirties that only three million newspapers were sold daily in
all China, to be read by perhaps one man in every twenty-
five. The Communists, in their successful drive for literacy,
have tried to simplify the written language by reducing
the number of characters to three thousand (there were still
eight thousand in common use in 1965) and by stripping down
the more complicated ones so that they are easier to memorize
and write, but this has served to introduce the further complication that there are now two written Chinese languages, for Formosa and the overseas Chinese have stuck to the original
ideograms. That suits Peking perfectly, for it means that the
"literate" young peasant or worker who has been given a limited
education in Communist China in new basic Chinese is largely
shut off from the deviationist writings printed in the more complex characters of the past, and is now enjoying the benefits of
a closed-circuit Communist culture. The masses are back where
they were when they relied on a small, literate elite to tell them
what was what. For a Communist student to whom "side" is
now reduced to this:

边

is not going to recognize it easily in its old form, which is this:

It has been said that Chinese is an essentially feminine language, dealing in concrete forms, so that abstracts cannot be
properly expressed. There is no word for size: the Chinese say
"big–small." No word for weight: they say "light–heavy." No
word for -ness, because while there may be (to use English
terminology) black ants and black despair, tall stories and tall

drinks, ugly situations and ugly sisters, there is no general concept of blackness, tallness, or ugliness. The ideograms are like a series of pictures, absorbed passively by the eye with all its Taoist spontaneity, whereas Western alphabetical script draws the reader forward along rails of writing as a man is taken along by a closely reasoned logical argument. Chinese, therefore, is not a language of ideas or of rational debate, some say.

But this argument can be taken too far. There is a curious superstition in the West that a mushy mouthful of romance jargon is more digestible to the reason of man than Anglo-Saxon brittle, although in fact the "impenetrability of matter" is perfectly well expressed by the "un-get-throughableness of stuff." Great fun can doubtless be had by translating Chinese literally. How amusing that *psychology* should be rendered by three characters meaning "mind-principle-study" (sic, sic, sic), that *sympathy* should be "together-feel," *aesthetics* should be "beauty-learning," and *inexhaustible* should be "use-not-finish"—until we realize that these quaint transmogrifications precisely reflect the true visage of the English words behind their Latin or Greek face packs. There seems no real reason to believe that the Chinese cannot feel abstract ideas just as keenly as a Humanities sophomore from Harvard plagued by psychosomatic fleas.

The trouble with Chinese is not indistinctness, but ambiguity. It has virtually no plural, no active or passive voices, no definite article, often no recognizable grammar as an English grammarian would understand it. It is capable of fine shades of meaning and of great exactitude when fully deployed. But, while highly idiomatic, it frequently has—in its less verbose form—about as much legal precision as can be found in the common expression "Long time, no see."

Ambiguity may be doubly dangerous in the mouths of the literal-minded, but to the Chinese the letter is nevertheless all-important. For as Chinese writing is a series of symbols and not a phonetic system, it has the inestimable advantage that it can be read and understood by people who pronounce the names of those symbols quite differently from one another. For centuries, Vietnamese was written with Chinese characters, some two thousand basic Chinese characters are still used in Japanese, and about twelve hundred in Korean, although these two languages do not appear to resemble any form of Chinese when spoken. All characters are also equally recognizable to Chinese from opposite ends of China, who speak dialects so widely at variance that they are almost separate languages.

For the complications of Chinese are not limited to the loopholes in the written language. In Singapore alone, six main Chinese dialects are spoken, and our amah cannot even talk to the servant next door except in badly mauled Malay, although they almost look alike, for Ah Fu talks Cantonese and Ah Sim talks Hokkien. Communist, Nationalist, and most overseas Chinese schools are now teaching the rising generation Mandarin, the national language based on the Peking dialect, but Chinatown is still a Tower of Babel laid out flat. This is one reason why it is difficult to romanize Chinese, for you cannot produce a phonetic script that will be easily understood by, say, an Englishman, a Frenchman, and a Hungarian, who must respectively read the same written word as *square*, *carré*, and *négyszög*. Show them a small drawing like this ☐, however, and they all recognize it at once. That is what the ideogram or character does for Cantonese, Hokkien, Mandarin, and Hakka speakers alike. But, conversely, this means that an Australian-Chinese friend whose surname is expressed by this character:

許

is called *Shü* in Mandarin, *Hui* in Cantonese, and *K'ou* in Hokkien. (The Australians cut through this complication in their direct antipodian fashion by calling him *Gin*.)

Separate romanized systems have therefore to be devised for separate dialects (especially when, for example, *li* means "one" in Mandarin, but "two" in Cantonese). But the experts have not been content with this multiplication of effort, for attempts to invent alphabetical Mandarin alone have produced a wall-to-wall shelf of books on different transliteration systems, so that the word for "thank" may now be spelled *xie* or *hsieh* or *sye* or in half a dozen other ways. The use of the "phonetic language," as romanized Chinese is called, is still very limited, therefore, and the difficulty of rendering most foreign names in Chinese remains. A string of four characters in a headline catches the eye. They make no possible sense at all. Murmur the Mandarin sounds for these characters and you get *Fu-Bu-Lai-t'e*. Run these sounds together in a debonair manner, while listening unobtrusively for anything that they might by any wild stretch of the imagination resemble. You get Fulbright, and may now proceed to the next square. Khrushchev is *K'o-lu-hsüeh-fu* or sometimes *Ho-lu-hsiao-fu*, and Eden becomes *Ai-Teng*. Ping has read Turgenev and Dostoevsky with even more diligence than I have studied *Peanuts*, but mention the Russian names of either of these writers, and she will not know whom you are talking about.

There are some sixteen thousand characters in the modern Chinese dictionary, but only some 420 monosyllables in the entire language. This means that one sound has to make do for many characters, each of which has a separate meaning. In my modest dictionary for ignorant barbarians, *ching*, for example, is the sound of nearly forty different ideograms, which have eighty meanings or more altogether, ranging through "pity," "bramble," "underground streams," "to cut the throat," "to regulate," "shinbone," "neck," "capital," "mirror," and so on. String together five of these all-purpose monosyllables in a short spoken sentence, and the computations in terms of the possible meaning of the whole will theoretically run into billions. In fact, Chinese is a tonal language, and it makes a difference whether you say *ching* with a flat, upward, swooping, or diving inflection. This aid to understanding—requiring a sharp ear and a nimble, musical tongue—is not the only one. But that does not make it any the less disconcerting that a Mandarin-speaker will pronounce the written phrase "Forty-four Dead Stone Lions" as "Ssu Shih Ssu Ssu Shih Shih."

Every unfortunate foreigner who has been hooked by the Chinese language has had the experience, while floundering through the shallows, of ordering soup and getting sugar, or salt and getting tobacco, for the words in Chinese sound the same. There are also the minefields of slang and everyday usage which cause casualties even among Chinese. (Moreover, Ah Fu is not, as many think, the lady's name, but Ah, Fu! The association has now become so close that they are inseparable, much as if enough repetition of conventional calls and greetings among Westerners had produced a corrupt practice by 1966 whereby the President of the United States and the Prime Minister of Great Britain were normally spoken of as Hi Lyndon and Oi Harry, and the French head of state, to his profound disgust, ended up as Alors Charlie. Ping can be called Ah Ping, and much of the time Ah Fu refers affectionately to our Alsatian dog Banner as "Ah Ban," which seems to make it all as democratic as tovarich, except that what the aristocratic Ah Ban calls Ah Fu is not recorded.)

The opportunities for punning in Chinese are obviously almost limitless, and the very first sentence of Lao Tzu—"The Way that can be spoken is not the eternal Way"—is strongly suspect, for "Tao" is used to mean not only "Way" but also "speak," so that the sentence might be rendered: "The Way that can be the Way is not the eternal Way," or "The speech that can be spoken is not the eternal speech." The "li" that represents the code of chivalrous propriety and ritual advocated by the humanistic Confucius is indistinguishable in sound and in tone from "li" meaning profit, or "li," the questionable cosmic principle of the neo-Confucians that was made to justify despotic monarchy fifteen hundred years later. At this point one begins to feel faintly uneasy, to suspect that the harmless play on words may, after all, hold a hidden hazard.

Punning leads the Chinese into a curious realm of self-delusion, superstition, and symbolism in which one thing tends to be represented by another, and therefore to have no reality of its own. The First Emperor is told that if he buries a myriad men in the foundations of the Great Wall, it will endure a myriad years, for their spirits will protect it. But either he or someone else suffers an unwonted twinge of conscience and avoids ordering a massacre by immuring Mr. Myriad, a hapless creature who was unfortunate enough to be born with the name of *Wan*, which is the sound of the character that means "ten thousand."

To the Cantonese, sugar cane is a symbol of gratitude, for in their dialect it has the same sound as "thank." For similar reasons, a bat symbolizes good luck (because they are both *fu*); a fish, fertility (they are both *yü*); heavily stylized characters are identified with longevity, or happy marriage; and the whole instinct for such formulae gets out of control until Chinese decoration on everything from a garden gazebo to a ten-story chamber of commerce is a garish mass of stereotyped symbols in green and red (lucky colors), of dragons (heavenly forces), cranes and pines (long life), bats and carp and auspicious ideograms.

The Chinese mind is often as stereotyped as Chinese décor, clad as it is in stiff clichés of prejudice and tradition. The neat pun, the symbol, the apt classical quotation are all part of a mental system of push-button tuning that tempts a Chinese to avoid bothering with the finer adjustments of original thought. His language delights him with its "pleasures-shallow-sorrows-deep" economy of idiom, and he would rather be concisely ambiguous than long-windedly lucid. Nothing, to the Chinese, could be more deliciously enigmatic for the uninitiated than my wife's full given name, for Ching Ping means "Apprehensive Ice." This is a drastic contraction of the classical tag in the ancient Book of Odes which reads:

> We should be apprehensive and careful
> As if we were on the brink of a deep gulf
> As if we were treading on thin ice

Literally:

> Apprehensive Careful
> As If Brink Deep Gulf
> As If Tread Thin Ice

All this shrink–think leads to situations in which a house is considered uninhabitable because its previous owner called it "Sunset Heights"—which implies that to occupy it is to pass one's peak. Richard Widmark's tight, dangerous smile earns him the conventional label "Laughing Tiger," and he is no longer an infinitely complicated animal called Richard Widmark but a stock character in a human puppet show. Too often the responses of Chinese are narrow and mechanical. For centuries they learned the Classics by rote, repeated improving slogans parrot-fashion, memorized words rather than remembered their wisdom. In 1966, teenage Red Guards expressed their revolutionary Communist zeal by scribbling and shouting endlessly the same fag-end phrases from the *Thought of Mao Tse-tung* and showed their atavistic obsession with symbolism by smothering their cities in red flags and red tags, by demanding that the red lights on traffic signals signify "go" and not "stop," and even by discussing how to rearrange the world so that East would always be to the left.

When I was last in China, officials always prefaced their answers to questions with the same robot routine until I found myself hearing it even in the rhythm of a railway carriage: "*Thanks* to the *lead*ership of *Chair*man *Mao* and the *Chi*nese *Communist Par-tee* . . ." No homily was complete without it. Chinese propagandists work like pile drivers, pounding their simple messages further and further into the Chinese skull, accustoming the Chinese mind to mesmeric strip-language of "Khrushchevian-splittism," "Western-imperialist-warmongers," and "All-American-imperialists-are-Paper-Tigers." Then there are the finger-counting exercises for easy memorization: the "three-anti" campaign of 1951 (anti-corruption, anti-waste, anti-bureaucratism); the "five-anti" movement against bribery, tax evasion, fraud, theft of public property, betrayal of national economic secrets; and in the army there are the "four good companies" and the "five good fighters," and so on.

The unwary accuse Mao of formulating a system of indoctrination designed to turn all China into one diabolical, chanting kindergarten, but "Overthrow-the-Ching, restore-the-Ming" was very far from being the first patriotic maxim when it was popularized nearly three hundred years before the Communists, for Chinese have a reverence for such things. As for the ideological numbers game, the *Book of Han Fei,* who lived two hundred and fifty years before Christ, has chapters on the Two Handles, the Eight Villainies, the Ten Faults, and the Five Vermin (conservative scholars, corrupt speechmakers, free-lances, draft-dodgers, and speculators). In the *Three Kingdoms,* the dying strategist Chu-ko Liang speaks of his treatises on the Eight Needfuls, the Seven Cautions, the Six Fears, and the Five Dreads of War.

The Chinese are neat, nimble-fingered people. They love a well-coined phrase or a snugly capsuled slogan, and this goes with their affection for a smart, economical trick or trap, intriguing metal puzzles that slide smoothly apart for the man with the knack, cute conundrums, and fantastically intricate carvings of three ivory balls inside one another. They recoil from the messiness of our untidy reality into their own wonderland of the pat answer and the solution ingenious. Three men want to divide seventeen oranges so that one gets half of them, another gets a third, and the other gets one-ninth of them. How is it done? A small boy comes along with one orange, which he throws into the pile. There are now eighteen. The first man takes nine, the second six, the third two. That accounts for seventeen of the oranges, and the small boy then takes his own back. This is the reality that delights the Chinese—reality with a magic orange in the wings.

An officer of the Empress Wu is much admired for the occasion on which he asked a corrupt judge how he should squeeze the truth out of a stubborn malefactor. The judge, famous for his

astuteness, suggested that a caldron be filled with water, a fire
lit beneath it, and the victim slowly boiled. The officer ordered
a caldron of water to be brought and a fire lit. This done, he
turned to the judge and said politely: "Now kindly step inside
the pot." It is very Chinese to praise the table-turning without
worrying too much whether it was justified or not, and the
phrase is still quoted today.

Poetic justice is often regarded, in fact, as a sort of legal pun.
No doubt many Chinese laughed appreciatively in Peking at the
end of the eighteenth century when Lord Macartney, the noble
envoy of His Most Gracious Majesty King George III, was
housed in a sumptuous mansion worth about £100,000 which
had been built out of the outrageous dues levied on the British
merchants in Canton. The origin of chop suey also amuses the
Chinese in the same way, for it is said that this beggar's hash
came into being in ruder Californian days when a group of gold
miners barged into a Chinese restaurant in San Francisco after
closing time, demanding food. The Chinese proprietor had nothing to offer but the day's leavings, which he then heated up,
scrambled together, and served. From that day onward, and
until the postwar proliferation of Chinese restaurants in the West
taught the with-it set from Wimbledon to Wisconsin the difference between lotus soup and lacquered duck, the white world's
favorite Chinese dish was this Cantonese equivalent of a dog's
dinner.

In this sense, life to the Chinese is a game of chess in which
the gambit, the ruse, and the little stratagem are often ends in
themselves. "Very Chinese story," commented Apprehensive Ice
when we walked out of the theater after seeing the film *The
Bridge on the River Kwai,* in which a British colonel, taken prisoner by the Japanese, builds a bridge for them and even gives
his life trying to save it, so obsessed by pride in his work that
he has forgotten it will serve the wrong cause. Similarly, in the
time of the Warring States, able free-lance strategists schemed
and fought across the board of China, so wrapped up in their

ploys that they sometimes brought disaster upon their home towns before they realized that they had been working for the worst enemy of their own native states.

There is no common denominator, no generic term that can embrace all the loosely linked manifestations of this slightly gimmicky quality in the Chinese mind which is so at odds with Taoist teaching, this preference for the truth in the clock rather than the time itself. From punning to poetic justice, however, they nevertheless have one thing in common: they confuse by seeming to clarify, for the more we try to tidy nature up, the more we obscure it. They are, in their neat suburban fashion, the enemies of the windy and shapeless open spaces of free inquiry in which alone truths can sometimes be found, if not truth itself.

20

Science and Fiction

To dismiss the Chinese as a race of irrational bigots would be to fall into their own error of wrapping up inaccuracies in spruce little aphorisms. In the struggle between Chinese science and Taoist unthink ("Do not seek to probe the workings of nature, and all things will then flourish of themselves"), science has at times scored startling victories, which were often unknown to the West simply because at the time the West itself was sunk in a trench of abysmal ignorance.

In some obscure way, the average foreigner tends to feel that silk, paper and printing, gunpowder, lacquer, and porcelain sum up China's material contribution to the urgent practical business of complicating life. Not that they are to be despised. China exported silk westward in Caesar's lifetime, and it was not until about A.D. 560, when a group of crafty monks smuggled silkworm eggs across Asia to Byzantium hidden in sections of bamboo, that the six-hundred-year-old Chinese monopoly came to an end. The Chinese made paper before Hadrian's wall was built, were block-printing Buddhist sutras by the ninth century, and had already manufactured porcelain movable type when the Battle of Hastings was fought. (It was the Koreans, however, who cast metal type and beat the Germans to the invention of modern printing by nearly fifty years.) Chinese hard-paste porcelain and lacquer first reached Europe in the fifteenth century.

Nearly three hundred more years passed before the Europeans could imitate them properly.

But a loose list of Chinese inventions from earliest times in fact covers an astonishing variety of everyday gadgets and their working principles. When the Roman legions were still in Britain, the Chinese were making wheelbarrows (which did not appear in Europe for another thousand years), watermills, seed-sowing mechanisms, and crank-operated rotary-fan winnowing machines that were not to be seen in the West until six hundred years later. In A.D. 132, the Chinese produced the first seismograph. On the cylindrical outer casing of this "earthquake weathercock" were eight dragon heads, each one facing toward one of the eight divisions of the compass, while beneath it squatted one of eight open-mouthed toads that sat in a ring around the instrument. Suspended inside the casing, it appears, was a pendulum which was connected by levers to each of the dragon heads and could therefore move in the direction of any one of the points of the compass. When there was an earthquake, the pendulum tipped in the direction of the tremor and tilted the dragon's head that pointed the same way, whereupon the dragon vomited a ball into the mouth of the toad below. Earthquakes which no one had felt were recorded in this way.

By the third century, the Chinese had a distance-measuring chariot, the miles it covered being automatically registered by the beats of a mechanical drum, and a "south-pointing" carriage fitted with sets of coupled-up gears so that a human effigy swivel-mounted on top of it always pointed south, whatever turns and twists the vehicle itself made. A Han dynasty general of Pythagorean inclinations flew a kite over the fortress city he was besieging, to determine the distance his sappers would have to tunnel to surface within it. In the fourth century A.D. there appears an account of "flying cars" based on the principle of the helicopter top that rises as it whirls, and it was the Chinese "bamboo dragonfly" that was derived from this which inspired the earliest

British experiments in aeronautics at the end of the eighteenth century.

Move forward to the Norman Conquest: sulphur matches have now been in use in China for at least a hundred years, and inquisitive men in darkened rooms have experimented with pin-holes of light and discovered the "photographic" inverted image. In a few years, the first silk-reeling and spinning machines with a treadle mechanism will be constructed. Before the fourteenth century is out, a set of mechanical bellows for metalwork will be in use whose revolving wheels, operated by a crank, are so coupled up that their motion is converted into the thrust of piston rods. This is simply the mechanism of the steam locomotive in reverse (in the steam engine, the piston drives the wheels).

Directions for mixing gunpowder are first found in a Taoist work of the ninth century, but there is a legend widespread in the West that the Chinese never put it to proper use. Instead of employing it to kill people in large numbers simultaneously and indiscriminately, they found nothing better to do with it than make firecrackers to scare off devils and amuse children, detractors declare. In the decade of the Chinese nuclear bomb it would be a mistake, however, to credit the Chinese with such remissness, for history contradicts this comforting tale. Three centuries before the English archers took the field at Agincourt, the Chinese were using gunpowder grenades enclosed in bamboo casing; by the twelfth century, their war junks were armed with catapults that threw explosive bombs; and by Shakespeare's day, they had batteries of rocket launchers mounted on barrows. Fire had always been a weapon of war, too, and more than nine hundred years ago the Chinese evolved a flamethrower and an incendiary rocket—the flamethrower being fed from a tank of naphtha equipped with a piston-operated pump.

Iron-chain suspension bridges up to three hundred feet long began to appear in China at the beginning of the seventh century, one thousand years before Europe's first, and more than seven hundred years before the Ponte Vecchio was opened in

Florence, Chinese engineers constructed a single-span stone bridge over a river on the same principles. They were drilling for brine and natural gas long before Christ was born, and rapidly reached depths of up to two thousand feet. Operating without any form of power, some of the workers rotated the drill, while others drove it into the earth by jumping on and off a pivoted beam that acted like a hammer. A hollow bamboo tube, fitted with a valve to bring up the brine, was then lowered into the shaft. The method may sound a little old-fashioned today, but it was still used when the first oil wells were sunk in the United States—the Americans called it "kicking her down."

This atticful of miscellaneous toys should not give the impression, however, that Chinese science consisted of a number of haphazard, relatively homey discoveries without any common foundation in mathematics or physics. The Chinese had a fully developed counting system one thousand years before the Romans. More than two thousand years ago, they understood quadratic equations and were using algebra to solve problems in geometry. Early in the Christian era, they invented the abacus, which every Chinese shopkeeper still uses today. He sees no reason to change. In 1946, an American technical sergeant operating an electric calculating machine competed against a Chinese working an abacus. The abacus proved faster and more accurate than the machine at subtraction, addition, and division, and was only a little slower at multiplication.

The Chinese were above all the most accurate observers of the heavens of ancient times. Nearly fourteen hundred years before Christ—and well before even Athens was built—they were registering on oracle bones not only eclipses of the moon but man's first record of a nova. In Cleopatra's day they began noting sunspots, and by the time Galileo had observed the first sunspots recorded in Europe, the Chinese had accumulated details of more than one hundred. Obsessed with their view of the universe as a delicate, carefully balanced mechanism in which they themselves were also synchronized moving parts, the Chinese were almost absurdly anxious that they should do everything important at the most auspicious moment, from the emperor who had to plow the ceremonial furrow that opened the spring sowing, to the housewife who was planning to take a bath. The study of the movement of the stars and the measurement of time were therefore almost sacred sciences, for these gave the Chinese the astrological calendar that constituted their bank of night-flying instruments in a dark, changing, otherwise unpredictable cosmos. By A.D. 140 they had started using a water wheel to turn an armillary sphere of the heavens, and by the eleventh century were rotating a celestial globe by means of a complex water-powered mechanical clock connected to it by history's first chain drive. Eight hundred years ago, Chinese sea captains were carrying both astronomical and marine charts in their ships.

Like Imperial concubines, the greatest Chinese inventions tended to have the oddest origins. In pre-Christian China, geomancers and astrologers used a divining board which was on two levels, consisting of a circular plane corresponding to the heavens suspended over a square base which was the earth. In the center of the "celestial board" lay a metal spoon representing the Great Bear that balanced on its bowl, so that the handle was free to turn and act as a pointer. Then, nearly two thousand years ago, the Chinese began making the Great Bear spoon out of lodestone.

For an unconscionable passage of time, the Chinese kept their "south-pointing spoon" strictly in the realm of magic. But by the eighth century they had found out about polarity and magnetic variation (thus establishing a comfortable six-hundred-year lead over the West), and then came the breakthrough. In 1044, armies of the Sung dynasty were carrying a "south-pointing fish"—a sliver of iron two inches long and half an inch wide, with a point at one end. Heated and then watercooled, this small blade was placed on top of the still, clean water in a bowl without breaking the surface tension, and would then point south. By this time the Chinese in fact have both floating and dry-pivoted compasses, and a few years later someone records of ships' captains: "In dark weather they look to the south-pointing needle, and use a sounding line to determine the smell and nature of mud on the sea bottom, and so know where they are . . ."

Western navigators have worked out from his courses the divisions of the compass card used by Cheng Ho, the great eunuch-admiral of the fifteenth century who sailed as far as East Africa. It was divided into twenty-four points, and these were in turn split into three, giving seventy-two subdivisions, which means that the doctored old sea-dog must have sailed his courses to within five degrees.

The legendary father of Chinese medicine compiled the first book of drugs two thousand years before Christ, and many tales about ancient Chinese doctors come down to us, if sometimes distorted by the fun-fair mirrors of antique legend. It was unquestionably a doctor who saved the future First Emperor from assassination in 227 B.C. by knocking a would-be killer off balance with his bag of instruments, and perhaps it was the memory of this, more than an unfashionable preference for the sciences over the humanities, that persuaded the ruler to exempt medical works when he ordered all the books in China burned.

A Chinese consulting room in Singapore will often be hung with wooden plaques, bearing a few characters in red or gold, presented by grateful patients. The usual formula for these testimonials is something like: "Hua To come to life again." As has been remarked, Dr. Hua To died under torture in the third century A.D., but before that regrettable episode, he performed many skillful operations, it seems, including one upon the general who was later to be worshipped as the Chinese God of War. Finding that the arm of this hero had been pierced to the bone by a poison arrow, the sensible doctor told his adult patient precisely what he was about to do to him: "In a private room I shall erect a post with a ring attached. I shall ask you, sir, to insert your arm in the ring, and I shall bind it firmly to the post.

Then I shall cover your head with a quilt so that you cannot see, and with a scalpel I shall open up the flesh right down to the bone. Then I shall scrape away the poison. This done, I shall dress the wound with a certain preparation, sew it up with thread, and there will be no further trouble."

The tough old veteran in fact played a game of chess while the surgeon performed his operation, a young boy holding a basin under the arm. "Although your wound is cured," the doctor admonished him later, "you must be careful of your health, and especially avoid all excitement for a hundred days . . ." The instructions have a very familiar ring, and were, as usual, ignored. Any fantasy in this story lies in the general's behavior rather than in Hua To's expertise, for a reliable historical work records this interesting excerpt from his writings: "If the patient has an internal disease that cannot be cured with medicines, he must be operated. Before the operation begins, he should be given a drug that will make him fall asleep as one dead drunk. If the trouble is in the intestines, part of the intestine must be cut away, the wound cleaned well with special medicines, and then sewn together. Keep the patient still in a comfortable sleep for three or four days. One month later, the patient will have recovered."

The Chinese have always been great herbalists, and in the sixteenth century they produced a *materia medica* that listed two thousand drugs and some eight thousand prescriptions which included iodine, kaolin, and ephedrine, a form of inoculation for smallpox, and a treatment for syphilis. By the mid-nineteenth century they had published a *Research into the Names and Virtues of Plants* that ran to sixty volumes and contained two thousand accurate drawings. Every Chinese pharmacy in Singapore displays rows of glass jars filled with fascinating dried roots, weeds, and grasses—some so expensive that they provide a profitable living for smugglers. Good Korean ginseng, for example, costs about US $1.50 for one-tenth of an ounce, for it has a great reputation not only as a general fortifier but also as a herb possessing those properties dear to old gentlemen of failing faculties. The ordinary Chinese of Singapore, a healthy lot who do not sicken easily, have enough faith in their own medical science to be very conservative and to stick very often to traditional remedies. In the old days the well-to-do families would run their own health-insurance system by paying a permanent retainer to a Chinese doctor. (But it is not true, as the "topsy-turvey land" school of thoughtlessness has it, that they stopped paying the doctor as soon as someone fell ill.)

This confidence was not unjustified, it appears. In 1965, Dato Lee Kong Chian, probably the richest and certainly the most affable of the fourteen Chinese millionaires that the tiny island of Singapore manages to sustain, was found to have cancer of the liver. He was treated in accordance with Western medical practice, and a section of his liver was cut away, but no one could make any promises about even his immediate future, for he was in his seventies. He then went to Shanghai, however, where two Chinese specialists examined him and instead of suggesting further surgery recommended prescriptions for certain potions, one to be taken twice daily, the other just before retiring. The ingredients are mainly herbs and seeds, but the eye, jinking nervously among the Latin names in the translation, is caught by alchemical references to peonies and ginseng, sage, arrowroot, and wheat-flour yeast, not to mention "roasted shell of soft-shelled turtle—4 maces" and "fresh shell of oyster—31.26 grains." A supporting tonic is also recommended, and this is compounded of red dates, rock sugar, and "snow-toad jelly." (The snow toad comes from the shores of frozen Lake Barkol in Chinese Sinkiang; the body is dried to obtain a gluey aspic for medicinal purposes.) Lee Kong Chian drank these witch brews regularly, and religiously followed the diet that was supposed to accompany them. His Western doctors were frankly astonished by the improvement in his condition, and all his friends agreed that he looked better than he had done for years.

Perhaps the most curious and controversial aspect of Chinese

medicine is the practice of acupuncture. Commenting ruefully
on an unwise and unnecessary action, Confucius is supposed to
have used the metaphor: "I must confess I plastered myself with
moxa when I had nothing wrong." He might have done, for the
allied therapeutical treatments of moxibustion and acupuncture
are said to be four thousand years old. In moxibustion, "cigarettes" of dried moxa plant, which has heating properties rather
like those of a mustard plaster, are applied to certain places on
the patient's body for up to thirty minutes, with the burning
end away from the skin, so that only the warmth is felt. In
acupuncture, very fine needles are inserted at these points. In
earlier times, nine different kinds of metal needle were used.
Today, however, the needles are usually made of silver or stain-
less steel wire. Only a few years after the unfortunate Dr. Hua
To died, a Chinese medical treatise listed 349 points at which
the patient might be pricked, and by the eighth century the
Chinese were organizing lecture courses and examinations in
acupuncture.

How does it work? The doctor first determines whether the
ailment to be treated is caused by "weakness" (an illness which
demands stimulation of the system of senses), "superfluity" (requiring a relaxation of tensions), or "hyperfunctioning" (spasms,
hyperacidity, etc.). The whereabouts of the symptoms also enable
him to say along which of the fourteen channels of the body that
carry the "vital force" the trouble lies. If stimulation is needed,
he inserts his needles at key points along the relevant channel
in line with the flow of the vital force. If relaxation or a slowing-
down process is required, he sticks the needles in against the
flow of the vital force. In certain cases the needles may be pushed
in over the affected part itself, but more often than not, they
are planted elsewhere along the sick channel. Where stimulation
is desired, the needles may be left in for up to half an hour (they
do not hurt the patient), but if they are being used to bring
a fever down, they are withdrawn as soon as the temperature
drops. The fourteen channels, carrying blood and nutrition

through the body, are connected to all the internal organs, so acupuncturists believe. Consequently, heart trouble may be cured by puncturing the forearm, or arthritis by sticking pins in the head.

There is incontrovertible evidence, the Chinese say, that acupuncture has been effective against a formidable array of ills, including sciatica, neuritis, neurasthenia and facial paralysis, bronchial asthma, diabetes, malaria, even infantile paralysis if caught within half a year of its onset. It will deal with acute conjunctivitis within forty-eight hours, with glaucoma, with tonsillitis, beriberi, and many other maimers and killers. Several Europeans—some of whom have especially flown out to the Far East for treatment—say they have been cured of their ailments with astonishing speed by acupuncture, after having exhausted the resources of Western medicine. The last of which I have a note was a certain Otto Kaufmann, who lost his persistent lumbago within two days of undergoing acupuncture in Singapore. The fulsome letter of thanks that this traveler wrote to his Chinese doctor carried a certain authority. Kaufmann was himself an Austrian surgeon.

The Manchu emperors would not countenance acupuncture for themselves, for the Imperial body might not be pricked, and as Western medicine began to seep in, the exponents of the ancient art dwindled steadily, until the Communists became the masters of China. Thereafter, Western and Chinese medicine were practiced side by side. In 1958, I walked out of the X-ray department of a modern hospital in Honan and straight into a treatment room opposite, to find myself face to face (figuratively speaking) with a naked young woman lying on her stomach, her body bristling with needles. Western medicine had failed to solve her problems, so Chinese acupuncture was being tried.

"A speck of rat's dirt will spoil a bowl of rice," the Chinese say, however, and there is more than one speck in the history of Chinese medicine. The achievements are sometimes impressive, but the diagnoses are often disconcerting. Acupuncture may cure gastroenteritis, but the prosaic European has always been a trifle worried by the questionable principles of anatomy behind this treatment: that the human body was a reproduction of the cosmos ("Man has 365 bones, corresponding to the number of days it takes the heavens to revolve"), that it was activated by a life force called "ch'i," and that illness came from discordant sentiments which disturbed the harmony and balance of this miniature universe. Causes of internal sickness were listed as joy, anger, desire, surprise, fear, grief, worry; of external ills: wind, fire, heat, cold, dryness, and humidity. The main organs were the equivalents of the five main elements of Chinese alchemy—wood, fire, earth, metal, water—and were easily affected by airs and vapors.

During the Sung dynasty there was indeed an academy of medicine, but doctors were also pounding up insects, reptiles, pearls, and jade to make potions. The spirit of inquiry had not led anyone beyond the point where a learned work could state: "Males have twelve ribs on each side, eight long and four short. Females have fourteen." If you have ulcers in the leg, stop eating salted fish, one diagnosis dictates. For salt makes the blood run downward, and fish provokes fever and ulcers. Eat more salt fish, therefore, and you are bound to have more ulcers in the leg. Even in this field, fine theories are spun intuitively, without anyone troubling to test them.

The Sung dynasty was overthrown seven hundred years ago, but modern examples of Chinese medical unreason are still a commonplace. In 1962 the Ministry of Public Health in Peking recommended that people should practice birth control by swallowing live tadpoles. Doctors still diagnose "too much fire" in the body, or "too little water," as if health and sickness were like good and bad weather. "Apply to the affected part," ran the instructions for one embrocation for wounds, cuts, burns, and fractures, "and then drink the rest of the bottle." In 1960 the Chinese Communists suddenly evolved a new, all-embracing medical theory that covered the whole field of sickness: health was a matter of ideological consciousness; it was a bourgeois-rightist deviation to fear that you might succumb to disease. "I used to fight against tuberculosis as a test of my revolutionary will and loyalty to the Party," one comrade declared half threateningly at a medical conference in Peking. "Combating it is a political mission." Medicine was ascribed only a minor role in the business of healing the sick: it was Marxist-Leninism that really pulled you through. This sort of "rat's dirt" also sullies the repute of state medicine under the Communists, who have in some ways gone very far toward putting their Hippocratic house in order (they have also been the first to make synthetic insulin). But in the old days healing was always a family affair in China, each doctor passing on his dubious knowledge to his son, and until modern times there was no proper control of training and practice, so that any quack could put up his plate. (Not that this entitles the Westerner to raise his hands in horror, for effective supervision of medical standards was only introduced in Britain in 1858.) Even today, the back pages of Chinese newspapers in Singapore and Hong Kong are filled with advertisements about the wonder cures of Chinese "gynecologists," who attract their patients by publishing repulsive diagrams of the most intimate organs, showing a flair for imaginative draftsmanship rather than a sound knowledge of anatomy.

Superstition rather than science also colors the Chinese attitude toward hygiene. "In this city there are fully three thousand public baths," writes Marco Polo of Hangchow, "to which men resort for their pleasure several times a month; for they believe in keeping their bodies very clean. I assure you that they are the finest baths and the best and biggest in the world." Hangchow was in fact a fairly sanitary city in the Middle Ages, and remarkably free from lice. Municipal boats removed the refuse from the streets, and once a year the town and its canals would be given a thorough cleansing. The rich had their private cesspools, and scavangers removed the rest of the nightsoil in buckets.

Marco Polo, coming from an unwashed and verminous Europe, was doubtless impressed and, as ever, ready to gild the lotus.

On the other hand, Daniele Varè described the Chinese city and the Jade Canal in Peking at the turn of this century as stinking of a rich mixture of sesame oil, garlic, manure, beetroot, and rotting corpses. In fact, the north, being colder, was always dirtier than the south, and the hard-bitten people of the Imperial capital often took their revenge by biting the fleas back: it was quite common in earlier times for them to be eaten, along with the body lice that so plagued the citizenry. On the other hand, the Chinese have been known to be very fastidious, and it is recorded that two colleagues of the redolent if renowned administrator Wang An-shih once forced him into a bath when he became unbearably dirty. Some not only scrubbed themselves and their houses but had their servants wash down the trees and scour and polish the stones in the garden with a kind of lunatic lust for cleanliness and order otherwise only seen in British army barracks. Nevertheless, to maintain the proper rhythm of the universe an educated man would only bathe every ten days in ancient times, so that the ideogram for "bath" and for the ten-day periods into which the Chinese divided the month was the same. And there are still many who will not wash on certain ill-omened dates connected, for example, with the Chinese zodiacal signs of the Hare and the Rat, for bathing then brings bad luck.

For the Chinese, hygiene is on one frontier of mysticism, and sport on the other. Between lies a no man's land of semi-magical physical culture utterly strange to the Westerner, who thinks of antiseptic bathrooms and eighteen holes of golf as the twin answers to debilitation, sickness, and early death.

21

Digging for Dragons

Turn a corner in a Chinese town in the early morning or at dusk and you may observe, with some kindly concern, an old gentleman of seventy waving his arms on the sidewalk, leaning over backward to a dangerous degree, pivoting on nimble feet, and then kicking a leg high in the air—and all of this at septugenarian speed as if he were some sort of slow-motion sot. But he is only practicing *T'ai Chi,* or Chinese shadowboxing.

T'sai Chi is within the realm of breathing control and of esoteric physical disciplines that promise almost supernatural rewards to their devotees, for they belong to the Chinese conceptions of "nurturing life" and "nurturing the body," which includes "the secrets that enabled the Yellow Emperor to enjoy twelve hundred concubines without harm to his health." Its movements so harmonize with the motion of the universe, teachers say, that an expert may concentrate his whole bodily force in his fingertips, master all nature, and live on to an excessively overripe old age. So while young men get up at dawn to perform exercises or practice Chinese boxing, their elders may at least make a few passes at their shadows.

For both bodily and mental hygiene are inseparable. If the body is to be in harmony with the universe, the mind must be also. Sport, therefore, becomes a religion in quite a different sense from the heathen devotion of the Anglo-Saxon athlete. It is that worship of natural rhythm which inspired judo and karate, which makes Chinese love acrobatics and take pride in being chosen for the back legs in a two-man lion dance (it takes several more years after that to graduate to the front legs). It meant that China's greatest poets were not pale, solitary dreamers but competent archers, riders, swordsmen, and charioteers, who would have understood at once the European student of Japanese archery who described how after five years of study he at last, to his great joy, learned to loose an arrow "unintentionally." They would have recognized that this was a step toward that mystical condition which makes a man invulnerable, almost immortal.

These considerations are surely of no consequence to the girl who wins eight gold medals for swimming at the Southeast Asia Peninsula Games, or the world table-tennis championship winners from Peking, it may be argued. Surely the hocus-pocus has been buried with China's past?

Has it? In April 1965, the Chinese Communist press published an article headed *Eliminate the Dregs from Shadowboxing*. This was not an attack on bloodsucking fight promotors and fixed bouts but upon abracadabra. "The martial arts in China are not without remnants of many feudal superstitions and beliefs," the article complained. "Large numbers of teachers of the art of shadowboxing have made a supernatural cult of the works and theories of its old masters." Many people say, for example, "that the Absolute is produced out of the Illimitable," and that this is the origin of movement and the mother of Yin and Yang. "After you have been trained in shadowboxing, therefore, you can spring atop the house. It will make you young again, turn white beard and hair into black, allow you to pass through the hottest days without sweating, the coldest without shivering."

In Chinese science, medicine, sport, and even the daily dozen, there is this infusion of speculative metaphysics and superstition, so that all progress has the hit-and-miss quality of an experiment in alchemy. In consequence, Chinese astronomy was always regarded as suspect, because it was simply the handmaiden of discredited Chinese astrology. The Chinese discovered the compass only in the course of practicing magical divination, and then left it for centuries in the hands of geomancers, who used it for siting graves. They found gunpowder while looking for the philosophers' stone, and employed it to make firecrackers to scare off evil spirits. They are condemned by many as unserious men who only applied the law of natural selection to the breeding of goldfish, the principle of the rotary fan to the cooling of palaces, and their knowledge of zoology (it has been said) to the art of cooking.

The tragedy of Chinese science was that it became the plaything of the Taoists—not the Taoist philosophers who believed in unlearning, but their degenerate successors: the alchemists, the magicians, the quacks, and the plausible charlatans who did not exactly reject knowledge but tended to make it up as they went along. Knowledge is known by the company it keeps, and for most scholars and mandarins medicine, for example, was part of the dud merchandise of the wandering Taoist priest, along with necromancy and fortunetelling, and only of interest to popeyed peasants. The Taoists did not study the laws of nature, but only fumbled after relative truths. They believed in guessing the answers intuitively and then shaving down the facts to fit them. They tested nothing, and their findings can only be described as pseudo-science. This may sound like ancient history, but some Chinese scholars even in this century have solemnly insisted that modern technological discoveries were known to both the early Confucian and the early Taoist philosophers, for they could divine them from the ancient and mystical *Book of Changes*.

Chinese pseudo-science is based on the Taoist principles of the Great Unity, of Yin and Yang, and of the Five Elements—wood, fire, earth, metal, water—which consume each other rather as three beats deuce but deuce beats ace in certain card games, so that there is no master. The five elements had their equivalents in the five seasons (the Chinese inserted an extra one to avoid having a blank file), the five colors, the five principal flavors, the five viscera, the five smells, etc. Ancient numerology provides further fine examples of this stuff: "Heaven is One, Earth is Two, Man is Three. Three times three is nine, and nine nine's are eighty-one. One governs the Sun. The sun's number is ten. Therefore, Man is born in the tenth month of development . . ." This passage goes on to assert, among other arresting conclusions, that in winter swallows and starlings go down into the sea, where they change into mussels.

Three of the principal occupations of Taoist quacks were the search for the philosophers' stone and for the Elixir of Life, and the gentle but profitable art of geomancy. Following in the footsteps of the great Chinese sorcerers, an agreeable young Bostonian arrived at Singapore University in late 1962 and set out to produce posterity pills, using the recipe contained in a seventh-century Taoist monograph on the preparation of the elixir. Unlike credulous emperors of former days who thirsted for everlasting life, Mr. Nathan Sivin of Harvard was imbued with a peculiarly American ambition. He did not want to eat the pill once he had concocted it. He only wanted to analyze it. However, he was unable to obtain the use of a two-thousand-year-old iron crucible for his experiment, and had to make do with a twentieth-century nickel laboratory oven. This was not up to the strain, and burst like a bomb. It may therefore be said that during the past twenty-two hundred years, from the charlatans who fooled the Emperor Wu down to the impeccably honest Mr. Sivin, Chinese alchemy has failed to deliver the goods.

Feng Shui—Wind-and-Water—is the Chinese term for the mysterious art of so locating anything, from an ancestral grave to the new premises of a bra factory, that it will enjoy the most auspicious topographical relationship with mountains, winds, waters, and the spirits of dragons. Water means prosperity, for example, and still water facing the premises means easy money. Mountains are the underpasses of dragons, and a good *feng-shui* expert will weigh the state of change of the universe and decide which range of hills the local dragon spirit is moving through and how far he has reached. Build (or dig) there, and fortune is yours dead or alive, for there is nothing luckier than to be on top of a dragon and his lair.

But the presence of the dragon is determined by tracing its arteries in the earth, so that this form of geomancy becomes not only a costly business but a dirty one. In *The Scholars*, *feng-shui* merchants asked to decide upon the site of a grave not only examine clods of earth carefully but break off pieces and munch on them thoughtfully, until one announces: "If you bury someone in this, you will bankrupt your family." However, another site set in mountains positively gristly with dragon veins is approved: "This plot will produce a Number-One Graduate. If you make your Fourth Uncle's grave here, and you only come second in the examinations, you can pluck out both my eyes," declares the geomancer. Elsewhere in the book, geomancers are amusingly exposed as quarrelsome scroungers, and the whole "science" as nonsensical charlatanism. But that was in the enlightened eighteenth century. One hundred years later, the Chinese general defending Ningpo cast a tiger's skull into the local Dragon Pool, believing that the dragon would then rise out of it and sink the invading English fleet. And when he decided to attack the British in the port itself, he waited for the hour, the day, the month, and the year of the Tiger (0300 hours on March 10, 1842), to make sure of victory. He lost.

Feng-shui remains *de rigueur* today. In prewar Shanghai, even the position of the boss's desk would be decided by some artful exponent of this craft. In Hong Kong, the rich still shower money on geomancers who pick the right burial ground for them to buy before they die, and there are many Singapore Chinese who would never allow an architect to build them a house before a *feng-shui* specialist had decided which way it should face. When a successful Chinese businessman does not wish to move from the cramped, filthy, and collapsing premises in which he first began to prosper thirty-five years ago, it may be precisely because he has been successful there. He can afford new premises, but he cannot afford to leave. Better the dragon you know, so to speak, than the dragon you don't.

Where the railway crosses the border between the Chinese provinces of Kwangtung and Hunan, there is a curious mountain upon whose summit stands a rock as big as a house but shaped like a chicken. This zoomorphic slab of stone has naturally excited the Kwangtung geomancers, who have long predicted that the spirit of the Golden Chicken would take the form of a Kwangtung hero. In due course, local boy indeed made good, for a man called Hsueh Yueh, born in the very county within which Golden Chicken Mountain stands, became one of China's most able generals. The geomancers were further vindicated when he was appointed regional commander of the military zone that included Hunan Province, for the stone chicken had its beak pointing into Hunan, but its bottom in Kwangtung. It therefore fed on Hunan but laid its golden eggs in Kwangtung, and a Kwangtung general with power over Hunan would presumably do the same thing: the people of Hunan were going to end up the poorer, and those of Kwangtung very much richer. The stubborn and pugnacious inhabitants of Hunan (which has given us, among others, Mao Tse-tung) were furious that this foreigner should be appointed over them, expected the worst, and proceeded to remedy the situation by climbing the Golden Chicken and breaking off its offending beak. Once more the potency of *feng-shui* was strikingly demonstrated. Hsueh Yueh was indeed forced to withdraw from Hunan eventually—and it was overrun by the Communists.

Feng-shui, born of an earthy animism prompts men to placate local spirits rather than dream of a heaven full of houris, has a certain coherence about it, for it belongs legitimately to the concept of a unified and harmonious universe. But decadent Taoism also bred many a rank superstition that has proved just as hardy an annual as the flying saucer. There is still a Taoist "Pope," the sixty-third successor of the first pontiff, who was last seen riding up to heaven on a dragon in A.D. 156. To millions of overseas

Chinese who positively have to know their lucky numbers, colors, and days, astrological almanacs sell like hotcakes. Precious children are not given their final names at birth, but described as "Dog" or "Rat," "Pig" or "Monkey," to allay the interest of jealous and greedy spirits who may be listening. (The absence of names on tens of thousands of birth certificates of Singapore Chinese led to sharp political exchanges in 1966, when their holders became worried that they would be unable to prove they were entitled to citizenship.) Men believe that a child born on the fifth day of the fifth month will commit suicide, that girls born in the Year of the Horse (one of the twelve signs of the Chinese zodiac) will never marry well. A man's horoscope is a must.

In 1965, the Chinese Communists began sending "truth squads" throughout the country to preach "revolutionary culture and scientific thought" in order to fight superstition. For Mao had not managed to kill the occult. Even the director of a medical clinic in South China had been caught worshipping an unlovable little clay image of the God of Wealth, while in the marketplaces soothsayers and fortunetellers were still doing a roaring trade in that illusory split second, so beloved of Western official spokesmen, known as the "foreseeable future." Work bulletins circulated to formation and unit commanders in the Chinese Communist Army revealed in 1964 that, among their other shortcomings, some soldiers dreaded sorcery more than sergeants. One reconnaissance unit refused to go out on sorties at night for fear of ghosts, and in another area a military telephone line that ran through a graveyard was left out of order for two years. No signal detachment dared to go and repair it.

The mysterious Orient has no monopoly of superstition, however, as every salt-throwing, ladder-dodging European with a horseshoe on his watch chain will doubtless admit. Europe has fathered a fine flock of clairvoyants like Old Mother Shipton, of spiritualists, witches, mediums, palm-readers and crystal-gazers, of penny-in-the-slot sorcerers of the mechanistic age that purport to tell you not only your fortune but even your weight. Nor has the rational West been above confusing science and "what the stars foretell," or creating its own crazy-chains to link some planet with the pancreas and the power of three.

In March 1966, the Weekend Magazine of *The Observer* contained an illuminating article which pointed out that in the Middle Ages European astronomy was the servant of astrology (as in China), and that astrology largely governed the practice of medicine. Four hundred years ago, popes consulted astrologers, and Paracelsus combined in himself all the stock-in-trade of a Chinese Taoist priest—doctor, palmist, and alchemist—predicting the future from the stars and diagnosing disease from the lines of the hand. This seems fantastic now, perhaps. Yet in World War II a man who has been called the official astrologer of the British government was supposed to advise Winston Churchill on the predictions that his vis-à-vis in Germany would be making to Hitler, and *Time* magazine has given its cachet to palmistry by saying that as an aid to medical diagnosis it is "as promising as it is new." Meanwhile, Old Moore's Almanac sells more than a million copies a year in Britain alone.

The back-to-Paracelsus trend has produced Western reflections on the Taoist theory of the harmonious cosmos in which man is part of the universal watch movement, and it was none other than Jung who said earlier: "Whatever happens in a given moment has inevitably the qualities of that moment." (*How profound! How obscure!* Lao Tzu might have whispered from the wings of history.) Meanwhile, in Hong Kong, British officials of the crown colony's administration responsible for the construction of roads and public buildings watch their *feng-shui* as narrowly as would any Chinese with one eye on a grave for his grandmother and the other on a managing directorship.

Irrational Europe and irrational China differ in one vital respect, however. In eighty-seven short years, the seventeenth-century West moved from Tycho Brahe, a brilliant astrologer-astronomer still loaded down with the mysticism of the Middle Ages, to Isaac Newton, who explained the universe entirely in terms of cold, natural laws without a flicker of the old fantasies. Like second-stage rockets, astronomy detached itself from astrology, chemistry from alchemy, science from superstition. There was no reason why Churchill should not consult a wizard if he wanted to: the Spitfire would still be turned out to sound specifications.

But during the crucial period between Galileo and Newton, the Manchus had moved into China from the wild north and were carefully preserving the matured civilization of the Chinese in its own pickle. Western technical progress was treated with disdain and suspicion. China closed up, and within her frontiers the Taoist con-men sold spells and amulets for malaria, astronomy was still dragged along in the dust of astrology, and Chinese science lay besotted by the fumes of alchemy.

There was more to this than the Manchus, however. The clerk with a set of conversion tables does not bother his head with monetary arithmetic, and for perhaps three thousand years the average Chinese has been tempted to shrug off the occasional free-thinking oddball among his countrymen who advocated "the examination of the nature of things" or "testing assertions against facts." For he has been in possession of the *Book of Changes,* the cosmic ready-reckoner that gave all the answers, and therefore discouraged all the real questions.

22

Chinaman's Chance

There is a rather unlikely story that it was the legendary King Fu Hsi who discovered the trigrams. It seems that when he was walking on the banks of a river in the province of Honan, North China, on a fine day six or seven thousand years ago, a winged horse with the head of a dragon and standing *approximately* eight feet five inches high climbed out of the water. The appearance of this hippogriff did not surprise the sovereign, who had the body of a serpent himself (for this was before men were accorded self-government), but he was struck by the curious black and white markings on its flanks. From these he devised eight trigrams, which were in fact the first, heaven-inspired form of writing, for each had a meaning, like this:

```
————                  — —                  — —
————   = Heaven       — —   = Earth        — —   = Thunder
————                  — —                  ————
```

Other combinations of these complete and broken lines signified mountain, fire, water, marsh, and wind.

The ancient Chinese, however, made their important decisions and foretold events by examining the cracks in oracle bones (the femur of oxen) or on a tortoiseshell when it split and fissured under heat. The more prosaic therefore believe that the trigrams were simply symbols representing the different patterns that these ominous lines would make, and that from the beginning they have been associated with the soothsayer. At some point before the birth of Christ, however, the trigrams were turned into hexagrams by putting one on top of the other, so that the resultant figure consisted of six continuous or broken lines. This gave not eight but sixty-four variations, each of which acquired its own significance. For example:

— —   — —
———   ———
— —   ———
——— = Masterly inactivity, while ——— = Revolution
———   — —
———   ———

The hexagrams summarize all the possible changes in the evolving universe that can be brought about by the interaction of Yang (continuous line) and Yin (broken line). They are the basis for the powerful sibylline work whose origins have been swallowed up in the mists far behind us: the *I Ching*, or *Book of Changes*.

The first, limited edition of the *I Ching* may have appeared in about 1200 B.C., or even before, and was full of peasant omens and enigmatic warnings, but interpretive texts and appendices were then added to it, the Confucians venerated it as a classic, and the Taoists adopted it as their bible. From time immemorial, it has told the Chinese when to make sacrifices, or whether to marry off daughters, how to win the next battle, or where to find fortune. The fingers of tens of thousands of scholars have, with nervous reverence, fumbled through its pages for today's truth. It is not a vulgar fortuneteller's manual, full of dark strangers and light comedy. Its devotees claim that it simply gives general indications as to how we should act to be in harmony with the changing universe at any given moment. Its oracular utterances must be interpreted intuitively.

How does it work? Place the *Book of Changes* on a table facing south, take fifty yarrow stalks, set one aside, and bunch the remaining forty-nine in the fist. Let them fall on to the table, divide them into two piles with a swift movement of the right hand, and by a system of further subdivision and of eliminating leftovers in groups of four, you end up with three little piles of stalks. These represent one line of a hexagram, and the number of stalks in each pile indicates whether that line is a continuous Yang or a broken Yin. Repeat the process twelve times until two hexagrams are built up, and then consult the *Book of Changes,* which devotes a chapter to the meaning of each one.

Setting the *I Ching* the unworthy task of deciding whether, as an expatriate in Singapore, I should buy a modest piece of Hampshire or not, I cast the yarrow stalks and checked the hexagrams with the *I Ching* in December 1965, to be told this:

First hexagram (No. 38: water, pool, marsh, joy, fire, brilliance, beauty): "The Estranged—good fortune in small matters . . ." There followed a lengthy commentary, and then advice on the position of the individual lines: "Regret vanishes! Do not follow the straying horse, for it will return of its own accord . . . He encountered his lord in a narrow lane—no error!" And so on. It looked as if I were about to become a landowner. I then turned to my second hexagram (No. 64), and got this: "Before completion—success!" However: "Before the little fox has quite completed its crossing of the ice, its tail gets wet." And later on: "Its tail gets wet—disgrace!" And although this was followed by much earnest talk of persistence, it was interpreted as persistence in halting now and only proceeding at a later date.

I do not own any of Hampshire—and the advice proved excellent.

An adept does not necessarily have to juggle with yarrow stalks: he may see a hexagram in a pattern of bamboo leaves, or in a teacup, or in a spilled box of matches. But for the most part nowadays Chinese find truth in the *I Ching* too obscure and complicated to decipher. They prefer debased forms of instant-oracle, and consult soothsayers who have made this *Book of Changes* the basis for simpler ways of divining the future. However, the drama of the Christian conscience springs not from the wording of the Ten Commandments themselves but from the principles which they buried, like some alien charge of dynamite, deep in the stony nature of man. The *I Ching* may not lie to hand in every Chinese household today, but it has propounded a law that has subordinated the conscious to the subconscious in millions of Chinese. "Look," says Mr. Wong, "trillions upon trillions of constantly changing factors make up the universe. For a man to say, 'Let us take all the factors into consideration and then come to a logical conclusion' is absurd, for deduction can never take everything into account anyway. Argue your way for hours toward the correct decision, and in many cases you stand no more chance of being right in the long run than if you had flipped a coin and saved yourself the trouble." But the indications given by the *I Ching* are bound to be right because the fall-out of the yarrow stalks is part of the inevitable Tao itself.

The Chinese never had a consistent scientific method that might have disproved this racy rationalization, and so they tend to back the inspired hunch against any forty thousand words of cerebration. In their philosophy the most precious thing a man may have is a good horoscope, the second is good luck, the third is good *feng-shui* (to be born in an auspicious place: to have one's grandfather buried over a dragon's lair), the fourth is merit derived from good works—for merit can bring good fortune—and only the fifth and last is an aptitude for brainwork. A great Sung dynasty poet wrote nearly one thousand years ago:

> Families, when a child is born,
> Want it to be intelligent.
> I, through intelligence
> Having wrecked my whole life,
> Only hope the baby will prove
> Ignorant and stupid
> Then he will crown a tranquil life
> By becoming a cabinet minister.

A people that believes it is better to be lucky than clever has derived even its parlor games from astrological and soothsaying practices. Playing cards were originally used for divination, and the common Chinese ancestor of backgammon and parchesi was based upon the magical hexagrams. There is nothing strange in this to a Chinese, for whom divination and draw poker belong to the same world of chance, and the philosophy that makes the Chinese the soothsayer's best customer makes him one of the world's outstanding gamblers, too.

A Chinese will bet on anything. In the Sung dynasty the rich would stake their houses, their horses, and their slaves on a game of backgammon, and in Ping's ancestral home the men came to the card table with bunches of large keys instead of money or chips—the keys to their huge rice granaries. During World War II long-distance truck drivers bringing salt and oil and other commodities into Chiang Kai-shek's stronghold in southwest China would sit in the little teahouses on the high passes, betting their entire cargoes on whether the last digit on the registration number of the next truck to come up the hill would be odd or even. And when they had lost all else, they would casually toss the ignition key of their own truck on the table for the final hazard. In Shanghai, men who have been mulcted to the pocket linings have been known to bet a finger of their right hand against a big kitty, and to honor their debt in this gory game of strip poker by chopping off the finger themselves when they lost, before the sporting company. When Ping was in a Singapore hospital in 1966, she found that the orderlies were placing bets on whether patients would survive or not, and on which day of the month they would be discharged. In Malaysia many Chinese are passionate "drainpipe" punters, wagering money on whether it will rain or not that day—and agreeing that it will have officially rained if one drop of water comes out of a preselected drainpipe. Most Chinese have a touching faith in their own intuition, and many hailed the institution of a state lottery in Nationalist China as a stroke of genius that would allow them to save the Republic's economy by making their own fortunes. I remember the crazy confidence of one Cantonese in Malaysia who said: "What do you mean, the chances of winning the lottery are 1,568,593,219 to one? The chances are even: either your ticket wins, or it doesn't." But then a Chinese will even draw lots to decide which doctor to go to when he is ill.

The "1984" school of experts on Communist China delights in depicting grim gangs of regimented peasantry living antlike existences in a permanent state of utter terror. But these essays in horror are usually written by people who have not been within one thousand miles of the People's Republic, where the men in charge tend to behave not so much like vicious paranoiacs as like the stern, more-in-sorrow-than-in-anger Victorian paterfamilias. In Shanghai, for example, it was discovered that many of the workers were so cowed by all the iron discipline that they had become poker maniacs. Somewhat untidy statistics revealed that in two years, three months, and eight days, card-carrying members of the local poker school had cost one plant alone 5,320 man-hours. The Communist cadres did not immediately attack them with knouts, however, but urged them to confess their "evil practices" to their fellows and to reform. The saddened culprits were then told to spend two hours a week studying current affairs and reading the works of Mao Tse-tung instead.

Devil-may-care gambling manners are the hallmark of the hero, for the Chinese have an affection for characters with a certain chivalrous panache who never do things by halves. When they drink, it is always "No heel-taps." If they stake their fortune, it is on the turn of a card. When they win, they do not boast or show off, for they know that they may just as easily lose tomorrow. When they lose, they shrug—and start planning to bounce back. When they are well-off, they are generous and easygoing, quick to share their luck.

The conventional Chinese, burdened with family duties and forced to be closefisted, has a wistful admiration for this big-hearted picaresque rogue that he knows as a "chianghuk'o"—a "man of the rivers and lakes." Product of the more perilous centuries of Chinese history, a chianghuk'o was a knight-errant *raté* with the integrity of a rough diamond and the morals of a monkey—restless, rootless, a man with no home and no responsibilities. Quick to cry out against injustices, he was the enemy of corrupt and cruel government, and usually kept on the move to escape arrest, playing the lone wolf and only participating in collective enterprises like banditry as a last resort. Easy-come, easy-go, he took his women where he found them, gave his money away impulsively when he had any, and quickly earned more without much difficulty, since he was bold as brass and not fussy about getting tarnished either. He was a gambler and a wanderer, but often full of good deeds. He would never stab anyone in the back, but was quite capable of smuggling opium if it paid.

The tradition is not dead. The transport drivers who ditched their profitable loads in order to give a lift to poor refugees fleeing before the advancing Japanese during World War II were of this breed, and it was typical of them that they might then stake their trucks on one straight bet to try to make up their consequent loss of income. Today, young Chinese businessmen who spend half their lives traveling tend to announce with a sort of airy modesty that can be heard thirty yards away that they are "just a chianghuk'o." However, in more robust times this romantic, happy-go-lucky, no-good do-gooder could be respected but not emulated—unless a man wanted to take the chance that the government might annihilate his entire family. His was a role for a Clark Gable, and in fact in Ping's view, the chianghuk'o is well personified in the West by the character of Rhett Butler, the disreputable hero of *Gone with the Wind*.

The Chinese tend to believe that style can beat the system, just as a bold and spontaneous stroke of the brush is the best. A Shanghai banker, hastily emigrating to Hong Kong as the Communists take over on the mainland, confidently uses ten dollars to cover loans of a hundred, opens a four-story restaurant when he does not even have the money to pay the electricity bill—and in consequence bursts into the news as a spectacular bankrupt.

Chinese investors, knowing that the British lease of the New Territories in the crown colony will expire in thirty short years, and that the Communists may then move in, build skyscraper blocks of apartments in the expectation that they will get their money back in fifteen or even five years. As a Chinese merchant once told a startled Hungarian friend in North Malaya: "European idea—have five dollars, do one-dollar business. Chinese idea—have one dollar, do five-dollar business."

When Singapore split off from the Federation of Malaysia in 1965, the Singapore Chinese at once acted on the fallacy that they were no longer involved in Malaysia's fight against Indonesia. Within twenty-four hours, therefore, a small *kongsi* of Chinese merchants had quickly convened to charter a ten-thousand-ton cargo ship and send it through the British and Malaysian naval blockade from Singapore to Java, loaded with goods that had been bought on tick from Communist China six months before. If it made a major Indonesian port, cash payments for the freight would enable the *kongsi* to deposit a down sum in the Bank of China, which would qualify it for a long-term credit from Peking as the balance for payment of a far larger consignment of cheap Chinese produce destined for a quick sale to . . . It never came off, but as a business venture it had a certain wild gypsy beauty of its own. Yet the outlook of a Chinese is not dictated by impetuous irresponsibility but by a conviction that fortune seesaws upon a knife edge. "I can pick up a million on the market just as quickly as I can lose it—and vice versa," he will remark. "So why not take a chance?"

A man must follow his instinct, the Chinese say, for there is no principle that is right in all circumstances, or any action that is wrong in all circumstances. Mr. Shih (says Lieh Tzu) had two sons: one loved learning; the other, war. The first expounded his moral teachings at the admiring court of Ch'i and was made a tutor, while the second talked strategy at the bellicose court of Ch'u and was made a general. The impecunious Mr. Meng, hearing of these successes, sent his own two sons out to follow the example of the Shih boys. The first expounded his moral teachings at the court of Ch'in, but the King of Ch'in said: "At present the states are quarreling violently and every prince is busy arming his troops to the teeth. If I followed this prig's pratings, we should soon be annihilated." So he had the fellow castrated. Meanwhile, the second brother displayed his military genius at the court of Wei. But the King of Wei said: "Mine is a weak state. If I relied on force instead of diplomacy, we should soon be wiped out. If, on the other hand, I let this fire-eater go, he will offer his services to another state and then we shall be in trouble." So he had the fellow's feet cut off.

Both families did exactly the same thing, but one timed it right, the other wrong. Thus success depends not on ratiocination but on rhythm. However, if Lieh Tzu had continued with the story, it might well have run something like this: "The fighting foreseen by the perspicacious King of Ch'in thereupon broke out. The warlike son of Mr. Shih who had been so honored in Ch'u was killed in battle, and his peace-loving brother was decapitated when the capital of Ch'i was sacked. However, of the two Meng brothers, one had been banished to a far frontier region and the other had been sent back to peaceful Lu. Since both were mutilated, neither could be pressed into military service. They therefore survived these troubled times and lived to a comfortable old age."

For many Chinese believe that the impulses of Yin and Yang provide an alternating current of fortune, that bad luck brings good, and good luck bad. When Ping was teaching at a school in Hong Kong, she left the window of her bed-sitting room open one day when she went to work, and when she came home, she found that a cigarette butt, carelessly dropped out of the window by someone on the floor above, had blown into her room and burned a huge hole in her bed. Her landlady, much upset, consulted a fortuneteller, who assured her that this bad luck would be followed by good: the destruction of the bed by fire and light meant that a phase of Ping's life was over. She did not need this couch any more, for she would get married. On the next day, we met for the first time.

Life and death, joy and sorrow, these are two sides of the same coin—and only a fool of a European yearns for one side without the other, a Chinese might add. Even dreams must be complementary to waking, says that imaginary old sage, Lieh Tzu: "The old servant of the rich Mr. Yin was worked so cruelly hard that he rose each day with a groan and fell down in his sleeping place utterly exhausted every night. But when he dropped off, he at once dreamed that he was a powerful lord who spent his time on pleasurable excursions and on delectable banquets and marvelous spectacles in his great palace. On the other hand, Mr. Yin, plagued during the day by the heavy responsibilities of wealth, fell asleep at night in his broad and costly bed to dream that he was a harassed old slave who was constantly being scolded and beaten. 'That is simply fortune righting itself,' a friend to whom he complained replied rather unsympathetically. 'Did you really expect to have your comfort and riches both ways, when dreaming as well as when awake?' "

Down must follow up, so there is no more tragic moment than when we reach the summit of our powers: "When the eye can see the tip of a hair, it is about to grow dim; when the ear can hear the whirring of the wings of a midge, it is about to become deaf. But if a thing never attains its limit, it will not turn back." All Chinese history preached this warning, for successive dynasties rapidly reached their zenith only to decline and fall with a horrible inevitability. The switchback destinies of famous men also bore this out.

The fate of Li, the peasant brigand who wrested the throne from the Ming emperor early in the seventeenth century, was an outstanding object lesson in accepting what time brings. Inflated with Dutch courage induced by heady astrological portents that indicated a glorious destiny for him, Li raised the standard of rebellion in Shensi because he felt sure he had nothing to lose. After defeating the Imperial troops, he entered Peking wearing a black patch over the empty socket of an eye that had been pierced by an arrow in battle, convinced now that he was destined for greatness, for it had been prophesied that a one-eyed man would sit on the Dragon Throne. And he did sit on it—for one day. Having delivered the capital up to rape and massacre and had himself hastily installed as emperor, he was obliged to decamp as soon as he had bundled up as much of the fabulous treasure of the Forbidden City as he could, for he was threatened by the Manchus and one undefeated Imperial Chinese army of two hundred thousand men. Heading back to the hills of Shensi, Li was soon harried by his enemies, brought to battle, and badly beaten. He lost everything but his life, and within two years had once again become no more than a bandit with a following of some thirty men.

Once a Chinese wins position and power, he not only fights hard to keep them but exploits them ruthlessly, since he knows they are ephemeral. When the king of Ch'in who became First Emperor of China in 221 B.C. heard of a plot to overthrow him, he not only annihilated the entire households of the conspirators down to their meanest slaves, but exiled four thousand families and his own mother on suspicion. He then threatened to kill any adviser who criticized him in council, kept a naked sword at hand when he conferred with his ministers, and thereafter showed that he meant business by dispatching twenty-seven men who remonstrated with him, one after the other. For his entourage, never had the sun shone so fitfully, and so never had hay to be made more hastily. More than two thousand years later, the warlords and the Nationalist generals, who held sway over the Chinese provinces in the twenties and thirties of this century, looted their fiefs with such unprecedented zeal and lack of scruple, for fear of being supplanted at any moment, that the people of Szechuan, for example, found themselves paying taxes for twenty years ahead.

It is typical of the Chinese that in their highly intuitive finger-game of stone-paper-scissors, there can be no absolute winner, for paper wraps stone, stone breaks scissors, and scissors cut paper. "The wooden mallet strikes the chisel—the chisel splits the wood," the Chinese say. Every dog has his day, and if it is true that men at the top must fall, then men at the bottom must rise. Chinese are therefore able to bear adversity with calm and fortitude, and are fond of quoting with a certain pride: "We sleep on fagots, and on waking taste the gall," from a not very improving tale twenty-five hundred years old. At that time the ancestors of the Vietnamese inhabited the kingdom of Yüeh, which stretched to the south of modern Shanghai. Their unhappy monarch, taken prisoner by the rival state of Wu to the north, passed three years of drudgery in the palace of its king, sleeping in the royal stables and grooming the horses daily. His bed was of fagots, and when he awoke he could reach with his tongue a lump of dried pig's gall that hung above him from a rafter, and so breakfast. Finally freed from this exile, however, he returned to his own country, and at once demonstrated that his wretched experience had not impaired his faculties by dispatching to the horsy King of Wu an incomparably beautiful young woman. This lady's many excellences so bemused the monarch that very soon he had exhausted his treasury to satisfy her exacting whims. The interests of national defense were shamefully neglected, and when the King of Yüeh attacked, Wu fell like a rotten peach.

Every Chinese low on his luck is a King of Yüeh whose day will come if only he lives long enough, including Chiang Kai-shek. The exiled Chinese professor in Hong Kong, struggling for a living by writing little essays for what comes to US $2.50 a thousand words, offers a chipped cup of weak tea with both hands, glances around his damp shack of a home, and quotes from Confucius with a certain gusto: "With coarse rice to eat, with water to drink, and my bended arm for pillow—I still have joy in the midst of these." In poverty, a man finds his own dignity and integrity. But there is more to his satisfaction than this. For misfortune must lead to fortune—and he has never had it so bad.

The Chinese have been despised for taking the line of least

resistance, for their docility, and sometimes for a cowardice that asked for a kicking. But the reed only bends so that it may straighten again at an opportune moment. Timing is all-important, a Chinese will say, for given enough patience, time must always be on your side. And his words carry weight, for in the course of a long and turbulent history he has sooner or later overthrown by violence every single major dynasty that his misruled him, with the sole exception of the Sung. Detractors seem to forget these things. Mao, of course, does not.

23

The Five-Aces Fallacy

There are distressingly greedy Chinese, and there are Chinese of insatiable ambition. But Taoist admonitions against futile striving, against looking upon the proud summit as anything more than the top end of a nasty fall, are like small, never still voices in the Chinese soul. The Westerner may dream of holding five aces, but the Chinese know that to be caught with them will bring nothing but grief.

Seeking no heaven, the Chinese looks for happiness on earth, and finds it best when he is modest in his cravings. "If you do not want your house to be disturbed by robbers, do not fill it with gold and jade," said Lao Tzu. "Wealth, rank, and arrogance add up to ruin as surely as two and two make four." "Reduce your desires," urge the Buddhists. "Be modest in all the seven passions," demand the Confucians. "Things bring misery," declare the Taoists. If you are a king, others will covet your throne and assassinate you. If you are a beautiful concubine, the jealous will kill you. If you are rich, you will be robbed or kidnapped. When Chuang Tzu was offered a high ministerial post, he declined it with the words: "I would rather be a live tortoise in the mud than a dead one venerated in a gold casket in the king's ancestral shrine." "Happiness," says Ping, "is wanting to be nobody."

China was known as the Middle Kingdom, and her people respect the principle of the Golden Mean that both Confucius and the Taoists have preached. The first instinct of most Chinese is to distrust extreme solutions, whether Legalist or Communist, and their philosophers have condemned both the hedonist and the ascetic, the whiz kid and the loafer. Their belief that what goes up must come down leads them to be moderate even in their readiness to bend to the wind. Do not anger a tiger by thwarting it, they warn, but do not please it by giving way to it in all things either, "for when joy passes its climax, we are bound to revert to anger."

The Chinese is in many ways a man of frugal tastes, for his sages have taught him that the more simple the props, the fewer the hitches. He did not sit in a chair until the ninth century, and his furniture is of unforgiving hardwood, straight-backed, angular, and remorseless. His traditional bed was a wooden platform, covered only with thin matting or old quilts. His traditional pillow was a neck-rest of porcelain, or wood. Even his opium couch leaves bruises on Caucasian buttocks. He is very much the vertebrate, and his women have backs like ramrods. His seduction by the furnishing fashions of an overstuffed Occident is often a matter of prestige rather than passion, and he may still prefer a diminutive and comfortless porcelain tabouret to his imported pneumatic *fauteuils*. Ping's bed looks like the twin of the great twanging thing I sleep on, with its spiral springs and its six-inch box mattress on top. Pull back the covers on hers, however, and there is nothing but an inch-thin kapok bedroll resting on bare boards. She would rather sleep on the floor than on foam rubber, any night.

The Chinese take pleasure in small and simple things, even in their art. They do not demand constipated canvases of crowded coronations, pompous mansions, or teeming battlefields. They love the quick, sparse brushwork that shows the movement of a grasshopper, some shrimps, a startled frog, or two chicks fighting over a worm. The Chinese does not observe nature but becomes one with it. He senses the beauty of the uncarved block of wood, and the absurdity of the imitation leaf made of jade

that takes three years to fashion. Taoist quietism, that freewheel-
ing philosophy a man of years may allow himself once his main
race is run, teaches him that he would do well to retreat to the
misty mountain tops, or to feel that beat in his bones as he fishes
among the whispering willows on the edge of a lonely lake. But
a cultured Chinese can be just as contemplative in a noisy crowd,
for he does not fight the current of life, he joins it. His mind has
triumphed over existence by accepting it, and his character is
essentially mellow. For him, sufficient unto the day is the happiness thereof. If he lives to be seventy, he will die without demur,
for death is part of the deal.

Some two hundred years ago the Jesuit missionary Louis Le-
Comte wrote: "The Chinese seem still more negligent as to their
gardens. [They] so little apply themselves to order them and
give them real ornaments, yet make grottoes in them, raise pretty
little artificial eminences, transport to them in pieces whole
rocks, which they heap upon one another, *without any further
design than to imitate nature*." There spoke the compatriot of
the gentlemen who arranged the grim gardens of Versailles as
if they were passing a geometry test. The Chinese artist abom-
inates a straight line on anything other than a wall. He loves
his rocks with their irregular broken shapes, the studied artificial
landscaping that magically imitates the perspective of grandiose
scenery. He likes oddly formed stones and gnarled trees, bamboo and falling water that give a sense of movement and spontaneity. He does not want the desicated disciplines of Descartes
in his own back yard, but wild pastoral anarchy (however cunningly contrived); not a dead intellectual exercise, but the living
earth. *Barbarians*, breathed Ping at the regimented rosebeds of
Europe—and for once with real venom. Kew Gardens was an
improvement, but there she admired above all the unintended
daisies.

Spirit, flesh, and nature merge, characteristics are swapped.
Ping describes an undulating tropical fish as "most musical." A
pollarded tree that refuses to stop spreading is "arguing back,"

a broken teacup has "lost its ear," a clever pupil is a "smart mouse," and a woman friend who always gets constipated in strange houses has a "shy bottom."

Among the Chinese, who have their own God of Literature, poetry has often taken the place of faith. During the T'ang dynasty it was virtually a state religion. For one thousand years thereafter it was also one of the keys to a successful official career, for candidates were required to write verse to pass the Imperial examinations. In the *Three Kingdoms,* Ts'ao Ts'ao tipsily declaims a fine stanza on the eve of battle on the theme "Stern toil is his who would the empire gain," for only a flair for the Muse could round off this splendid rogue in Chinese eyes. There was no childish division between arts and manliness in the Middle Kingdom, for it was ruled by cultivated mandarins, not a semi-literate squirearchy. It was a famous general commanding troops on the Great Wall who invented both the Chinese writing brush and the thirteen-string lute, and the superstitious commander who supervised the defense of Ningpo against the British in 1842 was a skillful painter in the ink-blob style. To write poems on war and anti-war, on rejected wives and parted friends, was the normal accomplishment of most educated men, and the guest who could not improvise at least a fragment at the dinner table was simply not one of us.

Although disciplined by the tonal values that took the place of the dactyl and spondee of Ovid's hexameters, the composition of verse eventually degenerated into an exercise in classical clichés and artificial metaphor. But the veneration of the Chinese for their great, shining heritage of poetry has never faded, and Mao Tse-tung has been careful to set the seal on his image as the compleat hero (sometimes in most unlikely quarters) by composing such strong, if roughhewn poems as *Chingkangshan* and *The Long March.* It was above all Taoism that influenced the poet's life and the poet's sense of beauty, so that we see him reflecting the Taoist's delight in the marvelous, wandering through the country with his friends, drinking deep to find spontaneity in the wine, and throwing off rounded verse with the sure instinct of an Asian fisherman casting his circular net.

Li Po, perhaps the greatest of Chinese poets, was born in A.D. 701. After listening patiently to the sterner tones of the moralizing Confucians, this wayward genius felt himself attracted by the soft voice of quietism at an early age, and joined a recluse in the hills to study Taoism. He then traveled in a leisurely way through China, forming little coteries with other poets and kindred spirits with names like the "Six Idlers of the Bamboo Grove." Given a post as court poet by the emperor, Li Po wrote verses to the plump beauty of Yang Kuei-fei and idled away the rest of his time with a group of convivial companions known as the "Eight Immortals of the Wine Cup."

He did not fail to make enemies, however. Yang Kuei-fei's brother, the Prime Minister, described the poet as a mediocrity who should be mixing his ink for him. The powerful Chief Eunuch added that Li Po was only fit to take off his shoes. One day shortly afterward, the emperor summoned his court poet unexpectedly. Li Po turned up drunk and wine-sick, and demanded loudly that Yang Kuei-fei mix his ink for him and the Chief Eunuch pull off his shoes. Packed off in disgrace, this yellow Irishman once more went into Taoist retreat, but became involved in an abortive conspiracy and was banished to a remote frontier post. However, he stopped so many times on the way to drink and argue and versify with friends that he still had not reached his undesirable destination three years later when an amnesty was declared. Traveling down the Yangtze, although this time toward the home of a friendly relative, he got drunk on the boat, it seems, leaned over too far while trying to embrace the moon's reflection in the river, fell in, and drowned. One still seems to hear his (freely translated) prophetic whisper:

> Among the flowers with a pot of wine
> But without a friend, though drinking free,
> I raise my cup to the luminous moon

Which gives me a shadow, and makes us three . . .
For when I sing, the moon responds.
I dance, and my shadow follows my light.
Sober we are forever good friends
And they only get lost when I get tight.
But we'll be joined forever, moon, shadow, and I,
When next we meet in the star-flecked sky.

More than half of all Chinese literature has been in verse, which is so close to painting that the artist usually brushes poetry as well as picture on to his scroll, so that each may strengthen the mood expressed by the other. And Chinese painting is very much a matter of nature's mood and rhythm, rather than of nature herself. In the West there are bedtime stories for children about painters whose cherries-in-oils were so realistic that the birds came and pecked at the canvas. The Chinese have their own anecdotes, but they are subtly different. The birds do not peck at the cherries because they look exactly like the real cherries the artist was copying. For the Chinese painter does not paint from real cherries. The birds peck, rather, because the imaginary cherries of the Chinese painter look like the spirit of all cherries, the platonic ideal of the fruit. The European dog may bark at the painting of the horse, because it looks so exactly like Old Dobbin. But the legendary Chinese painter refrains from painting in the eyes of his dream stallion, for fear that if it could once see, it would gallop away.

The Chinese does not set up his easel, sit down facing a lake, and then painstakingly paint just that lake. He studies lakes and mountains for a few years, and then settles down in an air-conditioned room in town, or in a pavilion in the country, or even perhaps on the shore of some lake, and paints lakes. He does not faithfully copy the reality of a scene, but "writes" his own conception of it in a quick freehand. The Frenchman Le-Comte once more obtrudes with his otiose opinions, complaining that "as painters, the Chinese do not study perspective." However, in this case the Chinese have replied with their own comments on Jesuit pictures. They show "skill in drawing and conscientious work but simply cannot be regarded as true paintings." For form is dead without spirit and movement, they say, and "still life" is a ridiculous contradiction in terms. Chinese painting has its manuals and laws, like most other arts. The primary colors are black, red, green, white, and yellow. The six cardinal rules of painting were drawn up fifteen centuries ago, and the Chinese have classified subjects into landscapes, figures, flowers-bamboo-birds-fishes, architectural, and misc. But they do not pretend, like some learn-now-pay-later threat in a small ad, that this is all there is to it.

In the work of the Sung dynasty artists, executed seven hundred years and more ago, a diminutive human figure might set the scale that revealed the grandeur of the distant, yet crowding mountains, but for the rest, a picture would be a calculated accident, an affair of swift, practiced spontaneity. There is no geometry in the Chinese landscape, and perspective is achieved not through line but through the lightness of the more distant scenes. The painter is always looking down from a height, so that the more remote the mountain peak, the higher it is in the picture. The whole effect is impressionistic, fugitive, dreamlike, with the foam of a great waterfall simply suggested by a complete absence of paint. The human eye is like the human intellect—incapable of taking in all factors—therefore a man must not try to paint truth in all its myriad detail, but only the principle of truth. Essence is of the essence.

Poetry and painting are united in the Chinese art form that has no real equivalent in the West: calligraphy. For writing is the abstract painting of the Chinese, expressing a rhythm and momentum, tension and strength that owe nothing to the subject. Dash off your signature irritably on a check, and it can be seen to have its own impetuous, serpentine life. Get someone else to trace it slowly and carefully on transparent paper, and the result—though an absolutely perfect replica of the original— is a dead worm. This is the effect that the Chinese above all seek to avoid, treasuring good, vivid handwriting as we might treasure a Turner, and respecting the man who produces it, whatever his sins. Inevitably, the reprehensible Ts'ao Ts'ao was also a fine calligrapher, and Mao has a tough, aggressive hand.

No Chinese art entirely ignores the Taoist dream of quiet harmony with nature. At least seven hundred years before Salome danced for Herod, the Chinese were striking a solemn music on bells and ringing stones; by Alexander's day they had adopted the pentatonic scale; and later they were to use a system of twelve notes of fixed pitch. Today a stranger may be appalled by the deafening nasal cacaphony of Peking opera, with its head-rattling percussion instruments and whining falsetto voices, or delighted by the still popular dramatic ballad of Wang Ch'ao-chün, whose theme dates back to the time of Celtic Britain. Few, however, can fail to recognize the exquisite pastoral quality of the Chinese lute, the two-stringed violin, or the bamboo flute that set the peaceful Chinese idyl to music with such simple poignancy.

Peace is the key to the Chinese arts, and above all to the Chinese art of living. The foreigner is sometimes flabbergasted by the crudeness, vulgarity, and mediocrity of much modern taste among the Chinese, whether it is the Tottenham Court Road T'ang of Singapore and Hong Kong, or the Socialist realism of Peking expressed in gaudy imitations of the worst Russian chocolate-box style. Ask a Chinese what has happened to his three thousand years of mellowing civilization and he will shrug resignedly: "Men have no time to take in beauty today. How can you look for taste when the first thing that ninety-nine Chinese out of a hundred must do is to stick up a colored poster of Mao or Chiang on their walls before they can even feel safe?" In fact, with the Chinese as with the Westerner, the best and most beautiful is still there, behind the peasant proliferation of plastic and chrome bric-à-brac. And so are the rebels.

As Roman Britain began to suffer the first serious onslaughts of Saxon pirates in the third century A.D., the golden age of the beatnik dawned in China. Weary of the bestial wars that had wrecked the three rival kingdoms into which their country was divided, disillusioned with a Confucianism that had failed to keep their world sane, frustrated scholars revolted against the whole social system and turned to Taoism for consolation. The age produced the renowned band of intellectual wine-bibbers known as the "Seven Sages of the Bamboo Grove" which was later to inspire Li Po's drunken little coteries.

The Taoist outlook of this distinguished group of scholars, poets, and musicians was well expressed by one of them who said that once he had drunk enough, the affairs of the world were of no more account "than so much duckweed in a river." Defiantly flouting convention and all Confucian propriety like his fellows, this eccentric drove around in a cart pulled by a deer, and followed everywhere by two servants. One of these carried a large jar of wine. The other carried a spade, and had been given instructions that if his master fell dead in the middle of some binge or other, he was to dig a hole and bury him then and there. But these men were no mere poseurs, and there was nothing artificial about their adoption of the simple, natural ideals that Taoism taught. Around them scholars were abandoning conventional Confucian clothes and donning the third-century equivalents of winkle-pickers and drainpipe pants. They were growing their beards and their fingernails longer and dirtier, washing less and drinking more, talking Taoism, reading, painting, versifying and carousing, and above all studiously ignoring organized society.

"Cool" must be the squarest slang of the twentieth century, for it was the catchword for manners and dress in Chinese anti-society seventeen hundred years ago. The alchemists had produced a poisonous "five-stone powder" pounded out of quartz, sulphur, and other minerals which was supposed to give men strength, potency, a long life, even immortality, and it became a fad of the intellectual rebels to eat this stuff. Its effect was to provoke a violent burning sensation in the body, followed by a sudden access of good spirits and energy. In considerable discomfort, the addict would then go for a long walk until he cooled off, take cold baths, and eat cold food (but with great quantities of hot wine). He wore cooler, looser, and sleazier dress, threw off his shoes and socks, and donned wooden sandals only. One of these "cool" characters received his guests in the nude and, when someone remonstrated with him, replied tipsily: "Heaven and earth are my home, my house is my dress. So what are you doing in my trousers?" This Chinese type, aping the old Taoist scholars, can be as rude, drunk, ill-clad, malodorous, immodest, and iconoclastic today. "Only now they manage it," Ping remarked once, "without necessity of eating 'five-stone powder,' or being able to write verse, draw fish, or tell rhythm from rhyme."

Toping is not a particularly Taoist rite, for a true Taoist should do all things in moderation, but in general the Chinese see drinking as one of the pleasures of a life that is to be lived as contentedly and agreeably as possible. To most Westerners, Chinese wine, distilled from rice or millet, tastes like firewater. Yellow Shao Hsing resembles a dry sherry, although it is served hot from a wine pot into the usual diminutive porcelain cups, but the famous Chinese white wines—Mao-T'ai, Mei-Kuei-Lu, Pai-Kan, and the formidable Kao-Liang best brewed on the offshore Nationalist fortress island of Quemoy—have the mule kick of bathtub gin. The English word "wine" is itself a misnomer when used by the Chinese, for their favorite Western "wine" is four-star brandy.

At a formal Chinese dinner, each person toasts all the others individually during the course of the meal, raising his little bowl, shouting "Kan pei"—"Dry Cup!"—and tossing his drink back in one. As there are probably twelve people around the table, this usually establishes a certain atmosphere of conviviality, and thereafter the guest may sip more slowly, drinking "Sui pien"— "as you please"—if he can. The foreigner may reflect with some self-satisfaction that this is far removed from the civilized and

obsequious wine rituals of the West. But it is always a mistake
to think that a Chinese does not appreciate a good thing, including the oldest, dirt-encrusted bottle in the cellar.

The eighteenth-century poet Yüan Mei wrote: "*Wu-fan* wine
is black in color; the taste very sweet and fresh. But its excellence is really beyond anything that can be put into words. I
was told that at Li-shui when a girl is born they always make a
jar of this wine, using high-quality dark cooked millet. They do
not open the jar till the girl's wedding day, so that it is drunk,
at the earliest, fifteen or sixteen years after it is made. When the
jar is opened, half has evaporated. What remains is so thick that
it is like glue in the mouth and its perfume is so strong that it
can be smelled even outside the room." In 1742 the teetotal
Captain Anson, maneuvering with his habitual skill to persuade
the Chinese viceroy at Canton to arrange for repairs to the
Centurion, declined to drink while entertaining three mandarins:
"But there being another Gentleman present of a florid and
jovial complexion, the chief Mandarine clapped him on the
shoulder, and insisted on his bearing him company." The Chinese drank five bottles between them without even getting
flushed.

In 1916 the famous Chinese wine *fen-chiu,* brewed from millet
and fermented with a yeast of beans and barley at Apricot
Blossom Village since the days of the T'ang dynasty, won an
award at the Panama-Pacific International Exposition. Described
as "light and sweet," it in fact has the thrust of export kirsch.
In about 1960 the Communists expanded the existing distillery
in the village and added others, while still using the two-thousand-year-old wells that had supplied the crystal-clear water for
the vintages that Li Po drank. The Communists have been busy
for years producing traditional Chinese wines, including a white-
lotus wine and a thoroughly reactionary laurel wine that was
only served at the royal board in "the Feudal Age." The European may recoil from these odd-sounding liquors, but everything
is a matter of taste. The Chinese were already importing foreign

wines during the Sung dynasty nearly a thousand years ago, but, as one historian has noted tersely, "they preferred their own."

They would certainly say the same of their food, for eating is one of the delights of the tranquil life to which the Chinese have devoted much time and poetic genius. The essential ingredients of heaven-on-earth must include bird's nest and shark's fin, duck's head, fish lips, fresh turtle and fruit bat, monitor lizards, two-month-old "hundred-year-old" eggs, and boiled, fried, steamed, stewed, or grilled snake for a cold winter. (In Hong Kong a dish of king cobra may cost more than US $16.) The Chinese loves his food, and his equivalent of one of our business banquets—say consommé, sole, steak, fruit salad, and cheese—would be a ten- or twelve-course meal in which the firm favorites would be Chinese cold hors d'oeuvres, shark's fin soup, sweet-and-sour yellow fish, deep-fried prawns with chili sauce, boiled chicken with ginger, Szechuan fried duck with dumplings and black pepper, and perhaps even that dainty little dish of dishes, fresh fried milk; rice and a light soup to follow all, of course. Many Chinese will fast for twelve hours before tackling such a dinner, and those who can afford this kind of thing often eat simply when at home, content with rice or noodles and a vegetarian diet most of the time. Large men from the West who carve up fourteen-ounce T-bone steaks with tooth-edged knives every day have a horrid fascination for these modest trenchermen, as they do for the Chinese at the other extreme—the gastronomical poets.

Poetry is a worthy substitute for religion, for like a well-cut gown on a badly designed woman, poetry can transform drab reality into dream. The poet in the Chinese not only prompts him to invent a dish that is a subtle mélange of cat, cock, and snake, but inspires him to call it "tiger-phoenix-and-dragon-fighting." We order "beautiful woman's rolling buttocks," and somehow the dish of pig's rump that comes along in due course seems all the more delectable. And who could resist a tea called "eyelashes of the swan"? The Chinese delight in the picture of Sui dynasty emperors consuming sucking pig fed on human milk, and one doubts whether the average customer who walked into a restaurant in Hangchow during the Sung dynasty and eagerly ordered "two-legged mutton" cared just whom he was likely to find himself eating. But he might be more particular about the dish that he honored with the more flattering title of "fragrant flesh," for this was not human but canine.

In about 500 B.C. the King of Yüeh, anxious to stimulate the production of battle fodder for use in his struggle against the Kingdom of Wu, presented a succulent puppy to each woman who gave birth to a baby boy (she only got a piglet if it was a girl). And when Wu was finally defeated, the Chief Minister of Yüeh, who had been largely responsible for the victory, immediately fled the country because he no longer felt indispensable. "For when the fleet deer is caught," he explained to a colleague, "the hounds are cooked."

This is not the earliest reference to dog-eating, however, for it was laid down during the Chou dynasty, which was founded in about 1050 B.C., that there were six animals suitable for the table: horse, ox, sheep, chicken, pig, and dog. Mencius especially recommended dog for the old, and to be a dog-butcher became an honorable if lowly profession. Three dog-butchers are among China's greatest legendary heroes, and a special mystique attaches to men who kill and eat dogs. Nevertheless, several hundred years ago scholars appealed to the people to be kind to dogs, declaring that to kill one was not the act of a gentleman, for the dog was by nature loyal, faithful, "and patriotic." The dog began to have his day, but it ended when the Manchus declared dog-eating a punishable offense, for this immediately made it a heroic gesture of defiance against the foreign usurper on the Dragon Throne. In the revolutionary hotbed of Canton, men gathered secretly not only to conspire but to cook. They were not alone in their tastes, however, for a friendly European at one point sent a valuable pedigree puppy to the loyalist Chinese Commander Li Hung-chang as a pet. A few days later he asked Li what the thought of it. "Delicious," Li replied.

The dog dinner is still popular with the South Chinese, who believe that it is good for malaria, kidney troubles, and old age. Nor did the Communists scruple to offer one to their guests when they invited foreign correspondents to Peking for a special press conference in 1965. (The Hong Kong Chinese newspapermen were delighted, but all the Western journalists funked it.) It is forbidden to cook dog in Hong Kong, and shops are fined fifty dollars or more if they are caught offering dog meat for sale. The only time that I was invited to eat it there, I was taken to a small farm hidden in a deep valley amid mountain scenery from a Chinese scroll. We ate standing up—in case we had to run for it, it was half jokingly explained—and when an acquaintance turned up unexpectedly in the middle of the main course, he was at once pressed to have some too, so that he could not denounce us afterward.

Men of discrimination do not eat just any kind of dog. There is a special Chinese cooking dog—small, woolly haired, and fattened up like the suckling pig, whose meat it also resembles when served (black ones with pink noses are best). It is not confused in the mind of a modern Chinese with a pedigree spaniel or a boxer: as a dog lover he reserves the right to love them all in different ways. Today, in fact, many Singapore Chinese are repelled by the idea of eating dog at all, it seems. Why? "Too much human-being nature," says Ping. Tastes change. A thousand years ago the Chinese attacked with gusto a dish of "two-legged mutton." Now they are queasy about touching "four-legged man."

But no one who reads the cookery book of the sardonic and fastidious Yüan Mei can doubt the bird-in-hand instinct of the Chinese for making the most of this world in a modest way. "Cookery is like matrimony," he writes. "Two things served together should match. I have known people to mix grated lobster with bird's nest, and mint with chicken or pork! The cooks of today think nothing of mixing in one soup the meat of chicken, duck, pig, and goose. But these doubtless have souls. And these souls will most certainly file plaints in the next world on the way they have been treated in this.

"Don't eat with your ears; by which I mean do not aim at having extraordinary out-of-the-way foods, just to astonish your guests. The chicken, the pig, the fish, and the duck—these are the four heroes of the table. Sea slugs and birds' nests have no characteristic flavors of their own. Don't eat with your eyes; by which I mean do not cover the table with innumerable dishes and multiply courses indefinitely. Just as a calligraphist should not overtire his hand or a poet his brain, so a good cook cannot possibly turn out in one day more than four or five good dishes. I used to dine with a merchant who would serve so much that by the time we had finished we had got through some forty courses. My host gloried in all this, but when I got home I used to have a bowl of rice gruel—I felt so hungry.

"Into no department of life should indifference be allowed to creep; into none less than the domain of cookery. Again, I am not much of a wine drinker, but this makes me all the more particular. Wine is like scholarship; it ripens with old age; and it is best from a fresh-opened jar. The top of the wine jar, the bottom of the teapot, as the saying has it . . ."

The difference between gracious living as practiced by a Manhattan millionaire and gracious living as practiced by an impecunious Chinese poet, is that the poet can carry it off more satisfactorily than the tycoon and, moreover, can do it from the third-floor back. In tune with nature, he feels intensely the pleasures of the simple act. He will taste tea, fly kites, practice calligraphy, or just talk airy nonsense—and live every moment, whether he is smelling the cool clean air on the heath or the acrid fragrance of black ink. In the old days men took their birds for a walk, solemnly carrying the cages before them, and in a worker's flat in Communist China I have watched faces wrinkle with pleasure within a stone's-throw of such forbidding premises as the Number-One Tractor Factory in Loyang as a cricket trilled briskly in a small bamboo trap suspended from the ceiling.

Several centuries ago, a peaceable emperor ordered quarreling warlords to settle their dispute by pitting crickets against one another, and in Macao today the autumnal cricket season draws crowds as enthusiastic as those at Wimbledon. On a small sand-topped table champion males from Hong Kong and the Portuguese enclave face each other after a night of mating. A trainer tickles them with a mousehair brush, whereupon they rush at each other, mandibles snapping, while the gamblers place their bets. In their discreet pursuit of happiness, the Chinese have invented dominoes and playing cards, backgammon and their own version of polo. They raced dogs and organized cockfights two thousand years ago, when football was also encouraged in the army as good training in bodily discipline and military strategy. The Han dynasty found agreeable or energetic ways of whiling away the shining hour, from checkers to the tug-of-war. Then came "elephant chess." Chess is still the game of the educated in the West, but Chinese laborers will pore over a board during a Hong Kong lunch break, and hundreds of off-duty workers will sit down and watch intently as the moves of two contestants are reproduced on a giant display wall in Shanghai. Played not with figurines but with flat disks on which are inscribed the characters identifying each piece, how different is this game from the version that was first to be heard of in Europe nearly five hundred years after it appeared in China?

The board is similarly divided into sixty-four, but the game is played on the lines, not on the squares. The European pawn, castle, knight, bishop, and king are matched in their moves by the Chinese soldier, chariot, horse, minister, and king, and the object of both games is the same. However, although there are sixteen pieces a side, Chinese chess has no queen and only five pawns. The numbers are made up by two bodyguards for the king that move like pawns, and two "cannons." These cannons transform the whole game. For the cannon moves in straight lines like a castle but may only take an opposing piece if another piece stands between them. An aggressive player is therefore constantly linking up his two cannons so that they can leapfrog over each other to attack enemy pieces. On the other hand, where the interposed piece belongs to the same side as the intended target, the player on the defensive has only to move it out of line to spike the enemy's guns, for now nothing stands between the cannon and its victim, and the cannon therefore cannot take it.

Today the legend of the supine, opium-smoking mandarin, or of the Chinese émigré with the glistening yellow skin whose love of exercise is limited to the ironing of shirts, must slowly fade. In Nationalist China a general orders his troops to dig a championship-length swimming pool and sets all available field kitchens to warming up water for it, so that his young sister can practice the 200-yard breaststroke in the Manchurian winter in preparation for the national trials. The consequences (she came in fourth and he lost a province to the Communists) cannot obscure his driving motive: his Occidental love of sport. In Malaysia twenty years later, a Chinese teenager streaks through the water to set up an all-time record for international gold medals. Western traditions of keen, competitive sportsmanship even become evident among Chinese Communist leaders, who urge their international table-tennis team to hit the ball "as if it were the head of Chiang Kai-shek."

The European, observing these mutations, may tell himself that the next-door Chinese is somehow no longer a Chinese, and the detribalized among the younger generation, dunked in the universities of the West, have certainly worn their pants and ponytails with conviction. But to imagine that those who still hold the levers of power today in politics, business, art, and war have somehow shed their three-thousand-year-old heritage altogether is like believing that a naturalized Pole has forgotten the land of Chopin because he votes Tory and can order a pintabitter at the corner pub as well as the next man. The ordinary Chinese is still drawn by his own traditions, by the call of Confucian convention and the allure of the Taoist dream world. He does not seize life by the throat like an enemy, but handles it like the package deal that it is, holding it as its awkward shape and ill-arranged center of gravity dictate. In such a situation, fumbling man can only keep his dignity by humbly renouncing it, and a Chinese preserves his face when necessary by laughing at his own pretentions.

He can be caustic about grandiose funerals that cross the hairline between the solemn and the ridiculous, facetious and cynical about pretentious projects whose failure betrays the flaws in a self-righteous society. His theory of ups-and-downs gives him a saving irreverence, so that when we are told that a certain grand gentleman has had forty-two pairs of trousers altered to conform with his new prominence, Ping says: "Forty-two pairs? For God's sake, how many bottoms he got?" This is the instinct which turned the Chinese defeat during the Opium Wars into an absurd farce that somehow deprived the British of any sense of victory—for most of the negotiations were conducted in ridiculous you-one-time-catchee-one-piecee-belong-me pidgin. The Chinese believe almost devoutly in the principle that the higher they fly, the farther they fall. Theirs is essentially an Achilles'-heel-on-the-banana-skin humor.

24

The Passive Voice

It is not difficult to see the Chinese as an unfortunate creature stretched on the psychiatrist's rack, torn between the teachings of the Confucians and of the Taoists. However, the *traumatic effects of philosophical dichotomy are not reflected among predisposed Chinese in a high incidence of schizophrenic psychosis.* In short, few are screaming lunatics—partly because, most happily, you cannot really write that sort of sentence in Chinese, but also partly because the two philosophies fit snugly enough into the minds of most men, like Yin and Yang. Confucianism and Taoism in fact differ to agree at certain points, and these are some of the interstices that give the structure of the Chinese character its firmness and shape. And they have filched much from each other. Moreover, both are practical in that they set afterlife at a discount and urge man to seek above all to be at ease and in harmony with this world. Both preach moderation, simplicity, and the Golden Mean. Confucianism fixes a man's duty and position in society, while Taoism rejects society and insists upon his personal freedom of mind. The product is often a highly individual being with an enviable sureness and poise. It is the blend that makes the Chinese bland.

He has discovered that there is a time for Confucianism and a time for Taoism, and like the modern neurotic who finally learns to drop his work and sit painting bad pictures for dear life, he has for centuries retired to those misty hills and the metaphysics of the "Old Master" for therapeutic relief from the ulcer-provoking duties and decorums imposed by Confucian precept. But happiness must not be so hotly pursued that conscience develops a stitch: the Taoist rice winner of the family may have to work like a slave for most of his whole life first, finding contentment as best he can in the very struggle that is supposed to destroy it. His philosophy may seem to excuse the slob, but it is not *le slobbisme*. He is against senseless striving, not plain hard work.

One of the oddest things about the Westerner, says the Chinese, is his constant wish that things were different. He is forever trying to alter the world to suit himself, while the Chinese alters himself to suit the world. His conservative Confucian instinct is against contrived change, and his naturalistic Taoist instinct tells him to flow with the stream, to make the most of things as they are. But even in the age of the air-conditioner and the seventeen-cubic-foot icebox, the European in the Malaysian monsoon season may develop that atavistic twitch at the corner of the jaw so dear to the "White cargo" school of colonial drama, and start railing futilely at life as his tropicalized chemical-fiber shirt flaps against his sweat-soaked body like a plastic raincoat.

"Really I worry about you do yourself some harm," says Ping sadly, pressing upon me an infusion of lotus seeds well known for its deleterious effects upon the spleen. "What is the good you go mad? Of course the amah stupid some time; if not stupid, won't be amah, more likely be milliner" (this word does not refer to someone who makes hats but one who has more than one million dollars). "Amah is amah. You want the elephant ivory to grow out of the dog's mouth?" The amah also shows this Chinese take-things-as-they-are outlook. "Don't worry," she confides to Ping in Cantonese afterward. "I didn't get angry when he shouted at me. After all, we have to remember he is only a barbarian." She might well have been echoing Ping, who once said to me firmly: "Now we make the rule: at least when the little dogs next door bark at you, you don't bark back. Okay?" That drained off the adrenaline for a while.

The submissive objectivity of the Chinese enables him to spare himself—at least for long periods of ominous calm—the aggressions now so fashionable in the West: the English behave like the English because they are English, and there is no point in complaining unless the day comes when you can change them, he believes. The Japanese ravaged China with a bestiality that perhaps only the knightly code of Samurai chivalry could inspire. The Chinese hated the Japanese, and many still refuse to talk to them even today. Yet they also accept them in a curious way. The Japanese were in a sense also victims of the drama; they had their role to play, and they played it with incomparable courage as well as with detestable ruthlessness. In Singapore they massacred fifty thousand Chinese, arbitrarily picking them up in the streets and mowing them down with machine guns by the truckload, or chaining them together in groups of four, flinging them into the harbor, and then turning their guns on them as they struggled. "Yes," replied Ping. "I know. They kill everyone. They behave like devils. But still not rubbish. Just Japanese."

Abstract goodness does not exist. The foreigner—American, British, Indian, Russian—is basically the same foreigner. The Russia of "Big-nose Devils" and the Britain of "Red-haired Devils" were for one hundred years the principal modern foreign powers with which the unfortunate Chinese had to reckon. The British were uncompromisingly acquisitive, holding on with the discreditable tenacity of the bulldog breed to their privileges, their extraterritorial rights, and their concessions in China. The Russians were the first to renounce their concessions. They sent advisers to the Nationalists and later gave massive military and economic aid to the Communists. But one was no more trusted as a friend than the other. The Chinese feels that a man who steals a loaf from you at least leaves you your soul but that a man who gives you one may be trying to buy you up. He makes no sentimental distinction between barbarian and barbarian. Each, quite obviously, is simply serving his own best interests at any given moment, whether he is looting or bestowing. The reasons for frowning on one and smiling on the other are purely pragmatic. Business is business.

This talent for suspecting motives, for refusing to be categorical in labeling these "sheep" and those "goats" makes a man circumspect about committing himself to be a partisan of one side or the other in any conflict, and the Chinese does not believe that he is foolishly falling between two stools but rather that he is sensibly stalling between two fools. An unrivaled prevaricator, he likes to give the answer that he thinks will please, rather than the one in his heart.

If a Chinese is interviewed for a job, he will follow as closely as possible the words, the tone of voice, and the manner of his future employer, and when answering questions will even word the first half of his reply in such an equivocal way that he can finish it this way or that, according to the expression on the face of his interviewer: "Of course I am a great admirer of the *Daily Express*"—pause to check—"as an efficient profit-making organization/as the spokesman of the people and the conscience of government." (Strike out whichever does not apply.) Life is like a game of bridge, and only a dummy puts his cards on the table.

There is an old story that a Chinese tailor, asked to make twelve silk shirts *exactly like this one,* copied the sample meticulously, including the cigarette burn on the lower chest, which the customer had overlooked. Why? "He doesn't like that 'exactly' probably," said Ping. "What is this 'exactly'?" There must be some reason, something about it that the customer keeps to himself. Maybe he is a secret-society man and the burn is a recognition signal? Everybody knows Westerners have secret societies: the Knights of Columbus, the Druids, the Ku Klux Klan, the C.I.A., all those . . . It is better to suspect the worst, to do precisely what is ordered, and then one cannot be blamed.

This analysis is borne out by the historical account of the first audience granted by the ambitious Duke of Ch'in to that abominable, specifically Chinese hero Shan Yang in the fourth century B.C. The duke asked the future Lord of Shang his views on international relations, without revealing his own feelings. The future Lord of Shang then discoursed righteously on the virtues of the sage-kings and similar cant, doubtless watching the greedy potentate's face with preternaturally narrowed eyes. The duke revealed nothing but later confessed himself bored by this moralistic prater. "But see him once more," a well-primed confederate of Shan Yang advised. The duke did, whereupon Shan Yang, surer already of his ground, sidled up to the ruler's mat in the way such fellows do, and submitted to his patron such criminal proposals that the duke, enchanted beyond words, did not even rebuke him for his presumptuous manner.

In a revealing passage, Han Fei instructs the counselor how devious he must be in dealing with the lord. Summarized, his advice would read like this: "The difficult thing about persuasion is not one's own talent or courage, but the state of mind of the prince and the problem of fitting one's arguments to it. If the ruler makes a wrong move and you preach to him, your life will be in danger; on the other hand, if he learns of a good scheme and propounds it as his own, but you disclose that you know where he learned it from, your life is again in danger. If you try to force him to do what he cannot, or if you try to make him give up what he cannot stop doing, your life is in danger.

"If you praise good ministers to him, he will think you are criticizing him personally; and if you praise lesser men, he will think you are allowing yourself to be bribed. If you talk to him of those he likes, he will suspect you are trying to manipulate him; if of those he hates, that you are trying to test him out. If you speak to him bluntly, he will think you ignorant, and if you overpower him with your eloquence, he will think you pretentious. If you are too brief in expressing your thoughts, he will think you too shy, and if you are long-winded, he will think you pompous and impertinent. Talk at large of the things he is proud of; quietly forget those he is ashamed of; if he has a very personal desire, persuade him it is his public duty to fulfill it; if he has something reprehensible in view, present its better aspects. If, on the other hand, he has some laudable objective in mind but cannot fulfill it, point out its obvious disadvantages.

"If he wants to show how clever he is, hedge him in with second-rate alternatives so that he will light upon the real solution. If you are recommending a course of action that you are particularly anxious he should adopt, speak broadly of its public virtues but hint less obviously at the advantage to his private interests also. Conversely, dissuade him from an undesirable course of action by a great show of the slight upon his repute that this will incur—while mentioning in passing the hurt to his own personal ambitions. Praise great men who have the same virtues as your ruler, but take care to play down the significance of their vices if these are also the same. Be sure you say nothing to vex him, and then in full time you may display your wisdom and eloquence to him, without risking trouble.

"At this point the art of counseling the ruler becomes perfect. Thus men who wish to influence kings must first discover their secret wishes and fears before opening their mouths."

The Confucian gentleman is a model of discretion. He believes that what is hidden is deep, what is babbled on the surface is as shallow as a brook and will not be taken seriously anyway. He holds himself in reserve, rarely committing himself without careful reflection, but remaining withdrawn and watchful. For just as space counts so heavily in painting, so silence counts heavily in dispute.

What may be civilized self-restraint in one man, may nevertheless just be deviousness and cowardice in another, and the Chinese themselves are very alive to this. In his essay *The quintessence of worldly wisdom*, Lu Hsün wrote sarcastically of the climate that encourages a man to be mealymouthed: "If you meet with social injustice, on no account rush forward to say what is right. Otherwise on your head be it—you may actually be called a reactionary. If someone is wronged or slandered, even if you know he is a good man, on no account rush forward to explain or argue his case. Otherwise you may be called his relative or accused of taking bribes. Don't worry about right and wrong, or straight and crooked, but try to agree with everyone. Of course, keeping silent is better still, and best of all is to give no sign on your face of what you are thinking in your heart."

The man of virtue is essentially quiescent and humble, Chinese philosophers agreed, and he shows his superiority by accepting insults calmly (Gentlemen are requested not to bark at the dogs). But a man can have too quick an eye for martyrdom and for the moral victories to be scored by not hitting back on those occasions when hitting back might be distinctly dangerous. The Chinese supinely allowed the Manchus to make them grow pig-tails as a sign of subjection, and this gave Lu Hsün the name for his central character in a bitter short novel attacking this sanctimonious pusillanimity, *The True Story of Ah Q.* In the chapters that give an "Account of Ah Q's Victories," this unc-tious poltroon rationalizes every beating he deservedly receives as a great personal success, gives himself the title of "Foremost Self-belittler," and reflects that if you take away "self-belittler" you are simply left with "foremost"—"So who do you think *you* are?" he would soliloquize to his departed tormentors.

"Ah-Q-ism"—the self-justification for servile submission—has been vigorously attacked by the Chinese Communists, and not encouraged, as their detractors might imagine. It has often per-suaded the foreigner that the Chinese are a nation of milksops, but it is matched by a formidable ability to watch and wait, to seize not only the right moment to capitulate but also the right moment to strike. Christ's injunction to turn the other cheek did not make a craven of the early Christian, and his Roman over-lords rightly refused to regard his as an innocuous heresy propa-gated by a bunch of spineless shirkers.

A Chinese nevertheless finds it easier to forgive, and to bear adversity with patience and fortitude, because his everyday pragmatism is complemented by his genius for dreaming. Chuang Tzu ended up by suspecting he was really a butterfly that was only dreaming it was Chuang Tzu; the émigré Chinese, scraping a living as a noodle-seller in some stinking Hong Kong side alley, bears his lot with benign resignation, for this present existence can be treated as mere illusion. "You cannot choose your life, but you can choose your dreams," Ping once remarked. "And if Chinese are clever at one thing, it is to get away from real world."

The escapist gambler lies back and dreams he is rich; the lazy man will dream of his success rather than work for it; the timid lover becomes a masher in the mind. The first move of an idle son who inherits his old father's flourishing business may be to put in a manager, and from then on he will strut around the town playing the dream role of the educated, active man of ideas and of affairs. To women, he will be scholar, tycoon, hero, superman, and in time may have difficulty separating this shining figment of his overworked imagination from the *flâneur* that he really is. In some cases the world of illusion is not only an ivory tower of strength; it is virtually impregnable.

From century to century the Chinese daydreamed their way through downtrodden lives until the day when thoughtful British and American merchants, their Bibles in their pockets and their tame missionaries aboard with them to translate, tacked up the coasts of Kwangtung and Fukien to sell their cargoes of "foreign mud" from Turkey and India. Once this enterprising campaign for providing the masses with opium was well under way, the Chinese no longer needed even a do-it-yourself imagination in order to dream. Lie back on the wooden platform in the dim-lit cubicle, your head on a porcelain pillow, while a ragged bundle of skin and bones crouches nearby, teasing the bubbling, black pill of opium, held over the flame of a small lamp, on the end of a long needle. When the heated opium is inserted into the thick, clarinetlike pipe, put the lips to the end that has just been scorched in the interests of hygiene, and suck the smoke into the lungs with one long inhalation. The pipe, still over the flame, crepitates evenly, and the air is filled with the sweet, black butterscotchlike odor that draws any customs officer east of Rangoon as aniseed draws a dog. Five more pipes, and there is no dragon-filled sleep, but the knotted mind becomes miraculously smooth, the body placid, the tongue marvelously fluent, the universe vulnerable as an oyster.

Opium is going out, TV coming in. The younger generation of Chinese on the whole rejects both the old drugs and the old dream worlds. But this is still a society so heavily masked in the cosmetics of mental make-believe that the commonest psychological tragedy among Chinese is that they may not have one single friend to whom they can show their true face.

25

The Emperor's New Clothes

Ping, who had met Mei Lan Fang in China when she was a young girl, said: "Even then, I was reminded at once of Yang Kuei-fei. For Mei Lan Fang also had gentle movements, beautiful voice for speaking, 'asparagus-tip' fingers, and was little bit plump." The comparison was historically apt, for Yang Kuei-fei was the fabulous concubine of the T'ang dynasty emperor who organized the first school of music and drama in the Pear Tree Garden of his palace, so that even today, more than twelve hundred years later, Chinese opera singers call themselves "Children of the Pear Garden." And Mei Lan Fang was hailed as China's greatest prima donna of all time. Unlike Yang Kuei-fei, however, Mei Lan Fang was a man.

Chinese drama flowered suddenly under the Mongol dynasty founded by Kublai Khan, some three hundred years before Shakespeare scribbled for a living. The suspicious Tatars employed foreigners like Marco Polo rather than Chinese mandarins in their administration, examinations were suspended, and so the scholars, finding their hands idle, turned to the mischief of playwriting. Mongol dynasty drama was, from the outset, a discredited "popular" art, actors were of ill-repute, and it was later decreed that women's roles must be played by men in the interests of propriety, as on the Elizabethan stage. However, unlike the English, the Chinese stuck to these willowy impersonators with their falsetto voices, and they are often the heroines of Peking opera even today.

Mei Lan Fang took no part in politics, but the day he died in 1961 was a day of nationwide mourning throughout China, and in Peking the Communist government decreed a state funeral for him. For the opera is a great and popular institution in China, enjoyed by millions all over the country who know the plays almost by heart, can recite the plots and sing the songs, and provide a huge, enthusiastic, yet critical public. Talking, chewing melon seeds, shouting at the peanut-sellers in the big open-air theaters as the musicians devote themselves deafeningly to their drums and the high whickering voice of some male princess attacks the ear, the Chinese audience consists very largely of half-literate people who have learned nearly all they know of history, and of verse, and of their long cultural heritage from storytellers and the stage. It was from these that so many picked up their Confucian tags and Taoist aphorisms, so that it would be safer to bet that an ignorant Chinese peasant could quote from Mencius than that a literate English farmer had even heard of Socrates.

The Chinese theater combines opera, ballet, drama, acrobatics, and spectacle, so that the trainee must be able to sing and dance, to act, clown, and mime, to fight with all the eighteen weapons in the traditional Chinese armory, to be a first-class acrobat—and still be able to imitate women better than women. To watch Mei Lan Fang walk across the stage in the role of a Chinese empress with bound feet was to believe the claim that he could carry a fine paintbrush between his knees while he did it.

Mei Lan Fang did not learn to act in the Western sense of the word, but to mime. He acquired the fifty-odd sleeve movements that express everything from concealment and revulsion to separation and sorrow, the stylized gestures of the hand that meant he (she) was swimming, or accusing, or inviting, mounting a horse, dismounting, crossing a threshold, opening a door (from the inside), opening a door (from the outside), drinking, sewing, stepping into a carriage, opening a window, and so on. He had to practice the steps that represented walking upstairs (and walking downstairs), moving like a ghost, leaning on a nonexistent cane. For in Chinese opera there were always magnificent costumes, but no realistic props or stage effects, and the only scenery allowed would be the city wall. The rest was fantasy.

A man enters downstage L. He wears a gorgeous padded costume with five flags rising from behind his head, and a long, waving headdress of pheasant feathers. His face is painted red and black, and he has a short mustache. A band of yellow silk crosses his robe, and he has seized one of the pheasant feathers of his headdress in his hand. Behind him stands an attendant, holding on each side of him a flag with a wheel painted on it. The scene is lit by a candle, and facing him is another fellow in a black costume, his face painted white and blue. This man's eyes are triangular, and he wears an upswept mustache. He is about to jump off a chair, while an extra stands by carrying a flag with the ideogram for "water" on it, and another waves a switch of horsehair. The man in the pheasant headdress sings a long bass aria, interrupted by occasional outbreaks from the gong and cymbal orchestra just off the stage.

The uninstructed foreigner cannot possibly guess what is going on. A Chinese, however, does not have to be familiar with the story, for all the clues are in the scene as I have described it. It is nighttime. Pheasant Feather is evidently a loyal, courageous, but somewhat impulsive general of crude ideas. He is riding in his carriage at the head of five regiments, and although he is ill, he has just ordered his army to advance against the enemy, taking advantage of the darkness. His adversary is an Imperial courtier —cruel, violent, yet also crafty and dishonest by nature. But his retreat has been cut off by a flood, and he is therefore cornered and about to drown himself in despair. A sudden change in fortune could occur, however, for somewhere on the scene there is a ghost. The Chinese late-comer would give this tableau one glance and not only take in the whole drama but almost certainly guess at once who these characters were, in history or fiction.

A man carrying a horsewhip is mounted, and one carrying a fan is a scholar, a man standing on a table while others run around him is invisible, and if he holds a long-haired whisk he is a spirit or fairy. A man with an oar is on a boat. Soldiers rolling off the stage have been killed in battle, and when heroes fight, their combat is a skillful, beautifully timed acrobatic dance to music with murderous-looking weapons, rather than a realistic encounter. The heavily and intricately painted faces of the characters make them look like devils rather than men, but every line in each mask tells its story (he is clever but treacherous; he appears to be of an honest disposition, but the chief minister had better be on his guard, for *this man is impersonating the real emperor*).

There is nothing more Chinese than this Chinese opera, with its symbols and its stiff canons, its etiquette and its tacit understandings, for these are the devices that for two thousand years provided a concordant surface pattern to a society which bowed to the yellow umbrella even if its prefect were not under it, and kowtowed when a mandarin passed carrying an Imperial decree on his back. Bound by the rules of a great conspiracy in convention, the Chinese conformed, playing their parts like pieces on a chessboard that do not crudely jostle one another in an attempt to occupy the same square at the same time but slip smoothly into their undisputed places with a decorum that deceives the alien eye and blinds it to the struggle on hand. Confucius had advocated ritual as a habit-forming discipline which would imbue men with the mystique of social sportsmanship. But he only succeeded in inspiring a split-level civilization in which the Chinese more often than not observed the rules to the letter in order to ignore the spirit of the game. He asked for gentlemen: he got players.

The European blunders through Chinese society, high and low, usually without an inkling of the reality beneath the appearances, so that even when the Hong Kong whore offers to pay her round of drinks at the bar, her American sailor boy thinks its kinda cute, and accepts. She goes through the motions, and he quite mistakenly takes them seriously. He hardly deserves the awful fate she silently wishes him for muffing his cue to say no. This *maquillage* on the skin of existence can sometimes be confusingly realistic. The demands of filial piety are met by a most convincing display of sorrow from professional mourners who can jerk out the tears to order, by young wives in sackcloth whose virtuous misery for the departure of their mother-in-law is only supect to those who know which local twopenny poet composed those touchingly elegant ejaculations of despair. But it is dangerous to be cynical, for there is a point at which ritual and reality must meet. Chinese believe that tears are not mere manifestations of uncontrollable emotion. They are, legitimately, the recognized expression of patriotism, loyalty, or filial piety.

At the end of World War II the Chinese army was drastically reduced and many impecunious officers (go anywhere, used to handling men) were thrown on the labor market. When a brigadier general of Chiang Kai-shek's own Whampoa Military Academy died without leaving a penny to pay for an honorable burial, veteran graduates some three hundred strong donned their best uniforms and their medals, and marched in protest to the tomb of Sun Yat-sen in Nanking. The colonel who led them intoned a threnody for Nationalist arms, whose theme was the age-old catchphrase: "When the birds are killed, the bow is put aside . . ." and three hundred officers wept bitter tears. The Chinese have one historical hero who was so ostentatiously lachrymose that Ping once described him as having "wept his way to victory." And in 1966 there were reports that Communist cadres were inciting the peasants to indulge in "mass crying" at hate meetings called "to remember past wrongs."

In August 1965 the conservative, predominantly Malay government in Kuala Lumpur ejected the small, predominantly Chinese island state of Singapore from the Federation of Malaysia. In a press conference recorded for television, Lee Kuan Yew, Singapore's Chinese prime minister, broke down and wept so bitterly that proceedings had to be suspended for some twenty minutes. Lee's grief was sincere enough. Human defense mechanisms are traitors, however, and he was in danger of facing the press with a quite deceptive and unbecoming composure if he failed to give way. It was meet that he should weep, and the tears were there, requiring no bidding. Chinese crying by numbers is like Christian churchgoing: laudable on the prescribed ritual occasion, if otherwise suspect.

Everyone knows the improbable tale of the emperor who walked stark naked through his capital while the entire populace conspired to uphold the fiction that he was clothed in new, fine-spun robes. Wherever it came from, this is a Chinese story and the story of the Chinese. It is even matched by a historical incident that occurred when the Grand Eunuch, wishing to test his hold over the Imperial court and to undermine the authority of his sovereign, presented the young weakling who had succeeded the great First Emperor with a deer, saying it was a horse. The monarch, who at least had eyes in his head, objected: "But this is a deer, not a horse." His courtiers, suitably intimidated, all told him it was a horse, however, and when he summoned his Grand Astrologer, that worthy warned him that if he thought the animal was a deer, he was suffering from delusions.

The Chinese are only too often ready to sweep the dust of reality under the carpet of appearance. Mencius notes that the proper course for a gentleman who cannot bear to see animals die, but likes his meat, is simply to keep out of the kitchen. Conversely, I have seen a foreign businessman who had playfully tapped a waitress on the head with the flat of his passport (weight: two ounces) peremptorily summoned by Communist Chinese authorities in Peking and asked why he had so viciously struck a state servant. Neither Mencius nor these Marxists were concerned with truth. The Chinese Communists may be rewriting history, but there is nothing odd about that: the Chinese have been rewriting it for centuries, and when accused of decadence during the Manchu era, some have been known to reply blandly that the Manchus were barbarians who let the Chinese down, and that the Manchu era is therefore simply "not part of the Chinese story."

When the foreign diplomatic missions in Peking were under siege in 1900, the Chinese government addressed a note to the British minister which suggested with some surprise: "It is possible that the foreign envoys do not fully realize the keen desire of the Imperial court to protect the legations." Astonished at complaints about the concentrated fire, however inaccurate, that is poured into the compound of the British mission, a Chinese mandarin describes it airily as "on about the same footing as the sounding of the drum at dusk and the bell at dawn." Moreover, when the hard-pressed little group of defenders in the legation quarter shoot back at their attackers, the Chinese government immediately protests that members of foreign missions are "firing into the city." Meanwhile, as the desperate battle continues to rage, the Chinese foreign ministry despatches a cart full of fresh fruits to the besieged British legation, with a message inquiring solicitously after the health of the diplomats sheltering behind its shot-scarred walls—six days before the neighboring Imperial Academy is fired in an attempt to burn the British and everyone with them.

When in 1743 Captain Anson sailed the *Centurion* out of the Canton estuary and past the Chinese forts which had failed so miserably to prevent his provocative sally upriver, his entourage up on deck remarked that the Chinese were determined to salvage their dignity. "The forts were now manned," one wrote, "with as many men as they could well contain, the greatest part of them armed with pikes and matchlock musquets." He went on to tell how one huge fellow particularly caught his eye, "dressed in very sightly armor . . . with a battle-ax in his hand." Observed through the glass, however, the armor turned out to be made of silver paper.

In England, the people of Hampstead rail against the man who put up the façade of a nonexistent bridge spanning nothing at the

far end of the Ken Wood lake. But when I pointed the sham
out to Ping, she thought it was perfect: "You need the white
bridge just that place, otherwise the whole scene dull. *Why it
must be real?*" There was no answer to this. When I asked her
once what the Chinese had admired most about the British at the
height of their power, she replied unhesitatingly: "Their falseness
in the diplomatic life, full of smart tricks always to fool the
people." (This was meant as a great compliment.)

The Chinese are masters at applying torque to plain terms.
Han Fei comments sardonically on the way that people will call
a man a "staunch friend" because he puts the Old Pals' Act before the public interest, will describe an official who is generous
with state funds as "benevolent," and those who make exceptions
of the law to suit their kinsmen as men of "loyal principles."
More than two thousand years after he wrote, a warlord's percentage on all narcotic sales is "the Tax to Discourage Opium,"
the Nationalists call the Communist anti-Japanese guerrillas "bandits," while those who settle quietly in Soochow without disputing the foreign occupation are "heroes of the Resistance." From
the earliest times the well-turned euphemism has beaten the
obvious truth. Drowning a child at birth to avoid future expense
has been "bathing the infant." The sexual act has been (rather
graphically) "the game of clouds and rain," and the grave is "the
land of pines." If you branded a person in the old days you were
"affixing the golden seals," and you might well be doing it during
that nightmare period of cutthroat fratricidal war known as the
"Era of Established Tranquillity." The heavy toll exacted in the
twenties by warlords who were raising funds for their brutish
soldiery was the "good-will tax," for it was supposed to finance
mercenaries who would only create ill-feeling by robbing the
peasantry if they were not paid. If anyone wished to refer in
Imperial China to the death of the reigning emperor, he might
only say: "When ten thousand years have passed," and when the
Dowager-Empress wanted the governor of Taiyuan to commit

suicide she simply remarked to him: "The price of coffins is rising."

Lu Hsün records that during the great "Buy Chinese" campaign of the thirties, smart shopkeepers loaded with large foreign stocks advertised them as "imported homemade goods." No one laughed. Are the Communists any different? When the American journalist Edgar Snow asked during a visit to China whether prostitutes still flourished, he received the answer: "Prostitutes? No. But there are still some women around who will make love for money." Chinese go by the label, and by the time the Communists have denounced the "American-imperialist-warmongers" for the millionth time, no Chinese peasant is going to think of the United States government in any other role, any more than "sonofabitch" can now be split up into its perfectly worthy component parts and given as a definition of Rin-Tin-Tin.

The instinct that enables a Chinese to move through this never-never-land with the practiced ease of an old inhabitant is his sense of "face." Honor is an affair of conscience and reality, but face is a matter of reputation and appearance. A loss of honor is a blemish on the skin, while a loss of face is a smudge on the make-up. A man of honor may only give a blind man a penny, but he does not rob him; a man concerned about his "face" may rob the blind man if no one is looking, but will ostentatiously give him a dime once enough people are. A Chinese may perform an honorable action not because it is dictated by his sense of honor but because it will give him face. Conversely, when a man is sued for a discreditable action, it is his loss of face, not his guilt, that worries his family.

The Chinese have rightly believed throughout their history that a man's "face" is his fortune. They have therefore been ready to ruin themselves and their families in order to give their son an impressive wedding and their parents an impressive funeral. Idle merchants will burn the lights at night in their offices to show how successful and busy they are, and if they go bankrupt, they will care more about the loss of face than the loss of money, for it also means a loss of credit. In Singapore a newspaper with a tiny circulation will charge the same advertising rates as the one with the biggest coverage in the country—but privately give a huge discount. Its proprietor would never admit that his was only a small sheet by publicly scaling down the rates.

In 1958 I tried to visit China on a British passport in which all the twenty-five countries for which it was valid had been entered by name, including China and Formosa. A Chinese security officer at the Hong Kong frontier noticed this and barked rudely that the People's Republic did not countenance dirty imperialist attempts to foist the "two Chinas" policy upon it, that Formosa was only a province of China in the hands of rebels, and that there was only one Chinese government. He then told me to get out. I protested that I had a valid visa granted by his own Foreign Ministry, but he was utterly unimpressed, and I was forced to withdraw with as much dignity as a man can muster while stumbling across the bridge that links China to Hong Kong carrying a heavy suitcase and a middle-aged typewriter.

Back in Hong Kong, I went to the crown colony's immigration office and explained my trouble. An official gravely took a bottle of Indian ink and a brush, drew a single black line on the passport that completely obscured the word Formosa, stamped the alteration, and handed the offending document back to me. On the following day I presented myself to the same Communist security officer at the frontier. He examined the passport and waved me into his enormous country with a smile and a few words of welcome. The fact that my entry visa was now a day out of date was neither here nor there. The word Formosa was not visible; all was well.

Much dissembling among the Chinese is prompted by a desire to save face. The Chinese history of the Opium Wars sparkles with "great Chinese victories" against the British, three of which, though purely imaginary themselves, are later multiplied, at the stroke of a writing brush, into "six crushing blows." The Canton forts, contemptuously bypassed by foreign warships time after time, are still described as "impregnable," and when the sick Lord Napier expires in Macao, he "dies from fear." In time the emperor himself began to doubt all these claims, well aware of the fine Chinese tradition in false reporting, but he was hardly in a position to glance down at his own naked body and shout: "But he hasn't got any clothes on!"

The international force sent to the relief of the foreign legations in Peking put down the Boxer Rebellion, which the Chinese court had deliberately encouraged, and compelled the guilty Empress Tzu Hsi to flee from the capital. But at an international ceremony that finally closed the episode, an iron-necked court official was nevertheless able to stand up and solemnly thank the foreign powers involved for helping the Chinese to suppress the Boxers. When peace was restored and the French units occupying one provincial city duly withdrew, the local Chinese at once put up a memorial stone describing how the French had "fled." The truth of the claim may be measured by the fact that a French corporal, happening to come back and ask what the inscription said, turned the stone around without anyone stopping him. But the Chinese, quite unmoved by this rebuttal, simply put it back in its original position after he had left.

A Chinese, however, thinks not only of his own face but of the face of others. He does not crush an opponent in public argument, leaving him with nothing to say and looking very much of a fool. He is content to let the man know that he could do this if he chose. He is just as sensitive about his image as the type of young European or American who seems to go through every minute of life as if he were "on camera" in front of a TV audience of 100 million personal admirers. This ham actor's play-this-cool, chew-that-gum antics would be comical were it not for his ill manners, his aggressiveness, and his desire to score off others. The Chinese, however, has to rub along smoothly in a crowded society in which "faces" are interdependent. His is, therefore, a code of forbearance. The master does not berate his servant in front of other domestics. The successful warlord does not necessarily decapitate his defeated enemy (for to lose your head is certainly to lose your face): he sends him abroad on some harmless "mission." When the Nationalist garrison commander surrendered Peking to the Communists in 1949, his capitulation was described as a "peaceful settlement."

The Chinese may appear ridiculous prevaricators in defeat, using absurd devices that would only fool men who are ready to be fooled without being convinced—in short, other Chinese. But the same concern with face often makes them gentle victors, for they have a habit of following up the *coup de grâce* with a cup of grace. When Lord Macartney tried to establish a permanent embassy for Britain in the Chinese capital in 1793, he was rebuffed with stinging condescension and then dismissed; but it took three months for Macartney's party to return overland to Canton and embark for England, and during this period they were treated with unstinted courtesy and generosity, were granted an Imperial allowance that in time rose to more than £3,500 a day, and were even provided regularly with milk (which the Chinese themselves did not touch).

Visiting Peking as Far East staff correspondent of *The Observer* in 1958 at the height of massive anti-British demonstrations, I was summoned by a vice-minister of the Communist government with whom I had requested an interview. He divided our meeting into three parts. First, he spent twenty minutes calling me a scurrilous imperialist who had consistently misreported on Communist China and put about the most damaging, unsubstantiated lies, an unscrupulous paid propagandist of reactionary forces whose only object was to blacken the name of the People's Republic, etc., etc., etc. Next, he gave offensively stereotyped answers to the written questions I had earlier submitted to him. He did this with cold civility, knowing that what he said could not possibly be of interest.

Finally, as I rose to say goodbye, he threw his arm around my shoulder, shook hands warmly, and said: "Well, I am sure that you are going to report in a most fair and objective manner on

FROM THE OUTSIDE, LOOKING IN 303

our country, and I want to wish you a most pleasant stay here."
My defense during the first two phases was to take careful written note of all his rudeness, but to take no notes at all of the
indigestible mouthfuls of statistics that he then served up to me
as information. I had no defense against the third, however. The
Imperial Chinese policy toward barbarians: "Awe first, and
soothe afterward"—which implied that the recalcitrant should be
chastened but not antagonized—had not been modified one whit,
it seemed.

The Communists very sensibly make use of the Great Chinese
Illusion when it suits them, and destroy it when it does not. They
reward a hard-worked, impoverished peasantry with praise and
laudatory citations, red banners, and flattering titles—firecracker
homage that gives face and shows favor. But they have also organized countrywide self-criticism campaigns in which hundreds
of thousands of citizens in need of "rectification" have been compelled to accept public humiliation, before being rehabilitated
and forgiven. Men have been forced to confess their "ideological
errors" in front of huge audiences of their own colleagues, who
have bullied and heckled them viciously, tearing their private
lives as well as their political behavior to shreds. They have been
ordered to write long *autocritiques,* confessing their faults and
recanting, and these have been torn up in their faces with demands that they write them anew. When I was in China in 1955,
distinguished professors, writers, painters, and other intellectuals
were in some cases writing their third or fourth *autocritique* under these conditions. "They are ripping the faces off them until
there is nothing left," a neutral Chinese sympathetic to the Communist regime commented to me. "Once that has been done, they
can remodel where the old face was." They were still doing the
same thing eleven years later, in 1966. Mao has always wanted
the Chinese mind to be a "blank sheet of paper" on which he
could write what he chose.

A modern Chinese youth does not have to be a Communist
to be anti-face, however. Many of the younger generation ostensi-

bly detest the whole dictionary of diplomatic euphemisms, the deceits and polite fictions that the convention involves. Yet it is still true that a Chinese schoolboy in Singapore will find it far more agonizing to own up and apologize for a misdeed than would his Western brother. But there is more in this than just a question of face, and although the European may be quick to say that the Chinese schoolboy simply lacks the moral courage of the young George Washington, many Chinese fathers would be just as quick to say that in the disgraceful episode of the cherry tree, both the future liberator of the American colonies ("Father, I cannot tell a lie") and his parent were obviously guilty of a moral turpitude that any decent Chinese boy should regard as beneath contempt—for the story should never have got out.

A Chinese feels entitled to believe that his most precious possession is a sense of shame. It is this which distinguishes him from the animals, which acts as the business end of conscience and prompts him to do good rather than evil. Shame is something to be conserved and not dissipated, and so to be hidden, not paraded. Moreover, it is something we should help others to hide also. But he has no sense of sin, for a sense of sin (he says) is the product of laws, whether the law is divine and reads in plain English "Thou shalt not kill," or is human and therefore requires ten lines of Anglo-Saxon archaisms and abominably mispronounced Latin to stipulate the punishment for a peccadillo. And the Chinese have as little regard for man-made laws as they have for god-made morality. To them the most notable thing about this famous Western sense of sin is that it prompts people to confess, while their own sense of shame tells them not to do so. For to confess "sin" to the universe at large shows a complete lack of shame on two counts: first, if true, it constitutes brazen publication of an evil act; second, to confess is in most cases to abdicate responsibility, to shrug off the lonely burden of conscience.

The European observes the Chinese make-believe world of face and damns it as hypocritical, but to the Chinese it is like someone who looks a fine figure of a man in a well-padded overcoat. There is nothing hypocritical about the overcoat, because everybody is aware that it is an overcoat and that underneath those massive square shoulders stuffed with wadding is the ordinary, uninspiring human form. The Chinese accepts the conventions of the overcoat's shape, and because he is not fooled by its deceits, they cease to be deceits. Life is therefore lived on two layers, and for the Chinese the one that counts is the one underneath. The outer layer of appearance is made up of advertised actions and loud words that may no more belong to the truth than the foam-rubber falsies belong to the unpretentious breasts they revaluate. All emotional prattle is insincere, all public gesture a fake. A Chinese prefers to believe what he reads between the lines—the unspoken thought that is like one of his "stop-short" poems (the words stop, but the sense goes on), the *sous-entendu,* the intuitively felt emotion.

It was said of Confucius: "When a friend sent him a present, though it might be a carriage and horses, he did not bow." For "thank you" to a Chinese is a cheap payoff. It may be used to strangers and shopkeepers and vague acquaintances who have done a small favor, but it is, like confession, an abdication from further obligation in an audit-minded society that double-entries all moral debt. "Thank you" is a surface phrase for workaday dealings with the community, and must be used with discretion, for it can easily be offensive. A son takes from his father without a word, and his silence itself means that he recognizes his great, snowballing indebtedness to his parents. Close friends who help each other and men who understand each other deeply do not let that inadequate little expression come between them.

An intimate shows gratitude, he does not voice it. True sentiment is only shyly revealed. Toasts are part of the polite, insincere surface convention, and to propose a toast that expresses in trite speech the intimate wish of lovers or friends may be to debase it in the most tasteless manner. Men who feel real emotion do best when they conceal it, hiding their misery or embarrassment behind a laugh. If a well-to-do man wants to help an impecunious friend, he might take wine to his house, settle down to a drinking session with him, and then, in strict privacy, press money upon him. If the other protested, the lender would say that he was so worried about his friend's difficulties that he himself would only be able to sleep peacefully if the money were accepted: "So you are really doing me the favor . . ." He would give the money, not lend it. The debt would, after all, be precisely the same.

A Chinese mourns, therefore, if he does not have one good friend with whom he has an instinctive understanding and to whom he can show his true face ("For we always have two," says Ping with pride, turning Western insult into Eastern boast). It is the one-faced white, with his heart on his sleeve and his honest, open manner, who is to the Chinese the very picture of a specious barbarian. And if anyone wants proof, he should count the number of times he says: "Thank you" in a single day. "European laugh at Japanese bowing and hissing one another," Ping once said. "Has never occurred you that by the time shopkeeper and customer in England have said 'Thank you, sir' and 'No, thank you, sir' six times, is no different?"

We adopted three Chinese boys, and they mooched around the house, taking everything without a word of acknowledgment until the inevitable explosion came. But it was for me to learn the lesson. The Chinese have a more delicate appreciation of personal relations simply because they also have a thick carapace of tough, almost cynical convention—for nothing has softer flesh than a hard-shell crab. The Taoists say that all things must be perceived intuitively, not analyzed rationally. And this counsel applies to the Chinese themselves.

26

The Dovehawks

"I impute their behaviour to the unparalleled pusillanimity of the Nation," a British man of God wrote of the Chinese in the eighteenth century, and indeed a strong body of literary evidence can be produced to show that the Chinese have been inclined toward the arts of peace rather than war. The British also have an anti-war literature, but this either is regarded as slightly treasonous ("But 'twas a famous victory") or, if of unimpeachable security rating, is simply ignored ("Thou shalt not kill"). Small wonder that in 1860 the Chinese emperor dropped an account of our island history with a sigh and remarked wearily: "They seem to be always at war, or going to war, with someone or other."

Confucius and Mencius, sickened by the dog-eat-dog struggle for supremacy in their own times, preached benevolence and not aggression, and Mencius described the idea of a war of conquest to end all wars of conquest as "worse than trying to get fish from a tree." The Taoists went further by saying that even to take the side of those who were in the right in order to discourage wars was the best way to start new wars. All conquest was fundamentally futile, for what did a parcel of land amount to when the country of the mind was limitless? Mo Tzu denounced conquerors as kleptomaniacs on a large scale, all wars as destructive and evil and ridiculously unprofitable. The poets joined the philosophers in their protest, and during the T'ang dynasty, the great Po Chü-i composed a famous anti-militaristic satire about an old man of eighty-eight who had lived a long and tranquil life thanks to a timely self-inflicted wound which enabled him to dodge the draft. A century later another poet wrote:

> Do not let me hear you talking together
> About titles and promotions;
> For a single general's reputation
> Is made out of ten thousand corpses.

Even the ruthless strategist Wu Ch'i warned: "The field of battle is a land of standing carcasses."

The first real break with a bloodthirsty past, however, came shortly before Ethelred the Unready in far-off England also started to pay the enemy rather than fight him. In A.D. 960, the officers of a Chinese army on the march mutinied against the throne and, in the best Roman tradition, forced their own general at the point of the sword to don the yellow robe of an emperor. The general reluctantly agreed to found a new dynasty, but was quick to reflect that soldiers who could mutiny and overthrow a sovereign once could do it twice. Once on the throne, therefore, he called upon all senior officers responsible for his being there to resign their commands and to retire to the provinces. In exchange, they would be given extensive lands and splendid residences, and would be allied to the personal family of their new emperor by a series of marriages.

On the next day the officers, feigning serious illness, all resigned, and the savage scrimmage for supremacy among rival families and contending generals that had shattered the unity of China for half a century came to an end. This was the beginning of the pacific Sung dynasty's sway over China, when soldiering was at a discount, men painted and played chess rather than draw a bow or wield a sword, and, like Ethelred, the emperor bought off his bellicose neighbors with tribute. The army was recruited from the lees of society and was regarded as little more than a refuge for drunken looters: "You do not use good iron to make a nail, nor a good man to make a soldier," the Chinese have said.

The Taoist belief that all truth is relative, that while one party may be right the other may not necessarily be wrong, encourages the instinct for compromise, and so does the Confucian principle of the Golden Mean. The Chinese, therefore, has a magnificent seat on a fence. He will swear to fight to the death, and yet will secretly parley with the enemy at the same time, for war and peace are complementary weapons and, having two hands, he may wield both simultaneously. In 1948 the vice-president of the Chinese Nationalists privately negotiated an agreement with their Communist enemies whereby Chiang Kai-shek was to be discarded and a Communist-Nationalist coalition government formed. The gambit failed. But a similar under-the-counter deal between an outwardly menacing Communist government in Peking and a bellicose Nationalist government in Formosa has for long been on the cards. It will one day emerge that they are not really enemies but just bad friends.

Lu Hsün was characteristically scathing about the tepid tea in Chinese veins: "Quixote is a Spanish fool," he wrote. "You will not find his counterpart in China. When Spaniards court a girl, they serenade her every day; when they feel religious, they burn heretics at the stake; when they make a revolution, they pull down churches and kick out their king. Our Chinese scholars, however, always accuse the women of seducing them, trace all religions to one common source, protect temple property, and allow the emperor to remain in his palace for years after the revolution." The Chinese love bullfights—but in Chinese bullfights the bulls fight each other, while the men look on. The public watches the warlords fight, he continues, and the warlords, from the safety of their barricades, watch their soldiers fight. For a Chinese likes any fight he can just sit out and observe in comfort.

The Chinese nevertheless developed a great capacity for stubborn, courageous, tireless defense, for "strengthening the wall and scorching the earth," but dynastic decadence eroded this also in time, for a soldier must have both status and a good cause. In the degenerate days of the Ming dynasty he felt he had neither, and these were followed by more than two hundred and fifty years of foreign occupation. It was during this period of martial disillusion and neglect that the Europeans were to arrive on the scene and see the Chinese warrior at his worst. After 1644, national defense was in the hands of Manchu "bannermen" who revealed an unsuspected talent for shedding their hard-riding history and sinking swiftly into a soft life of idleness and opium. They were supported by Chinese irregulars, who were little more than a rabble. An article in the *Chinese Repository* published by the British in Canton early in the nineteenth century said that the army's gunpowder often did not explode, but its cannons frequently did. It was a "stage army" in which sentinels were "undressed, unarmed, and half asleep" when called out. Their swords were often so rusty that they could not draw them, and daily rated spare soldiers would be hired, like film extras, to swell the number when necessary, riffraff dressed up in imitation tiger skins and taught to shout war cries.

When the Boxer Rebellion broke out sixty years later, the stories were the same: "Had we been fighting such people as the Zulus or Dervishes, we should have been polished off in a few days," one diarist wrote about the siege of the foreign legations in Peking in 1900, for there were only four hundred lightly armed men, desperately short of supplies, defending the long perimeter of the diplomatic enclave. A fantastically badly organized international relief column marched on Peking from the coast, yet this push through enemy territory turned into a race rather than a battle, for great herds of Chinese troops ran before the invaders, firing and looting villages as they fled. The concensus was that the Chinese soldier was an illiterate and ignorant peasant, poorly armed, ill-trained, and badly led, from whom it was unfair to expect more.

More than thirty years later, opposing generals were engaging in telegram battles, bracketing each other with barrages of in-

sults and threats and boasts, and only taking to their guns as a
last resort. Campaigns were won before they were fought, and
fought before any prepared defense positions had been constructed. The worthless warlords rigged their battles between
them, the loser was paid off and ran for the International Settlement in Shanghai before the first shot was fired. The winning
general automatically acquired the soldiers of his defeated colleague, since their resistance rapidly collapsed when they found
their commander had absconded. Peter Fleming remarked at this
time that the Chinese footslogger was too intelligent to serve
such traitors wholeheartedly, to risk his life in a fixed fight, or to
die for nothing at all. He nevertheless had qualities that went to
the making of a good soldier—he was strong, enduring, lived on
little. He was cheerful and he came from a race that took its
crafts seriously, he had courage and resource, and he would
be loyal to a good commander. He must simply be properly paid
and properly fed. The world was to learn how true these words
were. But the Chinese also had something that Fleming denied
him: military tradition.

War was the principal business of the state in ancient China.
Masters of cavalry and the unique crossbow, skilled in sophisticated tactics, and supported by durable soldiery capable of
handling a hundred-pound longbow with ease, Chinese commanders might well have inflicted upon Alexander the Great a
stinging lesson on the fallibility of famous generals, had he advanced far enough to encounter them. And one thousand years
later men were still writing verse like this:

> On Liu horse, white jade saddled, proud rode he
> from battle home in moonlight chill,
> While tower-top iron drums yet trembled, and blood
> in scabbard scarce congealed.

Or in Victorian vein:

> They swore the Huns would perish:
> They would die if needs they must . . .

And now five thousand, sable-clad,
Have bit the Tartar dust.

Kipling could hardly have done better, but then he also came from a nation of shopkeepers.

American military analysts now pay serious attention to the *Romance of the Three Kingdoms*, for it has gradually dawned on the West that the inspired trickery practiced by that legendary third-century slyboots of a strategist, Chu-ko Liang, remains as subtly influential among the Chinese as a sermon at mother's knee. Recognized as a worthy preceptor by Mao, carefully studied by the Vietcong guerrillas in South Vietnam, Chu-ko Liang was a "Sleeping Dragon," a sage in retreat who never wielded a sword, for the essence of the great Chinese military tradition has always been that brains baffle brawn. Persuaded to emerge and to act as counselor to the Han pretender in his struggle against the usurper Ts'ao Ts'ao, Chu-ko Liang quickly found himself the victim of jealousies in the loyalist camp and almost on the eve of a river battle was challenged to produce a stock of one hundred thousand arrows within three days on pain of death. He did not attempt the hopeless task of trying to manufacture the arrows in time, however, but arranged to have at his disposal "a score of vessels, each manned by thirty men, with blue cotton screens and bundles of straw lashed to the sides."

When the heavy evening mist descended on the river, these boats were roped together, floated down toward the enemy shoreline, and strung out in the gloom so that they were just visible. Ts'ao Ts'ao's ships hesitated to sally out against them in such ideal condition for a naval ambush, but at the same time their commander feared an assault landing. Ground troops were therefore brought up to line the river, and these saturated the threatening flotilla with a continuous hail of arrows, which embedded themselves in the straw-filled screens until by morning each of the little vessels looked like a hedgehog. Only when the sun came up and the mist dispersed did the lightly manned fleet move swiftly downstream, delivering to Chu-ko Liang the promised hundred thousand arrows.

The incident could well have been an allegory about Chinese Communist and Vietcong guerrilla forces that for years equipped themselves almost exclusively with weapons and ammunition captured from their enemies—Nationalist, French, American. During his struggle against Chiang Kai-shek in the thirties, Mao wrote: "We have a claim on the output of the arsenals of London as well as Hanyang and, what is more, that output will be delivered to us by the enemy's own transport corps."

Chu-ko Liang always fought with an economy of means well suited to the stripped-down revolutionary jungle armies of today, and never missed an opportunity to use cut-price resources, like water, or fire, or both. On one occasion he employed one force to pile sulphur, niter, and other inflammable materials on the roofs of the town which he himself was holding, a second to dam a river which the enemy would have to cross, and a third to wait in ambush at a ford downstream. He then quietly withdrew his headquarters into the surrounding country.

Ts'ao Ts'ao's main body moved against the town but was diverted by various ruses and only arrived at the walls at nightfall. Finding it deserted, his generals concluded that Chu-ko Liang had accepted defeat and had retreated, and they allowed their weary men to disperse into the houses, to cook a meal, and sleep. Chu-ko Liang's snipers then shot fire arrows into the town from outside, the highly combustible roofs were soon in flames, and Ts'ao Ts'ao's troops awoke to find themselves in a blazing inferno. Fleeing as best they could in their scorched and tired condition, they were ambushed on their way to the river and many were cut down, and when the remnant of their army finally reached the water, Chu-ko Liang's men smashed the dam upstream and most of the retreating enemy were overwhelmed in the flood that poured down upon them. Those that were left returned to land and hurried thankfully to the ford farther down, only to fall into the second ambush that had been patiently waiting there from the beginning.

It is often said that a commander of genius is worth several divisions, and Chu-ko Liang was once able to prove the point without fighting a battle at all. Hearing that a huge enemy force was advancing against a city in which he disposed of no more than three or four hundred men, "he ordered all the banners to be removed and concealed, and said if any officer in command of soldiers in the city moved or made any noise he would be instantly put to death. Next he threw open all the gates and set a score of soldiers dressed as ordinary people cleaning the streets at each gate. When all these preparations were complete, he donned the simple Taoist dress he affected on occasions and, attended by a couple of lads, sat down on the wall by one of the towers with his lute before him and a stick of burning incense." The intimidating horde of the enemy approached in a great cloud of dust, ready for battle. But seeing the ever cautious Chu-ko Liang seated peacefully on the wall and no one about but a few street sweepers, its commander assumed that some diabolical trap had been laid for him and, turning about, took himself off with his troops.

It is not difficult to see parallels between Chu-ko Liang's military card-sharping and the sleight-of-hand tactics of the Chinese and Vietnamese guerrillas. The "Sleeping Dragon" often succeeded in baffling his own side almost as much as the discomfited enemy, and never more than in the affair of the King of the Mans. The Mans, who were (and are) a minority people living in the wild hill country of southwest China, had rebelled against Chu-ko Liang's master. The "Sleeping Dragon," sent to suppress the revolt, defeated the Mans and took their king prisoner, but then, to the mystification of his entourage, asked this barbarian what he would do if he were released. "I shall return," said the king stoutly, "and when I have set my army in order, I shall come to fight you again." Chu-ko Liang let him go.

The King of the Mans duly raised another army, mounted another insurrection, was captured again, and again released. This happened six times, but on the seventh occasion that he found himself a captive before Chu-ko Liang, the discouraged chieftain yielded unconditionally. Chu-ko Liang then sent him back to rule his people. Instead of inviting constant trouble and suffering a continuous drain on his forces by trying to hold this sprawling territory with Chinese occupation troops, he let its own acknowledged but suitably chastened native ruler do the job for him far more effectively. Many Chinese remembered this story when the Communist troops showed how easy it was for them to pour across the northern frontier into India in 1962, and, having administered the lesson, withdrew.

Chu-ko Liang's spirit has never died among the Chinese, as Captain John Weddell found when, commissioned by King Charles I, he trod on the Dragon's tail in Canton. For as his little fleet lay at anchor in the narrows of the estuary one night, several junks were dimly observed drifting toward it on the ebb tide without lights. When they were close to the British ships, their skeleton crews jumped overboard and the approaching junks bursts into flames. Faced with the sudden menace of these terrible fireships, the British slipped their anchor chains and hastily drew off. "Balles of wylde fire, Rocketts and Fire-arrows Flew thicke as they passed us," wrote one appalled onlooker aboard. "Great and sodaine was the amasement and affrightt att such a tyme of the Nightt to see such a Fearfull Daunger redy to Destroy us . . ." The four ships escaped, but it was a narrow squeak. One hundred years later, two British frigates forced their way up the pasage toward Canton, scornfully challenging the obsolete Chinese forts at the entrance to stop them. But they had not reckoned with the viceroy, who ordered barges to be loaded with stones and then scuttled in a line across the narrows after they had passed, so that the invincible warships found themselves neatly locked up in a twenty-mile stretch of river, and quite incapable of doing anything about it.

However, the real Clausewitz of China lived long before Chu-ko

Liang and codified much earlier the principles that the "Sleeping Dragon" so often put into practice. The great Sun Wu probably wrote his *Art of War* when Philip was still king of Macedonia during the fourth century B.C., and had he not lived more than two thousand years before they were published, he might well have been accused of cribbing from Mao Tse-tung's somewhat later works on guerrilla warfare.

"If you know the enemy and know yourself, in a hundred battles you will never be in danger," taught China's greatest military master. But, just as the Chinese God of War is really a God of Peace, so, Sun Wu added, the proper object of strategy was to avoid combat altogether. "To win a hundred victories is not the acme of skill. To subdue the enemy without fighting is the acme of skill." The best policy is to take a state intact. To ruin it with much conflict is an inferior solution. How is this achieved? Sometimes one is convinced that Hitler was one of the few Europeans who had ever read Sun Wu in his day, and Europe was consequently made to suffer for its ignorance. Undermine the enemy first, counseled the guileful Sun Wu, and then his army will fall to you. Subvert him, attack his morale, hit his economy, corrupt him, sow internal discord among his leaders, and practice every possible deceit upon him.

A man is flogged mercilessly so that when he deserts to the enemy and tells him a pack of lies about his commander's intentions in a suitably resentful voice, he will be believed. Arrows carrying propaganda are shot into beseiged cities before an assault to spread false rumors and shake morale, kites bearing subversive slogans are flown overhead, and men are disguised and paraded before the walls to convince the inhabitants that important enemy officers have been captured and relief columns cut to pieces. Sun Wu has a special chapter on the use of five kinds of secret agents, including "double agents" and "expendable agents." "Expendable agents" are spies to whom false information about their own side has been deliberately leaked, so that if they are later caught and tortured, their disclosures will only mislead the enemy. "Sometimes I send agents to the enemy to make a covenant of peace, and then I attack," one commentator on Sun Wu disarmingly reveals. The Japanese may have had him in mind when they planned the bombing of Pearl Harbor. It was not surprising that President Johnson's peace proposals for Vietnam were dismissed in Peking as cover for "frenzied war preparations."

But it is not only in the preliminary softening-up period that a successful general staff practices every subterfuge and swindle in the book. "All warfare is based on deception," Sun Wu stresses. When you are capable, pretend incapacity; when you are active, pretend to be idle; when you are strong, feign weakness; and when you are near, seem to be far away. Always conceal your true dispositions so that you can "attack when the enemy is unprepared, and sally out when he does not expect you." Gradually a whole philosophy of fighting peculiarly suited to modern guerrilla war emerges, founded on the Taoist tenet that the soft and flexible outlasts the hard and rigid as tongue survives teeth. "Do not fight a static war, and do not besiege cities," warns Sun Wu. ("Bypass what he defends, hit him where he does not anticipate you," comments Ts'ao Ta'ao.) Attack what he does not protect, hold what he does not attack. Strike where he is weak, but disperse when he is strong. Only take calculated risks, and only carry out an assault when victory is assured. Use local guides, and when you bring the enemy to battle, be there first: "skilled commanders entice the enemy with something he is sure to take, with lures of ostensible profit await him in strength." Conceal your dispositions, causing the enemy to divide and spread, then use your strength against a fraction of his. ("My strategy is one against ten," Mao has said. "My tactics, ten against one.")

A descendant of Sun Wu once persuaded the enemy to believe that he was suffering badly from mass desertions by halving the number of cooking fires he allowed his troops to light each successive night; Chu-ko Liang did the reverse, progressively reducing the number of troops in a certain position every evening but doubling the number of cooking fires to make it look as if he had been reinforced. Deception, surprise, fraud, the ruse, the ambush, the sudden unexpected concentration of hidden force against a weak enemy, and the quick "vanishing into the ground" before a strong one—these are the tactical tenets that Sun Wu taught and that the Chinese and Vietnamese Communists have learned, so that Mao's jingle on the keys to his successful guerrilla war against Chiang Kai-shek ran:

> When the enemy advances, I withdraw.
> When the enemy halts, I harass.
> When the enemy avoids battle, I attack.
> When the enemy retreats, I pursue.

Employing these principles, the elusive Vietcong have time and time again made fools of sledgehammer forces five times their size, equipped with the most up-to-date weapons and strongly supported by modern air power. But behind these able contemporary masters of military thimble-rig stands Sun Wu, and behind him is the Taoist philosophy of flexibility which prompted him to write: "Adapt to the ground like water."

It follows that for those who reverence these shrewd, if sometimes infamous doctrines, "stupid, quick-tempered, and courageous generals are a menace," as Sun Wu indicated. Since war is a matter of stratagem, not strength, the ideal commander is not a calm, self-assertive pragmatic fellow with a solid West Point grounding in logistics, but a more reticent figure—subtle, enigmatic, a man with a certain mystique, an intuitive flair. The Chinese warmed at once to the personality and the story of Lawrence of Arabia. Here was a Chinese hero reminiscent of the intrepid Pan Chao, who lived in Nero's day.

In A.D. 73, Pan Chao, then a young officer on the staff of the Chinese commander-in-chief, was dispatched westward into the little-known wilds of Central Asia to find allies among the kingdoms of Turkestan against the Hun, who plagued the Chinese so diligently along the Great Wall. There is something oddly British about the fact that for this formidable task he was assigned only thirty-six men. He was therefore in no position to lay down laws when he found that the first king he visited was secretly entertaining a Hun delegation at the same time as his own, and was beginning to look upon Pan Chao with increasing disfavor as the days passed. So Pan Chao first tricked the official detailed to wait upon the Chinese embassy into telling him where the Huns were lodged, and then locked the fellow up. Next, he moved stealthily out to the Hun encampment at night and proceeded to surround it and set it on fire, while his drummers beat the assault as loudly as they could. The Huns, fearing that they were being attacked by a large force, and unable to see what was really going on, rushed out of their quarters and were immediately set upon by Pan Chao's men. Nearly all perished, for those who were not killed on the spot ran back into the huts and were burned to death. Pan Chao, who had not lost a man, now took the severed head of the Hun ambassador and calmly presented it to the king of this petty state, without any hope of being able to defend himself if his immediate execution were ordered. However, the overawed monarch not only hastily concluded an alliance with China but offered his son as a hostage for his future decorous conduct.

Jealous courtiers at home managed to engineer Pan Chao's recall to China after three years of wandering, but not before his fame and influence had reached as far as Kashgar, and four years later he was again allowed to set out, having promised the emperor that with a force of no more than a few hundred men he could unite Central Asia solidly against the Huns under the suzerainty of the Celestial Empire. In the seventeen years that followed, he kept his word. Consistently playing the tributaries whose loyalty he had won against those princes who still held out against him, he subdued the entire Tarim Valley, established himself as Chinese viceroy, and with a vassal army that had swollen to more than sixty thousand men advanced to the Caspian Sea. The Chinese were now the masters of all Central Asia as far as the threshold of Europe, and the venturesome Pan Chao administered more than fifty petty kingdoms on behalf of his Imperial overlord in the Chinese capital. In A.D. 102, this Chinese Lawrence finally retired to China, after thirty years in "the West," to die in a matter of months. In Kashgar there are springs named after him to this day.

27

Arms and the Han

"The cautious seldom err," remarked Confucius. "I do not want an associate who will attack a tiger unarmed or cross a river without a boat, dying without regret. He must be a man who acts with care, who is fond of adjusting his plans . . ."

From the accounts in the last chapter, the Chinese military tradition may appear to be founded on cunning rather than courage. "Do not thwart an enemy returning home." "Do not press a foe at bay." "Leave a way of escape for a surrounded adversary." These Chinese military maxims in particular will sound reprehensibly inglorious to the blood-and-balaklava school, unless it is realized that they also worked in reverse. Sun Wu defines "death ground" as the position in which troops are cornered and can only survive by fighting like tigers. But while it is a mistake to lure the enemy into such a trap, it is not necessarily a mistake to put your own men in it, say the ruthless Chinese strategists. After all, which side do you want to fight like tigers "When Han Hsin destroyed the State of Chao, he drew up his own army with the river at its back. The Chao troops, observing this, roared with laughter and taunted him: 'The General of Han does not know how to use troops.'" But the General of Han did know. He had smashed the camp cooking pots, chopped up his boats, and so deployed his men that they must do or die, defeat the enemy or drown. He accordingly proceeded to thrash the Chao army soundly and, after eating his breakfast, decapitated its overlord. This is widely acclaimed among Chinese as a classic example of sound professionalism.

For Sun Wu, the commander's power is absolute, and he must enforce obedience with an iron hand on all occasions. Having granted him an audience on the art of war, the King of Wu suggested to the great strategist that he might prove his ability by drilling the palace womenfolk. Sun Wu agreed, and so 180 beautiful girls were brought before him. These he divided into two companies, appointing the king's two favorite concubines to be their respective officers. Next he explained the conventional words of command, but every time he gave an order the irritating women giggled and failed to comply with it. "When orders have been made clear, but are still not carried out," said Sun Wu severely, after this had happened several times, "it is a crime on the part of the officers." Whereupon he ordered the two favorites to be beheaded. The king protested, but Sun Wu replied: "When the commander is at the head of the army, he need not accept all the sovereign's orders." The concubines lost their pretty heads, the next beauties in line were appointed company leaders in their places, and there was no more tittering on parade. The king— distracted with grief, appalled by such brutality, but secretly impressed—made Sun Wu his commander-in-chief.

Sun Wu insisted not only that those who retreat without orders should be executed but that those who failed to withdraw when they should must also be beheaded. Discipline must be harsh and invariable: "If troops are loyal but punishments are not enforced, you cannot employ them." This ferocious tradition is far from dead, and when Chiang Kai-shek was commandant of the Whampoa Military Academy, he not only instituted collective responsibility for any disobedience or lapse but stipulated that if the platoon (or company, or battalion) commander retreated with his unit without orders, he should at once be executed; if a squad retreated without orders from an officer, the entire squad should be executed. No one thought this particularly barbarous. It was less than three hundred years since the defiant ruler of the Chinese province of Szechuan had ordered all soldiers under his command to kill their wives so that he would not be bothered with camp followers—and had seen that the command was carried out.

Even today Communist soldiers may be seen strolling in Peking, carrying Chinese umbrellas of oiled paper to keep off the sun, but the world might quickly become a wiser and even sadder place if the image of the Chinese army as a sort of Gilbert and Sullivan chorus persisted. A foreign observer slightingly remarked during the Boxer Rebellion that as the Chinese "had no stomach for frontal assault," they had become adept at moving barricades forward at night. But there is more to war than brute force and bloody-minded ignorance. This game of grandma's steps was not only effectively used by the Chinese in Korea but proved an even more spectacular success at the battle of Dienbienphu, where the world's champion military moles, the Vietminh, gradually advanced their assault trenches nearer to the French redoubts under cover of darkness each night until they were almost on top of their enemy.

The Han people who moved out of their modest settlements in a bend of the Yellow River to create the great Chinese empire, and who finally smashed the Mongol hordes of the Great Khans and burned their stronghold at Karakorum, were in no sense cowards. The British first took note of this in 1839 during the naval engagement of Ch'üen Pi, off the Canton coast. They inflicted a humiliating defeat on the outmoded Chinese fleet, but their commander wrote of its admiral: "He bore up and engaged H.M. ships in handsome style, manifesting a resolution of behavior honorably enhanced by the hopelessness of his efforts." The admiral broke off the action when his tub of a flagship was awash, but fell in battle against the British during a subsequent engagement in which, as a British officer noted, "many of the Chinese officers boldly and nobly met their death." H.M.S. *Blenheim* fired a salute in Admiral Kuan's honor once it was known he had been killed.

The record of the "Sons of Man" for courage, intelligence, and fortitude has been impressively upheld during this century in spite of the scratch teams that the squabbling warlords put into the field in the twenties. By 1936 the world was beginning to hear details of the epic "Long March" performed by the Communist guerrilla armies under Mao Tse-tung, who led his followers on foot over more than six thousand miles of often wild, mountainous, and swampy country to set up a new stronghold in northwest China, running the gauntlet of ten Nationalist armies that successively barred his way through ten provinces. Constantly harassed, the guerrillas crossed eighteen mountain ranges and twenty-four rivers, fighting at least one action every day. They were engaged during the journey in fifteen days of major hostilities, and they faced such daunting hazards as the bridge of Liu over the Tatu River in west China.

The Nationalists had thoughtfully removed half of the wooden floorboards of this bridge, which was more than three hundred feet long and entirely suspended on sixteen iron chains, and they had prepared machine-gun positions which enfiladed it satisfactorily from the far bank. But the bridge had to be crossed, for the river was in roaring flood. Thirty barefoot Chinese Communists in the assault party therefore swung themselves hand over hand along the chains, their guns strapped to their backs, in the face of long, murderous bursts of fire from the Nationalist redoubt. Several were soon cut down and fell into the torrent far below, but comrades on the hither bank were giving them strong covering fire, and the chains and the splintered remnants of the bridge flooring afforded some protection once the rest were halfway over, so that one man was at last able to climb up on the planks and lob a grenade into the enemy machine-gun nest. The Nationalists tried to tear up the rest of the planking or set it on fire with paraffin, but Communist after Communist hauled himself up from the chains and ran through the flames to attack the redoubt. The Nationalists finally fled, and the great Red column crawled forward once more. One hundred and thirty thousand men and women set out on this grueling marathon; twenty thousand arrived at the other end.

The Japanese were soon to be startled by the stubborn defense that Chiang Kai-shek's none-too-well organized armies, largely made up of poorly fed, badly paid, underarmed, and ignorant conscripts, were to offer to their modern, professional forces in the struggle for China. In 1937, a quarter of a million Chinese, out of a defending force of 450,000, fell in the battle for Shanghai, recognized as the most terrible slaughter since World War I. According to Japanese estimates, the Chinese lost more than eight hundred thousand men in 1938 and again in 1940, but they showed a fantastic ability to recover, replacing anything from sixty to a hundred percent of the fighting soldiers of a front-line unit in a year. These conscripts, called up for the war from their villages, often had to walk for months, covering hundreds of miles on foot before they reached the unit or depot to which they were posted. Many fell sick, died, or went absent without leave on the way; yet about half actually reported for duty.

Before the situation stagnated, and neither the soldiers nor the peasants saw much point in doing more than to try to survive, Chinese Nationalist generals scored a number of brilliant victories against their formidable enemy which went unsung in a West desperately preoccupied already with its own war. In the struggle for Changsha, the key rail center at which my brother-in-law commanded the 99th Army under the overall direction of the redoubtable Hsüeh Yüeh, the Japanese were completely routed three times in succession in three of the fiercest battles of World War II, and were therefore never able to dominate the vital rail link from Hankow to Canton before 1945. Brigadier General Thomas S. Arms, who commanded the infantry training center in southwest China, wrote: "This is perhaps the greatest difference between a Chinese and an American soldier. The American soldier asks when he is going out of the front. But the Chinese asks when he is going back to the front. When a man has gone through the kind of hell a Chinese soldier has gone through in the last seven years and is still anxious to go back and get even with the enemy, you can't beat him, if he has the necessary training and equipment."

As the Japanese moved menacingly down the peninsula of Malaya, a British colonel in Singapore hastily threw together a little army of local irregulars, ranging from schoolteachers to secret-society thugs, which was contemptuously referred to behind his back as "John Dalley's band of Chinese cutthroats." Brought into play when matters were desperate, one company of this unorthodox force was deployed on the north shore of the island, where the Japanese assault could shortly be expected, with orders not to retreat. That night the Japanese attacked, cutting their way magisterially into the soft, disorganized British and Australian defenses, but Dalley was still able to make his way to the company position next morning. "It was a frightful sight," he said. "They had been blown to pieces. They had used up all their ammunition. There were no wounded to bring back. They'd stood their ground. They'd orders to stay and they stayed. And they all died." Some two hundred strong, mostly Chinese, they had fought a Japanese machine-gun battalion to the last man—except for a British officer who withdrew with five other ranks. On the flank, a complete Australian machine-gun battalion had also failed to stand firm and had pulled back in the night.

"Sacrifice a finger to save an arm," say the Chinese, whose strategy has often been shaped by their geographical and economic conditions. Their country is too big to conquer and occupy, and their industry has been too puny to support vast armies in any prolonged frontal offensive against a modern enemy. The flexible and foxy tactics advocated by Sun Wu have therefore always remained valid: do not try to hold land, lead the enemy on into this great, roomy trap, stretching his lines of communication out farther and farther until the slender thread will almost snap of its own accord. Once his troops are spread tissue-thin on the ground, anyone can poke a hole through his defenses if he concentrates strength at one point. The Chinese fought a largely guerrilla-type campaign against the Japanese, rarely seeking a

stand-up fight from fixed positions, for they are by blood and environment masters of the protracted nagging, harassing war that
will wear the adversary down. "Chinese are brave to run away,"
as Ping succinctly puts it. But if the vastness of China has encouraged commanders from Sun Wu to Mao Tse-tung to bypass cities, to avoid the clinches, and to rely on fast footwork in
order to tire the opponent out in the open, the vastness of the
Chinese population has often encouraged generals to envelop and
suffocate the enemy, to bury him under a dead weight of expendable cannon fodder in the grisly traditions of World War I.

To the practical Chinese commander, this is not necessarily a
descent from his intellectual position to the "sausage-grinder"
simplicities of Flanders. Even Sun Wu said: "When you outnum-
ber the enemy five to one, you may attack," and so the "human
sea" joins the hit-and-run guerrilla strategy of the Chinese as an
odd-looking bedfellow, but one that does not in fact offend the
Yang-Yin principle of matching opposites. In the narrow Korean
Peninsula the Chinese relieved their military claustrophobia by
falling back on their human-wave tradition and in 1951 threw
close-packed masses of yelling troops at the United Nations positions, drowning their enemy in men even as they were mown
down. They lost tens of thousands, but the tens of thousands that
survived took Seoul and forced the Americans to withdraw. In a
second human-wave attack in May of the same year, the Chinese
suffered about a hundred thousand casualties in five days, not
counting twelve thousand men who were taken prisoner. Perhaps
this could hardly be accounted imaginative of the commander,
but it would also hardly be accounted cowardly of the troops.
More than a thousand years before, a great poet had written:

> Men of China are able to face the stiffest battle,
> But their officers drive them like chickens and dogs.
> We have learned that to have a son is bad luck;
> It is very much better to have a daughter
> Who can marry and live in the house of a neighbor,
> While under the sod we bury our boys . . .

Yet sometimes even a Taoist believed that to keep the cosmos in kilter, a man must be ready to die.

The American answer to disconcerting examples of Chinese military competence and courage that discomfited the United Nations forces in Korea was to fall back on phony Fumanchuism. The ability of the enemy to move 250,000 Chinese troops secretly into North Korea was sneeringly dismissed by a senior officer as an example of concealment and deception "suited to the Oriental nature." The helter-skelter withdrawal of the American forces was perfectly comprehensible since they were "swamped by a yellow tide." When the British charged the German machine guns at Ypres, they were heroes; when the Chinese charged in Korea, a number of unappetizing little explanations were cooked up. They were doped, "hopped up with opium," said some. No, said others, they did not have to be doped, because the Chinese nervous system was not finely coordinated like ours and therefore their crude mechanism could not register our more delicate sentiments (like blue funk). They were, in fact, subhuman, and the mass frontal assault was the only tactic they knew. Their nervous insensibility accounted for their cruelty, for they did not really feel pain, so, of course, being cruel to them was not like being cruel to you or me . . .

Happily, the authoritative voice of Andrew Geer, the historian of the American marines, cuts short all this ugly cackle: "Human-sea frontal assaults are rare," he wrote in 1952, "and are ordered as a last resort when the necessity for victory dictates such a high cost. Actually there have been few such attacks made by the Chinese forces in Korea. Such tactics were reported as an excuse for the defeat suffered by United Nations troops."

Chagrin is nevertheless excusable in a certain type of American. "There is no doubt that a first-class fighting machine can be made of, say, 20,000 Bulgars or Turks. The same cannot be said of 20,000 Chinese without numerous qualifications," one lofty general officer had written before the Korean War, and many United States advisers earlier attached to Chiang Kai-shek's forces complained in addition that the Chinese were not mechanically minded and could not use modern weapons and equipment effectively. But, in Korea, the Chinese are suddenly "better artillery men than the Germans," and at Dienbienphu the ability of the Vietminh guerrilla army to handle radar and antiaircraft guns, field pieces, radio communications, and mechanized convoys efficiently is attributed to its Chinese advisers. It is a little difficult not to sympathize with the conclusion of some ill-disposed Communist commentators that the bad imperialist has once more been blaming his tools.

The key to all the contradictions in stories of Chinese cowardice and courage, pacifism and military prowess, appears in fact to be this: to the pragmatic Chinese, life itself is an exercise in the strategy of Sun Wu, a guerrilla operation which he will win and survive if he conforms, like water, to the ground. Balancing this, on the other hand, is a stiff, ruthless pride, the quality that gives a Chinese the courage he himself compares to the most precious jade: "for while it can be broken, it cannot be bent." The Communists extol what they call the "hard bone" characteristic in cadre and soldier, exemplified in history by the inflexible Confucian integrity of the castrated Ssu-ma Ch'ien, the banished Han Yü, the decapitated Shih K'o-fa.

There is no paradox here. In the guerrilla struggle for existence there are moments for footwork and moments for fighting. But, like the spirals on a dead straight drill, the dodgy fluctuations of Chinese tactics are redeemed by this iron steadfastness of ultimate purpose. A Chinese will not, therefore, throw away his life profitlessly in a pointless battle joined on badly chosen terrain for an inferior cause. But if the time comes when he can sell it at a price worth dying for, he sells. And that, to him, is the measure of valor. For while it is permissible for a Chinese hero to be a villain, it is not permissible for him to be a fool.

28

Requiem for an Assassin

The principle that it is better to win with one blow of the knife than to lose with ten thousand chariots is in the great Chinese tradition. No tale, therefore, is more steeped in noble purpose than the account of cold-blooded killing that Ssu-ma Ch'ien relates in his *Historical Records,* and whose hero is one Ching K'o.

We are approaching the fateful year of 227 B.C. In the West, Hannibal, a young man of twenty, is soon to shake the world, yet just fail to change the entire course of history. In China, Ching K'o is about to do the same: not with armies and elephants, however, but with a poisoned knife.

Ching K'o is introduced as a modest, pleasing sort of fellow, a cultured student of the Classics, a notable drinker, and a keen swordsman. But although he applied to study under the greatest master of the dagger of his day in order to perfect his knowledge of arms, that overproud champion dismissed him with contempt, for he was neither famous nor personally known to him. Disappointed, Ching K'o made his way to the state of Yen, and it was typical of him that although he had hobnobbed with learned scholars and great lords, he should go to live near the marketplace with a certain dog-butcher named Kao, for Kao was an old friend, an amiable drinking companion, and an accomplished lute player. Every day this likely pair strolled down to the market

331

to swill wine, to sing and weep and carouse until night fell and they staggered home.

But if there was carousal in the marketplace, there was gloom in the royal palace. Some time before, Prince Tan of Yen had offended the aggressive ruler of Ch'in who was destined to become the First Emperor. To make matters worse, the prince had given refuge to General Fan Yu-chi, who had also fled from Ch'in after displeasing the king. Royal counselors pointed out that this gave the King of Ch'in a valid excuse for invading Yen. "You have put meat in the path of the tiger," they said. Prince Tan's father, the King of Yen, had then proposed seizing the initiative and making war on this despot, but his appalled advisers had been quick to warn him that to send troops out against the redoubtable Ch'in armies would be "like trying to pluck a dragon's scale." It would be better to pack General Fan off to the Huns to the north without delay, so that Ch'in's anger would be deflected. Prince Tan objected stoutly: "He has come to me and I cannot turn a friend in need away before Ch'in has even attacked." "Are you ready to sacrifice your country for one individual, then?" asked his tutor. "You are holding a feather above a cooking fire, but is the feather safe because the flames have not yet reached it?" And he recommended to the stubborn prince that he consult one T'eng Kuang.

This splendid old man was a scholar, a statesman, almost a sage, but he held no office. When he was brought to Prince Tan, the prince hastened to the palace gate to welcome him, led him within, and humbly knelt before him. After their attendants had left them, the prince swore that the states of Ch'in and Yen could not exist in the same world and that he must somehow encompass the downfall of his enemy by strategem. What should he therefore do? T'eng Kuang, guessing what he might have in mind, protested that he himself was too old for conspiracy but that the prince might do well to talk to Ching K'o. The prince agreed to receive that gentleman, saw his honored guest to the gate, and earnestly enjoined him not to mention the subject of their discussion to anyone else. T'eng Kuang looked at the sky, smiled, and replied simply: "Yes."

The old man then sought out Ching K'o and instructed him to present himself before the prince, adding: "I have heard some say that if a good man behaves with propriety, nobody will distrust him. But today the prince found it necessary to warn me that what I have told you is an important secret which I should communicate to no other. So the prince distrusts me. And if a man is distrusted, he is no longer a gentleman. Therefore, go to the prince and tell him I am already dead. This will prove that I have kept silence." Whereupon he killed himself.

When Ching K'o gave the prince the news, Tan wept bitterly and beseeched Ching K'o to believe that he had intended no lack of faith: "But though he knew I had done wrong, yet he still sent you. Thus he forgave me, and heaven will not let Yen die." The prince then went on to explain his desperate situation to Ching K'o, and added: "We need a man, a hero who will go to the King of Ch'in bearing desirable gifts and who will then either persuade him to negotiate or, if this is impossible, kill him on the spot." The modest Ching K'o protested that he was not up to the task, but the prince pooh-poohed his misgivings, and Ching K'o finally accepted the commission. From then on, the prince laid splendid pavilions at his disposal within the palace precincts, always treated him with great respect, and sent him beautiful women, a limitless supply of wine, horses, gold, and all that any man of normal appetites could want. Ching K'o took all, said nothing, and set out to enjoy himself without much apparent thought for his hazardous future.

This put the perplexed prince in a quandary, for he could not tell Ching K'o to press on with the operation without seeming once more to show distrust. At last, he said tactfully to Ching K'o: "Ch'in are almost on our borders, so you must forgive me if I have no time to serve you constantly, which I assure you would otherwise be my wish." Ching K'o, who could take a broad hint, replied that his main problem was to persuade the King of

Ch'in to allow him into his presence, for the king was incensed with Yen and had in fact offered a reward of one thousand catties of gold and the landholdings of ten thousand families to the man who would deliver up to him the Ch'in defector, General Fan. "Now, if I could present myself to the King of Ch'in with General Fan's head, and also a map of the border area over which we are at least notionally to negotiate . . ." But the excellent prince repeated that Fan had nowhere else to flee and that he could not kill the man to whom he had given asylum.

Ching K'o then went to see General Fan himself, and found him full of sorrow and foreboding. "When I think of what I have helped to bring upon Yen, my very bones ache and I do not know what to do," he sighed. Ching K'o then confided that he had "a plan of revenge." "What is it?" the general asked. Ching K'o replied gently: "I want your head. With it, I can get to the King of Ch'in. Holding his sleeve with my left hand, I shall plunge a dagger into him with my right. And justice will have been served, both for Yen and for you." "Now you have pointed the way for me, and I am happy," exclaimed the hardy general, not blanching at this hideous suggestion. And drawing his sword, he resolutely plunged it into his throat.

His severed head was placed in a casket, and the prince ordered the murder weapon, a sharp knife tipped with poison, paying for it with more than one hundred measures of gold. Ching K'o had meanwhile been waiting for the arrival of a trusted henchman of his, but this man had still not arrived and the prince, now consumed with impatience, foisted on to him as his assistant a young boy whose main claim to fame was that he had killed his first man at the age of thirteen. "If I do not come back from Ch'in," objected Ching K'o bitterly, "it will be this child's fault. If I cannot wait for my friend, I shall go at once. Do not be certain, however, that I shall return." For this reason the court donned the white robes of mourning and accompanied Ching K'o as far as the frontier when he set out on his desperate enterprise.

Practical details have not been neglected amid the farewell tears. Ching K'o carries gifts to the value of one thousand catties of gold destined for the secretary of the King of Ch'in, who is to be bought over so that he will procure an audience for the assassin. This man duly tells his acquisitive monarch that the Prince of Yen will not fight him and only asks for a chance to live, and that he has therefore sent an ambassador who carries not only a frontier map but the head of General Fan. The gratified king agrees to give Ching K'o an audience and receives him ceremoniously in the palace. Seemingly unarmed, Ching K'o holds the casket containing the general's head and also a letter from his prince. His accomplice carries the map. But as they approach the throne, the young fellow's face gradually goes green with trepidation, and courtiers and attendants begin to look at the pair oddly. Ching K'o quickly makes a joke of it: "This barbarian has never seen a king before, he is so frightened that Your Majesty must forgive his manner." It is a nasty moment. "I do not think we need him," remarks the king to Ching K'o after a pause. "Let it be you who give me the map as well."

The map, the first ever mentioned in Chinese history, is like a Chinese scroll, and while the king grasps the baton at the foot of it, Ching K'o unfolds his end until the poisoned knife, hidden near the top, is suddenly exposed. Ching K'o moves fast. Releasing the scroll and grasping the king's sleeve with his left hand, he seizes the dagger and plunges forward to stab his victim. The king recoils in fright, the sleeve of his flimsy surcoat tears, and he is free. Hastily leaning back, he struggles to draw his sword, but it is a long ceremonial weapon, not easy to disengage from its scabbard while sitting. Ching K'o is almost upon him before he rises, stumbles backward, and then quickly rounds one of the pillars of the audience chamber, putting it between himself and his would-be assassin.

The job has been bungled, but all is not lost. For not only are the court officers apparently rooted to the ground, but they have no weapons: it is forbidden to carry swords or daggers when entering the hall of audience, and the nearest armed men are the guards below. These are not allowed to move unless the king personally gives the order, and the king is too shocked and pre-occupied to remember to shout. In one endless moment of silence Ching K'o advances warily to kill the fumbling monarch while the court stands as still as a painted frieze. But suddenly the spell is broken. Dr. Hsia moves.

"Sire, free your sword," shouts the royal physician and, swinging his medicine bag, clouts Ching K'o heavily at the same time. Ching K'o staggers, and the king, swinging his scabbard behind him so that he is able to draw, lunges forward and cuts him on the thigh. The desperate man, now bleeding profusely, flings his dagger at the king, but the king dodges and the knife sticks in the wooden pillar. Then the king comes forward again and drives his sword carefully into the doomed assassin. Ching K'o, bleeding from eight wounds, leans gasping against a pillar, laughs weakly, and chokes out: "I have failed to kill you, for the very reason that I did not wish to. I wanted to talk peace with you as my prince desired . . ." The guards close in and dispatch him, but he has saved the face of his own lord.

Six years later the King of Ch'in, having annexed Yen along with all the other Chinese states, proclaimed himself First Emperor of China. A physician had made possible the birth of an empire that was to live for nearly two thousand years until in the twentieth century another physician—Dr. Sun Yat-sen—signed its death certificate.

Meanwhile, Kao the dog-butcher changed his name, quietly moved from Yen to the new Imperial capital, and went to work with a wealthy and influential family as a servant. But his master, discovering by chance that he was a musician, ordered him to play at a banquet. When he began to strum, it was at once seen that he was no servant, for he performed with great skill on the new thirteen-string lute which had just become fashionable.

Kao's fame spread until he was ordered to play before the emperor, whereupon one keen-eared courtier murmured to his monarch that this rascal "played as well as Kao" and might indeed be Ching K'o's friend. "I don't care whether he is Kao or not," replied the emperor, and forthwith had him blinded so that he could safely keep him about the place and enjoy his incomparable music, whoever he was. In this he miscalculated, however, for the sightless Kao patiently learned the geography of the Ch'in palace, and at the same time secretly converted his instrument into an effective cosh by hiding a large lump of lead in its belly. Feeling his way by sound until he was near to the emperor one day, Kao slammed the lute down at the point where he judged Ch'in's head to be. But he missed, and the emperor, unhurt, ordered him to be killed at once. It was nevertheless the last time that he ever allowed anyone close to him during his short but terrible reign. The account of the extraordinary affair of Ching K'o concludes with the sad comment of the champion knife fighter who had so disdained the hero: "I made one mistake in my life: I never taught Ching K'o how to use a dagger."

This is no operatic synopsis. A bas-relief nearly two thousand years old, decorating ancient tombs found in Shantung Province in North China, depicts the climax of the melodramatic story. Everything happens at once: we see the dagger stuck into the pillar as the king dodges behind it, the doctor swinging his bag at Ching K'o while his assistant lies prone with fear on the ground, the fragment of torn sleeve floating to the floor, upon which stands the casket containing General Fan's head. The tale is more than just a bloody slice severed from Chinese history: it is a moving tapestry of the timeless Chinese world. The murderous, sometimes irresponsible, somewhat histrionic central figure is an unmistakable Chinese hero, a friend of scholars and princes who can sing a catch and improvise a poem, yet also a swordsman and a drinking pal of dog-butchers. He risks his life in a worthy cause—the assassination of a tyrant—and so he shows no servile gratitude to his prince, for they are involved in an enterprise in which obligations are not shrugged off with words but worked off with deeds.

The old scholar, T'eng Kuang, is a man of honor in the oldest tradition of chivalry, who must kill himself if he earns distrust, yet at the same time forgive the insult and fulfill his mission on behalf of his involuntary royal murderer. The prince shows the humble respect due from a ruler to a scholar, but is guilty of sacrificing the interests of his country for the sake of one man, of doing the right thing at the wrong time, for by granting General Fan asylum he brings down upon his state the implacable wrath of Ch'in. (Later, the prince's relatives cut off *his* head, and send it to the King of Ch'in in order to buy time, only to be crushed by the conqueror within five years. If the prince had chosen the wrong time for loyalty, they had chosen the wrong time for treachery.) The unflinching self-sacrifice of General Fan, the last words of the dying Ching K'o designed to spare his prince and also save his face, the whole dastardly plot as a common-sense substitute for hopeless hostilities, make this a tale of true heroism, known not only to every Chinese schoolchild but to every peasant who has seen the simplified Cantonese opera that is based upon it.

These are the Chinese. To the more incredulous Westerner, who thinks in terms of black and white and yellow, they are obviously unconvincing and cannot really exist. They are pinch-penny, yet they will gamble a fortune on the turn of a card? They are power-hungry, yet they will renounce all to go off and fish without bait? They are moderate, yet they throw up mobs of screaming fiends who smash crosses and bully sixty-year-old nuns? They are pragmatic, yet they proudly turn bony and defiant shoulders upon a world of ill-repute eagerly frequented by rival American and Russian sugar-daddies? They are described as irresponsible, distrusting all government, lacking all civic sense—yet they are known in Communist China to be for the most part a disciplined, honest, and obedient people who will not accept even a cigarette for fear that it may hold the seed, not of cancer, but of corruption?

How can all this be? It can be because the Chinese are themselves working models of the Yang-Yin principle, born extremists whose extremes simply interact. And when Confucius, recognizing this so sharply twenty-five hundred years ago, preached the Golden Mean, he inadvertently accentuated the whole process by creating a new form of extremism: moderation.

The more people were cautious and frugal and reserved, the more a man cut an arresting figure by being "Hao"—the bold, devil-may-care man of integrity. The more ruthlessly some scrambled for power, the more others saw their compulsive urge as a horrific disease, to be shied away from even at the risk of penury. The more they practiced Confucian moderation and patience, the more the Chinese were exploited and abused by their unscrupulous rulers to a point at which ideas of peaceful reform became impracticable, and the only redress lay in bloody revolution against all symbols of oppression. (A cunning destiny, in fact, has always maneuvered the submissive Chinese into Sun Wu's "death ground," where, his back to the wall, he has finally fought like a tiger.) And the more complaisant and venal the pragmatic parent in his subservience to the rich foreign foster-father in Shanghai or Singapore, the more Cassius-like became the son in his arid honesty and his cold disdain for barbarian benefits. For on the other side of the looking glass, pride comes *after* the fall.

These are the Chinese seen through the eyes of a barbarian. But a more disconcerting view is to come. For the barbarians must now be seen through the eyes of the Chinese.

From the Inside, Looking Out

29

The Saved . . .

Even in deep winter they would gather before dawn in an open, wind-bitten courtyard of the Forbidden City in Peking—great mandarins and generals, and sometimes a foreign potentate or ambassador, frozen-faced and with snow on their caps, but wrapped snugly enough in rich furs. Bells chimed, gongs crashed, and each man would kowtow deeply in the direction of an empty throne which he could not see, kneeling humbly on the stone flags. This done, all would be invited forward into the Palace of Heavenly Purity, and as they prostrated themselves once more, the strain of a curious antique air would steal through the chamber and the Imperial sedan, arriving from the Private Apartments, would approach the Dragon Throne before them. Then, if one stole a glance between numbed fingers, one might see him, facing south in the traditional position of the hierarch, solemn, silent, motionless as stone—the Emperor of China seated at the very apex of the world. For this was an Imperial Audience, and ordinary men were in the presence of the Son of Heaven.

The Emperor of China was not a god but a priest-king—a vicar of heaven charged with the duty of maintaining man and the Middle Kingdom in harmony with the universe. He alone performed the sacrifices addressed to heaven and earth, the rites of the spring sowing and of the winter solstice. In Manchu times a man could be beheaded merely for touching him, and when he

moved out, the road was guarded along its length and the populace swept off the streets, for none was allowed to look at him.
Reporting the presence of a powerful British fleet off the coasts
of China in 1840, his plenipotentiary wrote to the emperor: "But
these trifles do not merit a turn of the Holy Glance."

The Chinese expressed their ideal of cosmic harmony by the
phrase "Ta T'ung"—the Great Unity—and on earth that Great
Unity could only mean unity under the Imperial Son of Heaven,
for a pyramid may only have one apex. Farther west, people
might freely admit that their own particular monarch was not
the only king in the continent, but would dogmatically insist that
they worshipped the only true God (Christian, Hebrew, or Moslem) and condemn as heresy any attempt to claim a share of the
heavens for any other. The Chinese, on their side, were quite prepared to admit any number of gods into their capacious heaven,
but would dogmatically insist that theirs was the only true king,
and condemn as heresy any attempt to claim a share of the
world for any other on an equal footing. The Christian protested
that his alone was the true culture of heaven, the Chinese that
his alone was the true culture of earth. The Chinese, therefore,
did not think of China as the British thought of Britain, but as
Christians thought of Christendom: all men within it were
saved, whether or not they were ethnically of Han origin. All
without were benighted. But the Light of the World shone upon
them, whether they acknowledged it or—in their abysmal ignorance—did not.

"Chinese expansionism," that well-thumbed cliché of the professional anti-Communist, therefore took the form of a cultural
hegemony. It began some four thousand years ago when the
civilization of the Han people started to seep across the rest of
China from the valley of the Yellow River, slowly engulfing alien
tribes and kingdoms, and then uniting them through a common
philosophy and a common written language under a common
hegemon-king. And since no divine will had posted notices at any
given point saying "Chinadom ends here," it seeped on. The

culture absorbed neighboring peoples like the ancestors of the Vietnamese; it was carried into Korea by the sword, but it was embraced by the Japanese as an act of conversion. The Chinese never invaded or conquered Japan, but thousands of Japanese scholars and artists and writers visited China—notably during the great T'ang dynasty—stayed a while to worship, and then in their thoroughgoing way carted off to their own islands the spirit, the flesh, and the bones of Chinese civilization, from the Confucian texts to the tea ceremony, and from Zen Buddhism to geisha girls.

To the Chinese the states at the center of their culture were "ripe," and those on the fringe were "raw," but all were maturing within the same civilization, the same chopstick empire. Among the twelve million overseas Chinese in Southeast Asia there are hundreds of thousands who have never been to China and who are suspicious of Communism and distrustful of Chiang Kai-shek. But they have assiduously studied their own history and literature; they speak, eat, dress, sleep, think, and act Chinese. They are not necessarily loyal to the concept of a Chinese state or a Chinese nation: they are loyal to a Chinese culture, as any government that tries to suppress their language and their schools quickly finds out.

In China itself, this carnivorous culture treated any conquering invader much as stomach juices will treat a steak. In the fourth century the nomadic Toba Tatars overran North China, but by the end of the fifth century their emperors had prohibited the use of their own language and ordered all their people to adopt the Chinese tongue, Chinese customs, and Chinese dress. The Kitans invaded from the north in the eleventh century, were absorbed by Chinese civilization, lost their nomadic virility, and a century later were conquered by the Kins, who in turn were seduced by the Confucian society. The indigestible Mongols of Kublai Khan conquered, settled, were chewed up, and spat out. And then came the barbarous Manchus.

The manners of these warlike bumpkins in their early days of empire are described by a member of the Dutch embassy that visited Peking in 1655, eleven years after they had marched in. In an account of an official banquet of astonishing magnificence thrown by senior mandarins of the Imperial household, he tells how the Manchus ate vast quantities of underdone mutton, beef, and camel as if they had been fasting all day, and then: "According to the custom of the Countrey, were to put up what they left into their pockets to carry home. It was a very pleasant sight to see how these greazy Tartars stuffed their Pockets and Leather Drawers of their Breeches with fat Meat, that the Liquor dropt from them as they went along the Streets; so greedy were they in eating and carrying away, that they were more like Peasants than Courtiers." These were the people who were to become more Chinese than the Chinese, adopting and yet suffocating the civilization they had conquered, placing it with murderous reverence under an airless glass case.

The Chinese absorbed and adapted Buddhism from India, and they absorbed the Jews who migrated to China until these became utterly indistinguishable from other Chinese. But above all they absorbed conquerors—usually far smaller nations of less civilized nomads who quickly found that they must roll to the gait of the immense Chinese dragon if they were to ride it at all.

The frontiers of China began to set about one thousand years ago, and however much they expanded or shrank thereafter according to the fortunes of war, the Celestial Empire remained divisible into four concentric rings. The innermost was metropolitan China itself, which included Tibet and Mongolia. The second ring comprised the peripheral countries that China regarded as her tributaries, among them Korea and what is now North Vietnam. The third ring was principally formed by the Japanese—a sovereign people who had adopted so much from Chinese civilization that they could be said to acknowledge the cultural domination of Peking. And the fourth consisted of largely unheard-of countries like England which did not realize that the Emperor of China was in fact Emperor of the World.

In this pattern of intellectual dominion, only the tributary states seem to fit a Western design for empire. But in reality even they do not. For the Chinese had no true concept of colonization. If the vassal king behaved, sent tribute to Peking when it was due, accepted the gift of Chinese culture, and raised no standard against the emperor, he would be treated as a "younger brother" and largely left alone. If he misbehaved, a punitive expedition might be sent against him, so that the Pax Sinica could be restored (his people would first be "awed" and then "soothed"). If the Chinese failed to "pacify" the territory and their forces were defeated by the native army, no maps would be altered in China, and the intransigent state would still be a "tributary" to Peking, even if no tribute were forthcoming. A younger brother, however rebellious, remains a younger brother, the Chinese would say. One of the phenomena of the historical relationship between Vietnam and China was that every time a Vietnamese regime successfully repulsed a Chinese punitive expedition, its next move was to send a tribute embassy to the Dragon Throne with a request for formal recognition. (The American colonies behaved in a regrettably different fashion in 1776.)

The Chinese did not establish their loose dominion across land frontiers alone, however, for since earliest times they had been capable shipwrights. They had invented the sternpost rudder by Julius Caesar's day, about twelve hundred years before it appeared in Europe; they had the first fore-and-aft sails in the third century, a treadmill paddlewheel for boats by the eighth, and fighting ships equipped with rams and twenty paddlewheels by the twelfth. (When five of these appeared against fourteen paddle-steamers of the Royal Navy during the Opium Wars, the British inevitably thought the Chinese had somehow copied them.) Travelers to the great Chinese port of Zaytoun in the thirteenth century afterward described ships with fifty or more cabins for passengers, with four or six masts, and with double planking and watertight compartments (Europe copied the traditional Chinese transverse bulkhead in the last century only).

By the ninth century, the Chinese were sailing their big junks as far as the Persian Gulf, but it was during the fifteenth that they really showed their paces. In 1405 Admiral Cheng Ho set sail with a force of nearly twenty-eight thousand men in sixty-three ships. The biggest of these vessels was almost 450 feet long, had four decks, cabins with locks and keys, closets and conveniences, and buckets in which vegetables, herbs, and ginger were grown. This was the first of seven expeditions which took the "Three-Jewel Eunuch," as he was called, to Malaya, Java, Sumatra, India, Aden, East Africa, and down to Madagascar some sixty years before the Portuguese first sailed into the Indian Ocean.

These expeditions carried not only gold, silver, Chinese silk and lacquer, but a formidable force of fighting men, for their object was to show the Chinese flag, to spread the word of China's unique position as master of the world, to exact tribute from the weaker states en route, and to exchange courtesies and presents with those that appeared to be too powerful to intimidate (the presents received could automatically be recatalogued as "tribute" in any case). However, there are always impetuous men who will reach for a pistol or a sword when someone mentions his "way of life," and Cheng Ho's force was compelled to engage in some stiff fighting, although he tried to achieve his ends with ambassadorial suavity—whether these were to enhance the prestige and renown of his emperor, or to procure curiosities like giraffes for the court. He nevertheless imposed the suzerainty of the Celestial Empire over South Sumatra, Ceylon, and Malacca, and there is little doubt that the Chinese could have pocketed all Southeast Asia had they set about it at this time. But jealousies at court and China's chronic migraine—nomads in the north—combined to curtail these enterprises.

In 1522 the Imperial fleets defeated the Portuguese off Canton, and nearly a hundred and fifty years later the Chinese pirate Koxinga, champion of the overthrown Ming dynasty, threw the Dutch out of Formosa. The Chinese navy did not stay in port gathering barnacles during the centuries that followed, for its flotillas were constantly engaged against great fleets of pirates that infested South China waters. But the Chinese never became land-grabbers, and although they might depose an obstructive kinglet of Ceylon by force and take him back to China, this was simply to encourage among others good discipline and a proper observance of their tributary obligations to the Dragon Throne. They did not dream of holding down an empire on which the sun never set. To their way of thinking, they already had it—as long as they did not try too hard to prove it. One Vietnamese ruler was very typically allowed to call himself "Emperor" at home as long as he accepted the title of "Vassal King" in China.

"If you are not in danger, do not fight," Sun Wu had said. The military instinct of the Chinese was a defensive one, for since their earliest history they had been plagued along their frontiers by tough, stringy, horse-coping, nomadic barbarians from the steppes and deserts to their north and west. But few were Maginot-minded. They had learned from bitter experience that the Great Wall was not in itself enough to keep the hornets out, and the problem of garrisoning and supplying it had proved a headache from the beginning. Their own capitals (which moved with the march of history) were successively sacked, burned, or simply occupied and looted at leisure by the Huns in the fourth century, the Tibetans in the eighth, the Kitans in the tenth, then the Kins, the Mongols, and the Manchus.

Small wonder if they have felt crowded and jostled by ill-smelling neighbors of questionable intent throughout their history, and have sometimes used their own elbows savagely in what may have appeared an aggressive gesture but was usually a defensive reflex. The First Emperor secured one buffer state by marching into "Vietnam," which in those days stretched as far into present-day China as Canton. A century later the great fighting Emperor Han Wu-ti annexed a second buffer by breaking into North Korea. His main ambition, however, was to end the military importunities of the Huns by sandwiching them between

China herself and a new ally to be sought behind their backs in Central Asia.

More than two hundred years, therefore, before Pan Chao embarked upon his exploits, a certain Chang Ch'ien was dispatched into the Wild West with only one hundred Chinese followers, and struck out boldly into the perilous barbarian-infested wilderness to try to make contact with a remote but strong tribe that was last known to have been virulently anti-Hun. The Huns soon fell on Chang Ch'ien, took him prisoner, and held him for ten years. When he finally escaped from them, however, this resolute officer did not hasten home, but resumed his mission. After traveling enormous distances only to discover that his quarry had moved on, he finally ran the tribe to ground beyond the Oxus—to be told that they were now unwilling to turn back to the east to fight the Huns. The despondent Chang Ch'ien rested, and then set off on the long, hazardous road back to China, only to be taken prisoner again by the Huns. Once more he escaped, and was finally able to report personally to his emperor twelve years after his departure, accompanied by the one surviving member of his original party.

His mission had failed, but the information he brought back was of enormous value. This great explorer had been through Sogdiana and Bactria, the former Greek kingdoms that had originally been conquered by Alexander, and had traversed two thousand miles of desert and stony mountain pass to reach Parthia and the Northwest Frontier.

Another expedition sent to teach manners to the Ruler of Ferghana for refusing to provide the emperor with some of his famous blood-sweating horses (and for slaughtering a Chinese embassy in the process), subdued thirty-six petty kingdoms on its march across Central Asia, only to be defeated disastrously near Ferghana itself. But the Chinese had three mainsprings for military action: defending China, establishing buffer states against the barbarian, and upholding the prestige of the "Center of the World" by letting no humiliation pass unavenged. In 102 B.C., therefore, sixty thousand men set out to conquer the deserts again, and of these thirty thousand arrived to lay siege to the impudent horse-breeder's capital. Han Wu-ti got his thoroughbreds.

In the two millennia that followed, the Chinese steadfastly pursued their policy of accumulating peripheral padding against their tormentors. In 48 B.C., Hermaeus, last Greek king to rule in northwest India, passed under the suzerainty of China, whose tributaries and territories were to include not only Vietnam and Korea but also Mongolia, Tibet, Turkestan, Burma, and Nepal, in addition to Cheng Ho's maritime contributions. But the purely acquisitive instinct was rare among Chinese emperors, and the only enemies they would gladly have overrun inhabited just those barren deserts and steppes whose permanent occupation was for centuries both pointless and impossible. These were the barbaric milk-drinkers, skilled in war, threatening the very frontiers of the Middle Kingdom, and having "the heart of beasts." Marked by the same attributes, their modern equivalents come from San Francisco, Kansas City, New York.

30

. . . and the Damned

For Confucius, the Chinese world consisted of "All under Heaven." What lay in the shadow beyond this circle of light was benighted and barbarian. China could no more have "foreign relations," therefore, than a Christian church could contemplate an ecclesiastical alliance with a sect of stone-worshippers. Yet just as the medieval Christian will recognize with objective if reluctant approval the great Islamic traditions in mathematics and astronomy, so the Chinese would acknowledge in the "foreign devil" practical talents and merits, which, however, remained meaningless because he did not belong to the only true culture. Confucius could praise the "rude tribes" on the periphery of civilized China for showing far more virtue than the Chinese themselves—yet add almost in the same breath that only if a "superior Chinese" moved among them could they cease to be rude.

This Chinese sense of superiority, the familiar conceit of those who have the only true faith, was encouraged by the fact that China was surrounded on all sides not by other great civilizations but by nomadic peoples of a cruder culture. And when the barbarians from the more sophisticated societies of the West began to impinge uncomfortably on a tranquil empire, there seemed little to choose between them and their earlier counterparts. Hun or Hollander, they had the same gross faults, coupled with the same disconcerting military talents. The foreign devil with his agile, quick-firing frigate was at one with the creature of the desert whose primitive quality was somehow accentuated by his ability to draw a 150-pound horn bow accurately while galloping at full tilt down a boulder-strewn slope.

Since the emperor was master of the world, there could be no such thing as an "enemy" with which to dispute, but only "rebels" against his universal suzerainty. Christianity could not possibly be regarded as more than an impertinence, for it suggested that the Chinese had the universe all wrong, which was a contradiction in terms. The attitude toward the foreign devil from the West was well expressed by a Ming emperor who, in an edict issued against his rebellious brother's faction, wrote: "There is not a depraved priest, physician, soothsayer, rowdy, actor, or European, who is not of their gang." And this may be taken as a curtain raiser for the treatment accorded to all such rascals thereafter, starting with our Well-Beloved Cousin and Counsellor, the Right Honourable George Lord Viscount Macartney, Baron of Lissanoure, Member of the Privy Council of Ireland, Knight of the Most Honourable Order of the Bath and of the Most Ancient and Royal Order of the White Eagle, Ambassador Extraordinary and Plenipotentiary to the Emperor of China.

Dispatched with letters patent from King George III, Macartney and his suite arrived in China in 1793 with the task of persuading the emperor to improve "the connection, intercourse and good correspondence between the Courts of London and Peking, and of increasing and extending commerce between their respective subjects." To this end Macartney was furnished with "several presents for the Emperor of China from the King of Great Britain," including guns, clocks, telescopes, a clockwork model of the planetary system, and other Western wonders. The Chinese took due note of these, so that when after many vicissitudes the Marcartney embassy was embarked upon boats that would carry it from the port of Tientsin to the capital at Peking, a banner was hoisted on Macartney's vessel whose flaunting characters read:

"Tribute Embassy from the Red Barbarians." Like all the other countries of the world, Britain must be regarded as a dependency of China, and George III as a vassal king.

The noble Irishman was nevertheless received in audience and even given an elegant breakfast by the emperor, who showed himself most "affable and condescending." Macartney's hopes of a successful mission therefore rose foolishly. Three weeks later, however, an Imperial edict addressed to King George III was strapped to the back of a mandarin, who then carried it ceremoniously to Macartney's quarter in Peking accompanied by an escort of sixteen other mandarins. Typical passages of this revealing document read:

"We, by the Grace of Heaven, Emperor, instruct the King of England to take note of our charge.

"Although your Country, O King, lies in the far oceans, yet inclining your heart toward civilization you have specially sent an envoy respectfully to present a state message.

"Now you, O King, have presented various objects to the throne, and mindful of your loyalty we have specially ordered our Ministry to receive them.

"Nevertheless, we have never valued ingenious articles, nor do we have the slightest need of your Country's manufacture. Therefore, O King, as regards your request to send someone to remain at the capital for trade, while it is not in harmony with the regulations of the Celestial Empire, we also feel very much that it is of no advantage to your Country. Hence, we have issued these detailed instructions and have commanded your tribute Envoys to return safely home. You, O King, should simply act in conformity with our wishes by strengthening your loyalty and swearing perpetual obedience so as to ensure that your Country may share the blessings of peace . . . This is a special edict." Well did it reflect the advice of the emperor's Grand Secretary, who had urged: "These are ignorant foreign devils, and it is not worth treating them with too much courtesy."

Twenty-three years later Lord Amherst tries again, but the

Chinese emperors have now had enough of these barbarous importunities, and the prince regent who sent him is treated to a Celestial brush-off designed to end all Celestial brush-offs: "We fully recognize the spirit of reverent submission which animated you. We accept your tribute and to acknowledge your devotion have in turn conferred presents. However, your presents are of no interest or use. In future do not bother to dispatch them, for they are merely a waste of time. If you loyally accept Our Sovereignty, there is really no need for these state appearances to prove that you are indeed our vassal."

This haughty attitude was to mark all relations between the Chinese and those particular foreign devils who, at this point, had just finished off Napoleon and were undisputed masters of one of the greatest empires the world had ever seen. A quarter of a century later, the viceroy of Canton notes of Lord William Napier of Meristoun, who has been dispatched to China to protect British trading interests: "The said barbarian is of reasonable intelligence. His speech is said to be placid and slow. If he applies himself with perseverance, he may yet distinguish right from wrong." He does not, however, and it is not long before he is described in an official proclamation as a "lawless foreign slave" and a "barbarian dog." On the problem of making foreign devils behave, one great mandarin writes of Queen Victoria: "I am told it is she who issues commands, and it seems it would be best to start by sending instructions to her."

By the eighteen-sixties the Chinese, humiliatingly whipped twice over in the previous twenty years, begin to realize that the foreign devils are simply refusing to become part of the Great Celestial Act. But a Christian is no less a Christian for having been defeated in battle, and a prestigious Chinese military administrator therefore explains: "Everything in China's civil and military system is far superior to that in the West—only in firearms is it impossible to catch them up." The glimmer of light brightens a little with the passage of years—but only a little—so that Dr. Sun Yat-sen, destined to be the first president of the twentieth-century

Chinese Republic, is heard to say that China must learn science from the West, but, "as for the true principles of political philosophy, the Europeans need to learn them from China."

In the light of this tradition, was it really to be expected that the prophet Mao would go to the Muscovite mountain? "We must find our own national form of Marxism," he declared many years ago, and Liu Shao-chi, then the recognized party theoretician, explained: "Our party is powerfully armed with Marxist-Leninist theory, and also heir to all the splendid traditions of the many progressive men of thought and action who have illuminated the pages of Chinese history." The argument is the same: once given the machine guns, or mechanism, or Marxism, we must automatically be superior to all the others, for in addition we are the Chinese.

For more than three centuries, sheer ignorance of the dark barbarian world beyond the grace of Chinese culture has fed the humble veneration which the Chinese have accorded themselves. The spirit of curiosity that had illumined earlier dynasties, when foreigners might flock into China and Chinese expeditions were launched westward by sea and land, so shriveled that in the absence of first-hand knowledge or any desire for it any ridiculous fancy could flourish. In 1601 the Italian Jesuit missionary Ricci was described in a Memorial as "a mendicant . . . where he comes from it is impossible to say, the alleged name of his country being untraceable in our records." More than fifty years later a Dutch envoy was asked whether his country really existed, or whether the Dutch were not in reality marauding pirates without a homeland. In 1839 another Memorial to the Dragon Throne, submitted by an educated mandarin of the first rank, informed a doubtless interested emperor that if China cut off all exports of tea and rhubarb to England, she would quickly be brought to her knees, for her people could not live without these benefits (rhubarb was vital as a purgative to this tribe of particularly constipated barbarians, it appeared).

"Just so," says Ping. "We Chinese say about trade in those days:

Chinese send tea to England to make you into gentlemen; England send opium to China to make us into slaves." The Chinese did not believe the English knew what to do with tea, however, since they were not in fact gentlemen. The English recipe for making tea, according to the Chinese, ran something like this: "Put three teaspoonfuls of tea leaves into a warmed pot, pour boiling water over them (after bringing the pot to the kettle and *not* the other way around), and leave to infuse. After a few minutes, drain off and throw away the liquid, remove the leaves from the pot, mash them up thoroughly with fresh butter, and spread the mixture generously on thin slices of brown bread. Enough for four persons."

Merchants obeyed nuns, missionaries ate babies, and for smug decade after smug decade no one in the Celestial Empire thought to ask how the British had come to conquer all India, or why the French were so much better at making clocks than the Chinese, or the Dutch so much better at building ships. But have the Europeans been much better? "So Canton is down *there*," Mr. Stanley Baldwin, the British prime minister, once exclaimed, looking at a map with astonishment. "I always thought it was up *there*"—and he pointed to the coast near Tientsin. The two ports are at the opposite ends of China and about as far apart as London and Tunis.

To the orthodox Jew, his people are God's Chosen, and everyone else is a *goy*, however good. He stands to mix with his own, to be assimilated only slowly and with difficulty into the alien societies of the unbeliever and (in less hygienic days) the uncircumcised. He would only accept one of those as fit company for his sister on a desert island if he had first embraced Judaism. The orthodox Chinese—the Chinese Chinese, not the detribalized English-educated liberal—has the same deep sense of belonging to an exclusive race-culture-religion. And this communion among Chinese cuts across all political considerations, so that a Communist feels closer to a Nationalist than he does to a foreign Communist.

However bitter the political antagonisms between Peking and Taipeh, they are antagonisms within the extended Chinese family, differences born of perfect mutual understanding. The Communists and the Nationalists agree that their struggle against each other is a purely internal Chinese affair. Any suggestions from the Russians or the Americans that they may have a say in the matter will be violently rejected as the unwarrantable interference of rank outsiders; and it will be the Nationalists who castigate their generous American backers for their presumption, and the Communists who chastise the Russians for theirs.

The only power in international affairs that the Chinese Communists can depend on to reject the pernicious "two Chinas" policy, to insist that Mainland China and Formosa are one country, is Nationalist Formosa—they merely differ over who should be ruling the combined territories. The only sympathizers on whom the Chinese Communists could rely to approve of their invasion of India in 1962, to support unquestioningly their stand that Tibet was part of China, to be secretly proud and pleased when China exploded her first atomic bomb in 1964, were the Chinese Nationalists. The Nationalist government in Formosa in fact formally protested to Washington when certain American officials spoke of the McMahon Line as the internationally recognized frontier between India and China, although Peking had repudiated it.

The Nationalist Kuomintang in Taipeh is a revolutionary party and has a cellular structure not unlike that of the Communist Party in Peking. In Formosa as in China there is a one-party system, only slightly confused by the existence of other minor political groups that simply go to show how democratic everything is. The visitor to Taipeh and Peking meets with the same polite, watchful efficiency, the same eagerness to satisfy offbeat wishes— to be received by a Buddhist Superior, to visit a lunatic asylum, pass a night or two in a prison. In both places the weak-minded can find themselves spending from morning until midnight tramping around model factories, model schools, model farms, model hospitals, and model models, on a crowded prearranged schedule based on the philosophy that true hospitality to the stranger consists in showing only your best in the best of all possible worlds.

The two regimes have sprung from the same revolution. In 1962, one of them introduces a number of austerity campaigns on the occasion of the Spring Festival. First, it decrees a "simplification of New Year greetings," and Party members are asked neither to send nor to accept New Year gifts. At the same time a New Literary Movement is organized in the armed forces to establish a "National Literary Front," and to develop a "Revolutionary Literary Concept." A "Barracks Are Home" drive is also launched to make officers and men live as brothers, and an "Army Political Work Day" is inaugurated to ensure "full-scale implementation of political work and to indoctrinate every single soldier." Mao Tsetung at work in Peking? No, Chiang Kai-shek in Taipeh.

The common culture that united the disparate peoples spread over the vast territories of the empire did not weld them into a nation but into a unique civilization. In Imperial China a man could no more be a nationalist than he could hear the sound of one hand clapping, for there was nobody to be nationalist against. The physical focus of his loyalty was not the soil contained within a set of frontiers marked on a map, but an emperor on his Dragon Throne whose dominion was universal. The Chinese were otherwise parochial farmers, wary of the man in the next village, deeply distrustful of the "foreigner" in the next province. When refugees from the center and north were washed up in Hong Kong by the Communist wave that hissed down the length of China in 1949, the Hong Kong people lumped them all together as "Shanghainese" to distinguish them from their fellow southerners, whether they came from Peking in the north or Szechuan in the west. They were treated as rich cousins as long as they had money from which to be parted, and as foreign flotsam once they had been fleeced.

Nationalism, as against straight xenophobia, has been a hothouse growth in China largely fertilized by foreigners, particularly the Japanese. The first strong shoots appeared only in May 1919 when the victors of World War I calmly proposed to punish the Germans and reward their Chinese ally by taking over the German concessions in China and giving them to Japan. Violent student outbursts were organized, and the Chinese negotiators at Versailles were obliged to refuse to sign the treaty. But Sun Yat-sen had had to rub home the novel lesson—"Love your Country" —with a persistent propaganda campaign and by the introduction of patriotic symbols and rituals. However, in their exhausting war of attrition against the implacable and acquisitive Japanese, the Chinese showed themselves capable of such a startling efflorescence of national sentiment that everyone mistook it for the long overdue birth of a narrow and conventional patriotism.

The spell was nevertheless broken when, World War II over and the Japanese evicted, the Communists and the Nationalists, who had at least for a time joined forces against the invader, once more went for each other's throats. No man could feel intuitively the concept of China as a nation when the first question he had to ask himself was: which China? It still remains true to say that the vision of China in the eyes of the emigrant Chinese is—like any religious vision—golden, fuzzy at the edges. He sees the land of his ancestors perhaps as the Christian sees Jerusalem, the Jew sees Israel, or the New Zealander (but not the homesick English exile) sees England. It is the sacred soil of his forebears, the cradle of his culture, the site of his home village. If they could, the tycoon and the wash-amah alike might return there to die. But not to live.

Their environment may make young Chinese in Southeast Asia anti-colonial and progressist, but their blood responds to Mao the Marxist primarily because he has proved his potency as Mao the medicine man. Their fathers would be horrified at the suggestion that their adopted land of Malaysia or Thailand might go Communist, yet they also applaud Mao from afar. Both generations would have felt exactly the same about the Kuomintang if Chiang Kai-shek had not failed where Mao succeeded, if the Nationalists and not the Communists were sitting today at the head of affairs in the old Imperial capital of Peking, and controlling a civilization whose power to shake the world had been recaptured. The Chinese only venerate Communism as a faith insofar as they value it as a winning formula.

To many, Mao is like a brilliant surgeon of otherwise controversial habits whose theory, method, and sharp scalpel combined have given the loved one a new lease on life. But the real object of reverence is the patient, and his patient is China herself as the repository of the prestige of Chinese civilization and its people. It is this that makes impetuous young overseas Chinese arrogant, conceited, and contemptuous of the other races among which they live, proud of their heritage, and touchy about the Communist tonic that has given it new vigor and luster. Mao may have "stripped the faces" off a hundred thousand Chinese, but this is nothing when compared with his one great, unexceptionable achievement: he restored the all-important "face" that the barbarians had earlier so humiliatingly torn away—the face of China herself. And for this reason alone he is accorded the adulation that neglected Christianity would give to the pontiff who could organize a great religious revival, even at some sacrifice of traditional tenets.

31

Skill and Crossbones

"If," said the Lord of Shang, "in a country there are the following ten things: propriety, music, poetry, history, virtue, the cultivation of morality, filial piety, brotherly love, integrity, and prudence—the ruler cannot make the people fight and it will be dismembered as soon as the enemy approaches." The warning proved as prophetic as it was well-intentioned, for more than two thousand years later, the great, flaccid, peaceable, over-civilized Chinese empire lay at the mercy of predatory barbarians more interested in cash and carrion than in the Confucian ethic.

Worried on her frontiers by sinewy nomads of Tatar or Turki stock, the empire had enjoyed innocent enough relations with the more civilized peoples of the world, since for the most part these had the grace to live at a considerable distance. China sold silk to Rome, received embassies from Byzantium, gave asylum to defeated Persians. The Chinese imported Buddhism from India, and otherwise allowed Islam, Nestorian Christianity, Manichaeaism, and Zoroastrianism to flourish or die as they would, on the tolerant principle that one man's heresy is, after all, another man's faith. And when, in 1598, still another traveling monk came to Peking to expound his doctrine, the Confucian mandarins were somewhat suspicious, but the court was faintly intrigued. This mendicant brought pictures and images of the Celestial Lord and a holy virgin with him, and some bones of immortals in a bag—

all of which was of little interest. However, barbarian though he was, he not only spoke Chinese but had the scholarship and manners of a Confucian gentleman, and he made an excellent first impression.

He deserved to. Father Matteo Ricci had arrived in Canton in South China prepared to execute a carefully planned, long-term, thoroughly Jesuitical operation. He would convert the Chinese to Catholicism by taking on the Confucianists and defeating them in philosophical debate. For sixteen years he strived to acquire the language and the education of a Chinese mandarin to this end, but meanwhile found that there was another way to capture the attention of his quarry. For, although only a gifted amateur, he gained the respect of the Chinese by instructing them in mathematics, mechanics, and astronomy, giving them back the know-how they themselves had lost.

Jesuit missionaries who followed in his cannily placed footsteps were able to introduce the Chinese to a wide spectrum of Western knowledge, to modern maps and telescopes, clocks and cannon, in fact to almost every excellent thing the European had, including—if to a more limited extent—his God. However, modern anti-Communist governments would sympathize keenly with the emperor in the next century who suddenly realized that well over a hundred thousand of his subjects were under the ideological control of a foreign potentate in Rome, whose object was to undermine the Confucian foundations of his state. From that moment on, the Jesuits were encouraged to function as mechanics in the capital rather than as missionaries in the provinces, and a school of thought was founded that was later to equate the Christian evangelist with the Comintern agent.

Moreover, as the Manchu emperors, successively ignoring the effervescent world around them, disdainfully donned the blindfold and strutted arrogantly down the centuries toward the end of the Imperial plank, the Chinese lost their interest in mechanics, too. All that the barbarian had to offer were curiosities, luxuries, and ingenious toys, they remarked. The Chinese were superior to the West. Europeans could not, therefore, have anything to teach; they should only come to China to learn. For the most part they were anyway bandits, murderers, thieves, pirates, savages, and devils.

Before condemning this Chinese judgment on our great Christian civilization as perhaps a trifle harsh, it may be as well to consult the dossier:

At the beginning of the sixteenth century, seafaring Arabs trading with China saw their monopoly threatened by the arrival of the first Portuguese ships in Far Eastern waters, and at once tried to damn these interlopers in the eyes of the Chinese by describing them as pirates. The Portuguese, filled with the fervor of their holy Christian mission to convert or kill every heathen they encountered in the four known continents, played the part ascribed to them admirably. When they were weak, they traded, but when they were strong, they raided. In 1517, four Portuguese ships sailed up the Pearl River to Canton as if to do business, but almost at once started launching bloody little forays along its banks, looting and slaughtering until the Chinese viceroy was obliged to mount a military operation against them and flush them out. Twenty-five years after that, the incident almost forgotten, the Portuguese were allowed to settle and trade in Ningpo, but as soon as they were strong enough, they constructed their own fort in the city and once more began robbing, killing, and behaving like marauding gangs of freebooters. They were thrown out of Ningpo, only to repeat their performance in another major port seven years later. By 1557 the Chinese had had enough, and confined them to Macao.

When John Weddell appeared off Canton in 1637, the Portuguese not unnaturally took a leaf out of the book of the Arabs and told the Chinese that they would be well advised to treat the Dutch and British as thievish privateers. The Dutch had already killed and plundered along the Fukien coast thirty years before, and British and Dutch ships had looted and burned and sunk Chinese junks trading with the Philippines and the East Indies, cold-bloodedly murdering their crews. So the Chinese listened, and more misunderstandings and mayhem followed. In 1661 a Dutch fleet attacked a sacred island off the Chinese coast famous for its Buddhist shrine, supposedly inviolate and therefore undefended. The crews plundered its temples and beat the monks, and finally goaded the Chinese into forbidding foreign ships to trade at any port other than Canton. In the next century the Spanish massacred the big Chinese community in the Philippines in the cause of a Catholic Christ, while the Dutch slaughtered the Chinese in Java in the cause of a Protestant one. Relations did not improve.

And then, early in the nineteenth century, came the Opium Wars. Unlike syphilis (*Morbus Americanus*), opium was not actually introduced to China by foreign traders, but the big British and other Western dope-peddling companies could fairly claim to have popularized the habit and to have expanded the sale of the drug in a spectacular manner by putting it within reach of the common man. Since China bought almost nothing from the West, but the West imported silk, tea, rhubarb, and other Chinese commodities in great quantities, while traders soon found that unless they lit upon something to sell to the Chinese in bulk in return, they would have to go on paying for all their purchases in hard cash, which would be intolerable. The answer to this balance-of-payments problem was opium.

The Americans sold the Chinese opium from Turkey, the Portuguese sold them opium from northwest India, but it was when the British seriously developed the market that the sales graph really began to soar. In 1823, some six thousand chests of the forbidden drug, each weighing about 150 pounds, were smuggled into China, and by 1836 the figure had risen to more than twenty-six thousand.

The foreign traders were now confined to their thirteen restricted "factories" on the waterfront of Canton, and then only permitted to occupy them for the summer months, during which they were allowed no excursions, no womenfolk, not even lessons in Chinese. But the opium trade was mainly conducted from an offshore island, where the armed clippers from the West unloaded their black cargo and Chinese coastal vessels then transported it to the mainland. Local Manchu and Chinese officials were involved in the smuggling, while in Peking many outraged mandarins were less worried by the pernicious effects of the drug than by the thought that, were it not for the sale of opium, the foreign devils would be paying for all their purchases with solid silver. On the barbarian side, this great commercial enterprise was favored by the most respectable institutions, and the English East India Company was for long the biggest dealer in the dope. The Chinese appealed to Queen Victoria to suppress the commerce for humanitarian reasons, but in spite of much scandalized opposition the British parliament had already decided that there could be no question of foregoing "so important a source of revenue." Nobly supported, therefore, the trade continued.

On the one hand, the emperor not only repeated his edicts that the traffic must be stopped, but began to take steps to see that they were enforced. On the other, British and other Western companies, operating under the irksome conditions at Canton, were anxious to break China open to general foreign commerce. Incident led to incident, until the British government was neatly coaxed into making war on behalf of these eager shopkeepers. China lost and under the Treaty of Nanking of 1842 was obliged to open up five ports in which foreign traders might not only settle but would enjoy extraterritorial rights. She also ceded Hong Kong to Britain and was ordered to pay costs ($21,000,000). Righteous men had assured the Chinese that by opening up their country to general commerce with the outside world, they would kill the opium traffic, for it would no longer be necessary. But in 1850 the number of chests passing through Hong Kong exceeded fifty thousand.

This was only the first phase, however. Seventeen years later, fighting was resumed, an Anglo-French expeditionary force marched on Peking and burned down the gorgeous Summer

Palace, another treaty was signed, and more ports were opened. A second international expeditionary force rushed to the relief of the Legation Quarter in Peking during the Boxer Rebellion. Once more the court fled, once more a treaty was signed, and still more ports were opened. Thereafter, the Chinese customs and the Chinese postal and telegraphic services were virtually under foreign control, Western warships could navigate freely in Chinese waters, and Chinese coastal defenses were systematically dismantled to prevent any further misunderstandings. The great powers held territorial concessions of their own in all major Chinese ports, enjoyed exemption from trial in Chinese courts, and could station troops in their diplomatic missions and in their own special enclaves. They now began staking out their own claims to this or that portion of the rest of the prey, with a very natural disregard for the corpse's feelings. The British plumped for the valley of the Yangtze Kiang, the Germans for Shantung in the north, the Russians for Manchuria, the French for southwest China. Then in 1931 the Japanese annexed Manchuria and in 1937 struck with their armies against China proper, in time occupying most of her main cities.

Meanwhile, the barbarians were laying railway tracks, digging mines, and stringing out cables in a way that horrified the ordinary superstitious peasant. Burial grounds were torn up in the process, the spirit of Earth offended, and her very veins cut into as the shafts were sunk deep into the ground. The principle of *feng-shui* was outraged, and who could say what ominous, supernatural protest that eerie high-pitched hum in the telephone wires expressed? In the treaty ports the foreign devils seemed all alike—big, bad-tempered, arrogant men, among whom even the stupidest were powerful bosses. "Chinese and dogs not allowed," said the notices outside certain clubs.

Chinese and dogs not allowed! The great portraits loom, one after another, in a dim but splended gallery three thousand years long—Confucius, Mencius, Hsün Tzu, Mo Tzu, Lao Tzu, the virile and tyrannous Han Wu-ti, the poets of the golden T'ang dynasty, the cunning Chu-ko Liang, the intrepid Pan Chao—a hundred generations of men who have given an empire scholarship, administration, civilized living, painting and literature, heroism, loyalty, and wide cultural dominion. The Chinese were paying heavily for the fact that they had allowed themselves to be stranded with an anachronistic, inefficient, narrowly conservative society which was out of its element in the modern world: "A dragon in a puddle is the sport of shrimps."

There were those that wanted to move with the times, and in 1898 the young emperor himself made an abortive attempt to transform the comatose tortoise of a state he had fleetingly inherited into an electric hare: "If we continue to drift with our army untrained, our resources disorganized, our scholars ignorant, and our artisans without technical training, how can we possibly hope to hold our own among nations? There must be careful investigation of every branch of European learning, appropriate to existing needs." He was silenced by the Dowager-Empress and by the scholars, who had no intention of competing against other doctrines. After 1917, however, the younger generation began to clamor for "Science and Democracy." Chinese intellectuals were talking John Dewey and Bertrand Russell, and new reform movements were springing up: "New Tide" and "Chinese Renaissance." The Manchus had been overthrown. A clean wind of change was in the air.

But the Chinese felt humbled, bitter, determined to restore their face. Men who had visited the West came back to confirm that Chinese civilization was the only true one—the West had learned nothing but shamelessness, selfishness, and aggressiveness from its so-called technical progress. The barbarian remained the barbarian. Chinese pride fights an everlasting battle against Chinese pragmatism, but today as yesterday the Chinese only make minimum concessions to their former tormentors. The Communists could have won for themselves consular spy-holes in Singapore, Hong Kong, Malaya, and a dozen other places if they had agreed to establish full diplomatic relations with Britain after the

Labour government extended recognition to them. But they did not. The British embassy in Peking, under a chargé d'affaires, is still called the "British Office" by the Chinese, and has an inferior status that is punctiliously maintained.

Yet the British, confined to the "Canton factory" of Hong Kong (inviolate, since it is the channel for up to forty percent of China's foreign exchange earnings), are no worse off than the Russians. In the course of an unedifying half century, Moscow and the West vied with each other for China's hand. But the loser lost little. It was for the winner to find that there was no percentage in victory. For all marriages with China are, by definition, morganatic.

32

The Mandate Passes

Human affairs being essentially messy, the observer seizes with a sigh of relief upon such smooth, solid-looking sections of the past as the Victorian era or the T'ang dynasty, and blesses the historian who skips over periods of wrangling within the Saxon heptarchy or wars among the Italian states with such fine rolling phrases as "a century of confusion now followed, which only ended when . . ." The popular writer on China is no exception, so that the world hears of Han, T'ang, Sung, and Ming, but only scholars are obliged to plow through the niggling sailor knots of history—the Warring States, the Three Kingdoms, the Five dynasties—that tie one grand design to the next. There can be little doubt that the paperback pundits of the twenty-second century will treat the span of years from 1912 to 1949 in the same curt, highhanded manner.

The abdication of the Manchu dynasty in 1912 was the signal for a many-sided battle for Heaven's Mandate, in which, it seemed, any number could compete. At first the game lay between Yüan Shih-kai in Peking and Dr. Sun Yat-sen, the Republican leader in the south. But Chinese generals soon realized that they and their armies now represented the only real power in the land, and proceeded to carve up the country among themselves and then fight each other for the bits. The general who came out on top of the pile at any one time was in a position to make and unmake governments, to lay down his law to successive, almost impotent cabinets, and to coax money out of foreign states. The ragged soldiers of these warlords—vagabonds with modern weapons, no discipline, and pay six months in arrears—marched and countermarched against one another across the face of China, plundering and killing while their senior officers squeezed the rich merchants dry and wrung every cent they could out of the poor peasantry. The persecuted landowers deserted their estates, the civil administration crumpled, and the whole country fell among uniformed thieves.

But the Chinese revolution, of which this was an early and distressing phase, was not without purpose. Dr. Sun Yat-sen had already enunciated his three principles for a nationalist state: the warlords must be wiped out or won over and a period of military government and then of one-party tutelage must follow, until the masses were politically educated and ready for a constitutional republic with an elected parliament.

Sun Yat-sen died in 1925, and Chiang Kai-shek, inheriting his mantle at the head of the Kuomintang (KMT) or Chinese Nationalist Party, set out with a revolutionary army from Canton in the far south of China with the intention of rolling up the whole country like a mat. In this he may be said to have succeeded brilliantly, for by 1928 he had defeated the northernmost of the warlords and entered Peking. But the bread of victory was snatched from his mouth, for before he could put an end to the pox of foreign concessions and extraterritorial rights that disfigured the face of China, the Japanese invaded, took over most of the north in the succeeding years, and finally launched a full-scale war against a young republic that was still going through all the degrading torments of political pubescence.

The Kuomintang had twisted the teachings of Sun Yat-sen. China was ruled by Chiang Kai-shek and a small group at the top of the political hierarchy, not by the National Congress. Power was exercised through the sudden arrest and the firing squad rather than constitutional procedure, but was decently clothed in finely woven phrases reflecting the gentler moods of Confucius and Dr. Sun. Privilege remained in the hands of the more cooperative financiers and the landowners, the less scrupulous scholars were permitted to continue their depradations in the guise of officials, and "friendly" warlords who were confirmed in their fiefs began inventing more bizarre taxes than ever before. Graft, speculation, hoarding, profiteering, and the fiddling of contracts and requisitions were practiced on a grand scale, so that the honesty and frugal living of some high-minded revolutionary officials, and the puritanism widely practiced by those who took seriously the movement for a new civic-minded China, have since been forgotten.

Meanwhile, nothing effective was done for the men who represented four Chinese out of five—the peasant. Land reform looked handsome on paper, but landlords were still taking up to sixty percent of a farmer's crop as rent, there was no agricultural credit system, and so no alternative but to go to moneylenders, whose interest rates remained as fantastic as ever. The peasants therefore turned away from the Nationalists and toward their political enemies, and the Kuomintang soon found it necessary to announce a policy of "internal pacification before resistance to outside attack"—which meant that they were more concerned with liquidating the Chinese Communists than stopping the advance of the Japanese enemy.

The postwar era was marked by the even greater cupidity of get-rich-quick KMT gunmen, and by even greater proliferation of secret-police spies. Even opium dens were "protected" by Kuomintang officials, who closed them down if they failed to pay heavy bribes, confiscated their opium, and then sold it elsewhere. Inflation began to dig cruelly into the slender incomes of salaried officials and teachers, while speculators waxed fat and the men at the apex of the party rigged the exchange rate to suit themselves. Everything was obtained by bribery. To seek promotion or concessions or facilities without a fat billfold and a finger alongside the nose was, as the Lord of Shang once said of the corrupt state, "like baiting a mousetrap with cat's flesh."

In August 1948 the government introduced a so-called "gold yuan" which was solemnly declared to be worth twenty-five American cents. By January 1949 it had passed the one-million-to-the-dollar mark and was still galloping. The end was now near. In a few months the Nationalist Air Force would abandon Peking while the ground troops were still under Communist siege inside the capital, and take off for Shanghai after selling all its stocks of fuel on the local black market. Before the year was out, Chiang Kai-shek, one of many Asian leaders whose image of personal integrity and courage has been profitably complemented by the more dubious talents of thorough-paced scoundrels around him, would have withdrawn to Formosa.

What had gone wrong? "Employ foreign methods in order to protect Confucian ideas," the early Chinese progressists urged. Sun Yat-sen warned sadly that to wrench bits of Western political theory from their setting was like "plucking the flowers in a neighbor's garden to embellish the dying branches of one's own tree," but in vain. The first Republican parliament of 1912 was, accordingly, a model of corruption, with deputies auctioning their votes openly to the highest bidder. Having no real conception of their role, they simply behaved like venal mandarins and sold their favors accordingly. By the twenties it seemed to the Chinese that this so-called democracy was as liberal a cornucopia of chicanery, brutality, nepotism, and fratricidal war as the worst dynastic rule. Many even looked back sorrowfully on the rotten empire they had overthrown, for at least it had been administered by selected scholars and not by any jumped-up ignoramus of a careerist who climbed on to the party bandwagon or could pay his way into a lucrative post. The Chinese suddenly found themselves face to face with an animal they had never met before—the professional politician. And they quite understandably did not like what they saw.

Moreover, the Western democracies had behaved from the outset in as undemocratic a manner as possible. First they upheld the foreign Manchu dynasty against the revolutionaries, so that in 1897 Sun Yat-sen received the following answer to his application for permission to live in Hong Kong:

Sir,

In reply to your letter, undated, I am directed to inform you that this Government has no intention of allowing the British Colony of Hongkong to be used as an asylum for persons engaged in plots and dangerous conspiracies against a friendly neighbouring Empire, and that in view of the part taken by you in such transactions, which you euphemistically term in your letter 'Emancipating your miserable countrymen from the cruel Tartar yoke,' you will be arrested if you land in this Colony under an order of banishment against you in 1896.

> I have, etc.
> Sgd: J. H. Stewart Lockhart.
> Colonial Secretary.

So much for the future president of the Chinese Republic, three years before the ruler of the "friendly neighbouring Empire" set the Boxers to attacking the British legation in Peking.

In the next stage of the game, the empire having fallen, the Western powers financed General Yüan Shih-kai's counterrevolution in the north against the Republican movement in Canton, so that this discredited instrument of the Manchus was even able to make plans for his own enthronement as first emperor of a new dynasty, before the infuriated Chinese booted him out. In the years that followed, the Kuomintang gradually emerged as a republican party bent primarily on breaking the foreign hold on China, and the foreign powers therefore riposted by continuing to back its enemies. Disillusioned with the West and all its works, would-be revolutionaries were also disillusioned with the Confucian ethic, for it was quoted to justify the antics of all the sanctimonious ruffians of this uneasy age in turn: the die-hard reactionaries, the warlords, and then the Japanese. The Kuomintang regime was a police state, democracy was delusion, and the past was discredited and dead. Very early, the Chinese started looking around for a new dynasty and a new doctrine. And duly found it.

When Sun Yat-sen appealed to the Western powers to recognize his government and to help him crush the warlords, they flatly declined. What would happen to their tariff protection against Chinese competition in China itself, to their extraterritorial rights, their foreign courts, their garrisons, their warships on the Yangtze, their colonies in neighboring countries that had once submitted to the suzerainty of the Chinese emperor—if once Sun Yat-sen turned these people into a nation? Only one foreign power responded with a refreshing show of altruism: Soviet Russia.

Chinese intellectuals therefore began to study Marxism with new interest as a possible answer to China's problems. In 1921 the Chinese Communist Party was formed, and among its founder-members was a slightly uncouth library assistant from Peking University named Mao Tse-tung. In 1923 Sun Yat-sen, who had by then had quite enough of the West, accepted Russian aid and welcomed Russian advisers to the Kuomintang. Under a rather curious arrangement, Communists were allowed to join the KMT as individuals, and the Party was then reorganized on Communist lines with cells and commissars and a control commission, and groomed for dictatorship. Chiang Kai-shek was sent to Moscow for training, and subsequently became commandant of the Whampoa Military Academy in Canton, which was to prove the iron cradle of his power. The West seemed to combine ineffectual liberalism with efficient larceny, both of which could prove the ruin of China. The Russians advocated strong, centralized Party rule and showed respect for China's sovereignty. It was not very difficult to choose between them.

However, when the Communists began dominating his revolutionary government, Chiang Kai-shek decided on major surgery. In 1927 he abruptly turned on his Communist allies in Shanghai, massacred their leaders, outlawed the Communist Party, and packed his Russian advisers off to Moscow. Chiang had no intention of playing the role of an expendable Kerensky to any Chinese Communist Lenin: he also knew that "when the fleet deer is caught, the hounds are cooked," and he proposed to be the hunter himself, not one of the dogs.

Army units mutinied under Communist officers and launched a series of futile attacks against Chinese cities held by the KMT. They then drew back into the hills, and in the almost impregnable mountain fortress of Chingkangsham joined China's twentieth-century "Men of the Marshes" under that deviating ideological outlaw, Mao Tse-tung. For Mao walked where Engels feared to tread, and his heresy had the genius of simplicity: instead of basing revolution on the worker, he based it on China's pullulating population of peasants; instead of fighting for industrial rights, he promised land reform; and instead of attacking cities frontally, he read Sun Wu, Wu Ch'i, the *Three Kingdoms,* and the exploits of the heroes of Liang Shan Po, and put what he learned from them into practice. Modern guerrilla warfare and "Chinese Communism," were born as twins. Both survived.

For five years Chiang Kai-shek attacked Mao's growing force of guerrillas, but not until 1934 was he able to gouge them out of their mountain strongholds in southeast China, and then only to see them make the Long March up to the northwest, to establish themselves even more firmly in the caves of Yenan. The Communists armed the peasants, mobilized the masses in the forbidding hill country that they "liberated," and waged a well-conducted guerrilla war against the Japanese, while the Nationalists did little more than stonewall the hated foreign army. The KMT became increasingly uneasy and in 1941 ignored the Japanese and turned upon the Communists again.

The struggle for China between the Nationalists and Communists was to continue for eight more years. The Japanese watched it with ill-concealed satisfaction until 1945, when the Americans took over and watched it with ill-concealed alarm until 1949. The West was satisfied that Generalissimo Chiang

Kai-shek was legally entitled to reestablish his authority over all China at the expense of the Communists, but the Chinese, never impressed much by legal arguments, merely foresaw that if he did not compromise with Mao there would be no end to this murderous civil war. Sympathy for Chiang Kai-shek waned even among firm anti-Communists, and entire regiments sold their arms to the Reds or crossed over to them. The bell rang for the final round, and Mao swiftly knocked his enemy right out of the ring. Chiang withdrew to Formosa.

If Western strategy had suffered a terrible setback, Western democracy, at least, was unaffected. For democracy would have lost out, whichever side had won. Like Gorgonzola cheese, it is a taste which the Asian acquires with the greatest difficulty; it is only the Anglo-Saxon who persists in thinking that it is positively immoral of him not to like it.

33

The People vs. Democracy

From earliest times, the more thoughtful Chinese have shown much concern for the masses, so that even the ancient Book of History so venerated by Confucius himself warns:

> The people should be cherished,
> And should not be downtrodden.
> The people are the root of the country,
> And if the root is firm, the country will be tranquil.

The old Master, asked which was the most important to the stability of a state—food, weapons, or the trust of the people— replied that weapons and even food could be sacrificed, but "if the people have no confidence in the government, the state cannot stand." Mencius added: "Heaven has no fixed will, but sees as the people see, and hears as the people hear." Mo Tzu also championed the poor, condemning extravagance and prestige projects that hurt the economy without serving the millions.

Facile commentators are inclined to quote this sort of thing as evidence of a democratic tradition among Chinese philosophers and scholars. In fact, of course, it is firmly anti-democratic. The overdog is simply advised that he must treat the underdog well if he wants to remain overdog. There is no suggestion that within the four seas all dogs are equal. Frail as he is, man frequently ignored these sage counsels, and so the millions invoked the

379

power Mencius gave them to rise and remove the Mandate of Heaven from one emperor—but only to confer it on another.

The few are therefore admonished to be good to the many, and in the Book of Rites, the ancient classic which Confucius also edited, we find this strikingly early reference to the welfare state: "When the great Way was practiced, a spirit of public welfare pervaded the world. The aged were cared for until death. There was employment for the able-bodied, and means of sustenance for the young. Kindness and compassion were shown to widows and orphans, to those without children to care for them, and to those disabled by disease."

Mencius attacked excessive taxation and revived an old system of cooperative farming whereby eight neighbors would pool their resources and together cultivate a common field for the purpose of paying their dues. The economic adviser of the Emperor Han Wu-ti and the eleventh-century innovator, Wang An-shih, both hit out at speculation, stabilized prices, limited profits, and introduced state loan shops and low-interest agricultural credits for farmers. All this, of course, would evoke a far readier echo from the Kremlin than the Capitol.

Europe preserved its aristocracy, so that in progressive Labour Britain today the House of Lords still has hereditary scions as well as honours-list socialists. But in die-hard Imperial China the landed aristocracy enjoyed a short run only. First, some of their privileges were popularized, so that peasants started to marry officially and to worship their own ancestors, just like any duke. Then, in 221 B.C., the First Emperor eliminated the ancient fiefs entirely. Next, the Han emperors made all sons the equal heirs to their father's property, so that an estate quickly splintered into smallholdings, and if a man had no male issue, it was liquidated altogether. By Han Wu-ti's day, even the minor estates of gentry hardly figure in the land records. During the T'ang dynasty, a nobility existed whose members held equivalent rank as officials and whose lower grades were in fact filled from the mandarinate. However, these aristocrats owned no land but received revenue according to their title, a duke pocketing the taxes paid by three thousand families, a baron those paid by three hundred. More than a thousand years before the British invented life-peerages, the Chinese had an ingenious system for preventing the rise of a new hereditary aristocracy whereby the son always dropped a rank below his father, so that in ten generations even the direct descendant of a duke became plain mister.

Since "gentleman" ceased so early to be the definition of a hereditary lord and became instead that of a scholar-official chosen by a competitive examination, the Chinese quickly lost his respect for bloodstock. "All men are born equal—in evil," noted Hsün Tzu sardonically. "Therefore all have a chance to become sages through education." Great Chinese dynasties like Han and Ming were founded by men from humble country homes, and their descendants, even if Sons of Heaven, were kept close to the earth by the blood and chatter of plebeian imperial concubines.

The Chinese, moreover, has always had a talent for just the sort of proletarian cheek-by-jowl existence that repels the European, with his developed taste for rarified atmosphere. Crowded living is no problem to a man whose idea of an excursion into the country is to rape it with a busload of relatives and all their shrill progeny. Chinese people like to have Chinese people around them, the clamor of firecrackers, and the peremptory rattle of mah-jongg tiles. Even in the pre-transitorized seventeenth century a Dutch embassy to China, accorded a magnificent audience by the viceroy of Canton, noted that a band played so loudly all the time that there was "no hearing one another speak." A Chinese does not believe that his dignity depends on a discreet, depopulated setting. In the give-and-take family home of old, even newlyweds enjoyed little privacy with all the comings and goings, and people tended to do what they could and to take what they needed in what was very much a communal design for living.

But it was not, inside or outside the family, an egalitarian society. A Chinese proverb says: "Even your own ten fingers are uneven." The Chinese never entertained the manifestly absurd proportion that all men are equal, but only that they are born much the same. Otherwise they believed in the harmony of differences—not differences of inherited class but of rank and position, properly observed. "Heaven placed the people below, and gave them rulers and teachers," said Confucius—and heaven's object in doing so had been to destroy the concept of equality, for equality could only lead to anarchy and chaos. But if all men were not equal, they were still human. During centuries of neglect and oppression in which soldiers with long whips brutally lashed the streets clean of half-starved peasants before the four-man palanquin of this or that fastidious, overfed mandarin, there has also grown up an on-parade-on-parade off-parade-off-parade tradition whereby the proprieties must be observed between those of different rank, but their private relationship may still be founded upon the vulgar proposition that no man has more than two testicles.

Somerset Maugham made the point in an anecdote called "Democracy," which he wrote in the early twenties: An imposing mandarin arrives at a country inn for the night, to be told that the best room is taken. He and his attendants then make a great scene, raging up and down and shouting angrily, indignant at the grievous affront offered to so high and mighty an official. However, in time the turmoil abates and all is quiet. One hour later, Maugham goes into the courtyard to stretch his legs and there finds "the stout official, a little while ago so pompous and self-important, seated at a table in the front of the inn with the most ragged of my coolies. They were chatting amicably and the official quietly smoked a water-pipe. He had made all that to-do to give himself face, but having achieved his object was satisfied and feeling the need for conversation had accepted the company of any coolie without a thought of social distinction. His manner was perfectly cordial and there was in it no trace of condescension. The coolie talked with him on an equal footing."

The Chinese differed not only from the Europeans, however, but also from the Americans, for the Americans often confuse caste with cash, whereas in Imperial China the scholar-official came first, the peasant next, the craftsman third, and the merchant a bad fourth. The entire design might have been stenciled to order for the Communists, who have elaborated in China a pattern of society whose most important elements are the indoctrinated cadre (or "educated" scholar-official), the peasant, and the worker. The capitalist, of course, is not placed at all.

The cynical Chinese do not believe in popular politics, but in the use of power to keep power. "Who's got the army?" is the first question a Chinese asks when evaluating any political situation. After the ruling People's Action Party of Lee Kuan Yew had been returned again in the 1963 Singapore general elections, Ah Fu said he had naturally held the "winning ticket" by prearrangement in what she obviously regarded as a shady political process to be equated with a rigged lottery. When Ping explained gently that the results of general elections were not fixed in advance, she jeered at such ignorance: "This democracy is a Singapore thing," she reminded us cuttingly. "You are not Singaporeans—your husband is even a real foreign devil, all the way from England. So how can either of you know, anything about it?" The Chinese is nevertheless more at home with a revolution than a referendum.

It can be argued that most Chinese only have a garbled, fragmentary knowledge of their own cultural inheritance, revolutionary or otherwise. However, it is the very nature of a cultural inheritance that it becomes grotesquely buckled within the tiny confines of the public mind. Yet an Englishman has not lost his past because with the passage of years "God Encompasseth Us" has been corrupted into "The Goat and Compasses," nor will he have done so if "Dieu et Mon Droit" eventually appears on a tavern sign as "The Duck and Mandrake." It sometimes seems that Confucius has been reduced to a few misquotations, Taoism to a row of plaster saints and a bundle of fortunetelling spills, the ethics of centuries to meaningless marriages and burial customs, history to popular literature, and popular literature to a series of gaudy operas. But in reality the Chinese tradition is wide as well as deep—whether you think of chess, opera, or philosophy—and the Chinese outlook is nothing if not Chinese.

Liberal democracy is exotic, interesting, but not necessarily something to live with every day. For one thing, there is to a Chinese a certain foolishness about a system in which a party representing one half of the electorate spends much of its time trying to stop the party that represents the other half of the electorate from governing effectively. Could a better formula have been devised that would ensure a minimum of constructive effort, when all should be working together in harmony for the good of the country? The government's renunciation of power every four or five years is regarded by many as a hypocritical waste of time, and finally the one-man-one-ballot concept is manifestly unreasonable, unfair, unjust, and will lead to disaster unless the moronic majority are told how they should vote. Against this there is much to be said for benevolent despotism— given the people's power to wrench the Mandate of Heaven from the hand of the despot that forgets his benevolence. "In England you have general elections," a Chinese once said to me. "In China we have revolutions."

Western politicians and commentators are fond of describing Communism as vicious dogma and blind religion, but this is often just the reputation they themselves give to democracy among the Chinese. To describe a law, or a government, or the election of the committee of a women's sewing circle as undemocratic is at once to damn it for all time. All systems of administration that are not democratic are evil and must be destroyed with guns if they threaten democracy elsewhere. Once more, the Chinese notes, the West is hammering the table and arrogantly proclaiming one true faith. After Judaism, Islam, and Christianity, it is Democracy. And it does not seem to occur to its powerful evangelists that to try to ram it down the throats of others may in itself be regarded as an act of tyranny, that liberty must include the liberty to renounce liberty.

The West flaunts concepts like freedom and self-determination as if they were the silken banners of a holy crusade before whose devices all automatically fall on their knees. But the word freedom is a modern synthetic in Chinese, a relatively recent combination of two characters meaning "self," and "from" or "by." It embodies a new concept, borrowed from the West and laboriously explained to his people by Dr. Sun Yat-sen. Some say that it has a slight flavor of selfishness. Ping maintains it represents a right to do what you like, provided no other person is hurt, so that, on the contrary, it does not express absolute liberty of action as does the English word "freedom."

Again, neither the Chinese Nationalists in Formosa nor the Chinese Communists in Peking can possibly agree that there was ever such a thing as an abstract "principle of self-determination," for this would imply that the outside world would be right in demanding self-determination for Tibet, or indeed for Formosa itself. To a Chinese this is obviously bunkum. Both are historically bound to China (Formosa as a province, Tibet as a sort of vassal Holy See enjoying a chaplain-to-monarch relationship with Peking). They are part of Chinadom, and to talk of giving them self-determination is like advocating a referendum to decide whether the Isle of Wight should remain part of Britain. Moreover, to preach of "principles" in this context is to batter futilely against the fundamental Chinese contempt for what is legal, and its reverence for what is historically "natural."

There has evolved among Americans a picturesque legend that a very special relationship once existed between a wise, generous, and paternal United States already a century or more old, and the heathen, immature, stumbling, but hard-working Chinese ward with a case history three millennia long. Until 1950, America was ever at China's elbow with Christianity, or democracy, or dollars and guns and soldiers, and, of course, advice, so that when China went Communist it was as if an erring son had struck his indulgent father across the face. Not all Chinese saw this distressing affair in quite the same light, however. For many did not necessarily regard these brash barbarians with their penny's worth of history as father figures, and where Americans painted a self-portrait of kindly paternalism, the Chinese too often saw a mosaic of racial arrogance, insulting patronage, contempt, egotism, and hypocrisy.

The record of American treatment of Chinese immigrants on the West Coast of the United States in earlier years was, for a start, deplorable. They were kicked and beaten, stoned, lynched, subjected to every indignity by ignorant mobs, yet unable to testify against their white persecutors in court. Then, in 1905, the American government introduced the Exclusion Act in order to keep the Chinese out altogether, and the Chinese launched their first anti-foreign boycott in protest. To them, this was the first of a notable list of twentieth-century betrayals. In 1934, the United States govenment put into effect the Silver Purchase Act, which started an almost fatal leakage of silver from China at a time when the national economy was already dangerously anemic. The Chinese further remarked that the United States did not enter the war against Japan until they were blown into it by the obliging Japanese themselves at Pearl Harbor, and they accuse President Roosevelt of then selling out Chinese interests in Manchuria at the Yalta Conference in 1945 in order to coax Russia into the Far East conflict. The opponents of Chiang Kai-shek blame the Americans for backing him, and the Nationalists accuse them of betraying him by trying to blackmail him into a coalition with the Communists.

Middle-of-the-road Chinese say that the Americans are still unable to shake off their lofty parental complexes. They sternly discourage Chiang Kai-shek from either attacking the Communist mainland or talking to Peking, yet they authorize their own ambassador to conduct conversations with Chinese Communist representatives in Warsaw. In short, the trouble with the Americans, it seems to many, is that they do not know the meaning of the word independence. And so, as democracy stands at bay in East

Asia, the Chinese tend to turn away from the Land of Opportunity.

The Chinese experience of the West has hardly been a happy one. First came the century of humiliation, then came the generation of disillusion: disillusion with Western powers and disillusion with Western democracy. The Communists offered something else, however—the monolithic system of "democratic centralism," whereby the views of the masses would filter up from the humblest cells through echelon after echelon until they reached the Central Committee of the Party. Here they would be synthesized, and the correct line would then be decided, published, and thereafter universally applied. Since this correct line had its origins in the popular will of the Marxists at the lowest level, it must, of course, be regarded as sacrosanct and unquestionably obeyed.

About four hundred years before Christ, Mo Tzu wrote his famous chapter on "identifying with one's superior," or "agreeing upward." Beginning with an attack on democracy which might well have been directed at the French Fourth Republic of little-lamented memory, Mo Tzu starts: "In ancient times it may be said that every man's view of things was different. One man had one view, two men had two views, ten men had ten views, and the more the men, the more the views. Each believed his own views were correct, so that people spent their time condemning one another."

Mo Tzu—and President de Gaulle would doubtless agree—goes on to say that the basic trouble was an absence of rulers and leaders, and matters were quickly put straight once a proper hierarchy had been established. What follows may be summarized like this: the head of each family unified the views of all its members on what was right and wrong, and then submitted them to the local community leader, whose decision all would accept. The community leaders would in turn submit the sum of local ideas to the regional lord, and the regional lords would report in the same way to the king. "And what the Son of Heaven held to be right, all held to be right. Thus the world was properly ordered because the ruler was able to unify the standards of judgment throughout his realm."

The Chinese cast aside the bizarre gadget called Western democracy and picked up the faintly familiar-looking tool called Communism. From Mo Tzu to Mao, across twenty-three centuries of "Confucian" rule, the design in some respects hardly seemed to have changed.

34

The Chinese Puzzle

It is time to try and assemble the pieces of the Chinese puzzle, and to see if the picture answers two questions: Why do Chinese Communist leaders behave as they do? And do the Chinese like it?

In 1955 I idled at the entrance of a state store for foreigners in Peking and watched the wives of Soviet diplomats and technicians at play. Solidly built in the first place, these amiable ladies were adding to their ample presence by trying on Chinese sable coats of monstrous proportions and price, and simpering over smart duty-free watches which would have cost any cotton-picking Chinese peasant his earnings for the previous four years. The same thought seemed to have occurred to the knot of skinny, canvas-shod Chinese in faded blue denims outside, judging by the very special lack of look in their azoic eyes, and at that moment the obvious became obvious: the Chinese may have chosen Communism, but they had not chosen Russia.

The Americans and the Russians, the two peoples who have poured far more money, men, and missionaries into China than any other, enjoy a very special place in the hearts of the Chinese. For not only have they black records as imperialists, but in addition they are accused of treacherous double-dealing by the Nationalists and the Communists respectively. The Russians started out by gouging far more territory out of China than did Britain or any other imperialist power, so that although the young Soviet regime declared all Tsarist annexations in Manchuria null and void, at least half of the 700,000 square miles of former Chinese territory that Russia had filched remained and remains today within the borders of the Soviet Union, according to the Chinese. Sections of the Sino-Russian frontier that are still in dispute disfigure the torso of Asia like long, livid scars. Nor can Peking forgive the Russians for taking over "Chinese" Outer Mongolia and converting it into a Moscow-oriented independent republic.

Although Mao has in the past publicly acknowledged Chinese Communism's great debt to the Soviet Union, he discovered many years ago that you only had to scratch a Russian Communist to find a Tatar. At the time of the Japanese surrender in 1945, Soviet troops occupied China's industrial northeast, dismantled factories, stripped them bare of machinery and equipment, and shunted them off to the U.S.S.R. in looted Chinese rolling stock. Furthermore, Stalin told the Americans that he recognized the Nationalist government of Chiang Kai-shek as the only legitimate government of China. The Soviet Union, its depradations completed, did not, therefore, hand Manchuria over to Mao Tse-tung and the Communist forces that had in fact liberated much of the north from the Japanese, but to their "legal" Nationalist opponents. In the years of civil war that followed between the Nationalists and the Chinese Communists, the Russians gave the Communists very little assistance, and when Chiang Kai-shek was forced southward upon Canton, the Soviet embassy was the only foreign diplomatic mission that was ordered to withdraw with him. All others awaited the arrival of the Communists in Nanking. After 1950 the Russians sent military and technical advisers to China, but the Soviet Union made no move when advancing American forces raced for the Yalu River during the Korean War, and left it to the Chinese "human sea" to stop the rot—without benefit of adequate artillery. Moscow then demanded that Peking pay for every ruble's worth of Russian military aid received. Peking paid.

In 1956 the first sharp whispers of Sino-Soviet bickering began to reach the ears of the neighbors. In 1958, Khrushchev started to withdraw Soviet technicians from China, and Chiang Kai-shek's American jets were able to flit Mao's air force out of the air over the Straits of Formosa with their Sidewinders, because Moscow had declined to equip the Red Chinese Migs with air-to-air missiles. When Khrushchev chatted amicably with the archenemy Eisenhower at Camp David, Russia's treachery lay finally, fully, and indecently exposed.

Mao could claim that he owed much of his success to his stubborn rejection of Russian advice. It was the Russians who had insisted that the socialist revolution must be preceded by the "bourgeois revolution," and had coerced the Chinese Communists into an alliance with Chiang Kai-shek which led to the liquidation of the Reds in Shanghai in 1927. And it was the Russians who had urged the Chinese Communists to attack cities and to foment uprisings among the proletariat—with bloody and disastrous results. Mao's secret of success was that he flouted the Russians by organizing a peasant guerrilla army which was happily spared Soviet guidance. (There is a story that at the end of World War II Stalin sent Mao a book on partisan warfare and that Marshal Lin Piao declared after reading it: "It's a good thing we did not have this as our textbook before, or we would have been wiped out ten years ago.") Finally, in 1948 Stalin strongly advised the Chinese Communists to limit themselves to dominating the north, not to try to launch a grand offensive against the Nationalists for the control of all China. This counsel was sensibly ignored, and so Mao became master of the entire country by the end of the following year, despite the U.S.S.R.

China is gradually absorbing and modifying the foreign doctrine of Marxism-Leninism and this process of metabolism will not end with Mao's demise or cease until the alien origins of the gospel disappear into the Chinese juices. In 1949, leading Chinese Communists were already claiming that Mao had "added new truths to Marxism" and that his peasant revolution would be the model for all the downtrodden, colonized peoples of the world. By 1956 the Chinese were warning everyone against slavish copying of the Soviet Union. China could, however, "learn from Soviet mistakes." In 1958 a backward China launched the "Great Leap Forward" in a bold attempt to stand on her own feet in a modern industrial world, and Mao ordered the formation of the People's Communes, whose appearance would put Peking ahead of Moscow in the struggle toward a completely Communistic society.

There cannot be two suns in the sky, say the Chinese. Mao could not forever kowtow to Moscow, because no ruler of the Middle Kingdom could play vassal to a northern barbarian indefinitely and hope to survive. The Russian theory of peaceful coexistence with the capitalist countries—accompanied by a gentle middle-aged spread of Communism, as against vigorous world revolution—was therefore conveniently heretical, and gave him a respectable pretext for making a clean break with Khrushchev and his own bid for world Communist leadership.

As a comfortably established member of the world community, the Soviet Union might want peace and quiet, but the lean and hungry among nations and peoples of the submerged continents were waiting for revolution, not reconciliation, and they seemed to form almost a ready-made ideological empire for the pontiff in Peking. Mao therefore championed the cause of the world peasant uprising, calling Marx and Lenin to bear witness to his unorthodox orthodoxy, so that the planet ceased to be divided into capitalist and Communist, but became split into "coexistence" and "revolutionary" blocs, into have's and have-not's with not only America and Britain but also Russia on the wrong side among the rich.

Mao is a profound and outstanding Marxist theoretician, but he treats Communism as an instrument rather than as a creed. In Maoism he has the philosophical basis for a new cultural dominion, another Holy Chinese Empire with Peking once more as the center of the Asian world and himself as the infallible high priest of the one true doctrine. Communist and revolutionary

states will be "ripe" or "raw" according to their ideological development, and as one land after another veers to the left, China's
tributaries will once more be restored to her. Beyond the fringe
of light will remain the benighted anti-Communist barbarians.
But ultimately even these may be converted, so that world revolution and world Communism under Peking's spiritual leadership
will dovetail with the traditional Chinese concept of the Ta
T'ung, the Great Unity. Universal harmony is attained when all
opposition has been eliminated. "Just revolutionary war," therefore, equals peace, and so it is the "peace-loving peoples of the
world" who support the Vietcong.

This does not mean that China herself will embark on any
aggressive military adventures. "Asians will overrun Asia," Mao
once commented with sly semantical humor, meaning that, as in
Vietnam, the people must organize their own indigenous revolution. Chu-ko Liang did not tame the country of the Mans with
Chinese troops but with their own chastened and enlightened
king. True to the tenets of Chinese strategy, Mao would not try
to smash his way to suzerainty with Chinese armies on alien
territory, but rather would filter down the social and economic
cracks in his enemy's strength, trickling through the weak Western defenses against subversion, eroding from within the friable
soil of Asian political stability. Imperial suzerainty extended over
most of Southeast Asia, the Himalayan states, Burma and Assam,
and Korea, and it is primarily across these territories that the
Chinese dream of a new intellectual hegemony with the cadres of
fraternal Communist parties inheriting the cohesive role of the
Confucian scholar-official. But those cadres will be native, not
Chinese. The Chinese still regard the Vietnamese as "younger
brothers" and are therefore by definition "big brothers" themselves. China has no real tradition of physical possession beyond
what she considers her natural frontiers. She was never involved
in the undignified scramble for colonies and markets when the
going was good, for she sold her distinctive products with ease
and bought little from outside. Her people were poor colonizers,

for most of them were inexorably drawn back to China by their ancestral graves. Her "dependencies" were for the most part vassal states ruled by their own indigenous kings.

However, as Peking sees it, Chinese territories and tributary states along the frontiers of India were only lost because a rapacious and imperialistic nineteenth-century Britain peeled them away painfully from the skin of China herself. Mao therefore expected understanding from a newly independent India over the Sino-Indian frontier issue, and first bent upon Mr. Nehru his "tender regard." When New Delhi declined to give ground, however, the Chinese inflicted a disagreeable military lesson upon their presumptuous neighbor. For China has no tradition of coexistence either, since she has never recognized that there have been states of her own standing. The master only "coexists" with his pupil as long as the pupil does what he wants him to do. After that, he reaches for the birch. But the image of Mao as a modern Genghis Khan nevertheless belongs strictly to the realm of the fancy-dress ball.

For the Chinese Communists the world is divided into believers and infidels. "Neutralism is a sham," warns the mundane messiah in Peking ("He who is not with Me, is against Me," echoes the Christian memory—yet still fails to understand). It follows that Mao the infallible must never be seen to be wrong, must never be disproved in his role of the universal lawgiver. For this reason China's policies today are more often than not dictated, as they have been in the past, by considerations of face and renown. The pre-Christian Emperor Han Wu-ti who dispatched an army two thousand miles to chastize an impious Central Asian kinglet for refusing him a few horses, subsequently sent out more than ten peripatetic embassies to countries far and wide to make sure that all and sundry heard about his punitive expedition. He was afraid that if he was not known to have made a public example of the culprit, China might be regarded with contempt. He was also at great pains to receive foreign delegations in China and to overawe them with magnificent demonstrations of her power and riches. The Chinese Communists do precisely the same to-day, entertaining a wearisome and seemingly endless procession of politicians, Party members, trade unionists, and intellectuals from all over the world, and stunning them with an indigestible banquet of cultural and industrial sightseeing and speechifying that leaves them limp and adipose with reluctant awe.

Those who do not conform to the Chinese view must be corrected, impudence must at least appear to be punished, and old friends like Cuba who speak fair of Russia must be unfrocked and denounced for their heresy. But in the modern world a threat from one bully usually summons another to the victim's defense, so that the puniest of states can defy the most powerful, and there is no quicker way to lose face than to try to pull rank. The effect of this is cumulative, for the more China is mocked, the more arrogantly does she riposte in order to preserve her prestige. In consequence Peking has become the proper study not of the political mathematician but of the sympathetic psychologist.

The Chinese have a high boiling point. It has been remarked that they will contain their ire for centuries of misrule beneath a prudent and resigned exterior, until the final insupportable moment comes and they suddenly break out in violent and bloody revolution. It is in this lurid light that China's seemingly unbalanced behavior in international affairs must be observed. The prestigious Middle Kingdom patiently suffered a hundred years of humiliation at the hands of the barbarian and has only now emerged once more as a vast, unified power. Yet China is blackballed in the United Nations, cold-shouldered by the great, subjected to the intolerable affronts of second-rate states, preoccupied with the vital business of restoring her raddled face but frustrated by impertinent opposition at every turn. She is, therefore, ill-tempered and edgy, bent all the more on avenging the insults of a century. The Chinese nevertheless expect the perceptive to see the slimmer body within the aggressive, high-shouldered overcoat, to distinguish between words designed to preserve prestige, or to test reactions, or to conceal true intentions—

and the true intentions themselves. For China's words must literally be taken at "face value," and her leaders judged solely by their actions. The smaller the army, the greater the cacophony of crackers and drums, and the more Peking thunders that 700 million Chinese "will not stand idly" by in a given situation, the more certain can one be that China does not plan to *do* anything decisive or drastic about it.

The Chinese have no tradition of alliances, for none could be the equal ally of the Middle Kingdom, and they have no outside loyalties, for it has been the business of others to be loyal to them, and not vice versa. China does not believe in international friendships, for she knows that the only emotion shared between states is diplomatic cupboard love. She will only join international groups or fronts where the profit for Peking is clearly marked on the tag, and she will only tolerate the companionship of neutrals and non-Communists as long as they accept her paternalistic leadership. The Chinese, who keep such a careful ledger of material debt and moral obligation in their private relations, believe that aid without strings is a contradiction in terms. Any country that accepts American assistance has automatically forfeited its sovereignty, therefore, and any proposal that Washington might pour dollars into a contrite anti-Communist China must be seen as no more than a crude take-over bid.

Mao may be a Marxist of genius, but the "Men of the Marshes" morality still illumines his outlook. China herself is the fortress of Liang Shan Po, the hope of the wretched, the cheated, and the victimized in a world ridden with colonialism. The United Nations, the Western Powers, the Russians, and all reactionary governments constitute the brutal and corrupt mandarinate that has driven good men into the greenwood. International law is the tool of the imperialists, just as Chinese torturers and prisons were the instruments of iniquitous officials, designed to serve the rich and penalize the poor. Step through this looking glass and we see at once through fresh eyes that all is back to front: established order is simply a vast conspiracy to uphold injustice in the name of the law. It is the robber who is virtuous, the cop who is vile.

As Mao gets older, the arteries of Chinese policy harden. He has scarcely traveled outside China, and he judges by his Chinese experience. To him, capitalism means the foreign exploiters and their corrupt Chinese compradors who fed from the cadaver of his country until he and his armies drove them off. The alliance between Communists and Nationalists was murderously betrayed by Chiang Kai-shek in 1927: it follows, then, that any proposed rapprochement between the Soviet Union and America, or between America and China, must be seen as another "peace hoax." Mao rallied the have-not's of China and so revolutionized the republic: Mao, therefore, can champion the have-not's of the underdog continents and so revolutionize the world. Do not fight unless you are sure of winning, say the Chinese. Do not strive against something unless you can change it. "Do not shout unless you are certain of an echo." Mao, quite mistakenly, has felt certain of his echo in the world outside.

If Mao's short-think is inspired by ignorance, it is an ignorance compounded by bad reporting. The Communist movement throughout the world has at times been notorious for the way in which it has lied to its leaders by painting the situation in absurdly bright colors, for often the man on the spot does not dare to appear defeatist by admitting that in his neck of the woods the cause of Communism is losing ground. This foible of the Marxists only reinforces the great parallel Chinese tradition which earlier dictated that a provincial governor or southern viceroy would enchant the ear of the emperor in far-off Peking with legends of great victories against the barbarian when in fact the barbarian was, as is his nature, playing the very devil. In 1958, the Great Leap Forward turned into a slapstick stumble largely because none dared tell the latest emperor that his new clothes were virtually nonexistent.

It is dangerous for a Chinese ambassador or agent overseas to present a score sheet that makes nonsense of Mao's ideological arithmetic. The ingratiating Chinese, ever moving with the current, is in any case inclined to tell a man what he thinks he would like to hear, rather than the unpalatable truth. And to his knack for tactful distortion may be added his isolation from the local facts of life. Even in an Asian capital only three or four officials in a Chinese embassy perhaps one hundred strong are allowed to meet the local overseas Chinese, let alone the natives—and then only within the precincts of the embassy itself. For his part, the senior Chinese dignitary cannot search out the truth for himself on his brief visits abroad. In consequence, Mr. Chou En-lai successfully antagonized the governments of Africa and the Arab world in 1965 by describing their countries as "ripe for revolution," and Peking was blarneyed by the Indonesian Communists into believing quite mistakenly that they were strong enough to seize power under President Sukarno. Yet the Chinese have still not escaped their self-induced illusions.

The man-eating tiger is lord of his jungle, but a tiger will throw away a chance of moving behind the victim he is stalking if this means that he would himself be upwind, for a tiger naturally credits a man with his own sense of smell. The Chinese Communists, authors of a Chinese revolution organized in entirely Chinese circumstances, seem to generalize irrationally from their particular experience and automatically suppose that the Malay and the Burmese, the Algerian and the Ghanaian will have similar ambitions and thought processes to their own, and will therefore at once applaud and emulate them. The Africans are supposed to agree that China can hammer the table and demand that they denounce American imperialism, and yet still claim that she is respecting their non-alignment and refraining from interference in the affairs of other countries. "The Chinese always have two policies," Ping once said. "One official and one black market." And everyone else is assumed to have the same split-level sense of reality.

But one must not make the reciprocal mistake of failing to study the tiger. He may have the instinctive arrogance of the

Anglo-Saxon in Asia, he may seem uncharacteristically impatient, a stupid brute whose aggressiveness is sometimes an unmitigated disaster to himself. Earlier Communist successes may also appear to have acted like a shot of LSD on that fatal confidence which in any case so easily persuades a Chinese that he can achieve all things, tricking Peking into such absurd aerial adventures as the Great Leap Forward without care for the Great Look Forward that should have preceded it. The intoxicating sense of power has doubtless been further accentuated by the acoustics of a closed China, in which every word of the leader is dutifully echoed by a chorus of cautious millions.

Chinese often see it otherwise, however. Mao is in a hurry, for this is the crucial period during which he must make his bid for supremacy, before Russian influence becomes so preponderant that China can only sink to the unthinkable position of ideological tributary. And, being the weakling, China must of course strike first. There is no time to plan a methodical, well-coordinated advance with both wings keeping pace with the center. China must make a dash for the high ground, using bold and risky tactics, and be ready to take casualties and withdraw temporarily when makeshift planning and hasty execution earn her a bloody nose.

At home, China tried to break even with the major powers by launching herself into the Great Leap Forward in agriculture and industry. The attempt failed miserably. But nothing venture, nothing gain. The Chinese did not die from it, they learned from it, and they recovered from it by their own unaided efforts. "When the enemy advances, I withdraw . . . When the enemy retreats, I pursue." The Chinese treat diplomacy as an extension of war. They carry on to the scarred field of international relations the flexible traditions of Chinese guerrilla strategy and Sun Wu's first rule: "All war is deception." Their success or failure must not be judged, therefore, by the distance they retreated yesterday but by the net advance they have made since last week. The gallant attempt to coerce all Afro-Asia into condemning the Americans was another Great Leap Forward that ended on the fence of African resentment, but there was always the possibility that it just might have cleared the top bar.

Meanwhile, the more the Russians are driven toward a fumbling handshake with the Americans, the Chinese calculate, the more Moscow's influence will wane in the ex-colonial outbacks of Africa and Asia, and in the international Communist movement. Furthermore, although China's belligerent and intransigent attitude may seem to encourage this undesirable liaison, it is in fact a clear warning to the Soviet Union that she cannot flirt too intimately with the United States without splitting the Communist world in two. On the other hand, if China, having adopted so hostile an attitude toward the Russians, were to stop pouting and crook her finger, Moscow would at once drop Washington in order to be reconciled with Peking, because for the Russians there could be no real choice between capitalist and Communist suitor. In any case, the Communist bloc would certainly snap down the middle if the Soviet Union rejected such an opportunity to reestablish international Marxist solidarity.

There is no real hazard in Peking's spit-in-your-eye stance toward both the United States and the Soviet Union, the Maoists argue, for this is a classic *Three Kingdoms* situation: no two states want to fight each other to the bitter end, for fear that both will be crippled and the third will emerge as the real victor. The possibility that either the United States or the Soviet Union will attack China is regarded as remote, even if it cannot be completely ignored. Scoffing at the timidities of the "revisionists," therefore, hard-line Chinese Communists feel that they enjoy their favorite guerrilla advantage of extreme flexibility and are now the real masters of the situation. They can push matters as far and as hard as they like, or they can relax pressure, or they can even drop their dispute with Moscow entirely at any time.

It is, however, no coincidence that in the postwar era China should have reacted sharply to the "imperialist threat" in Korea and Vietnam, for these have been the buffers of the empire since the days of Han Wu-ti, and China's strongest reflex is still pro-

voked by tapping a defensive nerve more than two thousand
years old. To fear of the barbarian is added hatred of the "imperialist," so that today the United States is China's archenemy
twice over, and her strategy is primarily directed toward evicting
the Americans from their crescent of military bases and Asian
alliances around her. China in the role of Liang Shan Po is not
simply a political image to Mao but a topographical reality.
China's distances and China's masses combine to re-create the
vast stronghold around whose marshy and mountainous fringes
any invading army will flounder to its end. If the Americans attack, they will be "drowned in a great sea" of hostile Chinese.
Even if they use nuclear weapons, they will find that in war man
by the millions is the master of the megaton, the Maoists say.

This is the nub of the matter. Communist China, while still
adolescent as a nuclear power, has been created from a small and
wretched band of peasants and dissident soldiers inspired by the
spirit and the strategy of a venerable tradition of revolt. Rich in
men but poor in missiles, China shrugs on with an easy sense of
illusory comfort the military dogma which lays down that the
guerrilla fighting on his home ground is invincible. The Chinese
will close in on any invader so that he cannot kill their soldiers
without killing his own. Generations of secret societies with
names from the Chinese spectrum—Red Eyebrows, Yellow Turbans, White Lotus—have flung themselves against a well-armed
enemy, believing themselves equipped with a spiritual power
that would turn aside steel or—in the case of the Boxers—bullets.
Today, the Communists preach, the underweaponed Chinese soldier and militiaman are armed with the magic Thought of Mao.
It is this that will conquer the American imperialist without and
the treacherous bourgeois instinct within. A well-governed people
will "fight with sticks against sharp weapons," said Mencius. Belief and the bayonet beat the bomb.

It all sounds a most monstrous deception—except, perhaps, to
those who remember what they felt when they were bedded
down in a ditch on the coast of Kent in June 1940 with a Lewis

gun of World War I vintage (28 stoppages), and told to hold
England against Hitler's hordes. Victory was, in fact, unquestion-
able.

Peking etches its own perspective into the minds of young men
with outmoded machine guns who are ready to face the well-
preserved American bogy. For the corollary of Peking's contempt
for foreign opinion is Peking's concern for that of the ignorant,
patient, cautious, enigmatic, complaisant, cunning, yet amor-
phous 700-million-strong jury in China, which, like the College of
Cardinals in Rome, disposes of the Mandate of Heaven.

35

Mao Tzu

Mao Tse-tung does not struggle against his countrymen's sense of history. He moves with it, manipulating them through its flow. His policies, therefore, have been partly dictated by his constant care to present himself to the Chinese millions in the image of the recognizable Chinese hero. Cunning and unpredictable as Chu-ko Liang in his masterly strategies, a bold yet enigmatic dreamer like the peasant leaders of all great Chinese revolutions, he too descended from the misty mountains to change Heaven's Mandate. The scholar-poet with sword in hand, he championed the oppressed, treated his followers fair, and "made a noise in the east, while attacking in the west." Between swimming the Yangtze and penning poems in Peking, Mao has also remained for millions of his admirers that legendary Chinese figure, the infallible old fox.

He is, moreover, the emperor at the apex of the new Communist world, the vicar on earth of the new cosmic principle of Marxism-Leninism which orders the universe. In the best tradition of the Confucian ruler, he sets his people a good example, living a healthy and frugal life, and treating all with wisdom and fatherly understanding. His propagandists depict him as one whose word is gospel on every subject, from eating pounded chilies to economic theory, and when he wields a pick-ax during the excavation of the Ming tombs near Peking, "the great earth itself trembles." He is, in fact, the latest of a long line of Chinese supermen.

For two millennia the wide-angle lens of Chinese loyalty has focused on the ruler rather than the state, Confucian culture rather than the nation. Mao's Cult of the Personality therefore has an objective purpose no more pernicious than the idealization of a British queen as Monarch and Defender of the Faith. Where men formerly looked up to the emperor, they now look up to the seventy-three-year-old leader who swam nine miles in sixty-five minutes; where formerly they were urged to study the Classics as their unerring guide to correct living, today they are urged to study the *Thought of Mao Tse-tung*. This Thought of Mao makes the rice boil faster, is good for burns, increases the harvest, keeps the road-accident rate down, wins international ping-pong matches, and "changes heaven and earth." It is "the moral atomic bomb which our side alone possesses." Where Confucius advocated "li," Mao advocates Marxist-Leninist dialectics, and where the Confucians harked back to a golden age of sage-kings, Mao's historical materialism harks back to that golden age of communal freedom which, so Marx declared, preceded the era of slavery. It remains to be seen whether despotic abuses will be perpetrated in the sacred name of Maoism as they were perpetrated in the sacred name of Confucianism, once Mao also is conveniently dead.

To the Western observer, with his inflexible dogma of liberalism, China often appears as a monstrous empire of blue ants in which the crushed, terrified, half-starved millions crawl through their bitter days, wistfully dreaming of democracy. But that is not necessarily the view from the other side of the looking glass. China owes her very birth to the iron tyranny of Ch'in. The Chinese have long since resigned themselves to the fact that Confucian government-by-goodness is only practicable in a state so large when it is liberally dosed with dictatorship. Centuries ago, an autocratic Confucianism became sacrosanct state dogma, popular religion was despised as the opiate of the people, there was no true intellectual liberty, and dangerous deviations could be punished under the law. An often fanatically sectarian Board of Censors checked the activities of the mandarinate itself, much as the Control Commission of a Communist Party checks its officials and cadres. In short, the Chinese race-memory is restricted to a system in which an indoctrinated elite rules the country in accordance with an authoritarian ideology which in turn is founded on a "universal truth."

It can be fairly objected that the Chinese do not like "isms" or extreme solutions, and look askance at the inflexible doctrine that claims to be right in all circumstances. It was because they had an instinctive trust in the idea of humanistic, "reasonable" government that they so hastily discarded Mo Tzu. "My teachings are enough for every purpose," declared that hair-shirted bigot. "To try to refute my words is like throwing eggs at a rock. One may use up all the eggs in the world, but the rock remains the same." Mao sometimes sounds like Mo Tzu, and like Mo Tzu he preaches a somewhat joyless austerity that barks Chinese shins. But two millennia of intermittent turbulence and tyranny have intervened since Mo Tzu spoke, and the Chinese have learned to settle for less than the right to throw eggs. Four out of every five of Mao's charges are poor peasants who will quite happily accept an "ism" for the sake of peace and quiet. Their farming forefathers, who overthrew Ch'in and every decadent dynasty thereafter as if they were sorting out rotten fruit, were not the enemies of despotism but of its abuse. They did not demand democracy but a square deal. Mao has in any case turned upon them their own cherished hatred of government by making his a "government of the people," so that although the emperor may have derived his divine right from heaven, Mao derives his from the masses.

And they have reason to applaud him. Mao Tse-tung and his philosophy rescued their country from the knacker's yard of nations and the insults of a century. They united China under strong centralized government, poured new vigor into her arteries, gave her the face lift she so pitifully needed, and purged her of many ugly impurities. Today the foreigners have gone and all is now in Chinese hands. This is a wonder in itself.

Nor are they so disconcerted as a Western community might be by Mao's sweeping policy of socialization. They have heard all the arguments before. In 81 B.C. the pro-capitalist faction was already complaining that iron implements made in state foundries were dearer and of poorer quality than those turned out by private enterprise. The assembly belt was known in communally operated porcelain factories nearly four hundred years ago (the last man in the line adding the Chinese characters on the bottom of the pots that tell the reign and date of manufacture), and the "Yellow Turbans" organized "people's communes" some fourteen hundred years before that. Confucius and Mencius condemned "exploitation of the masses," and all early twentieth-century revolutionary leaders equated capitalism with foreign imperialism, so that not only the Communists but the Kuomintang pledged themselves to a policy of nationalization. Mao has in fact turned back to the Imperial system under which the Chinese state always ran the basic industries and essential transport services.

Meanwhile, there is nothing dismayingly unfamiliar to a Chinese about the Communist legal and police methods that seem so nightmarish to queasy Anglo-Saxons. He is accustomed to a law that protects the state rather than himself, and if he must suffer the importunities of the Chinese security police, he is at least spared the depredations of secret-society thugs. Mo Tzu advocated a system of "reporting good and evil to superiors," under which groups of families would be mutually responsible for each other and obliged to denounce each other's crimes or pain of dire collective punishment. It was to be expected that the Ch'in Legalists would also employ this formula (just as they stipulated that not more than five people might foregather); but even thirteen centuries after the First Emperor died, the "progressist" Wang An-shih introduced a "tithing scheme" whereby families were organized into units of ten, fifty, and five hundred. All members of these units were responsible not only for the crimes of any single member but for those committed by any strangers, relatives, or guests who happened to be among them at the time. Both the Manchu dynasty and the Kuomintang reinstituted this unamiable arrangement—the KMT confining it to areas suspected of being heavily infiltrated by the Communists. The Chinese, therefore, accept Mao's egalitarian spy system within which everyone informs on everyone else. Furthermore, a people whose books have been repeatedly proscribed and burned in the course of a long literary history do not necessarily object to Communist censorship any more violently than Roman Catholics object to the Index.

"Good government does not hold the people so firmly as good education," said Mencius. "Good government gains their wealth, good education their hearts." To the Chinese, who invented both paper and printing, propaganda and indoctrination are the devil they know only too well. Chanted slogans and mechanical responses, memorizing by rote and the reiterative skills of the parrot and the cuckoo, rewritten history and literature, and deer-is-horse brainwashing—the Chinese have long since had to learn to live with these. They do not think it curious if the government advises them that tadpoles make good contraceptives, for the information is derived from traditional Chinese medicine. Nor do they smirk if they are told that the Chinese first discovered America about fifteen hundred years ago, and "this shows that there has been a long traditional friendship between our two *peoples*," for they are a little hazy about the history of the Devil's Own Country anyway.

They glumly watched the fatal imbecilities of the Great Leap Forward and suffered the terrible years of hardship that followed, yet they quietly heard out the country's leading statistician when he excused his pipe-dream production figures by declaring that the proper purpose of his department was to "fully utilize statistical data to reflect great successes." They have seen overenthusiastic party cadres drive roads "straight as an arrow" through houses and cross rich fields, and others so inspired by the national appeal to make back-yard pig-iron in the villages that they decimated the chicken population in order to get feathers for primitive forge fans. They may resent the innumerable political meetings they have to attend, but they are not going to start a revolution over any of these things. For they can count their blessings.

Soldiers are disciplined, taxation is equitable, a man can eat at least two meals—if frugal ones—each day. There is work for all, and there are schools for the children. The establishment of the Communist regime followed half a century of division, unrest, and disaster. Today most people have food and security and the inalienable right to dream, and this at once means that far more than half of the families of China are better off than they were before the Communist conquest. For the time being at least, the Chinese are thankful for small mercies and are prepared to live by rice alone.

"You can kill a Chinese peasant by letting him sit down," says an old proverb. This has been the measure of his misery. Chinese may not like sleeping in factory dormitories, or feeding with strangers, or putting their children in crèches, or public confession, any more than would a European—but the European never had to sell his children to buy his next meal. It is not poverty that is to be feared, said the sages, but the imbalance between riches and poverty. The Chinese looks around at his fellow men and is ready to tighten his belt and face adversity cheerfully enough with the rest. The formerly landless peasant does not feel his lack of land; the gregarious Chinese with his crowding family does not recoil as violently as an Anglo-Saxon from communal living; and the man who can sleep on a wooden bench while three transistor radios are playing simultaneously in a Chinatown shop can stand loudspeakers incessantly blaring Communist propaganda and viciously scratched recordings of second-rate martial music, without becoming insane or insomniac.

The Communists have denounced family love as a form of exploitation ("Parents treat children as capital assets: children wait for their parents to die in order to inherit unearned income"), sons have been set to spy on fathers, men are encouraged to accept sterilization, and newlyweds are sternly enjoined not to think in terms of more than two children. Families are split up, and the student-sons are sent to till the land, or even to play pioneer in virgin fringe country a thousand miles from home. The older Chinese expert may raise his hands in horror at this blasphemous assault upon the sacred family system and predict an explosion. But by the end of 1966 that still had not come, because although millions of Chinese, especially among the older generation, may be deeply distressed by all this modern pekinoiserie, they balance it against the assets and decide there is no reason to riot. The Chinese family was in any case never permanently united. The children of the semi-serfs in the villages were often sold to distant households or were forced to set out to make their way in life independently. In the bigger families the sons left to take their examinations for the mandarinate, the daughters were married off elsewhere, the scholar-officials were sent to distant posts for years on end—or even exiled, if they were in the wrong faction. In later centuries Chinese emigrated to America and Britain, to Singapore and other centers in Southeast Asia. Those that remained behind were content as long as they had food and clothes and shelter. They might be sentimental, emotional, maternal, but they were not people who could afford frills and furbelows on their feelings, and they had always had to learn to make do with memories most of the time.

The women of Communist China stand arms akimbo and argue whether their life should be in the factory or in the home. None really believed that the "Saturday Night System" introduced in 1958, whereby all the women in a workers' dormitory would stay out late except the one whose husband was coming to visit her, was precisely glamorous. But many welcome a collective life that enables them to dump their children in a day nursery, and no girl wants to go back to bound feet and a baby every year. Communist China has given equality to women, and freedom from their parents to the young. And both like it.

The father may not. But since his son is taken away from him, his prejudices are not passed on so easily, and meanwhile a counterblast of Communist indoctrination is filling the ears of the boy in his new communal surroundings of school, university, farm, or factory. Both he and his father are being urged to opt for a three-pound cremation rather than a fancy Chinese funeral; to abandon the bourgeois, reactionary superstitions of the past like Buddhism or belief in the Kitchen God; to marry without fussy ceremony, dowry, or betrothal gift—and above all without wasting time and money on feasts, ceremonies, or capitalistic honeymoons.

The strength of Chinese traditional customs and prejudices may nevertheless be judged by the very weight of the Communist attacks upon them. The son is being warned against the dangers of Western influence, against winkle-pickers, tight trousers, pointed shoes, loafing, spending, underworking and overplaying, and thinking anything other than the Thought of Mao Tse-tung. For while the old may cling tenaciously to their customs, the young are—equally inconveniently—like the young everywhere. Some are ready to give wholehearted loyalty to their country and Party, are content to do what others do and only ask not to be sent too far away, but others dream of Beatle haircuts, a bulging bank balance, and a bookcase full of "poisoned weeds." Few of these children of the individualistic and go-head "Jews of Asia" yearn for private enterprise on a grand scale, however. The mercantile tradition is not universal. The poor of China never had enough money to run more than the market sidelines in vegetables, poultry, and pigs that they are allowed to start up after the failure of the Great Leap Forward.

On the other hand, the mutual-aid tradition of the Chinese anti-state, with its clans, its guilds, and its village associations, fits the Chinese admirably for their new world of trade unions and Party cells. Mao's problem has in fact been to transfer the hierarchical loyalty of the Chinese for his family and his closed club to the new network of the Party and to the equally sealed society of the Communist master-nation. A similar problem taxed the imagination of the Legalists and even of Confucius, who regarded virtue within the family as no more than a pilot scheme for virtue beyond it. In theory, Mao should succeed where they failed, for the extended family and the clan were founded on property and self-protection more than on love. Take away the property, prove that the state itself will protect the individual, and the clan begins to crumble like any other anachronistic castle.

However, the more that man is nationalized, the greater the danger that many Chinese will not serve the state but simply switch their loyalty from their families to themselves. It is one thing to strike the gyves from the ankles of a prisoner, another to serve him with a call-up notice after he has tasted the sweets of freedom. The very success of Mao's first Communist revolution, which rescued the poorer peasant from semi-slavery, in itself discredits a second Communist revolution thrust upon millions who by now have far more to lose than their chains.

Long before the "Great Proletarian Cultural Revolution" of 1966, Mao Tse-tung told foreigners of his private fears that "goulash Communists" inspired by revisionist ideas (peaceful coexistence with the capitalists, and a pragmatic approach that puts gracious living now before glory later) might be preponderant among the new generation of Chinese cadres that had seen nothing of the blood-and-iron revolution of his guerrillas or the "Long March" to Yenan. He admitted in 1964 that he doubted whether he and his old-guard contemporaries had any trustworthy heirs who would carry on the class struggle, firmly keeping the world divided into two rather than reconciling the two worlds of Liang Shan Po and corrupt imperialism so that they became one.

Counterbalancing the sectarian visionaries who hold out for permanent world revolution, and who put face and dogma before the practical advantages of compromise, there have always been the Chinese pragmatists who directly identified these inconveniently live prophets with dead loss, and who put sound economic development before crash socialization. Mao may believe that bold, aggressive tactics and mobilization of the millions are universal principles, as infallible in all fields today as they proved in the guerrilla struggle which he waged from the caves of Yenan some thirty years ago. But the Chinese Communist Party is shot through with seams of revisionist leaders and cadres who think that to continue to direct the Chinese revolution on an anachronistic basis of troglodyte Trotskyism is, as Han Fei said, to neglect the crops and stand beside the tree in the hope that a second rabbit will knock itself out against it. To them, Mao's revolutionary conservatism seems to add him to that long line of venerable Chinese philosophers who harked back to the "good old days" for their inspiration—in his case, the "good old days" of Yenan.

And they have had heavy weapons to hand to give firepower to their attacks: they could point to the catastrophic failure of the Great Leap Forward at home, to the collapse of China's militant foreign policy abroad, to her isolation not only from the rest of the world but also from her comrade states in the Communist camp, and notably to the disastrous effects of quarreling with the Soviet Union. To their chorus of objections could be added the voices of the professional soldiers who did not regard the human sea as the answer to the H-bomb, and who wanted Moscow's modern weapons more than the Mao Tse-tung's Thought.

The Emperor Han Kao-tsu once derided scholarship by scoffing: "I won the world on horseback, not by reading books." "Yes, but can you rule it from horseback?" came the swift retort—a retort that first inspired the prototype of what was to become the great Chinese mandarinate of scholar-officials. But whereas Han Kao-tsu acknowledged that war and peace were two different things, Mao seemingly did not. Instead, true to his instinct for unconstitutional action, he mounted a second revolution—the classic Chinese remedy for a problem that had once again been allowed to grow too big. But this time it was a revolution against his pragmatical, revisionist critics in the Central and Provincial Committees of his own Party. The natural allies of these "mandarins" were the younger officials who believed that the primary business of the Communist state was to provide them with better food, better homes, and better jobs. Their mass support came, in turn, from the sort of peasants who have been quoted as saying: "So long as we have grain, cash, and work points, everything is going fine . . . But politics is just beating air with air. Rather than waste good time on this, let us take the manure down to the fields."

The great witch hunt for "anti-Mao" intellectuals that began in 1966 was directed against a deeper resistance to the revolution, however. Almost the first victim was the playwright Wu Han, who was caught covertly criticizing the evils of contemporary government by dramatizing events under other dynasties, in the best tradition of the Chinese political satirist. Wu Han's play, *Hai Jui Dismissed from Office*, tells how a benevolent sixteenth-century mandarin returned to the peasants property that had been filched from them—and was made to suffer for it. The sinful implication that land should be given back to the peasants was crime enough to the Communists, but worse was the heretical suggestion that a bourgeois mandarin could act altruistically: a typical Chinese pragmatist, he was only trying to placate the underdog in order to perpetuate the privileged position of the overdog.

But beyond the bludgeoning of Wu Han in the foreground, the Communists said, all China lay locked in battle against Chinese Communism's greatest enemy: the humanistic Confucian principle that all men are fundamentally similar. For Mao preaches the inequality of man, that only the poor are honest fellows, and that to treat the rest as if they were entitled to the same rights would be to abandon the class struggle which is the very motive power of the revolution. The Maoists are therefore bent upon destroying the whole strain of Chinese scholarship that harbors this heresy, by sending the intellectuals into the factories and farms, and crossing them with the peasant mind much as emperors were crossed with plebeian concubines. They were submitting them to the purifying sheep-dip of "proletarian wisdom" at grass-root level in the hope of reproducing a new, hybrid mentality sweaty with socialism and feeding on "isms" rather than ethics. For Mao is essentially a man for masses—like the masses of anonymous, dedicated peasants who constituted the friendly water through which the sleek, sudden fish of his guerrilla armies first cleaved. To him the farmer, the worker, the soldier are the heroes; the ivory-tower intellectual, the "expert" and "technician," the villains.

The Chinese—ill-treated over the centuries, shy and cautious in the presence of a new, stern master—are still of uncertain temper. Democracy and the West they reject, but the uncompromising offer of Communism still sets them mentally dodging and skulking. They owe so much to Mao in so many ways, and yet they know that China has recovered her economic poise since the disastrous days of the Great Leap Forward not because socialist principle was upheld but because Peking permitted a heretical lapse into capitalism and peasants were allowed to organize their own private bits of business in the hitherto rigidly regimented People's Communes.

Hang a cage of Java sparrows on a tree, and while those inside will struggle to get out, those outside will struggle to get in at the food. Chinese youth overseas may clamor for Chinese Communism, but Chinese youth at home may one day ask whether the seed is worth the cage. Their ancestors married an ostensibly humanistic Confucian state to inflexible Legalist laws. Their descendants may marry an ostensibly inflexible Communist sectarianism to the profitable principles of pragmatism. As the old guard of Chinese revolutionaries dies off, its successors may betray Mao in the name of Mao, as their forebears betrayed Confucius in the name of Confucius, and China shake down into a new, more comfortable relationship with the capitalist half.

These were the dangers—dangers not of detonation but of dilution—that provoked the "Great Proletarian Cultural Revolution" and threw up the teenage Red Guards in 1966. The mob action of the Red Guards in publicly attacking all that was foreign, bourgeois, traditional, revisionist, or just pre-Mao, served two purposes: it provided an aphrodisiac for a sagging revolution and at the same time it struck a sudden daunting blow at the springy resistance to Mao's messianic Communism offered by people who have throughout history preferred coin in the hand to credit in some future heaven, Marxist or otherwise. "Power comes out of barrel of the guns." Mao himself, observing with some distress his own failing faculties mirrored in a wasting revisionism, may have seen as the obvious instrument for his second revolution the strong, armed, and indoctrinated Chinese army under the relatively youthful Marshal Lin Piao. From this, the concept of the militant Red Guards as the political shock troops and vigilantes defending Maoism is only one move to a man who thinks always in terms of the "mass line." In turn, their vigorous purification of an afflicted land might prepare the way for China's final communization before his death.

It might not, however. Lin Piao emerged in 1966 as Mao's heir apparent, but although he was ostensibly the most faithful exponent of Maoism, this might mean nothing. Neither Lin nor any other man could seize the effective leadership of the new mass revolution in China and put himself at the head of the Red Guards except as the champion of Mao's Thought. But once Mao has been not only glorified and canonized but also solemnly embalmed, his words will be open to new interpretations as other leaders, perhaps Lin Piao the first among them, swing China gently on to a fresh course. For the bourgeois instinct is like thrombosis, essentially a threat to the middle-aged. As a Communist state loses its youthful vigor, puts on weight, prospers, and settles down to a more sedentary political life within the community of nations, it becomes prey to this ill which is so derided when young. China found her own road to Communism: she will doubtless find her own road to revisionism, too.

But meanwhile there are two hazards. The first is that Mao's second revolution, which has provoked much cold resentment and some hot-blooded resistance, may be manipulated by leaders who lack the characteristic understanding shown by the illustrious old guerrilla himself, when he enjoins the overeager Red Guards to struggle against the revisionist enemy "not with coercion or force, but with reasoning." The second is that arthritic age may also have impaired Mao's own cental flexibility, the talent for "conforming like water to the ground" that has been the secret of his success.

Mao has in the past been a specialist in solving "contradictions," an advocate of exhaustive debate, of arguing everything out, so that no one is theoretically more alien to the blind worship of the "Thought of Mao Tse-tung" than Mao Tse-tung himself. No one has been more bitter than he in denouncing the "spontaneous capitalistic tendencies" which the Chinese millions so happily redisplay, but while he may have tried to thrust them forward suddenly toward ultimate Communism, he has always been ready to draw back when he felt resistance to be ominously strong, to retreat one pace now in order to advance two paces in the future.

The peace and unity of China have depended upon this sensitivity, this instinct for keeping the last straw in hand. For Mao and his successors face their most formidable and enigmatic challenge in the Chinese masses, who know how to bide their time and to dissemble under pressure in obedience to the same rules that Mao so well understands himself. If he has stripped their "face" from them, it has been very often to leave an unreadable blank or a baffling mask of acquiescence, the visage of a smiling land in which rice-Marxism is as common as genuine piety.

Mao the Master in Peking must always remember the great gallery of Chinese rebels whose latest portrait is that of Mao the "bandit" of Chingkangshan. This is his private looking glass. Han Fei wrote: "The beast called the dragon can be tamed and trained to the point where you may ride on its back. But on the underside of its throat it has scales a foot across that curl back from the body, and anyone who brushes against them is sure to die." Han Fei was speaking metaphorically of the Chinese ruler, but the Chinese ruler is and has always been, in the last analysis, the Chinese people. Today Chinese still quote with reverence the sayings of sages like Kung Fu Tzu (Confucius), Meng Tzu (Mencius), and Lao Tzu (Laocius), who lived long before Christ. The measure of Mao's success in riding the docile yet dangerous Chinese dragon will be whether men still quote Mao Tzu (Maocius?) a thousand years hence.

The Cast

(in order of appearance)

The Legendary Period

Emperor Fu Hsi	The Trigrams discovered (?)
Emperor Shen Nung	Founder of medicine
The Yellow Emperor	Founder of Chinese civilization
Emperor Yao	
Emperor Shun	The Golden Age
Emperor Yü, who founds:	

The Hsia Dynasty   c.1990–1557 B.C.

The Shang Dynasty   c.1557–1050 B.C.

The Chou Dynasty (feudal)   1050–221 B.C.   Divided into:
Early Chou   1050–722 B.C.
          841 B.C.   History accurately dated from here on

Spring and Autumn   722–481 B.C.   Age of chivalry

Duke of Sung   650 B.C.
King of Yüeh defeats Wu   500 B.C.
Confucius   551–479 B.C.
Mo Tzu   500–420 B.C.

Warring States   481–221 B.C.
                    The "Hundred Schools of Philosophy"

Strategist Wu Ch'i executed   381 B.C.
Sun Wu: "The Art of War"   c.350 B.C.

417

Shan Yang killed   338 B.C.

Lao Tzu   4th century B.C. (?)

Chuang Tzu   4th century B.C.

Lieh Tzu   4th century B.C. (?)

Chü Yüan: banished   295 B.C.

Hsün Tzu   298–238 B.C.

Han Fei: died   233 B.C.

Li Ssu   280–208 B.C.

Ching K'o's assassination attempt   227 B.C.

King of Ch'in overruns all six states of China   229–221 B.C.

The Ch'in Dynasty   221–207 B.C.

China united under the First Emperor

Kao, the blind lute player, fails to kill the emperor

The burning of the books

The Great Wall Built   214 B.C.

Liu Pang (future Emperor Han Kao-tzu) leads
      rebellion   209 B.C.

Han Hsin fights with back to the river

The Han Dynasty   206 B.C.–A.D. 220 Founded by:

Emperor Han Kao-tsu   206–195 B.C.

Emperor Hun Wu-ti   141–86 B.C.

Chang Ch'ien's mission to the west   138 B.C.

Li Kuang-li marches 2,000 miles to attack Ferghana

Ssu-ma Ch'ien compiles *Historical Records*

Li Ling captured by the Huns   99 B.C.

Imperial concubine Wang Ch'ao Chün married off
      to the Hun king   33 B.C

Red Eyebrows revolt, usurper Wang Mang deposed   A.D. 25

Pan Chao sets out for Central Asia   A.D. 73

The Yellow Turbans revolt   A.D. 184

The Three Kingdoms   221–A.D. 265

Chu-ko Liang (and the King of the Mans)

Ts'ao Ts'ao

Kuan Yü (God of War)

Liu Pei

Dr. Hua To

The Western Tsin Dynasty   265–317

The North and South Empires   317–589
Hsieh Ho lays down rules of painting   5th century

The Sui Dynasty   589–618
The Grand Canal is constructed
General Mu Lan turns out to be Miss Hua (?)

The T'ang Dynasty   618–907   Golden Age of Poetry
Hsüan Tsang's pilgrimage to India   7th century
Empress Wu   *b.* 625   *d.* 705
Minister Ti Jen-chieh (Judge Dee)   *d.* 700
Emperor Huang Ming acquires mistress Yang Kuei-fei   745
The Poets: Li Po   701–761
Po Chü-i   772–846
Tibetans capture Chinese capital at Ch'ang An   763
Han Yü   768–824
The poetess Yü Hsüan-chi is decapitated   *c.* 870

The Five Dynasties   906–960

The Sung Dynasty   960–1127   Great Age of Painting
Wang An-shih introduces economic reforms   1068

*The Partition between Kin (in North) and Southern
Sung Dynasties*   1127–1279
Hangchow at the height of its fame
Chu Hsi, neo-Confucianist   1129–1200
White Lotus Society appears   *c.*1250

Mongol (Yüan) Dynasty, of Kublai Khan (non-chinese)   1280–1368
The rise of the theater
Marco Polo in China
Lo Kuan-chung writes
Romance of the Three Kingdoms   1364 (?)

The Ming Dynasty   1368–1644   The novel comes into its own
Admiral Cheng Ho sails to Africa   15th century
Shih Nai-an writes *Shui Hu Chuan*
(Men of the Marshes)   14th century

Wu Ch'eng-en writes *Journey to the West* ("Monkey")   *c.* 1580
Chin P'ing Mei appears
The Jesuit Matteo Ricci arrives in Peking   1601
Captain Weddell arrives off Canton   1637
General Wu San-kuei and the Lady Ch'en   1644
Li Tzu-ch'eng captures Peking   1644
The Manchus take over   1644

The Manchu Dynasty (non-Chinese)   1644–1911
General Shih K'o-fa defies the Manchus   1645
Shao Lin monastery burned: the birth of the Triad   1670–1700
Captain Anson at Canton   1742
Wu Ching-tzu writes *The Scholars*   *c.*1750
Tsao Hsüeh-chin writes *The Dream of the Red Chamber*   1791
Lord Macartney sees the emperor   1793
Lord Amherst fails to see the emperor   1816
Empress Tzu Hsi born   1835
The Opium Wars   1840–1842
Grand Secretary Ki Shen dismissed   1840
The Defense of T'ing Hai   1841
Treaty of Nanking: Hong Kong ceded to Britain   1842
Taiping Rebellion   1850–1864
Lord Elgin burns the Summer Palace   1860
Treaty of Tientsin: China opened to the West   1860
Boxer Rebellion   1899–1900
International relief force takes Peking   1900
Dowager-Empress Tzu Hsi dies   1908
The Revolution: Sun Yat-sen is first president   1911
The Manchus abdicate   1912

The Chinese Republic   1912–1949
Yüan Shih-kai assassinated   1916
The warlord era   to 1927
Kuomintang and Communists collaborate   1924
Sun Yat-sen dies, Chiang Kai-shek inherits   1925
Chiang Kai-shek marches north to unify the country   1927
Chiang breaks with Communists   1927
Mao Tse-tung to Chingkangshan   1927
The Long March   1934–1935

Revolutionary author Lu Hsün dies   1936
Sino-Japanese War   1937–1945   (Hsüeh Yüeh holds Changsha)
The Communists overrun China, Chiang withdraws
    to Formosa   1949

The People's Republic of China   since 1949
    The Great Leap Forward   1958
    Mao breaks with Khrushchev   1958–1959
    The prima donna Mei Lan Fang dies aged 68   1961
    China attacks India   1962
    The "Great Cultural Revolution"   1966

Bibliography

PHILOSOPHY

The Chinese Classics, tr. James Legge, Oxford University Press, New York.
　Volume One: The Confucian Analects. The Great Learning. The Doctrine of the Mean.
　Volume Two: The Works of Mencius.
　Volume Three: The Book of Historical Documents (Book of History).
　Volume Four: The Book of Poetry (Book of Odes).
　Volume Five: The Ch'un Ts'ew. The Tso Chuen.
Confucius and the Chinese Way, by H. G. Creel. Harper & Row, New York; Peter Smith, Gloucester, Mass.
Chinese Thought, by H. G. Creel. University of Chicago Press, Chicago.
Three Ways of Thought in Ancient China, by Arthur Waley. Barnes & Noble, New York.
The Story of Chinese Philosophy, by Ch'u Chai. Washington Square Press, New York.
A Short History of Confucian Philosophy, by Liu Wu-chi. Dell, New York.
Chuang Tzu, tr. Burton Watson. Columbia University Press, New York.
Han Fei Tzu, tr. Burton Watson. Columbia University Press, New York.
Mo Tzu, tr. Burton Watson. Columbia University Press, New York.
Hsün Tzu, tr. Burton Watson. Columbia University Press, New York.
The Book of Lieh Tzu, tr. A. C. Graham, Paragon, New York.
The Sayings of Lao Tzu, tr. Lionel Giles. Paragon, New York.

The Way of Zen, Alan W. Watts. Pantheon, New York.

The Book of Change, tr. John Blofeld. Dutton, New York.

HISTORICAL CHINA

Records of the Grand Historian of China, tr. from the *Shih Chi* of Ssu-ma Chien by Burton Watson, Vols. 1 & 2. Columbia University Press, New York.

China: A Short Cultural History, by C. P. Fitzgerald. Praeger, New York.

A History of China, by Wolfram Eberhard. University of California Press, Berkeley.

A Short History of the Chinese People, by Luther Goodrich. Harper & Row, New York.

Europe and China, by G. F. Hudson. Beacon Press, Boston.

Lord Macartney's Embassy to Peking in 1793, from official Chinese Documents, tr. J. L. Cranmer-Byng. University of Hong Kong.

The Travels of Marco Polo, tr. Ronald E. Latham. Penguin, Baltimore.

The Tiger of Ch'in, by Leonard Cottrell. Holt, Rinehart & Winston, New York.

The First Holy One, by Maurice Collis. Faber and Faber, London.

The Empress Wu, by C. P. Fitzgerald. F. W. Cheshire, Melbourne.

Daily Life in China, by Jacques Gernet. George Allen and Unwin Ltd., London.

The Great Within, by Maurice Collis. Faber and Faber, London.

Foreign Mud, by Maurice Collis. Faber and Faber, London.

The Opium War through Chinese Eyes, by Arthur Waley. Dufour Editions, Chester Springs, Pa.

The Last of the Empresses, by Daniele Varé. Transatlantic Arts, New York.

The Siege at Peking, by Peter Fleming. Harper & Row, New York.

China's Courts and Concubines, by Bernard Llewellyn. George Allen and Unwin Ltd., London.

MILITARY

The Art of War, by Sun Tzu, tr. Samuel B. Griffith. The Clarendon Press, Oxford.

A Military History of Modern China, by F. F. Liu. Princeton University Press, Princeton.

The Red Army of China, by Edgar O'Ballance. Praeger, New York.

Selected Military Writings of Mao Tse-tung. Foreign Languages Press, Peking.

Mao Tse-tung: Strategic Problems in the Anti-Japanese Guerrilla War. Foreign Languages Press, Peking.

MODERN HISTORY

Revolution in China, by C. P. Fitzgerald. Cresset Press, London.

The Chinese Revolution, by Tibor Mende. Thames and Hudson, London.

A History of Modern China, by Kenneth Scott Latourette. Penguin Books, Harmondsworth, England.

Chinese Communism and the Rise of Mao, by Benjamin I. Schwartz. Harvard University Press, Cambridge, Mass.

Selected Works of Mao Tse-tung. Foreign Languages Press, Peking.

A Decade of Mao's China. The Perennial Press, Bombay.

Red Star over China, by Edgar Snow. Grove Press, New York.

The Other Side of the River, by Edgar Snow. Random House, New York.

THE ARTS

A History of Chinese Literature, by Herbert A. Giles. Frederick Ungar, New York.

Yuan Mei, by Arthur Waley. Macmillan, New York.

170 Chinese Poems, tr. Arthur Waley. Constable and Co., London.

A Lute of Jade, ed. J. L. Cranmer-Byng. Paragon Press, New York.

Three Hundred Poems of the T'ang Dynasty. Lien Yi Company, Hong Kong.

Tu Fu: Selected Poems, tr. Rewi Alley. Foreign Languages Press, Peking.

Poems from China, tr. Wong Man. Hong Kong Classical Translations Society, Hong Kong.

The Way of Chinese Painting, by Mai-mai Sze. Alfred A. Knopf, New York.

The Flight of the Dragon, by Laurence Binyon. Paragon Press, New York.

Peking Opera, by Rewi Alley. New World Press, Peking.

THE SCIENCES

Science and Civilisation in China, Volumes 1, 2, 3, 4(1) and 4(2), by Joseph Needham. Cambridge University Press, New York.

Notes on the Chinese Drugs Used as Cancer Remedy, by Professor Hsu-Yun-tsi'ao. Reprinted from the *Journal of South-east Asia Researches,* Hong-Kong, 1965.

Chinese Therapeutical Methods of Acupuncture and Moxibustion. Foreign Languages Press, Peking.

FICTION

The Romance of the Three Kingdoms, by Lo Kuan-chung, tr. C. H. Brewitt-Taylor. Charles E. Tuttle, Rutland, Vermont.

The Water Margin (Men of the Marshes) by Shih Nai-an, tr. J. H. Jackson. The Commercial Press Ltd., Hong Kong. Also Paragon Press, New York.

All Men are Brothers (Men of the Marshes) by Shih Nai-an, tr. Pearl Buck. Methuen and Co., London.

The Scholars, by Wu Ching-tzu, tr. Yang Hsien-yi and Gladys Yang. Foreign Languages Press, Peking.

Monkey, by Wu Ch'eng-en, tr. Arthur Waley. Grove Press, New York.

The True Story of Ah Q, by Lu Hsun, tr. Yang Hsien-yi and Gladys Yang. Foreign Languages Press, Peking.

Chin P'ing Mei, tr. Bernard Miall (from the German version). The Bodley Head, London.

The Dream of the Red Chamber, by Hsueh-chin Tsao, tr. Florence and Isabel McHugh (from the German version). Routledge and Kegan Paul, London.

Stories from a Ming Collection, tr. Cyril Birch. Indiana University Press, Bloomington, Indiana.

Sunrise, by Tsao Yu, tr. A. C. Barnes. Foreign Languages Press, Peking.

The Man Who Sold a Chest, tr. Yang Hsien-yi and Gladys Yang. Foreign Languages Press, Peking.

The Strange Cases of Magistrate Pao, tr. Leon Comber. Charles E. Tuttle, Rutland, Vermont.

MISCELLANEOUS

Triad Societies in Hong Kong, by W. P. Morgan. Government Press, Hong Kong.

Chinese Secret Societies in Malaya, by Leon Comber. Donald Moore Ltd., Singapore.

The Legacy of China, ed. by R. Dawson. Clarendon Press, Oxford.

My Country and My People, by Lin Yutang. John Day, New York.

The Wisdom of China and India, by Lin Yutang. Random House, New York.

Chinese Creeds and Customs, Vols. 1–3, by V. R. Burkhardt.

Chinese Festivals in Malaya, by Dorothy Lo and Leon Comber. Eastern Universities Press, now Donald Moore Ltd., Singapore.

The Chinese View of their place in the World, by C. P. Fitzgerald. Oxford University Press.

The Singapore Story, by Kenneth Attiwill. Frederick Muller, London.

The Selected Works of Lu Hsun, tr. Yang Hsien-yi and Gladys Yang. Foreign Languages Press, Peking.

Scratches on the Mind, by Harold R. Isaacs. Massachusetts Institute of Technology, Cambridge, Mass.

One's Company, by Peter Fleming. Jonathan Cape, London.

400 Million Customers, by Carl Crow. Harper & Row, New York.

On a Chinese Screen, by W. Somerset Maugham. Doubleday, New York.

The Chinese Unicorn, ed. by Thomas Rowe, printed for Robert Gilkey (private circulation).

The Prediction Business, by Virginia Makins. Article in *The Observer* (London) of March 13, 1966.

CHINESE SOURCES

Chinese sources consulted in the original included, among others:
   Shih Chi, of Ssu-ma Chien.
   Han Shu, of Pan Ku.
   Chan Kuo Ts'e, of Liu Hsiang.

San Kuo Chih, of Ch'en Shou.
San Kuo Yen Yi, of Lo Kuan Chung.
Tao Te Ching, of Lao Tzu.
Chuang Tzu.
Shui Hu Chuan, by Shih Nai-an.

Index